Tolley's
Charity Investigations

Mazars Neville Russell
Chartered Accountants

Andrew C Burgess MA (Cantab)

Tolley Publishing

Whilst every care has been taken to ensure the accuracy of the contents of this book, no responsibility for loss occasioned to any person acting or refraining from action as a result of any statement in it can be accepted by the author or the publishers.

Published by
Butterworths Tolley
2 Addiscombe Road
Croydon, Surrey
CR9 5AF
020 8686 9141

Typeset in Great Britain by
M Rules

Printed in Great Britain by
Hobbs the Printers Ltd
Totton, Hampshire

ISBN 0 75450 219-8

Preface

When I told people that I was taking a month out in the summer of 2000 to write a book about charity investigations, the reaction of many was surprise at the choice of topic (there then followed comments about golf handicap being reduced etc. – if only!). The idea that a charity should be subject to investigation is, for most people, as way out as imagining that their maiden aunt had been arrested for shop lifting. Yet it is a fact of life that charities are the subject of investigation by a number of authorities. There have been some high profile investigations by the Charity Commission in recent years which have had publicity in the press and there have been significant investigations by the Inland Revenue which have not had publicity.

Charities, in the main, are established for the best of motives and many people give of their time and effort to help such organisations achieve their objectives. Others give, often sacrificially of their money, to support charitable work. Charities operate against a backdrop of financial constraints – too many needs not enough money to meet them – a mass of regulations, and from members of the public, sometimes apathy and at times, outright hostility. Sometimes in the effort to stretch resources to fit growing need, administrative corners are cut and charities will, unfortunately, find themselves on the wrong side of authority. This is probably the backdrop to most investigation cases involving charities. There are, however, situations in which unscrupulous individuals have seen an opportunity for personal financial gain on the back of the goodwill of other people towards a particular charitable area. No one would argue that such people deserve to have the book thrown at them, but so often the charitable organisation suffers what is now termed 'collateral damage'.

Charities who, for whatever reason, find themselves the target of an investigation need to know what they face and how they can resolve the situation as quickly as possible with the minimum of risk to the assets and to the work of the charity. Their problem is that this will be their first experience of investigation whereas the official they are dealing with will usually be a veteran in the area. I hope that this book will help to redress the balance a little.

You will find background on the various investigation agencies – their organisation, powers and approach to investigation – the likely areas of investigation and practical help on how to cope with all aspects of investigation.

In one of the perceptive 'Peanuts' cartoons by the late Charles Schultz, one of the characters in a discussion about how to cope with problems remarks that there is no problem that is so big or so small that it cannot be run away from! Running away may not be an option when the problem is there, but avoiding the problem arising should always be considered good advice. The most efficient way of dealing with an investigation is to prevent one happening in the first place. I have therefore made a major part of the book a series of checklists aimed at encouraging charities to take a look at different aspects of their organisation, to assess the risks and where possible to eliminate them. Time spent on this may save considerable time and money.

I hope that my experience in dealing with tax investigations for most of the last 30 years – both in the Inland Revenue and in the profession as a tax partner at Mazars Neville Russell helping to serve some of our several hundred charity clients – will be of help to you. Experience is a vital ingredient in the investigation process – this is an area where charities may need, but don't want, the experience!

Finally it is appropriate to say thanks to a number of people. To my fellow partners at Mazars Neville Russell for encouraging me to write this book and for making it possible to have the time to do so. To various officers at the Charity Commission and the Inland Revenue who have answered questions and provided information, and to their colleagues who, over the years, have decided to carry out investigations which have provided some of the raw material for this book. To Gina Antczak at Butterworths Tolley for her practical support in getting the book out. Last, but never least, to my wife Christine and younger daughter Jennie who put up with an increasingly frantic husband/father during the summer of 2000 as the writing deadline loomed large.

Andrew Burgess
London   October 2000

Editorial note on spelling

The Charity Commission refers to their investigations as 'inquiries' but the Inland Revenue uses the spelling 'enquiries'. These conventions have been adhered to in this book so that 'inquiries' refer to Charity Commission investigations and 'enquiries' to Inland Revenue investigations.

Contents

Contents

Abbreviations and References

Law Reports
AC	Appeal Cases
AER	All England Law Reports
Ch	Chancery Division
SpC	Special Commissioners' Decisions
STC	Simon's Tax Cases
TC	Official Tax Cases

Legislation
Ch A 1960	Charities Act 1960
Ch A 1985	Charities Act 1985
Ch A 1992	Charities Act 1992
Ch A 1993	Charities Act 1993
Ch D	Chancery Division
FA	Finance Act
ICTA 1988	Income and Corporation Taxes Act 1988
LRMPSA 1990	Law Reform (Miscellaneous Provisions) (Scotland) Act 1990
TCGA 1992	Taxation of Chargeable Gains Act 1992
TMA 1970	Taxes Management Act 1970
s	section
Sch	Schedule
SI	Statutory Instrument
VATA 1994	Value Added Tax Act 1994

Miscellaneous
CIR	Commissioners of Inland Revenue
C & E	Customs and Excise
CGT	Capital Gains Tax
DSS	Department of Social Security
FICO	Financial Intermediaries and Claims Office (formerly Claims Branch)
IHT	Inheritance Tax
NAO	National Audit Office

Abbreviations

NICs	National Insurance Contributions
PAYE	Pay As You Earn
SMP	Statutory Maternity Pay
SORP	Statement of Recommended Practice
SSP	Statutory Sick Pay
VAT	Value Added Tax
VCO	VAT Central Office
VCU	VAT Central Unit

Table of Cases

Table of Statutes

Table of Statutory Instruments

Part 1: Participants in the Investigation

Introduction

The first part of the book must introduce the participants in the investigative process – the charity and the regulators. We need to understand who each party is, how they operate, and what their duties and powers are. Without that understanding the detailed comments on handling actual investigations would be set in an unhelpful vacuum.

The chapters in this part comprise

Chapter 1

Introduction

Introduction

1.1   Any investigation has at least two parties – the investigator and the investigated. The former must have rights to investigate and the power to impose sanctions if they find evidence of wrong-doing. The latter has obligations to fulfil in the face of an investigation but also has rights which may prevent the abuse of power by the investigator.

This book seeks to explore the rights and obligations of both parties in the context of the investigation of a charity. The investigated party will always be the charity but the investigating party could be one (or all) of the following:

- Charity Commission
- Inland Revenue
- Customs and Excise

A book about investigations must, necessarily, focus on what happens when an investigation takes place, but it must also have a sub-plot – how to avoid the investigation in the first place, or, if an investigation must inevitably happen, how to minimise the impact it will have. Investigations of any kind are disruptive. They focus the attention of key people away from the prime purpose which they have in running the organisation. They can be costly both in time and money spent on outside assistance. They can be emotionally and physically draining. They can in some cases bring adverse publicity which may have a continuing impact long after the investigation has ended. In the worst situations they could force the organisation out of existence. Prevention must be a top priority – that means being aware of the potential problem areas and ensuring that the organisation is not at risk in any of those areas. This book explores many of the potential risk areas for charities and highlights the significant issues. The discerning trustee will want to ensure that their charity is being fully compliant, and minimising the exposure to the worst that the regulators can throw at them.

Role of trustees

1.2   The public face of a charity may take many different forms depending on the objectives which it pursues. It might be in the provision of care in a hospice, a warm friendly welcome to a shelter over Christmas, an evangelist expounding his beliefs at a major rally, volunteers explaining the history of an historic building. It might be a major TV telethon, an advertising campaign on billboards, an envelope pushed through the door, people wearing fancy dress rattling collecting buckets. The charity world is diverse in its objectives, in its methods of achieving those objectives and in its methods of funding those objectives. There is, however, one common feature that links all charities and that is where ultimate responsibility lies.

That responsibility always comes back to one group of people we can collectively call the trustees. They may have a different title – they could be a board of directors, a council, a diaconate or a host of other names – but they have the same responsibility. That is to ensure that the work of the charity is directed to achieving the objectives for which it has been established, and that this work is carried out efficiently using the resources which have been or are being made available.

The message that President Harry Truman had on his desk in the White House read 'The buck stops here' and that message should be firmly in the mind of anyone and everyone who assumes a role as a charity trustee. Ultimately if there is a problem it is not the organisation which will take the blame but those who run the organisation. There is no shelter behind a name, however well known that name may be.

This book is intended to be a guide to those who are charity trustees. It will explain how to cope in the face of an investigation by the bodies already mentioned, but it should also be regarded as a guide to the best practice in key areas of charity life so that the assets and reputation of the charity and the trustees themselves are not threatened.

Charity

The basic concept of charity

1.3   There is no legal definition of 'charity'. Dictionary definitions suggest something like 'an institution or organisation set up to provide help, money etc to those in need' (*New Collins Concise English Dictionary*).

That definition would seem to be substantially deficient in the light of many activities which are accepted as charitable, and indeed there is a need to draw an important distinction between the concept of 'charity' as an organisation and 'charitable purposes' as the objectives which such an organisation seeks to carry out. The phrase commonly used in the tax legislation when granting a tax exemption is 'charitable purposes'.

It is not the purpose of this book to examine in detail the meaning of 'charitable purposes' – those who want a more detailed review can refer to Chapter 1 of *Tolley's Charities Manual*. A brief summary of the key issues follows in 1.4 below as an *aide memoire*. It is important to remind charitable organisations that they should always be clear for what charitable purposes the organisation was established because those purposes should govern and control all the activities they undertake. To carry out activities which were not in the fulfilment of the charitable purposes could be considered as a breach of trust by the trustees.

One other general point to make is that the use of the term 'charitable purposes' is not limited to any particular type of organisational structure (as we shall see there can be several different formats) nor is it restricted to what are known as 'registered charities'. The concept of registration is an administrative one and will be outlined below. The range of organisations which have 'charitable purposes' goes well beyond those which are registered charities.

The heads of charity

Statute of Elizabeth

1.4   The first attempt to legally define a charity occurred as long ago as 1601 when Parliament passed a law known as the *Statute of Charitable Uses*, which is sometimes referred to as the *Statute of Elizabeth*. The preamble to that Act listed objects which were considered at the time to be charitable. Many of them will now seem outdated at the start of the 21st century, but they do still provide some general parameters for the definition of charitable purposes. The categories referred to are:

(1)   relief of aged, impotent and poor people;

(2)   maintenance of sick and maimed soldiers and mariners;

(3)   maintenance of schools of learning and free schools and scholars in universities;

(4)   repairs of bridges, ports, havens, causeways, churches, seabanks and highways;

(5)   education and preferment of orphans;

(6)   relief, stock or maintenance of houses of correction;

(7)   marriage of poor maids;

(8) supportation, aid and help of young tradesmen, handicraftsmen and persons decayed;

(9) relief or redemption of prisoners or captives;

(10) ease of poor inhabitants concerning payment of fifteens, setting out of soldiers and other taxes.

The *Statute of Elizabeth* is no longer current law but it is still referred to from time to time in cases which have gone before the courts on the question of whether activities are charitable.

The four heads of charity

1.5　　The leading 'modern' case which set the measure for charitable purposes was the case of *Special Commissioners of Income Tax v Pemsel 3 TC 53* which was heard in 1891. That case had to consider whether income received from certain land was applied for charitable purposes. The lead judgment given by Lord Macnaghten in the House of Lords defined what have become known as the 'four heads of charity' or are sometimes referred to as the 'Macnaghten doctrine'. Macnaghten said that for an organisation to be considered as charitable its objectives must fall within at least one of the following heads:

(1) relief of poverty (now referred to as relief of financial hardship);

(2) advancement of education;

(3) advancement of religion;

(4) other purposes beneficial to the community not falling under any of the preceding heads.

The meanings of these heads have been considered in subsequent cases and are continually being considered by the Charity Commission as part of the process of registering charities (see 1.7 below). Some examples of each can be given as follows.

Relief of financial hardship would include:

● giving money to beneficiaries;

● providing food, clothing or housing;

● providing advisory services to those in need;

● providing support to other organisations which give help to those suffering hardship.

Advancement of education denotes an active organisation and includes:

● schools, colleges, universities;

● playgroups;

● work-related training organisations;

- research institutions.

It does not include political activities.

Advancement of religion has to relate to a religion which is founded on belief in a supreme being or beings and involves expression of that belief through worship. It includes the provision and upkeep of buildings for worship as well as paying priests. Although it is generally assumed that there is a public benefit to the advancement of religion, there may be some situations where there is no public benefit, e.g. an enclosed religious order whose activity consists only of private prayer and the organisation would not be charitable.

The fourth heading is the hardest to pin down and potentially can cover a wide range of activities. It is clear that there must always be an element of public benefit before an object can be charitable. Examples of what the Charity Commission regard as within this head would be:

- relief of old age, sickness or disability where there is no financial hardship;
- promoting racial harmony;
- resettlement of offenders or drug addicts;
- provision of help to victims of natural or civil disasters;
- provision of recreational facilities which are open to all;
- provision of recreational facilities for particular beneficiary groups such as the disabled or the elderly;
- promotion of industry and business for the public benefit.

Review of the Register

1.6   The Charity Commission recognise that the definitions set down over a hundred years ago may not be relevant to the needs of today and that there may be activities never contemplated by Macnaghten which should be regarded as charitable. They are currently undertaking what they have termed a 'Review of the Register'. The format of the review is based around discussion documents and then, following a period of consultation, the publication of revised guidance. You can keep up to date with the progress of the review and pick up copies of the various papers from the Charity Commission website which has a separate section on the review.

Two detailed reviews have been completed:

- Promotion of Urban and Rural Regeneration (RR2)
- Relief of Unemployment (RR3)

Three further discussion documents were published in March 1999 with a consultation period that ended on 30 June 1999. Further information is expected on these shortly. These documents are:

● The Promotion of Community Development

● The Recreational Charities Act 1958

● Maintenance of an Accurate Register of Charities

The progress of this review is not going to be rapid, but it will be thorough and will set down the markers for the concept of 'charitable purposes' into the new century.

Register of charities

Introduction

1.7 The concept of a register of charities was introduced by the *Charities Act (Ch A) 1960* and amended by the *Charities Act (Ch A) 1993*. The process of registration is one of the key roles of the Charity Commissioners and the maintenance of the register and the concept of public access to that register is one of the cornerstones of the public accountability of charities. The actual process of registration is part of the process of creating a charity and is not considered in this book.

The main purposes of the register are:

(1) to provide a permanent central record of property devoted to charity;

(2) to provide the public, including social workers and potential donors, beneficiaries and benefactors with information about charities, whether open to all or restricted to special needs and localities;

(3) to provide simple and authoritative means of determining whether an organisation is charitable in law, so what is registered as charitable shall be treated as charitable for all purposes, subject only to correction by the High Court.

It should be noted that not every organisation which is charitable is required to register. Organisations may be outside the need to register because they are:

● Exempt (see 1.8)

● Excepted (see 1.9)

● Small (see 1.10)

● Related to a place of worship (see 1.11)

● In Scotland (see 1.12)

The absence of a registration number should not be regarded as detrimental to an organisation which has clear charitable objects and falls within the groups above. Equally, it should be noted that just because an organisation has been registered, it does not mean that the Charity Commissioners approve of it. If the objects of the organisation are charitable in law and the constitution is otherwise satisfactory, the Commissioners cannot refuse registration on the grounds that they do not personally approve of the objectives or have fears as to how the organisation will be run. That is where their monitoring will play an important role.

The onus is clearly placed on those who are running the organisation to determine first if that organisation is charitable, secondly, if it falls within one of the groups which are not required to register and if it does not to ensure that it is registered.

Exempt charities

1.8   Exemption from registration is given by law (*Ch A 1993, Sch 2*) for organisations which generally have some other form of supervision approved by Parliament. Broadly the list includes:

- Universities

- Certain education bodies

- Major museums

- Church Commissioners

- Registered Societies within the meaning of the *Industrial and Provident Societies Act 1965*

- Registered Friendly Societies

Excepted charities

1.9   A further group of charities are excepted from the need to register by order or regulation. These include:

- voluntary schools which have no permanent endowment other than their premises [*SI 1960 No 2366*];

- funds, not permanent endowments, accumulated for the purposes of local units of the Boy Scouts Association and the Girl Guides Association [*SI 1961 No 1044*];

- certain religious charities where a specified trust corporation takes responsibility;

- certain charities for promoting the efficiency of the armed forces.

Small charities

1.10   A charity does not have to register if the income of the charity from all sources is less than £1,000 and the charity has neither a permanent endowment nor the use or occupation of land.

This definition changed in 1993 and that change has meant that groups such as parent teacher's associations, playgroups, branches of the Women's Institute and many 'private' charitable trusts which are funded only by deed of covenant or Gift Aid have had to seek registration.

Places of worship

1.11   No charity is required to register in respect of any registered place of worship, which is registered under the *Places of Worship Registration Act 1855*. This exception extends to a vestry or caretakers house situated on the same site as the place of worship and held on the same trusts, but it does not extend to any other buildings adjacent to the place of worship.

Scotland

1.12   There is no formal registration system in Scotland. The decision as to whether or not a body has charitable status rests with the Inland Revenue in Edinburgh. The *Law Reform (Miscellaneous Provisions) (Scotland) Act (LRMPS) 1990* which sets out the Scottish regime for charities, uses the term 'recognised body' which covers a body which the Revenue have accepted is entitled to income tax exemption as a charity and which is either:

● established under the law of Scotland; or

● managed or controlled wholly or mainly in or from Scotland.

[*LRMPS 1990, s 1(7)*].

Such bodies can call themselves 'Scottish Charity'.

Types of charity structure

1.13   There are three common types of structure which may be appropriate for a charity to adopt. These are:

● Company limited by guarantee

● Trust

● Unincorporated association

These are each considered below.

Company limited by guarantee

1.14   The traditional idea of a company limited by shares is not usually applicable to a charity because of the existence of shareholders who could receive dividends which would allow income to pass out of the company. In addition there could be a conflict between meeting the needs of the shareholders and the beneficiaries. Where the company is limited by guarantee, the members agree that in the event of the company being wound up, they will pay a specific amount (usually £1) towards the debts of the company. This limits their liability to that sum.

The company comes into existence when it is registered at Companies House in Cardiff. A company will have a Memorandum and Articles of Association. The Memorandum of Association sets out the basic constitutions of the company covering

(1)   the type of company;

(2)   where its registered office is located;

(3)   its aims and objectives;

(4)   its powers;

(5)   guarantees given by members;

(6)   what is to happen to the surplus if the company is wound up.

The Articles of Association deal with the internal running of the company covering matters such as:

(1)   the number of members;

(2)   management structure;

(3)   the election of the governing body;

(4)   the powers of a governing body;

(5)   the procedure for general meeting of members.

Having a limited company means that another layer of administration is necessary to deal with matters relating to the Companies Acts. For example, annual returns have to be submitted to Companies House.

Trust

1.15   A trust is a much older type of entity having its origins back in medieval times. The legal heart is the trust deed which sets out key matters such as:

(1)   who are to be the trustees;

(2)   how trustees are to be appointed or removed;

(3)   what the objectives of the trust are;

(4)   what powers the trustees have.

The latter point is vital, because it is the trust deed which empowers the trustees to act, and so it must be as complete as needed. The trustees must act in accordance with the trust deed to protect the interests only of the beneficiaries.

A trust obviously avoids some of the extra costs involved with a company. There will usually be costs involved in using a solicitor to draw up the trust deed.

Unincorporated associations

1.16 These are generally used where the organisation is made up of people with similar interests who want to benefit by disseminating information, sharing advice and experience or working together on projects. An unincorporated association will operate under a constitution which will set out, inter alia:

(1) its aims and objectives;

(2) the criteria for membership;

(3) the role of the committee which will govern the association;

(4) how the committee is to be elected;

(5) the process of arranging meetings of members;

(6) the election of officers;

(7) how the constitution is to be amended.

Comparison of structure

1.17 A comparison of the three structures can be made in simple tabular form as follows:

Type	Unincorporated association	Trust	Company limited by guarantee
Founding document	Constitution	Trust deed	Memorandum and Articles
Adoption of document	Members meeting	Signed by trustees and witnessed	Meeting of guarantors
Governing body	Executive or management committee	Trustees	Board or council of management
Legal features	No limited liability	No limited liability	Limited liability
	Not able to hold land	Not able to hold land	Can hold land
	Not able to sign legal documents	Trustees sign documents personally	Can enter into legal agreements

Type	Unincorporated association	Trust	Company limited by guarantee
Types of organisation	Small assets	Small group	Large organisation
	Local branch of national organisation	No time limit on trustees	Employees
		New trustees appointed by existing trustees	Deliver services under contract
	Membership		Enter into commercial contracts
	Fixed period for trustees	Simple administration	
	Trustees elected by members	Land and buildings permanent	Substantial landowners
	Outside representation		Risk ventures
		Grant making	
		Restriction on spending capital	

Trustees

Their importance

1.18   The different legal structures referred to above will create different titles for those individuals who are responsible for running the legal entity under which the charity operates. The key role of the trustees has already been identified at the start of this chapter and it is now appropriate to say a little more about the role and its responsibilities.

The only legal definition of a charitable trustee is found in *Ch A 1993, s 97(1)* which states that it means 'the person having the general control and management of the administration of the charity'.

Trustees could have actual titles which vary according to the nature of the organisation, e.g.:

- Directors of a charitable company

- Trustees of a charitable trust

- Management committee of an association

- Governors of a school

- Deacons or similar body in a church

It is therefore important that the group of people who are to be the trustees are identified at the earliest possible stage. Their role is absolutely vital and carries with it legal responsibilities and duties which those who are being asked to undertake the role should seriously consider before agreeing to be appointed. The Charity

Commission have produced a booklet (CC3), *'Responsibility of Charity Trustees'* which must be read by all prospective trustees. A copy of this booklet is provided in the information pack which the Commission send out to prospective charities.

In their booklet, the Commissioners state:

> 'Trustees must be selected for what they can contribute to the charity. They should not be appointed for their status or position in the community alone: this is the function of patrons. Trustees must be able and willing to give time to the efficient administration of the charity and fulfilment of its trusts. They should be selected on the basis of their relevant experience and skills and must be prepared to take an active part in the running of the charity.'

Ideally a group of trustees should comprise a mix of people, all of whom have sympathy with the objectives of the charity, but who each can bring specific gifts, abilities and interests including business expertise. As far back as 1989 the Charity Commission were noting in their annual report that many trustees were simply not up to their job – good intentions did not necessarily make for an effective organisation.

Duties and responsibilities of trustees

1.19 Trustees are ultimately responsible for the affairs of the charity and that responsibility is both a collective and individual one. That individual responsibility cannot be absolved by delegating matters to a subcommittee of trustees or to a chief executive. Any such delegation needs to be controlled and it must be clear that the organisation is answerable to the trustees who take the ultimate responsibility.

Trustees have a custodial role over the assets of the charity – both real assets and financial assets. If a loss of assets results from the negligence of trustees or, worse still, from their dishonesty, they may be personally liable for the loss incurred.

Responsibilities within the organisation of the charity must be clearly defined. This means that the remit of subcommittees should be stated clearly and arrangements made for reporting back their deliberations to the main trust body. Some minor administrative decisions can probably be taken in committee without risk, but these must be carefully identified and rules for exceptions put in place.

Where a chief executive is responsible for the day-to-day running of the charity, it is vital that their role is properly defined and controlled. The chief executive is a servant of the charity, not the controller of the charity, and must be directly answerable to the trustees.

It is important that the trustee body should contain people with sufficient experience to handle not just issues relating to the charitable objects but also issues relating to finance such as budgetary control and accounting issues. Financial naivety is not a trait which the Charity Commissioners will appreciate – if the expertise is not available on the governing body it should be brought in. However disdainful some may find the discussion of money in the context of a charitable organisation, it is a requirement.

In practical terms:

(1) Every trustee should have a personal copy of the governing instrument and should be aware of what it says about the responsibilities of trustees.

(2) At least one copy of that instrument should be available for reference at meetings.

(3) Formal minutes should be made of all trustee meetings. These should record all decisions made, future action planned, by whom and when.

(4) A record should be kept of the date and method of appointment of all trustees and the date on which they cease to hold office.

Beneficiaries

1.20 The beneficiaries are those individuals or groups of individuals for whom the charity exists. It may be very easy for the trustees to identify who the beneficiaries are – they are the needy whose practical needs are being met, they are the students in the school or college, they are those who are being racially harassed or whatever. There may be situations in which it is not so easy to identify the beneficiaries and in such cases the trustees should be careful to consider what it is they are providing and to whom. For example putting on a major pop concert to raise money is not a directly charitable activity. Those attending the concert are unlikely to be the beneficiaries of the charity.

The identification of beneficiaries and the recognition that the nature of those beneficiaries may change over a period of time should always be at the forefront of the minds of the trustees. Planning for every activity should consider how will this activity assist those who are our beneficiary group?

Public accountability of charities

Introduction

1.21 Charities operate in the public domain. Their objectives have a public element to them and it is right that they should be accountable to the public at large. Some of the obligations that are imposed are in the nature of taxation requirements and there is a legal responsibility but no public disclosure requirement. In the area of charity law, however, there has been an increased requirement imposed on charities to bring their activities into the public domain. There are five areas where this needs to be considered:

- Registration (see 1.22)
- Preparation of accounts (see 1.23)
- Audit (see 1.24)
- Publication of an annual report (see 1.25)
- Submission of an annual return to the Charity Commission (see 1.26)

It should be noted that, unless specifically stated, the requirements outlined below apply to excepted charities as well as to registered charities. They are only applicable to exempt charities where indicated.

Registration

1.22   The obligation to register as a charity has already been discussed. Part of the process of registration must be that details of what has been included on the register should be available to the public. There are a number of obvious reasons for this:

(1)   potential supporters want to know if the charity is one that they should support;

(2)   potential beneficiaries want to be able to identify organisations which may be of help to them;

(3)   public authorities who may wish to provide facilities for charities will want to establish the bona fides of the organisation.

The Register was computerised in 1990 and can be inspected at any of the three offices of the Commission. It can also now be accessed directly from the Commissioners' website. The information can be downloaded from the website for any purpose not connected with a commercial exploitation of the information.

The information contained on the register in respect of each charity comprises the following:

- Name of the charity
- Registered number
- Subsidiary number
- Other name(s)
- Correspondent

- Objects
- Area of benefit
- Registration date
- Governing document
- Area(s) of operation
- Details of subsidiaries

The information can be searched in four basic ways:

- for charities by name;
- for charities by charity object or name keywords;
- by area of operation; or
- by registered number.

On-screen instructions explain how to operate each search method, and details can be obtained very quickly.

Accounts

1.23   A charity's accounting records must show and explain all transactions and be sufficient to:

(1)   disclose at any time, with reasonable accuracy, the financial position of the charity at that time;

(2)   enable the trustees to prepare annual statements of accounts in accordance with regulations yet to be specified.

[*Ch A 1993, s 41*].

Accounts have to be prepared in accordance with regulations, although where a charity's gross income does not exceed £100,000, it will be able to elect to produce simply a receipts and payments account and a statement of assets and liabilities instead. The format of the accounts has to follow what is known as the Statement of Recommended Practice (SORP). This ensures that the accounts of all charities can be reviewed on a comparable basis. The terms of the SORP have been agreed between the Charity Commission and the representative accounting bodies. At the time of writing (August 2000), the SORP introduced in October 1995 is being reviewed and it is anticipated that some changes in the requirements will be published in autumn 2000 or spring 2001.

The Charity Commission expect the accounts of charities to follow the SORP unless there is some major conflict with the governing document of the charity, in which case the SORP requirements can be adapted but any material non-compliance with the SORP has to be identified and explained in a note to the accounts. A detailed review of the accounting requirements for charities is set out in Section C of *Tolley's Charities Manual*.

Audit requirement

1.24 It is not sufficient to know that the accounts of a charity have been produced in a standard format. It is necessary to know that those accounts are correct. That way, the public can see how the trustees have used the resources of the charity in the year and have the comfort of knowing that an independent person has scrutinised that use of resources.

The requirement for an audit is set out in *Ch A 1993, s 43*. A registered auditor must carry out the audit of a charity where the gross income or total expenditure exceeds £250,000 in either the current year or either of the two preceding years. A registered auditor is someone who is eligible to audit company accounts and will usually be a practising qualified accountant.

All other charities (except unregistered charities with income below £1,000 and unincorporated charities below £10,000) can opt to have their accounts examined by an independent examiner instead. The Commissioners have the right to guide trustees on the selection of an independent examiner and to give directions on the carrying out of an examination. An independent examiner must be an independent person who is 'qualified by his ability in, and practical experience of the practice of accountancy'.

The Commissioners monitor adherence to the rules and, if an audit or examination has not been carried out within ten months from the end of the charity's financial year, they have the power to appoint an auditor of their choice. The Commissioners are also given the overriding right to require a registered auditor to carry out an audit where they think this would be desirable even though the law would not otherwise require it. In this case the charity can choose its own auditor.

Detailed guidance on auditing of charity accounts is to be found in Part D of *Tolley's Charities Manual*.

Annual report

1.25 *Charities Act 1993, s 45* requires all registered charities to prepare an annual report which is to contain details of the charity's activities during the year and other information on the charity and its trustees as will be set out in regulations. The accounts are attached to the report, which must be sent to the Commissioners within ten months of the end of the financial year. This is an automatic requirement for charities with annual income or expenditure over £10,000. Charities below this level must still prepare the report, but will not be required to submit it to the Commissioners unless requested to do so. Any such request made within seven months of the accounting year end must be complied with inside the ten-month limit. A request made outside that seven-month period must be met within three months of the date of the request.

The annual reports kept by the Commissioners will be open to public inspection at all reasonable times. [*Ch A 1993, s 47*]. Any member of the public may obtain copies of documents either from the Commission or from the charity, subject to the payment of a reasonable fee.

The preparation of the annual report should be seen by charities as a positive requirement. It is not simply prepared for the benefit of the Commission, it is also an opportunity to let supporters or beneficiaries know what the charity has done during the year. A good report may help to attract new supporters and get the charity's message across more effectively to anyone interested in its work. The preparation of the annual report should provide the trustees with an opportunity to review the activities of the charity in relation to its objects and overall strategy. The publication of the annual report and accounts should be a major concern to the trustee body and positive encouragement is now given through various awards for the quality of charity accounts and reports.

Charity Commission News 9 reminded charities that they must respond positively to any request from members of the public or commercial companies for copies of the latest accounts and annual report. The following practical issues were noted:

(1)   any request in writing must be responded to within two months;

(2)   a reasonable fee may be charged – this must do no more than reflect the costs of providing a copy;

(3)   whilst the only obligation is to send accounts, it is considered good practice to send a copy of the annual report;

(4)   the latest accounts should be sent and this means the latest set to have been audited or examined;

(5)   the person asking for the accounts can use them as they wish, so the charity should point out any copyright which subsists.

Pro forma accounts prepared using the CC pack are subject to Crown Copyright on the design and guidance should be obtained from Taunton if necessary.

Annual return

1.26   Every registered charity (except those with annual income or expenditure below £10,000 per annum) has to submit an annual return to the Commissioners at the same time as submitting their accounts. [*Ch A 1993, s 48*].

The return for the last accounting period is the form AR8 which has to be completed in respect of financial years ending on or after 28 February 1999. A copy of this return is at Appendix 1. (The latest version of the return is form AR2000 for accounting periods ending between 29 February 2000 and 31 December 2000, this is to be sent to charities in October 2000 after this book has gone to press.) The requirement is to complete and submit the return within ten months of the end of the relevant financial year. Failure to do so is likely to be a trigger for Charity Commission interest in the charity.

The return is in two sections. Section 1 has to be completed by all charities and asks a wide range of questions about the charity and its organisation with subsections dealing with:

- Financial year
- Gross income and expenditure
- Internal management
- Fund raising
- Cash balances
- Trustees and trustee benefits
- Occupation of functional property
- Land and buildings
- Dealings with connected companies or connected trading companies

Section 2 is only required from charities with gross income or total expenditure exceeding £250,000 and asks for financial information to flesh out some of the details shown by the accounts.

The final page of the return has a declaration which must be signed by one of the trustees on behalf of all the trustees. The wording of the declaration states: 'I certify that the information given in this form is correct to the best of my knowledge and **has been brought to the attention of all the trustees.**'

The emboldened text appears on the return and emphasises again the collective role of the trustees. It is not sufficient for the chairman of the trustees to complete the form with the chief executive and send it off – effectively a copy of the return must be given to each trustee.

Hallmarks of a well run charity

1.27   The Charity Commission have published a booklet CC60, *'The Hallmarks of a Well Run Charity'* which should be required reading for every charity trustee. In it they examine the following characteristics which they consider identify the well run charity. Such a charity:

(1)   is formally set up with clearly documented aims and rules by which it will be run, and which should include the legal powers it needs to achieve its aims;

(2)   is run by a clearly identifiable body of people who take responsibility, and are accountable, for controlling the charity so that it is economically and effectively run;

(3)   manages and accounts for its resources well;

(4)   complies with all relevant legal and regulatory requirements;

(5)   acts with respect to the legal and human rights of the individual;

(6)   is able to show how its activities are, or will be, able to support its charitable aims;

(7)   is open in the conduct of its affairs, except where there is a need to respect confidentiality;

(8)   carries out its aims with regard to the requirements of those it is designed to serve, the community within which it operates and any relevant wishes of its donors;

(9)   conducts its external relations, fundraising and publicity in a way that enhances its own reputation and that of charities generally.

We will be returning to many of those issues as we proceed through this book.

The Regulators

Introduction

1.28   We turn now to consider the other party in the investigation process – the regulator. This will be a brief introduction to the three government agencies – the Charity Commission, the Inland Revenue and Customs and Excise – with which a charity is likely to have some dealing. To set the scene we consider the nature of the agency, how it is organised, its overall role as far as charities are concerned and a general summary of the legal framework in which it operates. More detailed consideration of investigation powers and activities is saved for later chapters.

Charity Commission

Development

1.29   Charities have always occupied a very privileged position in our society and, historically, the pressure for some sort of control over their activities appears to have surfaced in the early 19th century. After a number of false starts, an Act, known as the *Charitable Trusts Act* was passed in 1853. This Act set up a Body of Commissioners who were supported by a staff of inspectors with powers to enquire into the state of a charity, to give reliable legal advice to trustees, to sanction transactions in charity property and to control the bringing of charity law suits.

The system remained unchanged for a century until the role of charities in the evolving Welfare State became the subject of considerable public debate. A committee under the chairmanship of Lord Nathan was appointed in 1950:

> '. . . to consider and report on the changes in the law and practice (except as regards taxation) relating to charitable trusts in England and Wales which would be necessary to enable the maximum benefit to the community to be derived from them'.

The report of that committee eventually became the basis for the *Charities Act 1960* (the *1960 Act*). The Charity Commission emerged from that Act to replace the old Board.

Their role and powers have been considerably enhanced by the 1993 legislation, and it is readily apparent that they have a key role in the development and enforcement of the regulatory regime which surrounds charities today. The evolution of the Commission to what it is today has not been an easy process, and some would say that there is still a long way to go to achieve a perfect situation. The Commissioners have had to cope with a rapidly changing world where the concept of what is charitable has changed considerably, and where the pace of change in areas such as information technology is bewildering.

Legal constitution and objectives

1.30   *Charities Act 1993, s 1(1)* states:

> 'There shall continue to be a body of Charity Commissioners for England and Wales, and they shall have such functions as are conferred on them by this Act in addition to any other functions under any other enactment for the time being in force.'

This reflects the fact that the Commissioners were originally created by the *1960 Act*, and indicates the pivotal role that the Commissioners have in the regulatory framework for charities. The section goes on to give two general functions and objects for the Commissioners:

> '(3) The Commissioners shall (without prejudice to their specific powers and duties under other enactments) have the general function of promoting the effective use of charitable resources by encouraging the development of better methods of administration, by giving charity trustees information or advice on any matter affecting the charity and by investigating and checking abuses.

(4) It shall be the general object of the Commissioners to act in the case of any charity (unless it is a matter of altering its purposes) as best to promote and make effective the work of the charity in meeting the needs designated by its trusts; but the Commissioners shall not themselves have power to act in the administration of a charity.'

The roles are essentially on two levels – to provide support to the charitable sector as a whole but also, significantly, to get involved in the activities of individual charities. Charity trustees should recognise the benefits of using the Commissioners as a source of information and advice, but must realise as well that their own actions may be subject to the closest possible scrutiny by the Commissioners.

The Commissioners are required by the *1993 Act* to produce an annual report which explains what they have been doing and provides a useful insight into the current thinking of the Commission, the current issues that they are concerned about and their approach to those issues. The 1998 Report, published in May 1999, has on its front cover a single phrase which sums up the role of the Commission: 'Giving the public confidence in the integrity of charity'.

The Report starts by setting out three main objectives by which the Commissioners measure their progress. These are:

(1)   to ensure that charities are able to operate for their proper purposes within an effective legal, accounting and governance framework;

(2)   to improve the governance, accountability, efficiency and effectiveness of charities;

(3)   to identify and deal with abuses and poor practices.

The constitution of the Charity Commissioners is set out in *Ch A 1993, Sch 1* which provides that: 'There shall be a Chief Charity Commissioner and two other commissioners'. The chief commissioner and the other commissioners are appointed by the Home Secretary and are paid officials. The power exists to appoint up to two further commissioners.

The Chief Commissioner is given the power to appoint 'such assistant commissioners and other officers and such employees as he thinks necessary for the proper discharge of the functions of the Commissioners'.

Geographical organisation

1.31   The Commissioners have three offices located in London, Liverpool and Taunton. All three offices do the same type of work, but this is distributed between offices on a geographical basis. The location of a charity (usually found in the correspondent address) determines which office is responsible. The areas dealt with by each office are set out in Appendix 2.

The current addresses of each office are as follows:

London	*Liverpool*	*Taunton*
Harmsworth House	20 Kings Parade	Woodfield House
13–15 Bouverie Street	Queens Dock	Tangier
London	Liverpool	Taunton
EC4Y 8DP	L3 4DQ	Somerset
		TA1 4BL

There is now a single telephone contact number for general queries covering all the offices, and this is: 0870 333 0123. The number for hearing and speech impaired callers using a minicom is: 0870 333 0125.

It should be noted that the Commission does not operate in Scotland. Issues of charitable status are resolved by the Inland Revenue in Edinburgh and powers which need to be exercised under *Law Reform (Miscellaneous Provisions)(Scotland) Act 1990* are carried out by the Scottish Charities Office which is located at:

Crown House
25 Chambers Street
Edinburgh
EH1 1LA
Tel: 0131 226 2626

Functional organisation

1.32   The functional organisation within each office broadly breaks down into two main areas as far as charities are concerned – support and investigation. The former exists to provide help and advice to charities. It deals with issues relating to helping charities to function better, producing schemes to enable charity assets to be used more effectively, or perhaps to enable charities to merge to create a more efficient unit. Those engaged in the latter group are heavily involved in making charities accountable and reviewing the activities of those engaged in the charitable sector. It is their role that will be the focus of attention in later chapters.

The Commission has traditionally had a strong legal element in its staff. The production of schemes, the handling of property issues, trust law and so forth all requires a legal approach. In more recent years there has been a major move to recruit accountants and to develop the financial side of the Commission. This is particularly true of the investigation area where the examination of accounts and financial records assumes an important role.

Although the two main strands are separately organised there is a great deal of co-operation between the two groups. The investigation group will often refer issues they uncover to the support side to resolve with the charity because that is the best solution for the charity concerned. The support side may well uncover issues which require a more investigative approach.

Provision of information

1.33   The Commissioners have made considerable strides in recent years to widen the scope of their publications and to improve their readability and usefulness. A list of the current publications is maintained on the website, which has a brief summary of each publication and from which publications can be downloaded. Trustees should regard these publications as a first source of reference on issues that confront them. They will find the Charity Commission view on the subject and will gain an indication as to whether the issue is one on which they should seek detailed advice from the Commission. A list of the publications is at Appendix 5.

The Commissioners have a site on the World Wide Web the address of which is: www.charity-commission.gov.uk

The site is well presented and provides a useful way of keeping in touch with latest information from the Commissioners. As well as a home page there are pages dealing with

- Index
- About us
- News
- Publications
- Facts and figures
- Getting in touch
- Useful guidelines
- Review of the Register

A new development, and one which is being added to all the time, is the publication on the website of the internal guidance notes used by Commission staff. These are limited at present but will increasingly be an essential source of reference to trustees and advisors seeking to know the Commission approach on a wide range of problems.

Legal framework – England and Wales

1.34   For most of the latter half of the 20th century, the essential legislation governing charities was the *Charities Act 1960* (the *1960 Act*) which had eventually been enacted after a post-war review of the charity sector. In the late 1980s a series of highly critical reports was published pointing out that the legislation was unable to cope with the rapid development of the charitable sector. The outcome of this was the passing of the

Charities Act 1992 (the *1992 Act*) just before the 1992 General Election. The ink was hardly dry on that Act when much of it, plus the remaining powers of the 1960 Act, were consolidated into the *Charities Act 1993* (the *1993 Act*) which remains the prime legislation at present. That primary legislation is backed by a wide range of regulations.

Charities Act 1992

1.35   In its original form the *1992 Act* comprised 79 sections and 7 Schedules, but many of these were consolidated into the *1993 Act*. Certain provisions relating to the changing role of the Official Custodian for Charities remain in the Act, but these are of little lasting significance. The main areas of charity activity governed by the *1992 Act* are:

● Control of fundraising for charitable institutions (sections 58 to 64)

● Public charitable collections (sections 65 to 74)

It should be noted that at present this legislation has still not been formally introduced. The powers exist but the practical working of those powers has not been finalised.

Charities Act 1993

1.36   This Act is now the basic framework for all charity legislation in England and Wales. The *1993 Act* has 100 sections and 8 Schedules and is broken down into the following Parts:

Part 1   The Charity Commissioners and the Official Custodian for Charities

Part 2   Registration and names of charities

Part 3   Commissioners information powers

Part 4   Application of property Cy-pres and assistance and supervision of charities by court and Commissioners

Part 5   Charity land

Part 6   Charity accounts, reports and returns

Part 7   Incorporation of charity trustees

Part 8   Charitable companies

Part 9   Miscellaneous

Part 10   Supplementary

Charity trustees and their advisers need to be aware of the provisions of this Act because it provides the legal framework within which they must carry out their duties.

Scotland

1.37   The Charities Acts apply only to England and Wales. Some of the provisions are paralleled in Scotland by *Law Reform (Miscellaneous Provisions)(Scotland) Act 1990* which came into effect in autumn 1992.

Inland Revenue

Introduction

1.38   The Commissioners of Inland Revenue (usually referred to as the 'Board') are given the care and management of income tax, corporation tax and capital gains tax by *Taxes Management Act* (*TMA*) *1970, s 1.* The Commissioners themselves hold office by virtue of *Inland Revenue Regulation Act 1890.* The organisation over which the Board preside is a huge one – one of the largest of the government departments and one which has seen many changes of organisation over recent years as it has tried to come to grips with the demands of collecting tax in a very different economic, cultural and technical setting to that into which income tax was originally introduced in 1799.

The traditional Inland Revenue structure as far as the taxpayer is concerned has been based on the local district. That structure is changing and is being streamlined with many taxpayers finding that they no longer have a local tax office. The long established title of Inspector of Taxes is also being phased out to be replaced by 'officer of the Board' which the more traditional among us find less attractive!

As far as charities are concerned, the change in local district structure is not likely to have any major impact except in the area of employer compliance, because the Revenue have long recognised that the tax affairs of charities needed special attention. There are therefore two faces of the Revenue for charities:

●   the Financial Intermediaries and Claims Office (FICO), which deals with the tax affairs of the charity itself;

●   the PAYE district, which handles the tax affairs of the charity's employees and deals with the compliance of the charity with the requirements of PAYE.

Financial Intermediaries and Claims Office (FICO)

1.39   The Inland Revenue recognised many years ago that they needed to have a special unit to deal with the tax affairs of charities. This was largely because the work was primarily that of dealing with claims for repayment of tax and because the tax regime relating to charities was so very different from that governing other entities and individuals. The work in dealing with charities formed part of a division known as Claims Branch (Charity Division). That division has gone through a number of changes of title and identity and currently sits as part of a large unit which deals not only with charities, but also handles issues relating to major financial institutions (such as the operation of the tax deduction scheme for interest) as well as matters relating to advice on non-residence and the UK tax affairs of offshore trusts.

The main office is based in Bootle in what has to be regarded as one of the least impressive Inland Revenue buildings. There is also an office in Edinburgh (FICO Scotland) which has an important role for all charities in Scotland because it is the office which determines whether those organisations can be regarded as charities in Scotland. The offices are staffed by Revenue personnel who have come into the office from the main tax district network. They are not specialists in charity taxation, but they have to become so in a very short period of time because they are the Revenue's specialists in this area.

The role of FICO in respect of charities is to review the entitlement to tax exemption and to ensure that charities comply with the tax law as it affects them. The Revenue no longer have to establish the charitable status of organisations. As far as registered charities are concerned that is now the role of the Charity Commission, although that department does contact the Revenue as part of the registration process. In the days before the Charity Commission came into being, the Revenue were the arbiters of charitable status because tax exemption was the prime benefit of that status. FICO will still need to consider whether an organisation which is not required to register with the Charity Commission, is in fact an organisation which has been established for charitable purposes only. They have to take their own decision on this.

The basic work of the unit in FICO can be identified as follows:

(1)   Processing tax repayment claims made by charities – these are primarily in the area of Gift Aid and deed of covenant reclaims, although they would also include claims to transitional relief following the phasing out of tax credits on dividends. Official statistics published in the Report by the National Audit Office (NAO) on 'The Monitoring and Control of the Tax Exemption for Charities' (March 1998) – a document that will be discussed in more depth in Chapter 3 – show that in 1996/97 the Revenue processed 177,832 tax repayment claims from 46,500 charities. That number could well increase in future as the impact of the charity tax changes announced in *Finance Act 2000* work through the system. The approach adopted in the repayment process is largely a repay now check later one, although some more detailed checks are undertaken on the first claim made and on a sample of other repayments.

(2)   Charity audit visits to check on claims for repayment of tax on qualifying donations under the Gift Aid regime and formerly under deed of covenant donations. This usually involves a field visit to the charity and is discussed in more detail in Chapter 3.

(3)   The issue of self assessment returns to charities and the review of those returns. This is a modification of the old system of examining the accounts of charities that were submitted on a voluntary basis. The system of self assessment will be discussed in Chapter 3, because it is that system that establishes the investigation framework. In broad terms it will involve checking the entitlement to tax exemption on matters such as trading and fundraising activities. It also involves examining the accounts of companies which are wholly owned by charities.

(4)   Providing advice to charities on a range of technical issues such as the possible tax treatment of certain receipts, whether activities amount to trading which might or might not be exempt, etc. This part of the unit has been heavily involved in the implementation of the proposals of the Charity Tax Review and the author has found them to be very helpful in providing an interpretation on new and developing ideas. Charities who have interesting tax issues will find benefit in discussing them with the Technical and Advisory people in FICO before they implement them. Major problems can be easily averted.

Legal framework for tax exemption

1.40   The Inland Revenue are responsible for the operation of income tax, corporation tax and capital gains tax (CGT) and the legal framework for those taxes is set out in *Income and Corporation Taxes Act* (ICTA) *1988* and subsequent Finance Acts. Charities which are established as trusts will be in the income tax regime and charities which are companies limited by guarantee or associations will be primarily within the corporation tax regime. CGT is potentially payable by both trusts and companies.

The key income tax exemption for charities is set out in *ICTA 1988, ss 505* and *506*. This provides a wide range of tax exemption where income arises from specified sources and is then applied for charitable purposes. It should be noted that the section does not confer a blanket tax exemption on all income and that the application of the funds is as important as the source. Legislation in those sections, and also *ICTA 1988, Sch 20*, provides a quantitative test on the application side and needs to be carefully watched by charities. It will be discussed in detail later in this book.

It should be pointed out that where income does not fall into the Schedular system it will not be subject to tax. Items such as donations direct from the public which fall outside the 'qualifying donations' regime introduced by *Finance Act 2000* will simply be not taxable.

Charities which are within the regime for corporation tax will benefit from the same exemptions because *ICTA 1988, s 9(4)* simply provides that where Income Tax Acts provide an exemption from income tax, that exemption shall 'except as otherwise provided, have like effect for the purposes of corporation tax'.

Exemption from CGT is provided by *Taxation of Chargeable Gains Act (TCGA) 1992, s 256*, but again the exemption is conditional on the gain being applied for charitable purposes.

Employer compliance – organisation

1.41   Charities as employers have no special tax privileges. They must carry out the same duties as any other employer and are subject to the same regulatory regime as well. The Revenue organisation of employer compliance has gone through a number of changes in recent years, not least because from April 1999, the Inland Revenue assumed responsibility for the collection and administration of National Insurance which now also has to be regarded as a tax, particularly for employers.

Every employer has a district that deals with the tax affairs of its employees. It is possible, but often unlikely, that the district will be local to the charity. The Revenue went through a massive reorganisation of PAYE work in the late 1960s and early 1970s which led to the creation of large PAYE districts, the outposting of most London work to the north of England, and the creation of other regional centres. This was a prelude to the creation of large computer centres. However, operational problems with the first of these – Centre 1 which serves all of Scotland – put paid to that idea. Centre 1 still exists and deals with all Scottish employers. Many of the so-called London Provincial Districts have themselves now been merged into new districts in Manchester.

The role of the employer unit is to deal with the tax affairs of all the employees of each employer for whom the district is responsible. This will include issuing notices of coding, issuing returns where appropriate (not every employee is automatically issued with a return each year) and finalising the tax affairs of the employees. It will also be responsible for monitoring the routine PAYE compliance of each employer. The requirement to submit annual returns and the processing of those returns are part and parcel of the role.

It is useful for any employer to strike up a good working relationship with its PAYE district so that potential problem areas can be discussed before they become major problems. Certainly if you are planning any major changes in the remuneration structure of your organisation, it may be helpful to discuss these with the Inspector first.

There has been a significant change in the Revenue organisation of employer compliance in the late 1990s. The old system in the Revenue drew a clear distinction between compliance organised by Inspectors in districts and compliance organised by collectors. At district level the compliance concentrated on two key aspects:

- routine compliance with Schedule E and PAYE issues;
- detailed reviews of benefits in kind.

The collection side was responsible for the carrying out of PAYE audits, looking in detail at the operation of PAYE by employers. This took place at two levels:

- locally through the local PAYE audit group;
- nationally for large employers through the national audit group.

The structural organisation of the Revenue has been undergoing a major change over the past few years with the development of what is known as the 'new office structure' which is essentially creating separate administrative and compliance districts. In addition, with a project called 'new office development', there has been a move to integrate PAYE audit groups and traditional tax staff.

The end result is that the generic term for this type of work, no matter by whom it is carried out is 'employer compliance work'. The new basic organisation of employer compliance work is centred on the new style local compliance unit, which in many cases will combine the old employer compliance units and local PAYE audits, although in some cases there may still be an effective distinction between the two. It is the detailed operation of these units that is considered in Chapter 4 and in later reviews of the key investigation areas which affect charities as employers.

Legal framework – employer compliance

1.42   The employer compliance units operate primarily within the framework of the PAYE regulations which are centred on the *Income Tax (Employment) Regulations 1993 (SI 1993 No 744)* and subsequent amending regulations. These regulations take their statutory authority from *ICTA 1988, s 203(1)* which provides the basic principle of PAYE that where a payment is made of income which is assessable under Schedule E, the person making the payment must deduct tax.

Customs and Excise

Introduction

1.43   Like the Inland Revenue, Customs and Excise are a large department under the general auspices of the Treasury and the overall responsibility of the Chancellor of the Exchequer. Its visible face to most people is at airports and ports in the so-called 'red and green channels' supervising passengers arriving from abroad with the familiar phrase 'anything to declare?'. The department has for centuries fought a running battle of wits and often literal battle with smugglers around the coasts. Today that battle continues, particularly in the area of drug smuggling.

When the Government of the day introduced value added tax on 1 April 1973, it gave the administration of the new tax to Customs and Excise rather than to the Inland Revenue. Now it seems quite likely that, within a few years, the two departments may be merged into a single revenue gathering unit.

As well as administering VAT and customs duties, Customs and Excise also have responsibility for the administration of landfill tax, insurance premium tax, airport passenger duty and the new climate change levy introduced by *Finance Act 2000*. It is only the VAT area that is of concern as far as this book is concerned.

Organisation of Customs and Excise

1.44   Again, like the Inland Revenue, Customs and Excise are run by a Board, officially known as the Commissioners of H.M. Customs and Excise. They are supported by a Policy Directorate based in London which defines the tax base and deals with policy issues that might be arising at local level. Within that unit are specialists who deal with policy issues affecting charities, but they will not deal with the VAT affairs of charities directly.

There is no Customs equivalent to FICO which means that the VAT affairs of charities are dealt with within the local operational structure. This pivots around the VAT Central Unit (VCU) based in Southend which is the point to which all VAT returns are sent and all VAT payments are made. A regional structure of 14 Regional Collections has overall responsibility for the field staff who operate from the Local VAT Offices (LVOs) of which there are approximately 90 scattered around the country mostly in major cities. It will be these offices who will have responsibility for monitoring the VAT issues relating to the charities within their 'patch'. Some offices may deal with a large number of charities and individual VAT officers can gain some experience in dealing with the particular issues which charities face under the VAT regime. Other offices may have no real experience of dealing with charities and this can lead to misunderstandings and often inconsistencies. Evidence of such inconsistency of treatment needs to be drawn to the attention of the Policy Directorate.

The LVOs will be responsible for making what are referred to as 'control visits' to registered traders within their area to check that the routine operation of VAT is running correctly. They will also make 'educational' visits to newly registered traders to help them with any difficulties and to ensure that they properly understand the intricacies of the VAT system.

Within the local office there will be a small investigation team which can deal with local, civil fraud investigations.

Major investigations are now being handled by the National Investigation Service (NIS) which is staffed by fully trained investigators who deal with major criminal VAT fraud as well as drug-related investigations. Their activities are dramatised in the TV series *The Knock*. Charities will not, hopefully, need to have any dealings with this group.

Legislative framework

1.45   The main UK legislation is now consolidated in *Value Added Tax Act* (*VATA*) *1994* and subsequent Finance Acts. It must be remembered that VAT is essentially a European tax within the European Union and the UK has to have regard to various EU Directives that can limit the approach of Customs in developing VAT policy.

VAT has a language all of its own. It is a language where even basic things like 'exemption' mean something very different from their meaning when applied to income tax, and indeed to what might be expected in everyday English usage. Charities who get involved in VAT (and for many charities it has to be accepted that VAT is simply an additional cost to be borne in achieving their objectives) have quickly to come to grips with 'inputs' and 'input tax', 'outputs' and 'output tax', 'supplies', 'exemption', 'partial exemption' and 'outside the scope' as the more common words and phrases.

The appeal system in VAT operates through the VAT tribunals and is much more frequently used by traders, including charities, than the corresponding appeal system which exists for income tax. A regular flow of VAT tribunal cases adds to the body of interpretation. A number of these go on to the High Court and beyond, and because VAT is a European tax there is an increasing resort to the European Court of Justice. Cases which may originate in another EU member state can then become relevant to the interpretation of UK VAT legislation.

Framework of this book

1.46   Having set the scene, how will this book proceed? Essentially it falls into three parts:

- Part 1 looks in much more detail at the investigative powers of the three organisations introduced above. It will consider in each case:
    - Their legal investigative powers
    - How they identify cases for investigation
    - How they handle investigations
    - What powers they have to ensure co-operation
    - How they reach a conclusion to their investigations
    - What penalties and sanctions they can impose

- Part 2 looks at how charities can develop an approach to dealing with investigations. This is the practical heart of the book and examines the common tactics which can be applied in dealing with all three types of agency such as:

  - Coping with the first approach

  - Handling meetings

  - Progressing an investigation after the initial meeting

  - Negotiating your way to the best settlement

- Part 3 looks at the key investigation areas which charities can find themselves facing and looks at how these can arise, what the legal background is to each one and what specific action charities need to consider in each situation. This section also contains checklists to enable charities to look critically at their current position and so hopefully avoid major problems. The specific topics which will be covered are:

  - Governance issues and the role of trustees

  - Fundraising

  - Trading

  - Property

  - Membership

  - Payroll

  - VAT partial exemption

Chapter 2

Charity Commission Investigative Powers

An overview

Introduction

2.1   The Charity Commission identify one of their main objectives as being 'to identify and deal with abuse and poor practices'. This has become a more significant area of the work of the Commission, and more specialist resources have been directed towards it. The progress of the work has also been assisted by the development of a framework of legal accountability for charities put in place by *Charities Act 1993*. In particular the requirements to make annual returns provides a ready source of review material, although as we shall see, other sources of investigation cases are available as well.

Legal framework

2.2   The power of the Charity Commission to carry out inquiries stems from *Charities Act 1993, s 8(1)* which states that:

'the Commission may from time to time institute inquiries with regard to charities or a particular charity or class of charities, either generally or for particular purposes, but no such inquiry shall extend to any exempt charity.'

The power is deliberately drawn as widely as possible to give the Commissioners the ability to act in a variety of situations. It should be noted that the power extends to investigations into excepted charities but not exempt charities.

The remainder of *section 8* deals with the process of investigation and will be considered in detail below together with the provisions of:

Section 9   power to call for documents and search records

Section 10   disclosure of information to and by the Commissioners

Section 11   supply of false information to the Commissioners

The powers of the Commissioners to take action once they have an investigation in process are set out in *sections 18 to 20*

Scale of investigation work

2.3   The Charity Commission publish statistics on investigation work in their annual report each year and some of these are given below. In focusing on a specific area of work like investigations it is easy to get carried away with statistics on cases taken up, etc. without putting those figures into the overall context. The figures need to be set against the background of the number registered charities and the relative sizes of those charities. Figures on the Commission website show that at 31 March 2000 there were 159,424 charities on the register.

The 1998 Report of the Commissioners shows that in that year they opened 194 new investigations and completed 199 investigations where there was a cause for concern. Those cases were broken down into the following categories:

- Maladministration   89
- Deliberate malpractice   32
- Fundraising abuse   60
- Beneficiaries at risk   2
- Political activities   2
- Tax abuse   4
- Others   10

Those categories are very general and are simply a convenient way of recording results. In practice each investigation will be determined on its own facts and may actually fall into a number of categories. Examples of the investigations which fall into each group are given in 2.7 to 2.12 below

Investigation process

2.4   The process of investigation work falls into a number of clear stages:

(1)   Initial information indicating a potential problem – this can come from a variety of sources including members of the public, charity supporters, or from a review of the annual return.

(2)   Evaluation of the evidence and an initial review to see if the case needs a full investigation – in many cases this process either establishes that the concerns are not founded or enables the specific areas of concern to be cleared.

(3)   Investigation under the power in *Ch A 1993, s 8*.

(4)   Remedial action as necessary using the powers in *Charities Act 1993*.

Investigation organisation

2.5   Each of the three offices of the Commission has an investigation team, which comprises administrative staff who have some background knowledge of the charity sector and have investigative skills. They are able to call upon the legal and accountancy teams in each office for support where needed. They do have training on investigative techniques and questioning and a detailed Inquiry Manual is currently being produced, extracts from which should eventually appear within the public domain in the Operational Guidance Notes available on the Charity Commission website.

Charity Commission publication CC47

2.6   The Commissioners produce a range of publications including CC47, *'Inquiries into Charities'*. This explains in outline terms:

(1)   the types of compliants they consider;

(2)   how members of the public can alert them;

(3)   confidentiality;

(4)   what happens when they are alerted;

(5)   formal inquiries;

(6)   action to put things right;

(7)   auditors' and examiners' duties.

Types of investigation cases

Maladministration

2.7   This category really covers situations where the trustees have failed to carry out their duties in a competent fashion. Sometimes this may be caused by basic inadequacy which manifests itself in a lack of proper accounting records, a total lack of paperwork such as minutes and any real understanding of what is going on. Maladministration would also cover situations in which trustees obtain a benefit from their position which they are not allowed to receive.

Problems can arise in larger charities because of the sheer complexity of the organisation. In one case the Commissioners highlighted the excessive number of committees that existed and the lack of co-ordination between them. Rapid growth can also cause problems where the expertise of the trustees cannot cope. Perhaps specialist skills are needed which are not represented on the board. The existing systems which worked well at lower levels of activity cannot function property under a rapidly growing set of activities.

Similar problems can arise where a charity seeks to respond to a major crisis such as a natural disaster or the collapse of a political system. The Commission have noted in their reports that often the desire to respond positively to a situation overtakes a realistic assessment of whether the resources and expertise of the charity are actually up to the job.

A common problem which the Charity Commission have highlighted a number of times in reports is the failure of trustees to properly control a dominant trustee or chief executive especially where that person was the driving force behind the creation of the charity in the first place.

These areas and other governance issues will be considered in practical terms in Chapter 9.

Deliberate malpractice

2.8   Sadly there are those individuals who see the charity sector as a means to feathering their own nest and deliberately set out to exploit the systems or lack of them that they find. This obviously involves a degree of maladministration because if trustees had been on the ball such problems might not have arisen, but they go beyond just incompetence on the part of the trustees. Individuals diverting trust funds into their own bank accounts or enjoying improper use of trust assets would be basic examples.

It is noticeable that increased monitoring of the charity sector has resulted in this being a declining area of investigation work. The Report for 1991 showed that there were 168 cases of malpractice settled in that year but by 1998 that figure had fallen to 32.

Fundraising abuse

2.9   This has been a growing area of investigation and on the 1998 figures (see 2.3 above) was the second largest single area. The statistics show that each year between 50 and 70 cases are settled in this area. Common problems are:

(1)   the offer of funds from professional fundraisers who have not been appointed by the charity;

(2)   aggressive fundraising techniques being employed either by the charity or by fundraisers acting on their behalf;

(3)   too much money going to the fundraisers and not to the charity;

(4)   the use of bogus charities to collect money.

Point (4) highlights a significant legal issue relating to the jurisdiction of the Charity Commission to act in cases where those involved in the problem are not charities themselves. In their 1998 Report, the Commissioners give two actual examples of fundraising cases they have investigated. In one case, involving the selling of roses through pubs and clubs, criminal activity was uncovered and the matter was referred to the police who mounted a successful prosecution. In another case, the Commissioners investigated two organisations, neither of which was a registered charity, where one was raising money on behalf of the other which described itself as a 'registered charitable institution'. The Commissioners made orders prohibiting further fundraising and effectively drove the companies out of existence.

These cases prompted the following comment from the Commissioner (1998 Report, p. 23):

> 'The individuals behind these operations sometimes believe that, as their organisations are not charities, we have no jurisdiction over them. However, it has been our view, which has been backed up in a court judgement, that we do have jurisdiction over the funds they hold, if they have been raised via a charitable appeal.'

There are two cases in which the Commission have been successful in dealing with individuals who sought donations, and these cases have been upheld in another case which went to judicial review. What the cases show is that where a person acts as a fundraiser for a charity (whether he has been formally asked or appointed or not) he becomes in reality a trustee of the funds he collects. Those funds are funds held for charitable purposes and hence the Charity Commission have jurisdiction to act.

In the case of *Jones v Attorney-General* heard in 1976, charity collectors using open boxes had taken a commission out of the boxes with the knowledge of the trustee/founder of the charity concerned who was appealing against the decision to remove him as a trustee. In the judgment, Mr Justice Brightman stated:

> '. . . a person who solicits money for a charity is a trustee of the money for the purpose of handing it to the charity. A member of the public who puts money in the box is the donor of his contribution, not indistinguishable, in principle, from any other donor or settlor of trust funds. Unless the collector makes known to the donor his intention to retain a percentage of the contribution for himself, it seems to me that he has no possible title to that percentage.'

This judgment was followed in the 1995 case of *Regina v Wain ([1995] 2 Cr App Rep 660, CA)* which concerned an individual who ran events to raise money for a TV telethon. He put the money into a bank account, but then transferred sums to his own private account. Cheques were drawn to pay to the TV company but they were not honoured. Wain claimed that the money in the bank account did not belong to the TV trust, but it was simply an unsecured creditor. He was convicted of theft but appealed. In turning down his appeal, McCowan, LJ remarked

> 'It seems to us that by virtue of section 5(3) [of the Theft Act], the appellant was plainly under an obligation to retain, if not the actual notes and coins, at least their proceeds, that is to say the money credited in the bank account which he opened for the trust with the actual property ... . Whether a person in the position of the appellant is a trustee is to be judged on an objective basis. It is an obligation imposed on him by law. It is not essential that he should have realised that he was a trustee ... .'

Beneficiaries at risk

2.10   This will cover situations where the action (or lack of action) by the trustees actually puts individuals who are beneficiaries of the charity directly at risk. This could apply in a situation in which individuals who are in need of a particular type of care or treatment are not provided with that care.

Political activities

2.11   Charities are not allowed to engage in political activity unless they can demonstrate that it is being carried out exclusively on behalf of the beneficiaries in direct pursuit of a charitable object. General political campaigning in the charity's area of interest would not be allowed. The line is sometimes a very fine one and charities must be careful not to step across it.

Tax abuse

2.12   Obviously situations in which charities make incorrect claims to tax exemption are primarily matters for the Inland Revenue. The Charity Commission will become involved where it becomes clear that an individual has deliberately established a charity to take advantage of the tax exemption which it has. For example an individual could establish a charity to provide funds for relief overseas. The individual runs a company and arranges for that company to make a substantial donation to the charity on which it obtains tax relief. The charity makes a donation to an organisation overseas which purports to be an aid organisation. That organisation then lends the money back to the individual tax free.

Sources of investigation cases

Public information

2.13   A major source of potential cases for investigation comes from information either direct from members of the public, from individuals who have been involved as employees or possibly trustees of a charity, from MPs who pass on complaints from constituents, or from the media who pick up public disquiet on a particular issue.

Booklet CC47 explains how members of the public can contact the Investigation Division in the relevant office and asks that where possible they should supply:

- the name of the charity and its registration number;

- a summary of the complaint or concern with some background on what has actually happened;

- details of assets which may have been misused or are at risk;

- details of any documentary evidence;

- details of any attempts made by the complainant to get the charity to take action itself;

- details of any previous correspondence with the Commission on the charity or correspondence with any other public body such as the police, local authority, etc.

They also ask for the name and address of the complainant and they emphasise in bold text that they cannot promise to take any action based on anonymous information. The issue of confidentiality of information is a difficult one for the Commission. They need to be able to balance the rights of privacy of the individual against the need to rectify a problem in the charity concerned. They like to be able to put the information to the charity (unless it is obviously vexatious and provided out of malice). It has to be remembered that in some cases, even if the identity of the source is not revealed to the charity, the nature of the information provided may pinpoint the source.

Booklet CC47 does warn against giving false information and this warning has a statutory backing in *Ch A 1993, s 11(1)* which states that:

> 'Any person who knowingly or recklessly provides the Commissioners with information which is false or misleading in a material particular shall be guilty of an offence if the information—
>
> (a) is provided in purported compliance with a requirement imposed by or under this Act; or
>
> (b) is provided otherwise than as mentioned in paragraph (a) above but in circumstances in which the person providing the information

intends, or could reasonably be expected to know, that it would be used by the Commissioners for the purpose of discharging their functions under this act.'

The penalty on summary conviction is a fine and on indictment could be a prison sentence of up to two years.

Auditors and independent examiners

2.14   It is a requirement that charities which have gross income or gross expenditure of over £250,000 should have an audit and charities with an income or expenditure below that can opt for what is known as an independent examination (where income is below £10,000 neither audit nor examination is required). *Charities (Accounts and Reports) Regulations 1995 SI No 2724* requires reports to be made to the Commissioners by auditors or examiners in certain situations.

Auditors of non-company charities must communicate any matters identified in their capacity as auditor which are of 'material significance' to the exercise of the Commissioners' powers under *section 8* or *section 18*. In booklet CC47 the Commissioners indicate that this requires auditors to tell them about anything that:

(1)   needs to be investigated;

(2)   affects a current inquiry;

(3)   affects any action to protect a charity which the Commissioners might take;

(4)   indicates a significant loss or misuse of assets;

(5)   indicates a significant risk to charity funds arising from maladministration or misuse.

Auditors of charitable companies have no obligation to make the same disclosures but need to consider whether disclosure would be in the public interest.

The duties of the Independent Examiner in regard to the accounts are less rigorous and this is reflected in the reporting requirement which arises where there has been deliberate or reckless misconduct by one or more trustees. This would include:

- false accounting, theft, misappropriation or tax evasion;

- material application of funds for non-charitable purposes;

- attempts by a trustee to obtain benefits;

- failure to keep proper accounting records.

Annual returns

2.15   The introduction of the annual return was a key part of the process of establishing the accountability of charities. The format of the return has been modified and will continue to be modified. What is of more interest to the Charity Commission at the moment are those charities which have failed to submit their returns at all, or have been consistently late in doing so. Two return cycles have now been completed and the Commissioners have indicated that, although they could take proceedings to enforce submission, they prefer to deal with the matter through the inquiry procedure. The logic is that if the charity cannot organise itself to get in its annual return on time, there might be something amiss in its systems.

The intent of the Commissioners is set out clearly in their 1998 Report. Trustees who do not submit returns on time will get a polite reminder of their obligation. Failure to respond to that will cause the case to go to a small compliance review team which will adopt a 'more robust' line. Where that fails to obtain the return the case will be referred for evaluation and investigation. The Commissioners pointed out that attention was focused on charities with an income in excess of £250,000 during 1998/99 and that they would be looking at those with income over £100,000 during 1999/00.

Disputes in charities

2.16   The Commissioners may be come aware of issues involving a dispute within a charity. This may come from the media, or may indeed come from their own support group who may be trying to deal with matters at the level of trying to sort out a scheme or some other legal change. If it becomes clear that there is an underlying problem which might relate to administration or other matters then a review may be needed.

Inland Revenue and other public bodies

2.17   The Charity Commission and the Inland Revenue have a common interest in ensuring that charities conduct themselves properly. Problems of administration in the tax reclaim area may suggest a deeper problem. Issues related to trading or the use of trading companies may start with a tax problem but may suggest that assets of the charity are being put at risk possibly because of loans being made to support non-charitable trading ventures. The problem of confidentiality between government departments is one that lay people often find surprising but it has been an important part of the system for many years. In more recent years there has been a recognition that there are situations in which information available to one government department should be made available to other departments who may have an interest or concern in the same matter.

Charities Act 1993, s 10 provides a power to enable the exchange of information. *Section 10(1)* provides for any body listed in *subsection (6)* to disclose to the Charity Commission any information they receive and *subsection (4)* allows the Commissioners to make disclosure the other way. The bodies concerned are:

- Any government department (including a Northern Ireland department)
- Any local authority
- Any constable
- Any other body or person discharging functions of a public nature

The blanket reference to government departments is restricted by *section 10(2)* to exclude the Inland Revenue and Customs and Excise from the general permission. Those departments are, however, allowed to disclose the following information:

'(a) the name and address of any institution which has for any purpose been treated by the relevant body as established for charitable purposes;

(b) information as to the purpose of an institution and the trusts under which it is established or regulated, where the disclosure is made by the relevant body in order to give or obtain assistance in determining whether the institution ought for any purpose to be treated as established for charitable purposes; and

(c) information with respect to an institution which has for any purpose been treated as so established but which appears to the relevant body—

(i) to be, or to have been, carrying on activities which are not charitable, or

(ii) to be, or to have been, applying any of its funds for purposes which are not charitable'

Evaluation process

Statistics

2.18   The Charity Commission provide some statistics in their annual report on the number of evaluations carried out in each year and how those evaluations have been disposed of.

	1994	*1995*	*1996*	*1997*	*1998*
No significant cause for concern	691	544	352	669	478
Resolved by guidance	282	456	230	274	358
Formal investigation	397	255	280	245	194

Starting the process

2.19   The process of evaluation generally begins when a problem is brought to the attention of the Commissioners from one of the sources discussed above. Some cases are considered so serious that a formal investigation has to be opened immediately, but the majority of cases will go through this initial sifting process. The investigation section aims to clear 80% of evaluations within two months, although much depends upon the complexity of the points that arise.

The process will vary from case to case but will usually involve:

(1)   reviewing all the information about the charity held by the Commission in the form of annual returns, copies of accounts and any other information;

(2)   meeting with or corresponding with the individuals who have provided the original information to see what further information might be available;

(3)   putting written questions to the trustees on the areas of concern;

(4)   in more serious or complex cases, asking for a meeting with the trustees.

Trustees will be notified by the Commissioners when an evaluation process begins and they will be given an indication of what problems have arisen. It is important that all trustees are aware of what is going on and regard the matter as one of utmost seriousness. It would be fool-ish to regard it as some routine check being carried out. Bear in mind that the process is one which only affects a very small number of chari-ties – it is statistically not routine. It would be desirable to hold an emergency trustees' meeting as soon as it comes to the charity's atten-tion that the process of evaluation has been started.

If information is requested, it should by supplied as quickly but as com-prehensively as possible. If a meeting is requested, every attempt should be made to set that meeting up and all trustees should attend unless there are compelling circumstances. This is not a matter which the trustees should delegate to the chief executive or even to a small group of trustees.

Taking swift, decisive action will help the situation. An inability to respond in any meaningful way may simply confirm to the Commissioners that there is a serious problem in the charity which needs resolving. Again, statistically, there is only a 15%–20% chance of the evaluation turning into a full investigation, so it would seem that positive action can pay dividends and time and effort put in at this early stage may prevent the substantial drain of time that a full investi-gation will inevitably cause.

Around 50% of all cases are simply closed with no further action because the complaint made was groundless, or because it was not considered serious enough for any action to be taken. Where the complaint is really totally incorrect or vexatious, the trustees may still want to consider why someone should feel they have grounds for making the complaint. Where the complaint or information is trivial and no further action is taken, the trustees should not simply note the fact in the next trust meeting minutes but should take some time to look at the relevant area and make sure that what has been discovered is simply a minor blip that is unlikely to recur and not the start of something which could build up into a major problem at a later stage. Lessons should always be learned.

Guidance and support

2.20   Again the statistics show that between 25% and 35% of evaluation cases are closed by guidance being issued to the charity. This is usually done by the investigation team in the office passing the case over to the support section to sort out the appropriate action. This will be because there are some legal changes that may be needed in the organisation, perhaps an adjustment to the objectives of the trust, or some action in respect of trust property. Trustees should view this as a positive step and take full advantage of the advice being proposed – it is after all free consultancy advice from real specialists. It can be helpful to have long established procedures and documentation reviewed by an outside party.

Not every case will end at the evaluation stage. One in every five or six will become a full investigation.

Investigations

The opening

2.21   The charity will receive a formal notification when the Commissioners decide that it is appropriate to open a full investigation under *Ch A 1993, s 8(1)*. The action that should be taken is discussed more fully in Chapter 6. Where the investigation relates to a single specific issue it may be dealt with by one investigator. Where more complex issues are involved the investigation may involve two investigators. In each case they will be able to draw upon specialist legal and accountancy support as appropriate.

The formal opening may be followed up either by a very detailed letter setting out the information required or by a request for a meeting. Which approach is adopted will very much depend upon the circumstances of the case and also on any action already taken under the evaluation process. If a meeting has not happened under that process, it is likely that one will be required under the opening of an investigation, and that the investigators will want that meeting to be with all the trustees.

At this stage in the investigation the investigators are taking a neutral stance. As the Commissioners state in booklet CC47, para 18:

> 'Officers carrying out inquiries are under a duty to act fairly. They are concerned solely with the best interests of the charity and its beneficiaries. They **do not** represent the interests of either the complainant or the trustees.'

They will normally issue to the trustees a copy of booklet CC47(a) which explains the rights and obligations of the individuals.

Detailed investigation

What it involves

2.22   The precise format of the investigation is going to depend on the nature of the issues with which it is concerned.

An investigation which centres on the administration of the charity is going to involve a detailed review of working procedures in the charity. It is likely that the investigators will want to see minutes of trustee meetings, correspondence, internal procedures and standing orders. They may also want to interview individual trustees to find out just how much they are involved in the running of the charity and the decision-making process.

Where the investigation involves the running of a trading subsidiary, both bodies will come under review and the need for evidence will spread. This could involve a detailed review of:

(1)   the accounting records for both charity and company;

(2)   board meeting minutes for the company;

(3)   how the trustee body and directors relate to each other;

(4)   what control the charity trustees actually have over the company;

(5)   the financial links between the two and how these are controlled.

A review that looks at fundraising problems is going to consider the fundraising practices used. The involvement of external fundraisers, the terms of their agreements and specifically how the charity exercises control over their activities. The method of remuneration will also be considered. This will almost certainly involve the fundraisers in the inquiry as well.

It has to be expected that some investigations will focus very particularly on the activities of one individual, possibly the chief executive, or a founding trustee or a small group of trustees. The remaining trustees will want to consider how to react to this and what action they need to take to with regard to the position of these individuals and to ensure the smooth running of the charity's activities throughout the period of the investigation. Again these issues will be discussed in more detail in Chapter 6.

Powers to obtain information

2.23   The Charity Commission investigators are now armed with a formidable range of powers under *Ch A 1993, ss 8* and *9*. These can be summarised as follows:

(1)   Directing any person to produce accounts and statements with respect to any matter in question at the inquiry, where the person has or reasonably can obtain the information. [*s 8(3)(a)*]. This also extends to providing written answers to questions addressed to them on any matter relating to the inquiry. The individual may be required to verify accounts, statements or answers by statutory declaration.

(2)   Directing any person to provide copies of documents under his control which relate to the matter under enquiry. [*s 8(3)(b)*]. Again they may be required to verify the documents by statutory declaration.

(3)   Requiring any person to attend at a specific time and place to give evidence or produce documents. [*s 8(3)(c)*].

(4)   Taking any evidence on oath. [*s 8(4)*].

(5)   Paying a person's expenses in attending to give evidence or produce documents. [*s 8(5)*]. No one is obliged to go more than ten miles from his place of residence unless expenses are paid.

(6)   Ordering any person to supply them with any information in his possession which relates to any charity. [*s 9(1)(a)*].

(7)   Ordering a person to supply any document in his possession which relates to any charity. [*s 9(1)(b)*].

(8)   Taking copies of any documents of any court or public registry. [*s 9(2)*].

The use of orders under *section 9* rather than directions under *section 8* indicates a more formal approach to the investigation. There are enforcement powers in *Ch A 1993, s 88* which provide that if someone disobeys an order under *section 9(1)* they can be dealt with in the High Court as if they had disobeyed an order of that Court.

Statistics from the annual reports of the Commissioners indicate a steady rise in the use of orders to obtain documents, e.g. the number in 1996 was greater than the combined totals for 1994 and 1995. The 1998 figures show 172 orders being obtained in the year.

These powers do not require the prior approval of any other body or the courts, although anyone who felt that the Commissioners were not entitled to exercise a particular power in a particular case would be able to seek a judicial review of the action in the High Court. The powers, taken together, represent a formidable array and in reality leave trustees with little option but to comply.

Finalisation

2.24 The investigation teams aim to complete 90% of investigations within a year, and sooner or later all investigations are going to come to a point where they can be finalised. This will usually proceed in a number of stages:

(1) There will be a final meeting with the trustees at which the investigators will advise them of the outcome of their inquiries and the action they propose.

(2) They will draw up an action plan if they want specific action to be taken by the trustees.

(3) They will seek a written agreement from the trustees to that action plan and a timetable for implementation.

(4) Where appropriate the support section in the office will work with the trustees on the implementation of the action.

(5) In some situations more formal action under other provisions of *Charities Act 1993* will be required and these powers are considered at 2.25 to 2.29 below.

(6) The Commissioners may want to publicise the details of the investigation and this is discussed at 2.32 below.

The investigation teams are looking to try to add value to the situations and not simply to take punitive action against trustees or individuals. Trustees may not always see this as the outcome, particularly in the immediate aftermath of a closing meeting, but they should always seek to look beyond the immediate impact and consider the wider issues. The lesson must be that having experienced or endured one investigation, they would never want to experience another and must know what to do to ensure that this never happens again.

Remedial action

Basic power

2.25 *Charities Act 1993, s 18(1)* provides the power to take further action. It states:

> 'Where, at any time after they have instituted an inquiry under section 8 above with respect to any charity, the Commissioners are satisfied—

(a) that there is or has been any misconduct or mismanagement in the administration of the charity; or

(b) that it is necessary or desirable to act for the purpose of protecting the property of the charity or securing a proper application for the purposes of the charity of that property or of property coming to the charity,

the Commissioners may of their own motion do one or more of the following things . . .'

The first point to note here is that the powers can be exercised once the investigation has started and once there is evidence on which to act. The Commissioners do not have to wait until the completion of the investigation if they believe that action needs to be taken earlier. This may be particularly important as regards powers to suspend trustees, or to freeze charity assets.

The second important point is that these powers do not require any external approval such as that of the courts. The exercise of the powers is subject to review by the courts if those who are affected by the orders believe that the Commissioners have acted wrongly in imposing the relevant sanction. The Commissioners are therefore likely to act formally only in situations where they are content that the courts would back their actions.

Dealing with trustees

Suspension

2.26   The power to suspend is in *Ch A 1993, s 18(1)(i)* and applies to the suspension of 'any trustee, charity trustee, officer, agent or employee of the charity from the exercise of his office or employment pending consideration being given to his removal'. This power does not require that the trustee or employee should be guilty of any offence and the investigators are likely to use the power to prevent an individual who is the real target of the investigation from playing a continued role in the running of the charity.

In some situations the suspension may be lifted. For example in the recently reported case of the *Voice of Methodism Association* and the *VMA Board of Trustees*, the investigators suspended an individual who was the target of many of the complaints. Having appointed a receiver and manager, the Commissioners took the view that as that person was now running the charity, the suspension of the trustee could be lifted.

Removal

2.27   The removal of a trustee, officer, agent or an employee comes under a separate power in *Ch A 1993, s 18(2)*. The preliminary wording is the same as at the start of *section 18(1)* but the power to remove a trustee requires that the individual concerned 'has been responsible for or privy to the misconduct or mismanagement or has by his conduct contributed to it or facilitated it'.

Removal therefore requires a link between the individual and the problem. This is illustrated by the cases involving the Yorkshire Miners' Welfare Trust and the Yorkshire Miners' Welfare Convalescent Homes. In that case an inquiry decided that two individuals had been guilty of misconduct and mismanagement. The prime concern was their involvement as trustees of both charities, and their involvement in the making of a grant from the welfare trust to the convalescent homes which was in breach of the former's trust deed. There were also inquorate meetings and the two trustees failed to co-operate with the inquiry. The two individuals appealed to the High Court against the removal orders but their appeal was dismissed. The judge concluded that the two had knowingly persevered in breaching the terms of the charity's trust deed and had done so without apology or remorse.

The provisions of *section 20(3)* require that before the Commissioners make an order to remove a trustee or employee, etc., they must given them at least one month's notice of their proposal and invite representations to be made to them.

The Commissioners statistics show that 20 trustees were removed from office in 1998.

Appointment

2.28   Simply removing or suspending trustees is only part of the answer. The role of the inquiry is to preserve the charity assets and protect beneficiaries and this can only be done if the charity continues to exist. That means it requires trustees. *Charities Act 1993, s 18(1)(iii)* gives the Commissioners the power to 'appoint such number of additional charity trustees as they consider necessary for the proper administration of the charity'.

In some situations the prime need is to get the charity back on to a sound footing and that is best done by the appointment of a receiver (see 2.30 below). Once the receiver has completed his task, the Commissioners may decide to appoint new trustees to carry on the rehabilitation process and develop the work of the charity.

The Commissioners give an example of this approach in their notes on the Valley Books Trust in their 1996 annual report. The charity in that case was involved in the distribution of evangelical Christian books through a wholesale book business. The charity was run by a dominant founder trustee and the charity had made substantial losses on injudicious and unauthorised investments. The founder resigned as a trustee but continued as general manager and the remaining trustees (two of whom were in the USA) showed no inclination to take control. The Commissioners appointed a receiver and manager who was eventually able to bring the finances of the charity under control. Once the receiver had been discharged, a new body of trustees with considerable experience in the Christian book trade and who supported the doctrinal basis of the charity, took over the running of the charity.

Protecting property

2.29   This can take several forms and the Commissioners may:

- vest any property held by or in the trust for the charity in the official custodian, or they can require the transfer of trust property from anyone else to the official custodian [s 18(1)(iii)];

- order anyone who holds any property on behalf of the charity not to part with it without their approval [s 18(1)(iv)];

- order a debtor of the charity not to make any payment towards the discharge of his liability to the charity without their approval [s 18(1)(v)];

- restrict the transactions which may be entered into or the nature and amount of payments which may be made without their approval [s 18(1)(vi)].

The main power which is used is that of freezing the bank accounts of the charity (this happened on 37 occasions according to the 1998 Report). The restriction order would be used where, for example, there were agreements in place with fundraisers that were not appropriate. These powers are likely to be used during the course of the inquiry – indeed as soon as the investigators find that assets may be at risk. In cases where the situation can be quickly resolved, the action taken may be sufficient to allow time for the remedial action to be put into place. In situations where matters have become financially complex and dangerous the step of appointing a receiver and manager may be the only option available to preserve the charity's assets.

Appointment of receiver

2.30   The power to appoint a receiver and manager in respect of the property and affairs of the charity is set out in *sections 18(1)(vii)* and *19*. This power is given practical backing by the *Charities (Receiver and Manager) Regulations 1992 (SI 1992 No 2355)* which set out the basis on which the receiver or manager (referred to as the appointed person) is to act.

The receiver acts under the supervision of the Commissioners and the order appointing him may specify the powers and duties of the charity trustees of the charity concerned that the receiver is to assume. They can also provide that the receiver is able to exercise his powers to the exclusion of the trustees.

The *1992 Regulations* cover a number of administrative issues:

- The Commissioners can require a security. [*Reg 2*].

- The receiver's remuneration is to be determined by the Commissioners and is payable out of the income of the relevant charity. [*Reg 3*].

- The Commissioners can remove the receiver. [*Reg 4*].

- The receiver is required to make an initial report to the Commissioners, not later that three months after his appointment, setting out his estimate of the total value of trust property on the date of his appointment, his strategy for discharging his functions and any other relevant information. [*Reg 5(2)*].

- The receiver must submit an annual report within one month of each anniversary of his appointment setting out the value of trust assets at the anniversary, the actions taken in the previous twelve months, and changes to his strategy. [*Reg 5(3)*].

- A final report is required within three months of ceasing to hold office summarising the actions taken since the last report. [*Reg 5(4)*].

The recently reported case of the *Voice of Methodism* and the *VMA Board of Trustees* involved the appointment of a receiver, who happened to be a partner of the author. The two charities had similar objects and some shared personnel but had a history of friction both between the two and within each. In addition there was a dominant trustee on the board of trustees. The Commissioners had concluded that there were severe shortcomings in the governance of both charities and after attempts to agree a basis for going forward failed, the Commissioners opened a formal inquiry under *section 8*.

The Commissioners concluded that there had been misconduct or mismanagement and that they needed to act to protect the assets of the charities. They froze the bank accounts, suspended the dominant trustee and appointed a receiver. The specific tasks given to the receiver, apart from the day-to-day running of the charities, were to control and rationalise the financial records and bank accounts, producing statements of account, locating and valuing assets and debts and determining whether there had been any loss of funds, or evidence of misappropriation.

The receiver was able to report that the funds emerging in 1995 were not greatly dissimilar to those which existed in 1990 and that there was no evidence that assets had gone missing. He indicated that there had been profligacy and that a lack of proper investment had damaged the funds. The conclusions he came to broadly confirmed the concerns which the Commissioners had had. In addition, the receiver had found that the dominant trustee had liquidated the investment portfolio and put the money on deposit without any discussion or the taking of any professional advice. This action had resulted in a real loss of income.

The receiver had formed opinions on and made recommendations about how and why the administration had degenerated and what would be necessary to provide a sound base for the future. The Commissioners accepted those findings and have used them to provide a basis for the Scheme which is being put in place to resolve the problem.

Making a scheme

2.31   *Charities Act 1993, s 18(2)(b)(ii)* provides that the Commissioners may make a scheme for the administration of the charity where they find evidence of mismanagement or misconduct or there is a need to protect assets. This power can be exercised by the Commissioners unilaterally. This mirrors the power to make a scheme which exists in general in *section 16* of the Act. The making of a scheme is legally binding and gives the Commissioners the opportunity to impose a solution, especially where the parties are for some reason reluctant to accept new ideas.

The provisions of *section 20*, require that a scheme shall not be submitted to the court or to the Secretary of State for an order giving it effect unless they have given a month's public notice of their intention and invited representations to be made to them.

In the case of the charities of the *Voice of Methodism* and the *VMA Board of Trustees* discussed above, the scheme is going to contain the following provisions:

(1)   amalgamation of the two charities;

(2)   restatement of the objects (the Commissioners are not competent to determine a doctrinal basis);

(3)   adequate provisions for membership and subscription and a requirement that a membership list must be maintained;

(4)   the election of trustees from the membership but excluding those who were trustees of either charity;

(5)   the creation of an electoral process;

(6)   proposals for the conduct of committee and annual meetings.

Publicity

2.32   There are signs that the Commissioners want to give more publicity to the results of their inquiries. Some reports in abbreviated form have appeared in the Commissioners' Annual Report in most years. In more recent times there has been a policy of giving details of inquiry reports on the Commission website and certainly there are details of the *Voice of Methodism* case and also the *Roy Castle Cancer Trust* inquiry on the web.

Chapter 3

Inland Revenue – FICO Investigations

Introduction

A changing scene

3.1   Those who work in tax on a regular basis know that it is an area of constant change certainly as far as legislation is concerned. This affects both practitioners and the Revenue. For the latter, recent years have seen not only substantial changes in legislation but also major organisational changes as well.

The office dealing with charities – the Financial Intermediaries and Claims Office (FICO) – has not been much affected by the organisational changes in the Revenue which have had their major impact at local district level, although it has had its local problems, caused by the state of the building it occupies in Bootle. The two major areas of legislative change that are just starting to have a major impact on FICO are:

- The introduction of self-assessment
- The impact of the charities tax review

The background to self-assessment is dealt with at 3.3 below. These changes are gradually having an impact on the regulatory regime for charities and charities will start to notice the effect over the next couple of years as the new regime really takes hold. The self-assessment regime brings with it a new approach to investigation work and FICO will have to adapt its arrangements to work in this new regime.

The impact of the charities tax review is going to take time to work through. The major change which will affect the work of FICO will be in the new Gift Aid regime which largely replaces the old deed of covenant arrangements which were the source of many successful audits by FICO. The new regime, although spared many of the legal intricacies of deeds of covenant, will bring compliance problems for many charities and will, in the author's opinion, lead to a lot of initial work for FICO which it will find very 'rewarding'. The background to the new arrangements is discussed in Part 3.

In this chapter we will look at the legal background to the investigation work at FICO, how that work is organised and what potential penalties lurk for charities who become entangled in the web.

National Audit Office Scrutiny

3.2   The National Audit Office (NAO) is part of the operation of the Comptroller and Auditor-General, and is effectively the Government's own internal watchdog on the operations of other government departments and public bodies.

In 1998 the NAO published a report, on 'The monitoring and control of tax exemptions for charities' (*HC 575 Session 1997–8*). The report followed a detailed review by the NAO of the work done at FICO in Bootle and Edinburgh (the office which deals with Scottish charities). The report provides an interesting insight to the operation at FICO, what it consisted of and how efficient it was. The report was critical of a number of aspects of the compliance operation and it is likely that its recommendations will be put into practice by FICO. The comments and recommendations will be picked up in the relevant parts of this chapter because they help to give a flavour of the Revenue approach that is likely to develop over the next few years.

The report contains many statistics and some of the detailed figures will be looked at below. The following give an overall picture of the charity sector and the overall FICO base. The NAO put the overall charity population in 1998 at 300,000, comprising:

● Registered charities in England and Wales	184,000
● Registered charities in Scotland	24,000
● Registered charities in Northern Ireland	7,500
● Churches not requiring registration	40,000
● Other non-registered charities	43,000
● Other bodies including museums, universities	2,000

FICO maintains a database of 84,000 charities that have made a claim for tax repayment or have applied for charitable exemption. They also have a 'dormant' range of 213,000 charities whose last repayment was more than three years earlier. In 1996/97, FICO Bootle processed 177,832 tax repayment claims from 46,500 charities. FICO Scotland processed 12,660 claims from 5,300 charities.

Self-assessment regime

3.3   The introduction of self-assessment for companies with effect from accounting periods ending on or after 1 July 1999 completes the introduction of self-assessment into the UK tax system. Charities have been somewhat confused by the whole exercise, because, as non-tax-payers (usually) they do not see how the regime applies to them. The position for income tax purposes has not been helped by the fact that up to and including 1998/99 no special return has been available for charities. The notes that follow set out the position as it now is.

Revenue officers talk about giving charities the 'protection of self-assessment'. Charities may feel that they would rather not have the system at all and may wonder how it offers them any protection – it certainly can mean more work. What the Revenue mean is that charities are able to benefit from the legislative control of investigation work and this can ward off the excesses of over-zealous inspectors and give charities some certainty in their financial position. Charities may remain unconvinced!

Framework of self-assessment

3.4   There are three broad elements in the framework of self-assessment and they apply to both income tax and corporation tax. These three elements are:

- Issue of and filing of the tax return
- Calculation and payment of tax
- Right of enquiry

For the sake of completeness we will consider all three areas, although in practice the second area is not likely to apply to charities. We will also draw the distinction between the income tax requirements and the corporation tax requirements where appropriate.

It is also important to note that there is a part of the self-assessment regime that relates to claims for tax relief made other than in a return. This is of direct relevance to charities because of the procedure for making a claim for tax repayment on deeds of covenant and Gift Aid using the R68 procedure. These procedures broadly mirror the procedures for returns and are looked at in detail at 3.12 below.

Notification of liability

3.5   *Taxes Management Act (TMA) 1970, s 7* imposes an obligation on an individual or trust to notify the Revenue if they have become liable to pay income tax or CGT. This obligation must be discharged within six months of the end of the tax year in which the charge arose. So for the tax year 2000/01 the effective time limit for notifying chargeability will be 5 October 2001.

The obligation on companies is imposed by *TMA 1970, s 10* which has a time limit of twelve months from the end of the accounting period in which chargeability arose.

Charities need to be aware of these limits if they do receive income, e.g. from non-exempt trading activities, which should be declared. The onus is very much on the taxpayer. Waiting for the Inspector to send you a return could prove very expensive – the maximum penalty for failing to notify chargeability is an amount equal to the tax on the income not notified. The assumption will be that the charity should know if the income is taxable – if in doubt they should have sought advice from the Revenue. The requirement to notify chargeability does not apply if the income in question has already suffered tax at the basic rate.

Returns

3.6   No taxpayer comes into the full self-assessment regime unless they have been issued with a return, although a part of the regime deals with claims made under the Taxes Acts and that will clearly affect any charity that makes a repayment claim.

The issue of a tax return, whether an income tax return or a corporation tax return, immediately imposes on the recipient a requirement to file that return by a specified date known as the 'filing date'. For income tax purposes, those charities which are trusts will be required to file the return by 31 January after the end of the tax year to which the return relates, so for the 1999/00 tax year the returns issued in April 2000 must be filed by 31 January 2001. For a company, the filing date remains the same as it did under the old Pay and File regime – twelve months after the end of the accounting period to which the return relates. A charity with a year end of 31 December 2000 would need to file its return by 31 December 2001.

Income tax

3.7   For the years up to and including 1998/99, the issue of income tax returns to charities was a little haphazard, and the position has been complicated by the fact that the trust return which was issued is not directly relevant to charities. This caused considerable confusion for charities especially where the charity only had income covered by the *section 505* exemption.

For the tax year 1999/00, the Revenue have prepared special charity pages as part of the trusts and estates return. These pages are repro-duced as Appendix 3. The Revenue indicate that where a charity is required to complete the return they should submit the charity accounts as well, otherwise the Revenue do not wish to see the accounts.

The return falls into seven parts:

Part 1   asks for details of tax reference and charity registration number. It then asks two questions which require a 'Yes or No' answer – is exemption being claimed and has the income and gains been applied for charitable purposes?

Part 2   confirms the return period and that accounts are being submitted. A reason must be given in box 5 if accounts are not being submitted.

Part 3   deals with repayments of tax. It asks for details of amounts already claimed and allows space for a further claim to be made at box 10.

Part 4   requires a breakdown of the exempt income of the charity for the period. Where income is not exempt it should be shown on other parts of the main trust and estates return.

Part 5   asks for a summary of expenses and charitable payments made.

Part 6   is a summary of assets and details of disposals made in the year. The question about qualifying loans is part of the anti-avoidance measures which are considered in Chapter 7. This applies also to the figure given at box 39.

Part 7   is the formal claim for exemption.

Corporation tax

3.8   As far as charities which are in the scope of corporation tax are concerned, the Revenue have indicated that they will be issuing a notice to file in a number of cases. They will not necessarily issue a return to a charity every year but it is likely that over a period of time most charities may receive a return. If a return is issued, the charity must complete it and file it. The issue of these returns is in the hands of FICO and it will be deliberately selective in its choice of charities. FICO now also has all the files for trading subsidiaries of charities, and it will control the issue of returns to these companies. These are likely to be issued annually and again must be completed and filed.

A new return, CT600, was issued for self-assessment purposes and a copy of the 1999 version is at Appendix 4 together with the special form CT600E to be used by charities.

A charity must complete CT600 and will show on that return any income which falls outside the charity exemption. If there is any corporation tax payable, the calculation of that tax must be shown on the return.

Form CT600E represents the supplementary pages for a charity return, and will be the charity's claim for exemption from tax in respect of the income shown on the return. The first page of the return contains a claim for exemption which must be signed. The return then goes on to require details of the exempt income, breaking it down into the following categories:

- Total turnover from exempt trading activities
- Investment income
- Income from UK land and buildings
- Deed of covenant
- Gift Aid or Millennium Gift Aid
- Legacies
- Income from other charities
- Other donations
- Other sources

The return then requires details of expenditure shown in the charity accounts as follows:

- Trading costs in respect of exempt trades
- Expenditure on property income
- All general administrative costs
- All grants and donations made within the UK
- All grants and donations made outside the UK
- Other expenditure

The next part of the return requires details of charity assets showing both consideration received from disposals made in the year and the amount held at the end of the year. Separate details have to be shown of:

- Tangible fixed assets
- UK investments
- Shares in and loans to controlled companies
- Loans and non-trade debtors
- Overseas investments
- Current assets

In the final part of the return, the charity is to indicate if all loans and investments are within *ICTA 1988, Sch 20*. The value of any non-qualifying loans must also be shown. The charity has to indicate if it controls one or more subsidiary companies.

A trading subsidiary will complete only form CT600.

Penalties

3.9   Both the income tax and corporation tax provisions have penalties for submitting returns late, which are automatically leviable unless a reasonable excuse can be shown. The initial penalty for income tax is £100 if the return is not submitted by 31 January and a further £100 is leviable if the failure continues beyond the 31 July after the filing date. Where failure continues beyond the next 31 January (i.e. the return is at least a year late) the penalty becomes a sum equal to the tax shown on the self-assessment.

Provisions exist to allow a taxpayer to amend a return at any time within twelve months of the official filing date, although this facility is not available if the Revenue have already given notice of an enquiry. The Revenue have the right to correct any obvious error which may have been made and must do this within nine months of the date of actual submission of the return.

Where a taxpayer fails to submit a return, the Revenue have the power to issue a determination of the tax liability for the relevant year and that determination remains in place until the taxpayer submits a self assessment. This power can be carried out at any time up to five years after the filing date for the relevant year, although in practice the Revenue are not likely to wait that long.

All in all the message must be – get the return in by the official filing date.

Record-keeping

3.10   One important facet of the return regime, which will impact on all charities, is the requirement contained in the legislation that every item on the tax return must be backed up by relevant records. There are actually provisions that allow the Revenue to issue a penalty of up to £3,000 if records are inadequate. The more likely route is that entries on returns will simply not be accepted and tax liability may accrue as a result. This could apply to charities in matters such as records of payments made where there is no evidence to show that the payment was applied for charitable purposes.

Not only must records be maintained, they must also be retained. Where there is a trade being carried on the period of retention must extend to five years from the filing date (letting of property is regarded as a trade for these purposes). In other cases it will be one year from the filing date. In both situations, records must not be destroyed if the Revenue have given notice of an enquiry.

Calculation and payment of tax

3.11 The system of self-assessment imposes on the taxpayer the requirement to calculate their liability to tax and to arrange for that tax to be paid on the due dates without the Revenue issuing assessments. Interest is automatically charged if payment is made late.

Under the income tax system, tax is paid in three instalments in respect of each year. Payments on account, based on the previous year's liability (known as the 'relevant amount') are payable on 31 January in the year of assessment and on 31 July after the end of the year of assessment with a balancing payment being made on 31 January after the end of the year. So for the tax year 2000/01, the payments are due on:

- 31 January 2001 (50% of 1999/00 tax)

- 31 July 2001 (50% of 1999/00 tax)

- 31 January 2002 (tax as calculated on self-assessment less payments on account)

Obviously if the payments on account exceed the ultimate liability, the excess will be repayable. It is possible to make a claim to reduce payments on account to the estimated liability (known as the 'stated amount').

The corporation tax system requires a single payment nine months and one day after the end of the accounting period. So a charity with an accounting date of 31 December will pay any tax due on the 1 October in the following year. There is a requirement for companies with profits of over £1.5m a year to make quarterly payments on account during and after the accounting period, but these provisions are unlikely to apply to charities or to trading subsidiaries of charities.

Claims under the self-assessment regime

3.12 Provisions in *TMA 1970, Sch 1A* deal with procedures for making claims which parallel those for returns. The rules apply to claims made other than on a return and without these special rules there would be no way of regulating such claims. Where a claim is made on a return, that will fall within the return rules described above.

The provisions on claims allow for an amendment of a claim and also for the Revenue to correct a claim and well as to make enquiries.

The enquiry regime under self-assessment

Introduction

3.13 Under the pre-self-assessment regime, the Revenue could instigate an investigation into a taxpayer's affairs only if they were not satisfied that the return submitted was complete. Those provisions no longer apply under self-assessment and have been replaced by giving the Revenue the right to enquire into any return. They need no grounds for mounting such an enquiry, although in some cases they will commence an enquiry because of information they hold. This power of random enquiry is formidable and there are powers in the legislation to provide some checks and balances. This new enquiry pattern will be relevant to charities and indeed the FICO Inspectors see that regime as giving charities 'protection'.

The enquiry rules apply not only to the submission of the return but also to any subsequent amendment of that return by the taxpayer. The rules also apply to enquiries into claims.

Commencing an enquiry

3.14   The Revenue has a fixed period of time in which it can commence an enquiry. This is being referred to as the enquiry 'window' and will normally be a period of 12 months after the official filing date of the return (or the amendment to the return).

> *Example*
> A charity submits its return for 1999/00 due on 31 January 2001 on 15 October 2000. The Revenue have until 31 January 2002 to commence an enquiry.
>
> The same charity submits an amendment to that return on 12 March 2001. The Revenue have until 11 March 2002 to commence an enquiry into the amendment. Any inquiry started up to 31 January 2002 could include both the original return and the amendment. After that date only the amendment can be subject to enquiry.

The enquiry window is extended if the return is submitted late. In that case it runs until the next quarter date after the first anniversary of the submission of the return (or the amendment to the return). For these purposes the quarter dates are 31 January, 30 April, 31 July and 31 October.

> *Example*
> Another charity does not submit its return for 1999/2000 until 19 May 2001. The enquiry window will run until 31 July 2002.

Once the 'window' closes, the Revenue can no longer enquire into the year concerned unless an enquiry into a later year allows the Inspector to make what is known as a 'discovery' in respect of the earlier year. This would happen if it became clear that an error spotted in a later year had been going on for a number of years. The concept of discovery is not a new one and there are established legal principles relating to it. Whether a discovery can be made may well depend upon the facts that were available to the Revenue at the time the return was first made or, if there has been an earlier enquiry, at the time of that enquiry.

The Revenue have to give a formal notice to the charity when an enquiry commences. This is known as a 'section 9A letter'. The Revenue do not have to give any reason for the enquiry and will not do so, although the purpose may become clear. They will take the view that any initial approach is a neutral one because they are simply making enquiries and not making an allegation that the return is incorrect. In practice few enquiries will be undertaken without some clear grounds for so doing.

The formal letter is usually accompanied by a separate letter requesting further information. Where ordinary traders are concerned, if that letter asks for details of books and records, then it is likely that there are serious problems. With charity investigations, it is more likely that the enquiry will centre on a particular aspect, e.g. trading, and the questions will be of a factual nature aimed at gaining further information about the activities concerned.

One enquiry per return

3.15   The Revenue can only make one enquiry into each return. This has the practical effect of meaning that they will look at everything whilst they are in, unless it is clear that there is a simple explanation for an issue which allows only that aspect to be considered. Giving the Revenue an excuse to come in on a relatively minor point could be the opportunity for a major review and care over small details could be very important.

Information powers

3.16   The Revenue have always had some formidable powers to obtain information, but many of the more stringent of these, most notably *TMA 1970, s 20*, which is used in major enquiry cases, requires the consent of an Appeal Commissioner. When the self-assessment rules were introduced the Revenue included a new power at *TMA 1970, s 19A* which gives them the right to require the production of information. This does not require the consent of the Commissioners, although appeal can be made to the Commissioners if it is considered that the request is unreasonable. The right is expressed as requiring the taxpayer to act within a specified time (not less than 30 days):

(1)   to produce . . . such documents as are in the taxpayer's possession or power and as the officer may reasonably require for the purpose of determining whether and, if so, the extent to which the return is incorrect or incomplete or the amendment is incorrect, and

(2)   to furnish the officer with such accounts or particulars as he may reasonably require for that purpose.

The key question to be considered in every case is whether the information being requested can be reasonably required. It would probably not be unreasonable for an Inspector to want to see the accounting records of the charity, or the trading books and records. It would be unreasonable for a request to be made for the private bank accounts of the trustees. Where the taxpayer believes that the request is unreasonable, he can appeal within 30 days of the date of the notice requesting the information and can take that appeal to the appeal Commissioners who will determine whether they accept the reasonableness argument.

Bringing an enquiry to an end

3.17   An enquiry is formally concluded by a written notice from the Inspector that he has completed his enquiries and has concluded that the tax which should be shown in the taxpayer's self-assessment should be a specified sum. [*TMA 1970, s 28A(5)*]. Where that sum is greater than the original self-assessment the law allows the Inspector to ask the taxpayer to revise their self-assessment within 30 days. [*TMA 1970, s 28A(3)*]. If they don't do that, or don't do it sufficiently then the power exists for the Inspector to decide the amount of the self-assessment. [*TMA 1970, s 28A(4)*].

Taxes Management Act 1970, s 28A(6) contains an interesting power that did not exist in pre-self assessment days. The taxpayer has the right at any time in the enquiry period (prior to the issue of a completion notice by the Revenue) to ask the General Commissioners to direct the Revenue to issue a closure notice if they believe that there are no reasonable grounds for continuing. The onus of proof is on the Revenue to persuade the Commissioners to keep the enquiry going. This power should provide a brake on the activities of over-zealous Inspectors who simply do not know when to let go of a problem.

Specific power of enquiry on Charities

3.18   Specific legislation which grants the right of enquiry in the case of a charity pre-dated the self-assessment regime and is found in *Finance (No 2) Act (F(No 2)A) 1992, s 28*. This states that where a charity, or other body which can seek exemption under *ICTA 1988, s 507 or s 508*, has made such a claim, and the claim results in the repayment (actual or potential) of income tax or a payment of tax credit then 'The Board may require the body to produce for inspection by an officer of the Board all such books, documents and other records in the possession of or under the control, of the body as contain information relating to the claim'. The power can be used not only against a charity but also against a heritage body or a body engaged in scientific research.

The power to require the production of basic records is a formidable one. It is not, for example, available as a matter of course in investigations into traders, although a similar power exists in the area of PAYE investigations. There is no requirement that it should be used only in cases in which the Revenue believe that an excessive claim may have been made. The power is seen by the Revenue as a key part of their policy of 'pay now examine later' which has allowed them to speed up the processing of repayment claims made by charities. It is the price that charities have to pay for that service.

The power as it stands in the legislation is, however, only one of inspection of books of account, documents and other written records. It does not allow the Revenue to ask any questions they like about the charity's affairs. There are other powers that can be used to elicit information from either the taxpayer or a third party and it should not be assumed that charities are outside the scope of such legislation.

Approach of FICO to investigation work

General compliance objectives

3.19   The primary objective of the work of FICO is to ensure that the bodies which qualify for tax exemptions obtain the benefits of those exemptions and comply with their tax obligations. To achieve these objectives the Revenue have a staff of around 80 people of whom about half are engaged in the processing of repayment claims.

The more senior staff are engaged in the more complex areas of looking at the accounts of charities, and there has been an attempt in recent years to bring some technical and investigation experience into the FICO team.

Three types of compliance review

3.20   The compliance work is divided into three areas. Each of these areas has very distinctive characteristics and tends to be carried out by different groups in FICO. Each was looked at in some detail by the NAO review. The three areas are

(1)   the checking of repayment claims;

(2)   audit visits;

(3)   review of accounts – now the formal self assessment enquiries.

Each will be considered in turn.

Repayment checks

Selection process

3.21   The repayment section has to handle just under 200,000 repayment claims a year from over 40,000 charities. Many of these charities are small and, for many excepted charities, the repayment of tax in respect of Gift Aid and deeds of covenant, is their only exposure to the regulatory regime.

A decade ago the process was a long and tedious one with each claim being checked and a range of background information having to be submitted. For example all deeds of covenant had to be sent in, and all Gift Aid certificates had to be submitted. Charities could wait several months for a repayment. Now the process is one of 'repay now, check later' and the aim is to pay 95% of claims within ten days of receipt. The range of information which has to be submitted has also been substantially reduced and is being reduced still further under the new Gift Aid procedures. Basically no additional documentation will now be required with the claim form, which will list the total being reclaimed. The procedures for making reclaims are set out in Chapter 5 of *Tolley's Charities Manual*.

Repayment claims are checked against the list of charities on the databases to ensure that they are from bodies which qualify for charitable exemption. Larger claims are subject to arithmetical checks. The claims details are passed through a computer which provides an analysis based on a points system which includes changes in the charity since the last claim and the size of the claim but not (at least at the time of the NAO report) any risk associated with the compliance history of the charity.

The NAO report states that three categories of claim are submitted for a more detailed check to ensure that they meet legal requirements and that any supporting documentation matches up. Those three groups are:

(1)   all first claims;

(2)   all claims over a certain (unspecified) amount;

(3)   a small sample of other claims.

The NAO was critical of the absence of any assessment of compliance history in the computer process and also of the fact that no records were kept of the charities which made errors, meaning that persistent offenders could not be identified. A recommendation was made that this information should be collated and considered as an element in the risk profiling.

The statistics in the NAO report put the tax recovery on the repayment claim checks at around £2m for 1996/97. This is against total claims of in excess of £400m on deeds of covenant and Gift Aid alone.

As far as the charity is concerned, any amendment to their claim will be dealt with in writing and in most cases there will be no further action taken.

Tax to cover checks

3.22   One important part of the repayment process is that of ensuring that donors have paid sufficient tax on their own income to cover the tax being reclaimed by the charity. This is referred to as 'tax to cover'. Again as part of the streamlining process (and also as a reflection of the improved tracing procedures in the Revenue) very little information is now required about the donor. The new arrangements will require only their name and address.

FICO sends out details to local districts of all Gift Aid claims over a specified (but unnamed) level and asks for notification if insufficient tax has been paid. The job of dealing with the unpaid tax in these cases falls on to the local districts dealing with the donors. It is the donor who must make good any deficiency and FICO will always repay the charity. It is interesting to note that the NAO report states that the recoveries in districts rose from £172,000 in 1994/95 to £600,000 in 1996/97. The checks also uncovered systematic abuse of the system by a group of charities involving potential losses in excess of £2m and that these were being reviewed by the Revenue Special Compliance Office.

The NAO was very critical of the lack of follow up by FICO to the dissemination of information on tax to cover and also on the lack of any annual exercise to provide assurance that the risk to public funds was being kept to a minimum. The prospect of a much wider range of claims being made under new Gift Aid will make the problem worse unless FICO has already taken steps to improve the situation

Audits

Selection process

3.23   The use of audits is aimed at monitoring the validity of claims to repayment in respect of deeds of covenant and Gift Aid. The recent changes will mean that future audits will focus on the Gift Aid aspects, although any review that looks back to 1999/00 and earlier will consider the validity of deeds of covenant. Essentially the reviews are going to focus on the documentation and audit trail and on the question of donor benefit. These issues are discussed in depth in Part 3.

The statistics in the NAO report show that in 1996/97 FICO Bootle carried out 828 audits and FICO Scotland, 200. Of the settlements in Bootle, 38% yielded a monetary recovery for the Revenue and the overall yield in 1996/97 was just under £1m.

Prior to 1997, FICO selected audit cases on the basis of a minimum annual claim of £5,000 and the auditor's judgment. The NAO, as part of their review, identified one church with annual repayment claims of over £100,000 which had never had an audit. They also pointed out that 20% of the 6,400 charities making the largest claims had never had an audit.

The NAO report notes that from April 1997, FICO Bootle introduced a risk-targeting system which would concentrate resources on the larger claims. The largest 6,400 would be audited on a three to ten-year cycle – the frequency of visits being dependent upon an assessment of risk built up from:

(1) whether there has been a previous audit;

(2) the size of the annual repayment claim;

(3) the size of claim in respect of investment income;

(4) previous audit history;

(5) charity type.

The remaining 40,000+ charities would be audited on a sample basis.

Approach – single sites

3.24 The basic audit approach is to:

(1) carry out a visit to the charity;

(2) prepare a report to the charity within six weeks;

(3) agree a settlement if that is appropriate.

Before a visit takes place there will be some preparatory work usually reviewing the claims history and, in the case of non-church charities, having a review of the charity's most recent accounts undertaken by an accounts inspector. The NAO notes that this latter practice yields 'productive results'.

For very small charities the visit has been replaced by a desk-based audit because this is considered to be a more productive use of time by the auditor. The average total time for a desk-based audit is stated to be 5 hours as against 13 hours for the full audit.

The visit to the charity will in many cases be to the home of the treasurer (certainly in church cases). The visit can take up to a day depending on how many individual items there are and how good the record-keeping is. Essentially the auditor is looking for an audit trail to establish that the sums received came from the particular donor. In the case of deeds he will want to be satisfied that the deed is valid and that the right amount of repayment has been claimed. Common problems include:

● claiming for payments received before the deed was signed;

● claiming for the 'theoretical' amount due under the deed rather that the sum actually received;

● claiming for payments made after the expiry of the deed.

The situation is likely to change under the new Gift Aid regime and we can expect to see a strong emphasis on the audit trail. Documentation and evidence will be the key particularly where cash receipts are concerned. The question of donor benefit will also become more significant as more claims are made.

The auditor will expect to deal with most items in the course of the visit and will discuss any problems at the time. He will prepare a report which will set out the extent of the review and will detail all the items which are wrong and quantify the errors. One thing that he will seek to establish is whether the errors are peculiar to the year reviewed or whether they should be seen as symptoms of a wider problem. He may decide to extend his review to an earlier year and then decided if a wider approach is needed.

The negotiation of a settlement will usually involve a repayment of the tax overclaimed, will probably involve interest and may also include a penalty element depending on the view that the auditor takes of why the problem has arisen. The principles of interest and penalties are discussed at 3.31 and 3.32 below.

Approach – multiple sites

3.25 There are situations where substantial claims are made on behalf of a number of different claimants by a central body. For example a diocese may make a claim on behalf of all the constituent churches. This saves local treasurers the task of making claims and also reduces substantially the number of individual claims received in the Revenue. The Revenue audit approach in these cases is to take a sample of cases and review the records for these. Errors found are noted and on overall error rate is calculated which is then extrapolated across the total population for the year of review and earlier years as well.

In one case seen by the author, the Revenue took a sample of 15 churches from a population of 400. It found an overall error rate which it initially set at 1.29% and extrapolated this across the full sample for six years. For a discussion on the validity of this approach and how to deal with it in practice see Chapter 11.

Self-assessment enquiries

Selection process

3.26 This is the area of the work of FICO which is likely to change as a result of self-assessment. It previously dealt only with accounts investigations work, which meant that the compliant charities which submitted accounts were likely to be targets but the charities that did not comply were not investigated. The introduction of self-assessment will enable the process to become more focused and allow the formal investigation powers to be used to great effect.

The aim of this type of work is to concentrate the compliance effort on some of the key technical areas such as:

- Non-exempt trading activities
- Non-charitable expenditure
- Use of subsidiary trading companies
- Use of tax avoidance

The NAO report indicates that in 1996/97, FICO Bootle carried out 56 accounts investigation cases and FICO Scotland 69. Interestingly the Revenue achieved a monetary settlement in 64% of the Bootle cases and 100% of the Scotland cases. The statistics also reveal that over a five-year period, Bootle achieved a 'result' in 63% of its cases, and Scotland in 78%. The total yield in Bootle in 1996/97 was £3.5m, which included an exceptional case where the settlement was £2.2m and covered eight years. The Scottish cases yielded just under £200,000.

The Revenue have now gathered all the files for wholly owned trading subsidiaries into FICO and this has enabled an improved approach to investigation work. The process for dealing with accounts was first of all a rapid scrutiny which eliminated a large proportion of cases (3,171 out of 3,830 reviewed in 1996/97). A second stage scrutiny looked at previous accounts and any other information held on the file. The NAO calculated that the time taken to carry out the initial review was two minutes per set of accounts. No records were kept of the review or the reasons why the cases were not selected so that in future years there was no guidance available. The NAO had strongly recommended a more structured approach.

The NAO was critical of the approach of concentrating on the compliant charities who submitted accounts and suggested that it should take into account factors such as:

- Activities
- Compliance history
- Information from the Charity Commission and Customs and Excise

The NAO was also critical of the fact that only 43 of the largest 323 UK charities with gross income over £5m had been subject to review. They made a strong recommendation that prime attention should be paid to the larger charities.

The information given in the NAO report suggests that there was little actual passing of information from the Charity Commission or Customs and Excise at the time of the report but this may have changed.

Approach

3.27 As already mentioned, the introduction of self-assessment has meant considerable changes. In the first instance the Revenue are no longer dependent on the voluntary submission of accounts to provide their starting sample (indeed they have specifically asked that charities who do not receive a tax return should not send in their accounts). The Revenue will select their initial sample through the cases to whom they send income tax returns or give notice to file corporation tax returns. They do not expect to send a return to each charity each year and are likely to send some charities a return only very periodically. Larger charities may expect to receive a return on a more regular basis and some large charities will almost certainly receive a return each year. The requirement will be to submit accounts with the return.

The returns will be scrutinised and particular attention will be paid to parts 4 and 5 of the income tax return and the sections on income and expenditure on the CT600E. Particular areas which are of interest to the Revenue will be:

(1) the relationships between the charity and trading subsidiaries;

(2) funding arrangements for those subsidiaries;

(3) fundraising activities and whether these should be exempt;

(4) property transactions;

(5) any investments in unquoted companies;

(6) substantial payments overseas.

Under self-assessment a decision has to be taken as to whether or not to instigate an enquiry under *section 9A* or *section 11A*. This has to be done even if there is a single question the Revenue need to resolve. Where it is not proposed to issue a *section 9A* letter, the file will be put away, although if further information came to light before the relevant 'enquiry window' closed, the Revenue would still have the option to take up an enquiry.

What will be of more particular interest than the *section 9A* letter will be the accompanying letter which sets out the queries. If this contains a few simple items then it is likely that the Revenue are simply trying to resolve single issues and that will be the end of the matter (subject to the fact that a foot in the door might enable the Revenue to open up an Aladdin's cave!). A letter with many queries and a request to have a meeting or to review books and records must be viewed as a full enquiry and everything is open for scrutiny. Such a letter should be immediately referred to the whole trustee body and regarded as a very serious issue.

It is likely that the enquiry will proceed by a combination of meetings and correspondence until the Inspector reaches the point where he is satisfied that he has everything he needs and can take a decision on how to resolve the issue. In some situations the case will depend on quantifying an error that has arisen, in others it may be ascertaining facts so that a view can be taken on whether an activity is within the charitable exemption. This may involve other Revenue specialists outside FICO and can add considerably to the time involved in settling the case.

If the case is likely to involve an appeal, FICO may well submit the case to the Revenue Solicitor for a opinion and this can be a very slow and frustrating process.

Once matters have been sorted out the case will proceed to a settlement with the possibility of tax, interest and penalties being involved. The formal approach will be to require a revision of a self-assessment (which may originally have been nil because of tax exemptions). In practice the approach will be to seek a settlement by means of what is known as a letter of offer (see 3.35 below).

Proceeding to a settlement

Assessment procedures

3.28 Where the inspection finds irregularities in the repayment of tax on deeds of covenant or Gift Aid and the Revenue need to take steps to recover some or all of the tax repaid, they can do so by raising an assessment under *TMA 1970, s 30*. This is an unusual form of assessment because it treats the tax recoverable as the subject of the assessment rather than the more usual approach of charging income at a rate of tax to give a taxable sum.

The assessment should be made within six years of the end of the year of assessment to which it relates. It is open to the Revenue to raise an assessment out of time where they can argue that the charity is guilty of fraudulent or negligent conduct in its action in claiming repayment. This is discussed further in the context of penalties below.

Where the assessment is in an agreed amount and is used as a simple way of ending the enquiry process, the charity need take no further action other than to ensure that the tax is paid within 30 days of the date of issue of the assessment to avoid any interest charge.

In cases where the enquiry relates to income or gains that have not been subject to repayment, the assessment will be in the conventional form for years before 1996/97. In self-assessment cases the process will be that of amending a self-assessment.

Where the assessment is not agreed, the charity must ensure that an appeal is entered within 30 days of the date of issue of the assessment in order to keep the matter alive for further debate and decision. The same process must be followed where the Revenue amend a self-assessment in the absence of any amendment by the charity.

The option to appeal

Right of appeal

3.29   Where agreement cannot be reached on the point at issue, the Inspector will raise an assessment and an appeal will be entered or the Inspector will amend a self-assessment and an appeal will follow. That appeal must then be determined. That can be done by continued negotiation between the Revenue and the charity, and certainly that should continue if there are grounds for so doing. If the arguments have been made but no agreement reached then the matter must go to the Special Commissioners for a decision.

All appeals by charities lie to the Special Commissioners rather than to the local General Commissioners. The Special Commissioners sit in London and usually only one Commissioner will hear the appeal. The Commissioners are independent of the Revenue and are appointed by the Lord Chancellor. The Special Commissioners usually have a legal background and some familiarity with tax law and practice.

There is usually a delay in having an appeal heard by the Special Commissioners because their time is limited and there are great demands upon that time. This allows time for the preparation of the case and also to pursue any avenues of negotiation.

Process of appeal

3.30   There is obviously a cost in time in preparing and conducting a case before Commissioners, but it is not necessary for expensive representation. The charity may present its own case before the Commissioner and will receive a very considered and fair hearing. In the case of *Battle Baptist Church v CIR and Woodham* which was heard in 1995, it was the church treasurer who took the case to the hearing. Admittedly he was an accountant in practice, but this was the first time he had taken such a case. The Revenue were represented in that case by a representative of the Board's Solicitor. They will usually gear their level of representation to that chosen by the appellant. If the appellant uses tax counsel, the Revenue will usually do the same. Obviously costs are an issue that both sides must take into account.

It is not necessary that the point at issue involves a considerable amount of tax – again in the *Battle* case, the tax involved was a few thousand pounds. Sometimes there is a principle at stake and the issue cannot be settled by compromise.

The proceedings are relatively informal, and take place in a non-confrontational atmosphere. They will be attended by the two parties, the Special Commissioner and a clerk. The onus of proof rests with the appellant, which presents its case first, the Revenue respond and the appellant has a final summing up. Where witnesses are relevant to present facts they can be called by either party and will be examined by their party and cross-examined by the other side.

Once all the arguments are heard the Special Commissioner will go away to make a decision. This is usually delivered in writing some time after the hearing. Where the losing party considers that the decision is wrong on a point of law, they must express dissatisfaction to preserve any right to take the matter on to the High Court.

Special Commissioner cases are now reported, although anonymity can be given for the taxpayer. There have been a few cases involving charities which have been heard, but it seems that charities have less resort to the Special Commissioners than they have to the VAT tribunal. This could also of course reflect a greater willingness on the part of the Inland Revenue officers to reach a settlement, even by compromise, than their colleagues in Customs and Excise.

The issues involved in deciding whether to fight or settle are discussed in Chapter 10.

Interest

3.31   The Revenue have the right to charge interest on unpaid tax. They view this as nothing more than commercial restitution for the fact that the charity has had the use of the funds and not the Revenue. In pre-self-assessment days, the starting point was that interest is due 30 days after the date of issue of the assessment. However, if the assessment relates to a period several years earlier, the Revenue may be entitled to charge interest on that tax from what would have been its due and payable date if the assessment had been made at the correct time. They can only do this for years prior to 1996/97 where the tax that is now being assessed was lost because of a failure or error on the part of the taxpayer. In technical jargon they refer to this as 'culpable tax'.

Under self-assessment the date on which tax should have been paid is clearly established and account must be taken of whether a liability for one year would have triggered a requirement to make payments on account in a following year. If it does, then interest will also run from the dates of those payments on account.

Where tax has been over-repaid, the interest charge will be related back to the date of the original repayment.

Although there is technically a right to mitigate the interest charge, this is rarely done. If it seems likely at an early stage in the enquiry that some tax is going to be payable to the Revenue, it might be worth considering making a payment on account, which will have the effect of stopping the interest charge running on that amount. In larger cases that could represent a significant sum.

Penalties

The right to charge

3.32   The Revenue have the right to charge penalties in three main types of situation:

(1)   Where a charity fails to produce documents for inspection, the Revenue have the power under *TMA 1970, s 98* to seek a penalty of £300 and a continuing penalty of up to £60 per day until the failure is made good. They need an order from the Appeal Commissioners to do this, and will not normally seek to take such action.

(2)   Where the charity has income which is not covered by an exemption and has failed to notify chargeability, the penalty will be due under *TMA 1970, s 7* and will be the tax due in respect of income which was chargeable.

(3)   Where a charity submits an incorrect return or claim, the Revenue will seek to argue that the incorrect submission was the result of fraudulent or negligent conduct on the part of the charity, and are able, under *TMA 1970, s 95 or s 96* (if the charity is a company), to levy a penalty on the full amount of the tax difference between the correct amount and the amount actually due or repaid.

Example
A charity makes a repayment claim in respect of deeds of covenant which results in a tax repayment of £10,000. Inspection by the Revenue shows that a significant number of the deeds of covenant were not valid, and as a result the repayment claim should only have been £6,000. The Revenue, if they were able to show that the error was a result of the fraudulent or negligent conduct of the charity, would be able to levy a maximum penalty of £4,000.

Fraudulent or negligent conduct

3.33   There is no definition in the taxes acts of 'fraudulent or negligent conduct', and there are often grounds for argument with the Revenue as to whether an offence has been committed and if so what. Consider various possibilities:

(1)   A charity has made tax reclaims in respect of 'deeds of covenant' which were fictitious. Accounts entries were made to turn general donations into deed payments but, on inspection, the Revenue

uncovered the position. They would undoubtedly view such action on the part of the charity as 'fraudulent' conduct. A deliberate attempt has been made to obtain tax to which the charity was not entitled.

(2)   A charity makes a claim in respect of deeds of covenant which relate to real individuals, but which on inspection were found to have been signed after the date of the first payment. The Revenue may well have grounds for arguing that the charity has been neglectful in making claims which it knew were not strictly valid because the payments were not strictly under a deed.

(3)   A charity has made a disposal of a property gifted to it and claimed it was a capital gain. The Revenue argue that the disposal is technically a trade which is not exempt and seeks tax. The charity accepts the position simply to save further costs in fighting the matter. The Revenue then seek to charge interest on the grounds that the charity should have known that the transaction was a trade. The author would take the view that a dispute on a tax technical issue cannot be negligent conduct and no penalty should be levied.

Each situation must be looked at on its own facts and there are clearly degrees of culpability. Any attempt by the Revenue to argue for an automatic penalty should be resisted. Whilst accepting that ignorance of the law is no defence, the Revenue may have to accept that, in the case of charities, the people who are involved in processing claims may be volunteers without any level of experience in such matters as these.

From the charity point of view, however, carelessness in putting together claims and simply not checking that the basics of deed payments or Gift Aid payments are correct, must be accepted as negligent conduct, and the matter then comes down to one of degree and mitigation.

Mitigation of penalties

3.34   The law sets out the maximum level of penalty that can be charged, and the Revenue then have the discretion to mitigate that maximum by reference the facts of any case. The basic approach is to start with the maximum penalty of 100% and then to consider three areas of mitigation each of which carry a maximum percentage abatement which is deducted from the full penalty, The areas which are considered are:

(1)   Disclosure up to 20% abatement

(2)   Co-operation up to 40% abatement

(3)   Size and gravity up to 40% abatement

A key element in the negotiation of any settlement with the Revenue is the negotiation on penalties. Where the tax is substantial, the maximum level of penalties will be high and each percentage point will be worth a large amount. The process is discussed in Chapter 9 together with some background on the issues to consider in each mitigation category.

Letter of offer

3.35   Once agreement is reached in a case where interest and penalties are involved, the Revenue will want to settle the matter using the letter of offer procedure. This is an arrangement which avoids the need to make a number of assessments. The charity agrees to sign a formal letter offering an agreed sum in settlement. This letter is sent to the Revenue and when they respond accepting the offer, the two letters form an enforceable contract.

It is usual for the letter of offer to specify payment within 30 days of the date of the letter indicating Revenue acceptance. There may, however, be scope for some extension of that time limit, but this must be agreed before the letter of offer is signed. Where the charity is looking to pay in instalments, the Revenue will want a significant part of the final sum as a down payment and will also want to charge forward interest to cover the instalments.

Chapter 4

Inland Revenue – Employer Compliance

PAYE obligations of charities as employers

Introduction

4.1   The treatment of charities under the PAYE regime is no different to that used for any other employer, and the obligations of the charity as an employer are the same as for any other employer. Most charities have only a small number of employees relying very heavily on volunteer support for the manpower required to meet their objectives. Simply having one employee means that the PAYE operation clicks into gear and there must be an awareness of what has to be done. For the Revenue's part, the PAYE system provides the opportunity to leave the employer to do much of the work and gives the Revenue a policing role. That policing role is active and is growing and, ominously, is extremely successful. The Revenue's statistics suggest that in three out of four cases reviewed they get additional tax, often with interest and penalties as well.

This chapter looks at the mechanisms of PAYE and the obligations that are imposed on the employer. It highlights the organisation of the employer compliance effort in the Revenue and explains the sanctions that the Revenue have at their disposal.

Cardinal principle of PAYE

Introduction

4.2   The PAYE system was introduced during the Second World War as an attempt to overcome the problems of issuing 'half-yearly' assessments to all employees. The aim was to devise a system to ensure that as far as possible the correct tax was deducted during a tax year and therefore no formal assessment would be required. The big advantage to the Revenue, of course, was that much of the work then devolved on the employer, and the Revenue's role became more supervisory. Subsequently, the system has developed and become more sophisticated and for the majority of employees it actually achieves the desired result of collecting the correct amount of tax during the year.

ICTA 1988, s 203

4.3   The statutory basis for the PAYE system is found in *ICTA 1988, s 203* and this section provides the cardinal principle which all employers should take very careful note of. *Section 203(1)* states:

> 'On the making of any payment of, or on account of, any income assessable to income tax under Schedule E, income tax shall, subject to and in accordance with regulations made by the Board under this section, be deducted or repaid by the person making the payment, notwithstanding that when the payment is made no assessment has been made in respect of the income and not withstanding that the income is in whole or in part income for some year of assessment other than the year during which the payment is made.'

There are five very significant principles that emerge from this subsection, and all should be committed to heart by every charity that has any employees.

There must be a payment

4.4   This may seem an obvious statement, but it should be one that alerts the employer. Potentially, every time a transfer of cash takes place between an employer and one of his employees, whether that is in the form of actual cash, or a cheque or a credit direct to the employee's bank account, the employer should be considering the impact of *section 203*, and the possibility of operating PAYE on the payment. Most employers would recognise the making of the basic wage or salary payment as a payment within the section, but many may not recognise that a payment of subsistence, or mileage expenses is also a payment within the section. As such, PAYE should be considered, unless the employer has a dispensation from the Revenue which allows such a payment to be made without deduction of tax.

The relevant time is when the payment is made

4.5   Not only does the employer need to recognise that they have made a payment, they need to know as well when they made the payment. There are now specific rules set out in *ICTA 1988, s 203A* which stipulate when a payment is to be treated as being paid. Most of these rules relate to directors and are probably not directly relevant to charity situations. Charities should note that if an employee becomes entitled to receive a sum, that is the likely date for operating PAYE and not when the sum is actually paid.

The income must be assessable under Schedule E

4.6   Schedule E is one of the old schedules of our income tax system, dating back to the early taxing Acts where the types of income liable to tax were set out in Schedules to the Act. The scope of Schedule E is set out in *ICTA 1988, s 19(1)* which states that tax under the Schedule is to be charged 'in respect of any office or employment on emoluments therefrom . . .'.

It therefore follows that PAYE can only be applied to a payment made in respect of an office or employment. A payment made to someone who is self employed, or to a limited company, will be a payment of income which is assessable under Schedule D. This means that the terms of the relationship between the user of the service and the provider of the service must always be considered. If that relationship is governed by a contract of service, then the relationship will be that of employer and employee, and therefore the income received by the worker will be taxable under Schedule E, with the consequence that it will fall within the provisions of *section 203*. If, however, the relationship is governed by a contract for services, the income will be received by the worker in the capacity as a self employed individual, and will be assessable to tax under Schedule D.

The importance of this distinction means that the status of the worker must always be carefully established, so that at the time payment is made, the user of the service knows whether they are within the scope of *section 203*. If the wrong decision is made, the responsibility will rest with the payer.

Tax must be deducted

4.7   This is the action required. There must be a physical deduction of tax at source, and also in practice that must be followed by an accounting of that tax to the Revenue. Failure to deduct tax means that the payer of the remuneration is in breach of the legislation, and can be called to account if the failure is later uncovered as may happen when, in the course of a PAYE investigation, it transpires that an individual who has been treated as being self employed should have been treated as an employee.

The responsibility for tax deduction rests with the payer

4.8   This is the final principle, and pins the burden for the operation of the PAYE system on the payer of the income. In most cases this payer will be the employer, but there is new legislation, introduced at a late stage in *Finance Act 1994*, which puts the burden for deducting tax on to other parties in certain specified situations. The legislation is in *sections 203B* to *203E*, and seeks to close up loopholes in the system where the Revenue believe that PAYE is not being operated properly. It is not likely that these provisions will affect charities except in very specific situations. What charities must keep firmly in the forefront of their minds is that this principle means that if there is a problem unearthed where tax should have been deducted, the Revenue will come to the charity as the employer for the tax not to the individual who received the money. For example if a charity engages the services of a consultant on what it believes to be a contract for services (Schedule D) and the Revenue successfully argue that the arrangement is an employment, the Revenue will expect the charity to pay the tax even though they have already paid a gross sum to the individual. The problem of determining if an individual is employed or self-employed is considered in more detail in Part 3.

Summary of employers' responsibilities

During the tax year

4.9   The employer has a number of responsibilities which need to be kept in view during the tax year. These include the following:

(1)   to have a deduction working sheet for each employee for whom PAYE should be operated;

(2)   to operate a system of tax deduction on each payment using the code number given by the Revenue to operate the tax tables;

(3)   to pay over the net monthly tax deducted from employees by the 19th of the following month;

(4)   where tax is paid on a quarterly basis, to make payment by the 19th of the month after the quarter end (i.e. 19 July, 19 October, 19 January, 19 April);

(5)   to ensure that all new employees who do not hand over a P45, go through the P46 procedure as appropriate;

(6)   when an employee leaves, to provide them with a P45 and send part of the return to the Revenue;

(7)   to complete a P46 (Car) on a quarterly basis.

At tax year end

4.10   At the end of each tax year every employer must send a number of returns to his tax office:

Form	Information	Date
P14	Must be completed for all employees for whom a deduction working sheet has been used at any time during the year. Summarise each employee's pay, tax, NICs, earnings for NICs, SSP and SMP. Note that under the self-assessment procedures a version of this form known as a P60 must be supplied to each employee by 31 May	19 May

Form	Information	Date
P35	Employer's Annual Statement, Declaration and Certificate is essentially a summary of the forms P14 being submitted. There is a series of questions on the front of the form P35 to be answered by the employer, the answers to which may result in further enquiries by the Inland Revenue. On the reverse of the form summary information is given about each employee	19 May
P38A	Details of employees for whom a form P14 has not been submitted who were paid in excess of the weekly PAYE threshold or any employees taken on for more than one week; and any other employees who were paid more than £100 in the year who have not already been entered on the form	19 May
P11D	For directors and employees paid at a rate of £8,500 per annum or more, details of the emoluments which have been provided during the year and which have not been treated as pay for PAYE purposes. Under the self-assessment procedures, a copy of this return must also be provided to the employee by the same date	6 July
P9D	Return of benefits and expenses for employees below P11D threshold. Under the self-assessment procedures, a copy of this return must also be provided to the employee by the same date	6 July

Charities must ensure that their PAYE systems are capable of meeting all of these deadlines.

Investigation powers of the Revenue – general

The changing approach to employer compliance

The Revenue

4.11   The last few years have seen a marked change in the Revenue approach to compliance by employers. Gone are the days when the work was seen as something done by collectors of taxes and junior district staff. The Revenue were already going through a process of change before the merger with the Contributions Agency took place in April 1999. That merger has widened the scope of compliance visits and increased the resources for the Revenue. The only consolation for the employer is that they will now only get one visit when they might have had two in the past.

Employers

4.12   If the Revenue have changed their approach, it appears that employers have not. This is still seen very much as a Cinderella area of compliance even in very large operations where compliance is often left to junior members of payroll staff. If specialist tax people are involved it is very often as an adjunct to the more senior duties of corporate tax. On the internal audit side the focus is often on ensuring that there is no leakage from the system via expenses claims, etc. The fact that there may be a major loss because of a huge tax bill is overlooked.

In charities where the resources are not so great there are other priorities for people's time and effort. The amounts involved do not seem too great and it is easy to let matters slip. In some situations there may not even be an appreciation that a tax problem might be building up.

Lots of little makes a lot

4.13   One of the features of employer compliance visits is that the figures involved in individual aspects can seem very trivial, but an error of even a hundred pounds spread over 500 employees soon adds up to a major problem. If that is multiplied over a six-year period, the figures can become colossal – the author is aware of major employers where overall settlements in excess of £1m have been concluded. The compliance function is a messy one, it deals with technical areas which people think they understand but don't understand at all or where a kind of folklore exists about what is possible. Again for charities the amounts may, in absolute terms, be lower than for large commercial organisations but in relative terms they can become very substantial.

Role of employer compliance

4.14   Employer compliance review work usually consists of a full review of an employer's remuneration package. The review can include:

- the operation of PAYE and Class 1 NICs on employees' and directors' remuneration;

- expenses payments, benefits and other rewards provided to employees and directors;

- the operation of the Construction Industry Tax Deduction Scheme.

Within the overall context that the Revenue sees its role as collecting the right amount of tax at the right time, the aims of the Employer Compliance unit are to

(1)   help and encourage employers to comply voluntarily with their statutory duty to give timely and accurate information and to remit PAYE deductions when due;

(2)   deter the evasion or late payment of tax by demonstrating that the risk and consequences of detection make it unwise to do so;

(3)   detect irregular practice and thereby deter non-compliance;

(4)   recover any duties underpaid.

Reviews are therefore carried out with the objective of achieving the aims set out above, namely to ensure that:

- the amounts of PAYE, NICs and subcontractors contributions paid over to the Revenue are the full and correct amounts which an employer/contractor has deducted or for which the employer/contractor is accountable;

- frauds by employers/contractors, pay clerks or other employees are brought to light;

- all non-cash benefits have been returned correctly on forms P9D/P11D as appropriate.

The amalgamation of the National Insurance function into the tax function which took place on 6 April 1999 creates a single employer compliance agency. Although the rules for calculating NIC do differ in detail from the tax rules, many of the basic principles are very similar, in particular the need to deduct NIC from payments and to account for both the primary (employee's) contribution and the secondary (employer's) contribution during the year.

Basic legislative power for PAYE inspections

4.15   The basic power which allows the Revenue to carry out investigations into employers is set out in *Income Tax (Employment) Regulations 1993 (SI 1993 No 744), Reg 55* which reads as follows:

'Inspection of employer's records

1.   Every employer, whenever called upon to do so by an authorised officer of the Board, shall produce the records specified in paragraph (2) to that officer for inspection, at such time as that officer may reasonably require, at the prescribed place.

2.   The records specified in this paragraph are:

a)   all wages sheets, deductions working sheets, certificates given in accordance with regulations 29(1) and 30(1) (other than those which the employer has sent to the inspector) and other documents and records whatsoever relating to the calculation or payment of the emoluments of his employees in respect of the years or income tax periods specified by such officer or to the deduction of tax from such emoluments; or

b) such of those wages records, deductions working sheets, certificates or other documents and records as may be specified by the authorised officer.

3. "The prescribed place" mentioned in paragraph (1) means:

a) such place in the United Kingdom as the employer and the authorised officer may agree upon; or

b) in default of such agreement, the place in the United Kingdom at which the documents and records referred to in paragraph (2)(a) are normally kept; or

c) in default of such agreement and if there is no such place as referred to in sub-paragraph (b) above, the employer's principal place of business in the United Kingdom.

4. The authorised officer may:

a) take copies of, or make extracts from, any document produced to him for inspection in accordance with paragraphs (1) and (2);

b) remove any document so produced if it appears to him to be necessary to do so, at a reasonable time and for a reasonable period.

5. Where any document is removed in accordance with paragraph (4)(b), the authorised officer shall provide:

a) a receipt for any document so removed; and

b) a copy of the document, free of charge, within seven days, to the person by whom it was produced or caused to be produced where the document is reasonably required for the proper conduct of a business.

6. Where a lien is claimed on a document produced in accordance with paragraphs (1) and (2), the removal of the document under paragraph (4)(b) shall not be regarded as breaking the lien.

7. Where records are maintained by computer, the person required to make them available for inspection shall provide the authorised officer with all facilities necessary for obtaining information from them.

8. By reference to the information obtained from an inspection of the documents and records produced under paragraphs (1) and (2), the collector may, on the occasion of each inspection, prepare a certificate showing:

a) the amount of tax which it appears from the documents and records so produced that the employer is liable to pay to the collector for the years or income tax periods covered by the inspection; and

b) any amount of such tax which has not been paid to him or, to the best of his knowledge and belief, to any other collector or to any person acting on his behalf or on behalf of another collector.

9.   Paragraphs (1) to (5) of regulation 54 shall apply to the amount shown in a certificate under paragraph (8), with the modification that summary proceedings for the recovery of the amount of tax, or such part of it as remains unpaid, may be brought at any time before the expiry of twelve months after the date of the certificate.

10.   The production of a certificate under paragraph (8) shall be sufficient evidence that the employer is liable to pay the amount shown in the certificate pursuant to paragraph (8)(b) to the collector in respect of the years or income tax periods mentioned in the certificate.

11.   Any document purporting to be a certificate under paragraph (8) shall be deemed to be such a certificate until the contrary is proved.

12.   For the purposes of paragraphs (1) and (2), such of the wages sheets, deductions working sheets, certificates and other documents and records mentioned in those paragraphs as are not required by other provisions of these Regulations to be sent to the inspector or collector shall be retained by the employer for not less than three years after the end of the year to which they relate.'

The provisions need some explanation and elaboration.

When and where can inspections take place?

4.16   *Regulation 55(1)* provides that the answer to 'when' is to be whenever the Revenue want. The approach is deliberately random and flexible. The Revenue can decided how often they will visit a particular employer, and although the usual time span is several years between visits, they leave themselves the option of doing a follow-up visit shortly after an investigation which has thrown up real problems.

The answer to 'where' is in *Regulation 55(3),* and will usually be the most convenient location which is agreed between the parties. This will usually be where the payroll and other records are kept.

What documents can be examined?

4.17   The Regulations specify the obvious, but the use of the word 'whatsoever' in *Regulation 55(2)(a)* allows the Revenue to expand that basic list as appropriate. The Revenue indicate that the following records could be examined:

- wages sheets and deduction working sheets;
- all records for wage earners (including part-timers and casuals), salaried employees, directors and executives;
- time sheets, clock cards and tachograph records (where appropriate);
- cash books;

- petty cash records and vouchers;

- relevant ledger records;

- cheque stubs showing payments to employees;

- any other records used in calculating or containing entries for pay, benefits and expenses;

- forms P46;

- if appropriate, sub-contractors' records.

There can be no excuse that the records cannot be examined because they are on computer, because *Regulation 55(7)* provides that access must be given to those records. The collector also has the right to remove or copy records. [*Reg 55(4)*].

For how long must documents be kept?

4.18   There is a legal requirement in *Regulation 55(12)* to keep records for three years after the end of the year to which they relate. Employers may be delighted to throw away records after this period, but it should be borne in mind that in an investigation, the collector may decide to go back at least six years as part of his settlement. He will not be prevented from doing this by an absence of records, and given that the onus of proof in tax matters rests with the taxpayer, an absence of records could seriously weaken the case.

In practice, this Regulation will be overtaken by the new provisions in *TMA 1970, s 12B* which are being introduced as part of the procedures relating to self-assessment. These provisions will require all taxpayers including the self employed, partnerships and companies, to keep records needed to support entries in their returns (which effectively means in support of entries in accounts), and to retain those records until five years after 31 January following the end of the relevant year of assessment. This is a complex formula, but in reality imposes a require-ment to retain records for almost six years from the end of the tax year.

Settling the investigation

4.19   *Regulation 55(8) to (11)* provides the formal basis for resolving an investigation – the issue of a certificate by the collector showing the tax due. It is usual for this to emerge after negotiations with the employer, but the power would allow the collector to issue a certificate and enforce payment if no negotiated settlement was reached.

Legal powers within NIC legislation

4.20   The legislation setting out the appointment of and powers of Inspectors concerning NICs is in *Social Security Administration Act*

(SSAA) 1992 and specifically at *section 110*. This power is still available although it is under review. *Section 110(2)* provides that:

'An Inspector appointed under this section shall, for the purposes of the execution of those Acts have the following powers:

a)   to enter at all reasonable times any premises liable to inspection under this section.

b)   to make such examination and inquiry as may be necessary for ascertaining whether the provisions of the Act are being, or have been, complied with in any such premises.

c)   to examine, either alone or in the presence of any other person, as he thinks fit, in relation to any matters under the Acts on which he may reasonably require information, every person whom he finds in any such premises or which he has reasonable cause to believe to be or to have been a person liable to pay; and to require every such person to be so examined.

d)   to exercise such other powers as may be necessary for carrying the Acts into effect.'

It will be noted that these powers are significantly greater than the powers given to compliance officers under the PAYE regulations. In the first instance the power is given to enter premises – the Revenue have no such power, only the power to require the production of documents. In practice the Inspector can enter any premises where he has reasonable grounds for supposing that people are employed. The only exception is a private residence where no business is being conducted. [*Sec 110(3)*]. However, if he had reason to believe that a business was being carried on in a private home, he would have right of entry.

The second significant power is that of the right to interview any person that the Inspector finds on the premises, or anyone else who he believes to be a person liable to pay contributions. The Revenue power is limited to the examination of documents, there is no legal power to interview anyone, although in practice they do speak to people. The Agency power also extends beyond people working for the employer, e.g. if there was a dispute as to whether someone was employed or self employed, the right would exist to interview that individual.

As if those powers were not enough there is the final right in *section 110(2)(d)* which enables the Inspector to exercise such other powers 'as may be necessary' – quite a formidable right, and one that can be exercised without any apparent supervision.

Power to obtain documents

4.21   *Section 110(6)* requires that the Inspector is to be given 'all such documents as he may reasonably require for the purpose of ascertaining whether any contribution is or has been payable or has been duly paid, by, or in respect of any person'. Records which are usually required are:

- deduction working sheets;
- wages book;
- cash book, cheque book stubs, petty cash book and petty cash vouchers;
- minute book;
- record of payments of PAYE and Class 1 NICs;
- certificate of reduced liability;
- form RD950 where only secondary contributions are being made;
- age exemption certificates;
- contracting out certificates;
- accident book;
- sick notes.

In practice, these are not significantly different to those which can be required by the Revenue. However, some relate very specifically to contribution matters which have no parallel in tax

The process of an employer compliance review

Types of employer compliance review

4.22   In the new style Revenue organisation of employer compliance there are essentially three types of review which will be carried out

(1)   Combined review – which will combine the review of PAYE procedures with the review of benefits and expenses. It will include a review of all aspects relating to directors.

(2)   Schedule E only review – which deals with benefits and expenses only and will include a review of directors.

(3)   PAYE review – which looks only at the operation of PAYE and should not include any detailed review of directors

In all cases the review will follow the same pattern:

(1)   research the background;

(2)   approach the employer;

(3)   obtain all relevant information;

(4)   examine all the necessary records;

(5)   calculate any liability found to be due, together with penalties and interest where appropriate;

(6)   settle the case.

Selection of cases for review

4.23   A variety of sources are identified, and each is considered in some detail below. Some of these areas will not be particularly relevant for charities.

(a) Accounts Inspectors

The examination of charity accounts in FICO may identify matters to be investigated as far as the charitable exemption or the application of funds are concerned, but even if this does not happen there may be situations in which the Inspector believes that potential PAYE irregularities may have arisen. Examples would be the presence in the accounts of large amounts of payments for consultancy work, particularly in the area of fundraising, or a deduction for casual labour, payment of commissions or fees on which PAYE was not operated, or wages payments where there is no evidence of a PAYE scheme.

(b) Review of forms P38/P38A

This return is required from employers and shows details of individuals to whom a payment has been made in the year but for whom no deduction working sheet was held. Compliance managers are advised to estimate how many cases the office might handle from this source in the following six months, and then ask the local districts to stockpile a number of forms for review. The review is aimed at identifying those cases where entries on the form may indicate a PAYE or NIC failure. Charities will be reviewed here in just the same way as any other employer in the district.

In some cases, the compliance group is advised to make a quick telephone check with the employer to determine whether an inspection visit is needed. This call can obviously be of critical importance since, on the answers given, may hinge the fact of whether or not an investigation takes place. You should ensure that you have internal procedures to direct any call from a Schedule E compliance officer to a senior person in the firm rather than to the wages department. The officer should advise you at the start of the conversation that a PAYE inspection is being considered and that certain matters require clarification. At the end of the call you should try to ascertain from the officer if the inspection will be carried out. The officer may be non-committal on the matter because he is waiting to take a further opinion from his compliance manager. You should be advised shortly after the call whether or not a visit is going to be made. The Revenue Manual makes it clear that the employer must be advised where a decision is taken *not* to carry out an inspection.

(c) Reports by Employer Section

The Employer Section in the office which deals with routine PAYE issues will be able to identify potential cases where P11Ds seem deficient or are non-existent. They will also provide information about employers who submit forms P38/P38A.

(d) Reports by Collectors

Collectors involved in routine compliance of PAYE may come across situations where they believe that additional untaxed payments are being made. They will also be able to highlight those employers who are consistently dilatory in making their regular PAYE payments. Making sure that monthly or quarterly payments to the collector are always made on time can eliminate this source.

(e) Own research

Compliance groups are told to be on the look out for potential sources of cases for inspection. Local knowledge of a particular employer may suggest that there is a high turnover of staff or that regular part-time or casual labour is used, or there are more staff employed than the latest P35 would suggest. A scrutiny of job adverts may reveal that employers are offering potential staff incentives such as free travel to work, or the adverts may want self employed labour for work which would traditionally be done by employees.

(f) Reports by the public

What the PAYE compliance officer can spot and be aware of can also be spotted by members of the public. There are always those who feel obliged to report abuses of regulations, and this applies in all aspects of Revenue investigations. Sometimes the information is prompted by malice and is given anonymously – such information is not usually relied on and certainly not as the only trigger for an investigation. Sometimes the information comes from a knowledgeable source, e.g. an aggrieved ex-employee, and is obviously detailed. If the informant is prepared to identify themselves then the information may be taken more seriously.

(g) Reviews of P11D

Compliance managers are told to review P11Ds and claims under *section 198* (the section dealing with expenses claims) looking for tell-tale signs that an investigation might be appropriate. These will include:

- All company cars have business mileage over 18,000 miles

- A company car was withdrawn but not apparently replaced

- A company car was sold during the year – was it sold to an employee?

- If a company car was changed during the year was the mileage evenly spread?

- Have employers uprated the costs of benefits from one year to the next?

- Specific interest in areas such as:
  - General expenses payments
  - Travel and subsistence
  - Entertainment

(h) Mistakes on year end returns

This was the biggest single source of cases for the old Contributions Agency and will presumably continue to be a source for the new Employer Compliance Groups. The checking system in Newcastle that processes the annual P35, looks for errors and inconsistencies, and when it finds them the papers may be passed to the local unit to pay a visit. Some errors may be obvious and can be cleared up by a phone call, but a number of mistakes may lead the Revenue to conclude that the employer really does not know what they are doing, and should be visited at an early opportunity.

This is an area that employers can clearly influence by ensuring that their year end returns are correct and consistent. The type of mistakes that can generate interest include:

- missing off NI numbers;

- payment of an unusual number of non-standard contributions;

- the level of contributions paid is inconsistent with the other information on the return.

Organising the visit

4.24   Once an employer has been selected for inspection, a formal procedure swings into action from the local audit office. About two weeks before the proposed date of the visit, the compliance manager will inform the employer that a visit is planned in a specific week. It is not usual at this stage to give a precise date and time for the visit, although this can be requested subsequently by the employer. The employer is also sent copies of two Revenue leaflets:

- Code of Practice Booklet 3 which explains how the inspection will be carried out and advises the employer of his rights and responsibilities;

- Leaflet IR71 which provides a background to PAYE inspections, including information on the records which will be required, the procedures to be followed where irregularities are discovered, liability is disputed and/or the employer is not happy about the conduct of the investigation.

The employer is quite at liberty to request a specific time for the visit, after all, the visit is going to be an inconvenience so there should be some choice over when the inconvenience will be! The employer should respond to the notice with a request for a specific appointment and the compliance officer is under instructions to comply with that request wherever possible. If the employer leaves it too late, the compliance officer may already be out on visits and a specific time may not be possible. An employer should always aim to respond by return because as one of a number of employers who have been advised of a visit, it may still not be possible to get the most convenient time.

The employer will be asked for some basic information about the payroll records. If the records are computerised, the compliance manager has to decide if the compliance officer allocated to the job is experienced enough to handle the inspection.

If the employer chooses to ignore the notice completely he or she will almost certainly receive a telephone call from the compliance officer asking for the information requested. If compliance officers are unable to contact the employer, they will simply turn up during the period which was specified on the notice and expect to carry out the inspection.

Employer Compliance Group practice

4.25   The Employer Compliance approach is to proceed in two phases, with phase 2 only being implemented where phase 1 indicates areas of concern. Phase 1 will comprise a review of records for a set twelve-month period – usually the twelve months ending with the date of the inspection. In some cases the compliance officer may decide to carry out a brief selective review of some records for earlier years as part of phase 1. The compliance officer will move into phase 2 when any of the following apply:

- fraud is suspected;
- the initial inspection reveals omissions from or understatements on the P35;
- the Inspector in the district has already reported suspected irregularities.

The phase 2 review will cover all aspects of compliance in the preceding six years prior to the one in which the inspection commenced. Officers are told that they do not need to review all records for all years, but should bear in mind that what they are trying to do is to identify the amount of duty underpaid and the degree of culpability involved.

The officers are given specific instructions on how to deal with computerised records. They will ask if the system will produce any exception/rejection reports and if there are any for the period being reviewed in phase 1, they will want to see them. Compliance officers are under strict instructions never to use the employer's computer system even if invited to do so, and will always ask the employer for print-outs where necessary. In that case they will ask for confirmation that a complete back-up of the program and data files exist to avoid any suggestion that the Revenue might be blamed for any loss.

They will ask questions about computer security measures to identify who has access and the ability to amend records, so that they can establish the possible scope for manipulation of the records.

Opening meeting

4.26   The visit will start with a discussion about the PAYE issues. There will be some general questions about the nature of the organisation and what it does. These questions are in reality aimed at identifying for the compliance officer the areas on which he should direct his attention in the limited time he has available to carry out his visit. There will followed some more detailed questions usually based on a very comprehensive questionnaire that compliance officers use.

This opening meeting is the most critical part of the review and it is important that the employer should be prepared for it and conduct it as carefully as possible. Detailed notes on the approach to be adopted can be found in Chapter 7.

Review of records

4.27   Following the initial discussion, the compliance officer will move to the detailed review of the records. This will be based probably on a sample for one year, although if the records are substantial and time is short then this may be reduced to a smaller sample based on a six-month or even three-month period. If this is going to the case the employer should point out to the officer any particular seasonal factors which might be present and could distort the usefulness of the sample for drawing wider conclusions.

The field review, as it is known, will comprise several distinct reviews as follows.

Review of wages records

4.28   The starting point for the review of records will usually be the wages records. This is largely done to see what precisely is included so that when other areas are reviewed it is known if particular items have been included on the payroll. The wages records themselves are really of little overall interest but the other matters to be considered will include areas where potential problems could easily lurk such as:

- a review of procedures for dealing with casual staff;
- how students are dealt with;
- what procedures are adopted for UK-based employees working abroad;
- what procedures are adopted for any overseas employees working in the UK.

Review of petty cash

4.29   The petty cash vouchers will often be a fruitful source of investigation 'goodies' for the Revenue. Items which will attract attention will include:

- vouchers for round sum expense claims;
- purchase of sandwiches for internal lunches;
- cash items paid to casual labour, cleaners, etc.
- payment of small items such as newspaper bills which might be for the benefit of individuals.

Review of cash book

4.30   The cash book review will highlight the existence of items such as:

- payments to consultants – the compliance officer will look for the same names appearing on a regular basis;
- payments to limited companies with 'personal' names (this will be of more interest in identifying the recipient – the new so-called IR35 rules place no obligation on the payer to operate tax);
- payments of expenses to employees and senior executives. Travel and subsistence expenses will be a common area of review;
- so-called *ex gratia* payments made to certain employees may appear in some charity situations.

Review of purchase ledger

4.31   The review of the purchase ledger will focus on a review of invoices paid. This is an important area of the review for commercial operations but will not usually be a significant area for a review on a charity. Obvious payments to regular suppliers will be ignored, but in commercial cases the attention of the compliance officer will focus in particular on payments to third parties which could indicate benefits enjoyed by directors. The presence of such payments in a charity are likely to have consequences well beyond the PAYE area. There may be limited items such as:

- invoices for travel – looking in particular for accompanying partners and spouses;

- utility bills relating to domestic premises, e.g. telephone bills for a home line;

- invoices received 'for consultancy services rendered' from individuals or companies.

End of the visit

4.32   At the end of the visit, the compliance officer will usually want to sit down with the person responsible for PAYE issues and discuss the findings of the review. They may want to explore in more detail why particular actions have been taken (or not taken in some cases), they may want some further information and they may also indicate some areas where they are going to go away and think about the position. Unless the matters are easily dealt with it may be better for the charity employee to note the details of what is being said or requested and agree to follow this up after the meeting.

After the visit

The first letter

4.33   The visit may appear to be very amicable, but then the tone may change when the first letter comes back from the Revenue. This letter will usually set out in detail the areas of irregularity uncovered at the visit. Hopefully it should contain no surprises, but sometimes additional items appear which were not discussed at the meeting. These may be items that the compliance officer simply forgot about, but will often be matters which they did not want to raise at the time until they had had time to think through the precise implications of what they had found.

The letter should also set out the detailed computations of the tax and/or NICs involved in the irregularities uncovered. This may well come as an unpleasant shock, because what appears at the final meeting to be a number of small items, can add up to a large overall bill when aggregated together. Matters will be made worse of course, if the officer or Inspector decides to go back beyond the year reviewed and take into account potential liabilities for earlier years.

Draw up a control list

4.34   A general feature of this type of investigation is that there are usually a number of independent issues which are identified. It is helpful at this stage to draw up a list, probably using the headings in the Revenue or Contributions Agency letter, and to then keep this list as a working control to show the stage that each issue has reached. This will be discussed in more detail in Chapter 8.

The first objective question to ask is which points should be accepted, which should be fought? Are the figures all correct? Items which are agreed should be confirmed back to the compliance officer so that the decks are then clear for items which are disputed.

Continuing the arguments

4.35   Having decided if particular points are to be fought, the next question is how best to fight them. Again details on tactics in this area will be considered in Chapter 8 and some of the specific areas relating to arguments on employment issues are looked at in Part 3. If negotiations on some points are exhausted without agreement then the matter may have to be resolved formally using the General Commissioners.

Eventually all the points will be settled and the case can move through to a final stage of agreeing a settlement with the Revenue which will comprise:

- Tax payable by the employer
- NICs payable by the employer
- Interest
- Penalties

The tax and NIC liability will emerge from the different strands of the enquiry. Remember that in many situations it is the duty of the employer to operate tax and so the Revenue will look to the employer for recompense in these areas. In some cases, such as benefits in kind, the employer has no obligation at all to operate tax, but does have an obligation to provide a return of the benefits to the Revenue. The Revenue will often look to the employer to settle this liability rather than have to collect the tax from the employees concerned and there may be considerable pressure to do this. That pressure will be compounded by the fact that the Revenue may want to calculate this tax on a grossed-up basis, i.e. regarding the benefit received as net of tax – this can make a significant financial difference. This approach may represent a real dilemma for charities; would such a payment be a proper use of charity funds? The key will be in the relationship with the employees and the level of communication – employees may be prepared to accept the reality of the situation which is that the benefits in question are taxable and it is their liability to make the payment.

Interest

Introduction

4.36   The Revenue have not always been able to charge interest on PAYE liabilities but that position changed in the early 1990s and it is now common, except in very simple cases of innocent error, for the Revenue to seek an interest charge.

Regulation 51

4.37   This regulation now provides for a general interest charge where tax is overdue on Schedule E liabilities where the employer should have deducted tax and paid it over to the Revenue. Any tax which should have been paid over by an employer carries interest from 14 days after the end of the relevant tax year. So a liability established in 2000 in respect of, say, the year 1998/99 will potentially carry interest from 19 April 1999. The rate of interest is prescribed as the 'official rate' of interest which varies in accordance with the general base rate.

Basic penalty calculations

Introduction

4.38   We have already noted that employers have a statutory duty to submit certain returns on time and to ensure that those returns are completed correctly. Failure to comply with these requirements may render the employer liable to pay penalties depending on the circumstances of the case. There are two stages to the calculation of the penalty:

(1)   To establish that an offence giving rise to a penalty has been committed and the maximum amount of the penalty which is due under the law – this is considered below.

(2)   To consider the actual amount of the penalty which will be charged – this will involve consideration of the mitigation of the penalty which is considered in Chapter 12.

Situations in which the Revenue will not charge a penalty

4.39   The Revenue will not charge a penalty in circumstances in which the employer agrees to take on the tax liability of an employee, e.g. where the employer pays the tax on a payment that represents the settling of a pecuniary liability of an employee, or where the employer agrees to meet the tax on a benefit in kind.

TMA 1970, s 98

4.40   This section allows penalties to be charged in two basic situations which will arise out of a compliance visit:

(1)   Where any person fails to furnish any information, give any certificate or produce any document or record required under the PAYE regulation he can be liable to a penalty not exceeding £300. The penalty would apply to each P46 not submitted in respect of casuals and to any P11Ds not submitted.

(2)   *Section 98(2)* provides for a penalty of up to £3,000 where a person fraudulently or negligently furnishes, gives, produces or makes any incorrect information, certificate, document, record or declaration. A P11D that is shown to be incorrect would attract this penalty.

It can be seen that in a PAYE audit where there are large numbers of documents involved the maximum penalty level could be substantial.

Compliance officers who wish to consider penalties under *section 98(1)(b)* for failure to submit P11Ds or under *section 98(2)* for making incorrect returns, are required to submit the case to head office before they start negotiations on a penalty. The types of situation in which the Revenue are likely to seek penalties are:

- Cases where the employer has refused to settle the employees' tax. Charities which feel that they should not meet this liability because of the possibility of the payment not being considered charitable should resist the imposition of a penalty on other liabilities which the Revenue are seeking to impose simply because of a slavish following of the book. It is hoped that the Revenue would be sensitive to the charity's position in such a case.

- Second offences, e.g. where there has been a previous voluntary settlement of liabilities on employee benefits and there is a repetition of the situation in later years. There is not a lot of argument against this.

- Incomplete settlements, e.g. where further benefits are discovered for the same period for which a voluntary settlement has been negotiated. Again this can be difficult to argue against.

- Very large cases, which category would not include the typical charity case but is more likely to apply to a major commercial employer who in the Revenue view 'should know better' but gets in wrong.

- Blatant cases where the omission from P11Ds appears to be a deliberate attempt by the employer to conceal employee benefits. Again this is hard to argue against.

TMA 1970, s 98A

4.41   This section was introduced to give extra weight to the Revenue attack on PAYE non-compliance. The section effectively covers two types of situation

Failure to make year end return

4.42   A basic failure to make a year end return on a P35 by the basic deadline of 19 May after the end of the tax year to which it relates, will be the trigger for an automatic penalty. The initial penalty which can be levied on the basic failure is prescribed in the section to be twelve times what is described as the 'relevant monthly amount'. This is defined in *section 98A(3)* as being £100 where there are 50 or fewer employees, and where there are more than 50 employees it is £100 for the first 50, an additional £100 for each subsequent group of 50, plus £100 for the final group if less than 50. This means that if an employer has 102 employees, the 'relevant monthly amount' will be £300, and the initial penalty would be £3,600.

If the failure to make the year end return continues after the initial penalty has been imposed, an additional penalty of the relevant monthly amount can be levied for each month or part month for which the failure continues. If, in the case of the employer with 102 employees, the return was actually submitted on 20 July, the Revenue could impose two monthly penalties totalling £600.

The position takes an ugly turn where the failure continues for more than twelve months. At that point the Revenue can charge a tax-based penalty. This is based on 100% of the tax underpaid after 19 April after the end of the tax year to which the return relates. In practice, compliance officers are told not to seek the full amount of the penalty on a late return, but only a maximum of 100% of the tax underpaid as a result of culpable irregularities. They should only do this if there are obvious culpable irregularities, no return has been submitted at the start of the review and the employer does not have a reasonable excuse for not submitting the return.

Making an error on the year end return

4.43   Where a P35 return is submitted but is shown by the compliance visit to be incorrect, a penalty can be levied under *section 98A(4)*. This penalty is a maximum of 100% of the tax underpaid as a result of the error.

Negotiating the settlement

4.44   The overall settlement process will involve negotiations to mitigate the level of penalties; this process is discussed in more detail in Chapter 12. The final part of the negotiation will involve the setting of a date on which the final liability should be paid under the terms of the letter of offer. The normal period will be 30 days, but there may be grounds for charities seeking a reasonable extension of this period.

Chapter 5

VAT Investigations

Introduction

5.1   Many smaller charities have total income which is well below any VAT registration limits and have to accept VAT as a cost, although they can obtain some relief from certain zero-rating rules particularly in areas such as new buildings and advertising. However, for a significant number of charities, VAT presents an interesting dilemma – they recognise that it may be a cost to them and they want to minimise that cost, but the only way to achieve that is to bring themselves within the full VAT system with all the administration that this entails.

This chapter looks at the obligations that the VAT system imposes and the ways in which Customs and Excise administer compliance with that system. Before getting into the detail of that it will be helpful to deal with the basic concept of 'supply' which underpins the whole system.

Concept of supply

5.2   *Value Added Tax Act (VATA) 1994, s 1* provides that: 'Value added tax shall be charged, in accordance with the provisions of this Act . . . on the supply of goods and services in the United Kingdom . . .'. At the core of the legislation is the concept of the act of making a supply. Much of the complexity of the legislation derives from determining whether or not a particular activity constitutes the making of a supply and, if a supply is made, whether or not it is in technical terms 'taxable', 'exempt' or 'outside the scope'.

Outside the scope

5.3   The concept of a supply being 'outside the scope' derives from *section 4(1)* which refers to tax being charged on supplies made by a taxable person 'in the course or furtherance of any business carried on by him'. If a supply does not fulfil that condition then it will be regarded as a supply 'outside the scope of VAT'.

The meaning of 'supply' is found in *VATA 1994, s 5* and *Sch 4*. One immediate point to note, which is of considerable importance to charities, is that 'anything done otherwise than for a consideration' is not within the definition of a supply. [*Sec 5(2)(a)*]. In other words, services provided free of charge by a charity or goods given away by a charity are not supplies and the activities that generate those services will not fall within the scope of VAT.

Taxable and exempt

5.4   The legislation defines two types of supply, taxable and exempt, and the basic definition in *section 4(2)* is not particularly helpful, 'a taxable supply is a supply of goods or services in the United Kingdom other than an exempt supply'. There are currently three rates applicable to taxable supplies:

- Standard-rate – 17.5%

- Lower-rate – 5%

- Zero-rate

At first glance there would seem to be little difference between zero-rated and exempt. Indeed as far as the purchaser of the supply is concerned there is no difference in the end result. For the supplier, however, the distinction is crucial from the point of view of minimising the impact of VAT on goods and services he acquires. In very general terms, where a supply is exempt, the person making that supply will not be able to recover VAT on the goods and services he needs to produce the supply. Where the supply is zero-rated, a recovery of VAT is allowed.

Details of items which are zero-rated (e.g. food and books) are contained in *VATA 1994, Sch 8* and those which are exempt (e.g. education) are listed in *Schedule 9*. Items which do not appear in either of these lists can be assumed to be standard-rated.

Business activities – general

5.5   As already mentioned above, the basic legislation uses the phrase 'in the course or furtherance of a business carried on' to describe the sphere of activity within which VAT is chargeable. There is no comprehensive definition of business, just as there is no comprehensive definition of trade for income tax purposes. However, some guidance on the meaning is provided by *section 94*.

According to *section 94(1)*, business includes 'any trade, profession or vocation'. Those words define what is taxable under Schedule D for income tax purposes and so it can be seen that the VAT definition has a much wider scope than the income tax definition. Indeed, any charity which is carrying on a trade for income tax purposes should have no problem in satisfying Customs and Excise that it is carrying on some business activity.

The question of whether or not a charity is carrying on a business is one which is often at the centre of disputes between Customs and charities. The situation usually arises when there is either a large amount of VAT potentially payable by a charity (in which case Customs will try very hard to demonstrate that a business is being carried on) or where there is a large potential VAT recovery for the charity (in which case the charity will try to argue that it is carrying on a business and Customs will usually try to resist the claim). This is an area of both planning and compliance which must be considered by many charities. The issues that need to be thought about will be dealt with in Part 3.

Obligations of the VAT system

5.6 Once a charity potentially falls within the VAT system, three significant obligations fall to be considered

(1) the obligation to register;

(2) the obligation to make VAT returns;

(3) the obligation to account timeously and correctly for VAT.

These obligations are the same for charities as for any other business. There is no separate charity regime as far as administration is concerned and, as was noted in Chapter 1, there is no special Charities Unit to deal with VAT issues in the way that FICO does for income tax purposes. We will consider the theory of each of the obligations in turn before considering the compliance methods used by Customs and Excise and the sanctions available to deal with those who fail to meet their full obligations.

The obligation to register

Introduction

5.7 The fact that a charity is carrying on a business and is making taxable supplies does not mean that it must charge VAT on those supplies. It only has to do so if it is 'registered' for VAT. The converse is, of course, that a charity can only obtain relief for VAT it has suffered provided it is registered. The statutory provisions for registration are contained in *VATA 1994, Sch 1*. Customs and Excise produce a leaflet 'Should I be registered for VAT?' (leaflet 700/1/94) which sets out the procedures in detail.

A video to help newly registered traders to get their VAT 'right first time' is now available. It is a key part of the 'Learn About VAT Menu' which Customs have developed as part of a VAT education drive. The video is accompanied by a booklet which expands on the information. Both video and booklet are available free of charge and can be made available in Welsh, Cantonese, Gujarati, Hindi, Punjabi and Urdu on request.

Registration limits

5.8   The basic registration limits are expressed in terms of the value of taxable (standard- and zero-rated) supplies made in a specified period. A charity with both taxable and non-taxable supplies need only be concerned with the level of the former to determine whether or not it should register.

It is important to remember that the turnover which must be considered is the total taxable turnover from all activities. It is not a case of applying the limits separately to individual activities to see if each activity would require registration. For example a charity may have charity shop sales of £35,000, income from a conference of £5,000, sales of books of £8,000 and sales of Christmas cards of £5,000. None of these activities would breach the registration threshold, but taken together they total £53,000, which does exceed the registration threshold as at March 2000. The charity should register for VAT and should account for VAT on the conference receipts and the sales of cards. The fact that the bulk of the income arises from zero-rated activities does not affect the position – zero-rated supplies are taxable supplies and must be taken into account in calculating whether the registration limit is breached.

The current rules on registration contain two alternative tests. A person becomes liable to register if:

(1)   at the end of any month the value of taxable supplies in the period of one year to the end of that month exceeds the current registration limit (registration is not necessary if he can satisfy the Commissioners that the taxable supplies in the next year will not exceed the current deregistration limit); or

(2)   at any time if there are reasonable grounds for believing that the value of his taxable supplies in the period of 30 days then beginning will exceed the current registration threshold.

Notification

5.9   The first registration requirement means that charities which are not registered need to keep a careful watch on the level of all supplies which are potentially taxable. Where the level of such supplies is steadily increasing the need to register may well arise in just a few months.

The onus to register rests on the charity which must notify Customs and Excise within 30 days of the end of the month in which the registration limit is breached. For example if the registration limit is breached in February 2001, registration must be notified by 30 March 2001.

Registration will usually be effective from the end of the month following the month in which the limit is breached. In the example registration would be from 1 April 2001.

Where the second registration limit applies, the charity must notify Customs and Excise before the end of the 30-day period by reference to which liability is going to arise, and registration takes place from the beginning of that period to ensure that the large receipt bears VAT.

Registration should be made on Form VAT1 which is included in leaflet 700/1/94. Details on how to complete VAT1 are set out in the leaflet. Once the form has been checked, an advice of registration will be sent, showing the VAT registration number and the date of registration. A certificate of registration will be sent shortly afterwards. Customs and Excise state that a reply should be received within four weeks, and advise applicants to chase where that period is exceeded.

If an individual is liable to be registered, they should start keeping records and charging VAT immediately, even if they have not included VAT in their prices. They cannot show VAT as an item on an invoice until they have a registration number. They can adjust their prices to include VAT and explain to any customers who are VAT registered that tax invoices will be sent later. They must do this within 30 days of receiving their registration number.

Penalties arise where there is a failure to register and these are discussed in 5.38 below.

Cancelling registration

5.10   Once registered, it is possible to terminate the registration at any time provided Customs and Excise are satisfied that the value of taxable supplies in the next twelve months will be below a figure known as the deregistration limit. This changes each year and is always less than the registration limit. Customs notice 700/11 'Cancelling your registration' provides full details on how to deregister and the consequences of doing so.

Zero-rated supplies

5.11   Where a charity can satisfy Customs and Excise that all its supplies, although taxable, will in fact be zero-rated and Customs and Excise use their discretion, the charity can be exempt from registration. The onus remains, however, on the charity making the supplies. Care must be taken to ensure that all supplies are zero-rated which, given the complexities of the scope of zero-rated products and the fine distinction between standard and zero rating in some situations, may be very difficult. Where there are appreciable standard-rated inputs there may be a positive advantage in being registered.

Voluntary registration

5.12   It is also possible for a charity which is making taxable supplies below the registration limit to ask for discretionary registration. Businesses which do not have to register but wish to do so are no longer required to show a compelling business need to register. They need only satisfy Customs and Excise that they are making taxable supplies in the course of a business.

Customs and Excise policy in respect of the treatment of retrospective voluntary registration applications is that they will be restricted to a registration date no earlier than three years before the current date. This three-year restriction will not, however, apply in the case of obligatory registrations where the law requires a business to have been registered from a particular date by reason of its turnover. Customs have no discretion to limit backdating to three years in these circumstances.

The only real advantage of voluntary registration would be to obtain relief for heavy VAT suffered on goods and services used. The disadvantage is that all the requirements of the VAT legislation must be complied with even if the level of taxable supplies is very low. As a result the administrative costs may be excessive and possibly outweigh the financial gains.

There are very few situations in which it would be beneficial for a charity to seek voluntary registration. Where there is income outside the scope, e.g. donations, only a proportion of any input tax would be reclaimable and the additional administrative costs would be excessive.

Registered person

5.13   The preceding paragraphs all assume that there is a single entity, the charity, which is considering registration. Some charities are organised on a branch or local group basis and there are circumstances in which each separate part of the organisation may need to be registered separately. Customs and Excise usually consider the constitution of the organisation. If it provides for central control of local branches Customs and Excise will require a single registration. This will, of course, mean that all the local branches must submit relevant details to the centre in order for a single VAT return to be made. Where, however, the constitution provides that each local branch is to be autonomous, then the onus is on the local branch to register if necessary.

It might be tempting for charities to look to split their activities in order to avoid the administrative hassle of registration. Before such a step is taken the charity should give consideration to the nature of its supplies and level of input tax and also to the provisions of *Schedule 1, para 2*. These provisions give to Customs and Excise the power to direct that persons carrying on a business which has been artificially split mainly to avoid the need to register for VAT, should be treated as a single taxable person.

Impact of registration

5.14 Once a charity has registered for VAT it is obliged to charge VAT on its taxable supplies and this will involve the issue of VAT invoices. The VAT invoices must be issued and must contain some basic information as follows:

- Name, address and VAT registration number (including the country prefix where sales are being made to customers in another EU member state)
- Identifying reference number
- Time of supply
- Date of issue of the document
- Customer's name and address
- Type of supply
- A description which identifies the goods or services supplied
- Total charge excluding VAT
- Rate of any cash discount
- Total VAT payable
- VAT registration number of the recipient where the supply is to an EU customer

Obligation to make VAT returns

5.15 VAT returns must be made by all registered traders on a quarterly basis unless annual accounting is used (see 5.18 below). The period covered by a return is known as a 'tax period'. The return looks extremely simple, and requires only a few figures to be entered. How simple it is in practice depends on the completeness of accounting records, and how easy it is to extract from those records the required information. Customs and Excise leaflet 700/12/93 'Filling in your VAT return' provides guidance and points out some common errors. Essentially the return requires the following information for each tax period:

Box 1   Output tax on supplies made

Box 2   VAT due on acquisitions from other EC member states

Box 3   The total of boxes 1 and 2 which represents total output tax

Box 4   Input tax reclaimable

Box 5   Difference between boxes 3 and 4. If box 3 exceeds box 4 you pay the difference to Customs and Excise. If box 4 exceeds box 3, they will make repayment to you

Box 6   VAT exclusive total outputs

Box 7   VAT exclusive total inputs

Box 8   Total value of all supplies to other EU member states

Box 9   Total value of all supplies from other EU member states

Unless the cash basis is being used, output tax must be included even where this has not been paid by the customers. Input tax can be claimed even if the creditors have not yet been paid. Account must be taken of credit notes issued and received.

The return must be completed and submitted to the central VAT office within one month of the end of the return period. Failure to do so can lead to compliance problems in the form of the 'default surcharge' which is described at 5.40 below.

Mistakes in the return are also penalised by what is known as the 'mis-declaration penalty' which is explained at 5.41 below.

Obligation to account for VAT

General requirement

5.16   The registered trader simply calculates the difference between the VAT he has charged in the return period and the VAT he has suffered and accounts to Customs for the difference. Where supplies made are heavily dominated by zero-rated supplies there will probably be a net repayment due to the charity.

The complications arise because for many charities it is not simple exercise of looking at all outputs being taxable. There are always likely to be some 'outside the scope' transactions in the form of donations and could also be exempt supplies particularly if fundraising activities have been taking place or if investment income has been received. Many charities face the complexity of coping with partial exemption claims which will affect their VAT recovery. (For background information on partial exemption please see Chapter 11, Part 4 of *Tolley's Charities Manual*.)

Cash accounting

5.17   This scheme is available, with Customs and Excise's approval, to registered businesses with an annual taxable turnover of not more than £350,000. The business must also show that all returns and payments to

Customs and Excise are up to date and it must not have been guilty of any tax offences.

Under the scheme, tax is accounted for on the basis of cash received and cash paid rather than by reference to the date of issue of tax invoices. The main advantage is in giving automatic relief for bad debts. This may not be of any particular consequence for many charities.

A charity will usually have its income in cash and will not, it is hoped, have a bad debt problem. On the other hand it may well be a net repayment business, particularly if its outputs are zero-rated. In that situation it may gain a cash flow advantage by having its tax repayment before it pays its creditors. A move to cash accounting could remove that advantage and leave the cash flow of the charity adversely affected.

Annual accounting

5.18   This scheme is also available to registered businesses with an annual taxable turnover of less than £300,000. The requirement to have tax returns and payments up to date is also present and in addition the business must not be registered in divisions or regularly submit repayment claims. This latter point alone will preclude many charities from taking advantage of the scheme.

Where the scheme is put into effect the business will pay nine monthly payments by direct debit, calculated according to the tax payable in the previous year but taking account of expected changes in turnover, trading and inflation. At the end of the year an annual return will be made and the final balancing payment made. Charities who might qualify should consider the possible adverse impact on their cash flow position if the direct debit payments turn out to be too high. Charity income can be highly volatile and problems could easily arise.

Two recent modifications of the scheme provide:

(1) quarterly interim payments for businesses with an annual taxable turnover of £100,000 or less;

(2) no requirement to make interim payments where annual taxable turnover is below £100,000 and VAT payable is less than £2,000 annually.

VAT compliance powers

Power to assess tax due

5.19   Customs have the power (*VATA 1994, s 73*) to raise VAT assessments in a wide variety of circumstances including where:

(1)   a person has failed to make VAT returns;

(2)   a person has failed to give Customs and Excise the facilities necessary to verify those returns;

(3)   a person has failed to keep any documents;

(4)   Customs and Excise believe the returns to be either incomplete or incorrect;

(5)   an incorrect repayment has been made or a claim to input tax wrongly made;

(6)   tax has been deliberately evaded or lost as a result of dishonest conduct resulting in a conviction;

(7)   penalties, interest or surcharges apply.

The assessment must be made to the best of the judgment of Customs and Excise – in practice the best judgment of the individual officer who is looking at the case. The taxpayer must be notified of the amount of the assessment.

VAT assessments must be made no later than three years after the end of the accounting period to which they relate, although the normal basis will be the later of:

●   two years after the end of the period to which the assessment relates; and

●   one year after evidence of the facts to justify the making of the assessment comes to the knowledge of Customs.

Power to demand information

5.20   Apart from a requirement to notify Customs of any changes in registration details, a person who is concerned in the supply of goods or services in the course or furtherance of a business must supply Customs with any information they might reasonably require and any documents they may require. In practice any request for information has to be put in writing.

Power to enter premises

5.21   Customs have the formidable power of being able to enter at any reasonable times any premises used in connection with the carrying on of a business. This can be enhanced by the issue of a search warrant.

The power to enter and inspect premises extends to those premises which are being used in connection with the making of taxable supplies and the goods that are supplied are on the premises. The general understanding is that VAT officers should inspect with their eyes and search with their hands.

Power of arrest

5.22   This ultimate power exists in cases of fraud and the use of false documents in committing a VAT offence. It is used only in the most serious cases but the warning needs to be given!

VAT investigations

Types of visit

5.23   A distinction needs to be drawn at the outset between the routine type of VAT visit – referred to as a 'control' visit – and an investigation. The former is part of the routine compliance programme and most registered traders, including charities can expect to receive such visits. The frequency of those visits will depend on what is found and how that is dealt with.

A VAT investigation is likely to be undertaken only where there is a suspicion that the trader may have committed some kind of VAT offence.

Triggers to investigation visits

5.24   A control visit needs no trigger, but a decision to undertake a more vigorous VAT investigation will usually require some particular factors to be present such as:

- a poor compliance record in submitting returns and paying over the tax;

- references from other VAT offices which relate to dealings between traders – a control visit to another trader might spark an investigation;

- large repayment claims made by a newly registered trader;

- information, anonymous or otherwise, from the public, other traders, etc. – charities are not always popular with local traders who feel that they are at a competitive disadvantage;

- local knowledge and expertise – this may be difficult where charities are concerned because even if there is a concentration of charities in a particular VAT collection area, they are likely to be so diverse that any comparisons are going to be very difficult.

Role of the VAT Central Unit (VCU)

5.25   The central processing unit in Southend runs various checks on the VAT returns it receives and these can lead to visits being made if the particular VAT return throws up inconsistencies. For example a trader who has consistently been one who paid over VAT each quarter suddenly having a large repayment.

Control visits

Purpose

5.26   Customs would see the two prime objectives of control visits as being:

(1)   to enforce compliance with the VAT legislation;

(2)   to maximise the collection of VAT (interestingly the Inland Revenue are now making greater play of their objective to ensure that people pay the 'correct' amount of tax).

The control visit provides a direct opportunity to meet these objectives by getting to the heart of how the trader runs whatever business he is in, and how he maintains the records from which the VAT calculations are made and the returns prepared.

Format

5.27   Visits will usually be carried out at the premises of the trader. In larger charities this may be the central point where the VAT return is processed. The visit will usually start with a discussion with the person responsible for the VAT return so that the officer can make sure that they know what they are doing. This may be particularly important in the case of a charity where there are complications such as partial exemption.

The practical side of the review will focus on reviewing the last accounts of the business and comparing turnover against outputs and certain expenses where VAT would have been borne against inputs. In the case of a charity where there have been claims for zero rating perhaps on building work, or advertising or the purchase of certain medical aids, the checks may be to satisfy the inspector that the claim to zero-rating is in order.

Where a charity has a number of branches which report figures in to a central point to complete a single VAT return, the VAT officers will want to satisfy themselves that those procedures are working both in terms of the accuracy of what is being submitted by the branches and the method by which the figures are being compiled in the centre.

Frequency of visits

5.28   Control visits are a routine part of VAT compliance, and decisions on the frequency of control visits will be determined by the views taken at a local level of the risks present in any trader situation. Some may be perceived as being a greater risk and will therefore receive more frequent visits. It is likely that every trader will be visited at some time and so a charity should not draw any adverse conclusions when they have their first visit. If the habit becomes regular, then the trustees should start to be concerned that something serious is amiss. The factors that are likely to be taken into account in determining how often to make a visit include:

- size of turnover;

- complexity of the business activities (some of the issues relating to charities – particularly partial exemption – can be much more complicated than those affecting ordinary fully taxable traders);

- complexity of the accounting records;

- past history of the business;

- unexpected variations in the VAT returns;

- local initiatives to target particular risk areas (this is more likely to focus on specific trades where there are known risks or current avoidance schemes).

Investigation techniques

5.29   The type of review which will be undertaken on a control visit will depend very much on the nature of the trade which is being reviewed. Typically, the VAT officer may:

(1)   sample batches of invoices to see that the correct rate of VAT has been charged;

(2)   sample batches of purchase invoices to see that the correct input tax has been claimed;

(3)   check that credit notes have been correctly dealt with;

(4)   check that carry forward items in the accounting records have been correctly dealt with;

(5)   check the application of partial exemption rules;

(6)   if a particular retail scheme is in use, check that it is being properly applied;

(7)   check supplementary information such as orders, sales correspondence, bank statements to ensure that they are consistent with what has been shown on the VAT return;

(8)   compare the accounts and the VAT returns;

(9)   ascertain if there are any unusual issues which need review.

Typical problems for charities

5.30   There is a wide variety of problems which charities can encounter under the VAT regime. This is well evidenced by the number of VAT tribunal cases which deal with charities and must represent only a fraction of the issues which are dealt with. Some of these cases come about because charities are claiming the benefit of certain zero-rated provisions rather than being registered traders. The broad issues that appear to cause regular concern are:

(1) the issue of whether or not a business is being carried on and if so how many businesses, which may emerge under the new building rules where there can be no zero rating if a building is to be used for the purposes of a business, it may also arise where a charity wants to be registered as carrying on a business so that it can recover input tax;

(2) whether the exemption for welfare activities can apply, which can include arguments as to whether activities are carried on 'otherwise than for profit'

(3) partial exemption calculations and in particular the use of schemes which differ from the normal practice

(4) application of the zero-rating for the supply of medical and similar goods to what are known as 'relevant bodies' such as hospitals. Issues also arise as to what items constitute aids for handicapped people.

(5) zero-rating and advertising has been a constant cause of argument as charities have tried to shift the boundaries outwards and Customs have resisted. (this may become less of a problem following the new provisions implemented after the charities tax review, although some of those provisions may provoke their own arguments.)

(6) arguments as to what constitutes education and can therefore qualify for exemption;

(7) issues relating to membership;

(8) how admission charges should be identified and the application of specific exemptions surrounding cultural bodies and sports centres;

(9) the whole area of fundraising events and whether they qualify for exemption or not (again this is an area of change following the Charities Tax Review);

(10) A major area of contention is the area of building and repairs.

In Part 3 of this book we will examine several of these issues which are of general application across the charitable sector in some detail specifically:

(1) the issue of a business activity will be considered in the overall context of trading;

(2) the exemption on fundraising will be considered in chapter dealing with that subject;

(3) issues relating to building will be dealt with in chapter on property;

(4)   other issues will be dealt with in chapter on VAT

There is a detailed review (including a review of relevant cases) of the whole area of VAT and charities in Chapter 11 of *Tolley's Charities Manual*.

VAT assessments

The process

5.31   The issue of VAT assessments usually follows on from a control visit where irregularities have been found. The trader may also be required to make specific changes to their accounting systems to prevent further problems. Where the assessment is not disputed, tax should be paid.

A VAT assessment should always be carefully check to ensure that it is technically correct, i.e.:

- It is addressed to the right person

- It properly sets out the basis of charge and is calculated correctly

- It is made for the correct accounting period and is made in time

Made to 'best judgement'

5.32   The assessment must always be made to the 'best judgement' (*VATA 1994, s 73*) and the charity should always consider this if they receive an assessment. It is not necessary that Customs should have undertaken a very detailed audit of all the financial records, but they should have acted reasonably based on what they have seen. The figures may be disputed and the logic of the assessment may be disputed.

Not surprisingly VAT tribunals have had to consider the question of what 'best of judgement' means and in one case that went before the High Court, Woolf, J summed up the criteria as follows:

> 'What the words "best of their judgement" envisage, in my view, is that the Commissioners will fairly consider all the material placed before them and on that material, come to a decision which is reasonable and not arbitrary as to the amount of tax which is due.'

> *Van Boeckel v Customs and Excise [1981] STC 290*

It is not open to the trader to argue that the assessment is invalid just because he does not agree with either the concept of being charged the tax or the amount of the tax. Those issues can be argued out before the tribunal.

Right of appeal to VAT tribunal

How the tribunals are organised

5.33 The VAT tribunals operate as part of the Lord Chancellor's Department and are therefore independent of Customs and Excise in the same way that the General and Special Commissioners are independent of the Inland Revenue. They are set up under the terms of *VATA 1994, Sch 12*. They operate through three main centres:

- London (LON)
- Manchester (MAN)
- Edinburgh (EDN)

Each office deals with appeals from VAT offices within their specific areas. There are also hearings held in other locations effectively as outposts of the main centres so that there is greater local access for the trader.

The tribunal operates under a president and a number of chairmen (currently 43 are on the panel) and tribunal members. The chairmen are lawyers with at least seven years' experience and the members are lay people. A chairman can sit alone to hear an appeal or can have one or more members with them.

They are supported by administrative staff in each of the three centres. These include clerks who actually sit in the hearings and assist the chairman in administrative issues.

Appealable matters

5.34 Not every dispute can be taken to a Tribunal. The full list of issues on which appeals can be taken are set out in *VATA 1994, s 83* which contains a very lengthy list. Significant issues which can be heard include (the letters are the subparagraphs of *section 83*)

- (a) the registration or cancellation of registration of any person under this Act;
- (b) the VAT chargeable on the supply of any goods or services;
- (c) the amount of any input tax which may be credited to a person;
- (e) the proportion of input tax allowable under *section 26*;
- (g) the amount of any refunds under *section 35* (relating to construction of certain buildings);
- (n) any liability to a penalty or surcharge by virtue of any of *sections 59 to 69*;

- (p) an assessment;

- (q) the amount of any penalty, interest or surcharge specified in an assessment under *section 76*;

- (r) the making of an assessment on the basis set out in *section 77(4)* in cases of fraud;

- (s) any liability of the Commissioners to pay interest under *section 78* or the amount of interest so payable.

Appeal procedure

5.35   There is a formal procedure which has to be followed in order to have an appeal heard. The administration is all handled by the relevant appeal centre not by Customs and Excise. It is a requirement that all VAT affairs of the appellant are up to date and VAT has been paid where appropriate. It is also a requirement that the tax which is in dispute should be paid or deposited with Customs and Excise, although this requirement can be waived either by the department or the tribunal if they consider that a payment would cause hardship to the appellant. This can be particularly important for charities where cash flow may be a major consideration.

Once the case comes to a hearing, the procedure is not dissimilar to that used in appeals to the Commissioners in tax cases; the detailed work in deciding to appeal and conducting an appeal will be discussed in Chapter 13 below.

Correcting errors in VAT returns

5.36   Where a trader finds a mistake in a VAT return before Customs and Excise discover it, there is a strong incentive to take action to correct the problem quickly. The error should be corrected through the return for the most current period. If at the end of that period the overall effect of the error is less than £2,000, the trader can simply deal with it through adjustments to the current VAT account. If the error exceeds that figure a separate notification to Customs must be made.

Where the error is disclosed voluntarily and is in excess of £2,000, interest can still be charged on the tax. There will not, however, be any exposure to the misdeclaration penalty regime.

Interest

5.37   Interest is payable at a prescribed rate where an assessment is raised for an under declaration or an overclaim of VAT. [*VATA 1994, s 74*]. Typically interest can be charged in the following circumstances:

(1)   VAT has been overclaimed by the taxpayer;

(2)   VAT has been underpaid to Customs and Excise;

(3)   'VAT' is included on an invoice by an unregistered person;

(4)   no returns have been submitted;

(5)   there has been a loss of tax to the Exchequer;

(6)   a voluntary disclosure has been made but the net error exceeds £2,000.

Interest can also be charged where an assessment is avoided simply because the trader makes the payment of tax concerned. In that case the interest will run from the date on which the tax should have been paid to the date on which it was actually paid. Interest is calculated from the date that the tax should have been paid to the date of issue of the assessment. In the case of an excessive repayment claim, interest will run from seven days after the date of authority to pay was issued by Customs and Excise. Interest is payable on receipt of the assessment and further interest charges will be incurred if the assessed tax is not paid within 15 days.

Penalties

Failure to register

5.38   Penalties arise where a trader fails to notify registration within the statutory period unless he has a reasonable excuse. [*VATA 1994, s 67*]. The penalty is calculated as a percentage of the VAT due from the date when registration should have taken place to the date when notification is made or Customs and Excise become aware of the need for registration. The penalty levels are as follows (subject to a minimum of £50):

- registration no more than nine months late 5%;

- over nine months late but no more than 18 months late 10%;

- over 18 months late 15%.

The penalty is subject to a 'reasonable excuse' argument, as are a number of the VAT penalties. This concept is discussed below.

Giving an incorrect certificate for zero rating

5.39   There are a number of situations in which a charity can give a certificate to a supplier where they are entitled to zero rating in respect of a supply they receive. For example on the new building of what is known as 'relevant charitable property'. If that certificate is given incorrectly, Customs can charge a penalty equal to the tax which should have been payable. Customs have the power to charge this penalty where the error arises, there does not have to be any evidence of deliberate error on the part of the trader who gave the certificate. This can be an important area for charities in the light of zero rating for land and also zero rating for the supply of goods for handicapped people.

Default surcharge

5.40   The basic requirement is that a VAT return must be sent in quarterly, together with the amount of VAT due. Failure to do this will trigger the default surcharge procedure which operates on a 'totting up' basis. The offence occurs when either the return and the tax are sent in late or the return is sent in on time and the tax is paid late.

The procedure operates rather like a yellow card in football. If you default, Customs and Excise will issue a surcharge liability notice warning that any default in the next twelve months will trigger a default surcharge on the VAT involved. Once a notice has been issued it remains in force until a twelve-month default free period has elapsed. Where a notice is in place and defaults take place they are calculated on a sliding scale – 2%, 5%, 10% and then 15%. No default surcharge assessment will be issued for an amount of less than £200.

Misdeclaration penalty

5.41   Where an error is made in a VAT return a penalty can be applied. The penalty rate is 15%, although there is a separate rate which applies for dishonest conduct and this starts at 100%. The penalty will arise when the tax misdeclared is the lower of £1m and 30% of the 'relevant amount' for that period.

The definition of 'relevant amount' depends on the nature of the offence. Where an error has been made, the 'relevant amount' is to be the gross amount of tax for the period, i.e. the total of tax paid and tax claimed on the return. Where the offence is that of failing to draw the attention of Customs and Excise to an error, the 'relevant amount' is the true amount of tax for the relevant period.

Penalties can only arise if three out of twelve VAT periods contain significant errors, and no penalty will be due unless Customs and Excise have first issued a warning and a penalty liability notice.

Reasonable excuse

5.42   Most of the penalty provisions contain the power for the penalty to be removed if the taxpayer can show a reasonable excuse for not complying with the relevant matter. The tribunal have had to consider many arguments as to what constitutes a reasonable excuse and a number of general principles have emerged. The overriding requirement is that the trader must provide evidence to show that his circumstances fell outside the normal hazard of trade, or that there was some element of inescapable or unforeseeable misfortune. The crucial question is: 'Was the trader faced with a difficulty which could not have been anticipated and that a person acting in a reasonable manner could not have overcome?' If the problem persists, the trader will be expected to show that all reasonable steps are taken to overcome it – what is regarded as a reasonable excuse the first time round is unlikely to be given sympathetic treatment the second time.

Customs and Excise give guidance to their officers in considering the validity of a claim to reasonable excuse. They point out three basic questions which must always be considered:

(1)   Has the problem been around for some time?

(2)   Did the difficulties arise immediately before the due date or did the trader have time to put matters right (i.e. were the circumstances unforeseeable and/or inescapable)?

(3)   Has the trader used the same excuse before?

Exclusions from reasonable excuse

5.43   *Value Added Tax Act 1994, s 71* specifically excludes the following from being a reasonable excuse:

● 	lack of funds to pay any VAT due; or

● 	reliance on any other person to perform a task, where there has been a delay or inaccuracy on that person's part.

Customs do point out that whilst lack of funds does not in itself constitute a reasonable excuse the underlying cause of the lack of funds may do so.

Factors affecting reasonable excuse

5.44   The success or otherwise of a claim to 'reasonable excuse' will depend very heavily on the particular facts in relation to the offence which is being considered. The following factors may be considered by VAT officers.

Insufficiency of funds

5.45   Although the legislative intention is that insufficiency of funds can never in itself constitute a reasonable excuse, the cause of that insufficiency, i.e. the underlying cause of the default, might do so. In one case a trader claimed that the failure of a major customer to pay his bills led to a cash shortage which caused the inability to pay Customs. The court accepted the argument and Customs now note that in considering a claim of insufficiency of funds the VAT officer should determine whether:

(1)   the trader could have reasonably foreseen the insufficiency of funds or was he faced with a sudden cash crisis, e.g. sudden reduction or

withdrawal of overdraft facilities, sudden non-payment by a normally reliable customer, insolvency of a large customer, fraud,
burglary or act of God such as fire;

(2)   the trader received enough money before the end of the period to
pay the VAT due;

(3)   any payments been received during the periods concerned (details
of outgoings may also be relevant) – if so whether the trader paid
part of his VAT on time;

(4)   steps have been taken to overcome the difficulties, e.g. the trader
has tried to collect overdue debts or obtain alternative finance to
cover the VAT due;

(5)   the trader is tied to a single (or very few) customer(s);

(6)   any actions by the department contributed to the grounds of
appeal, e.g. investigations, failure to answer trader's correspondence or failure to make prompt repayments.

Return and/or payment sent in time

5.46   *Sections 59(7)(a) and 59A(8)(a)(i) of VATA 1994* allow traders to
appeal on the grounds that:

'(7) . . .
(a) the return, or as the case may be, the tax shown on the return, was
dispatched at such a time and in such a manner that it was reasonable
to expect that it would be received by the Commissioners within the
appropriate time limit

(8)
(a)(i) that the payment on account of VAT was despatched in such a
time and in such a manner that it was reasonable to expect that it
would be received by the Commissioners by the day on which it
became due.'

Vat officers are told to consider the following questions:

●   Does the trader have proof of posting or, for payment on account
traders, evidence of when the bank payment transfer was initiated?

●   Was the date of signature on the VAT return after the due date?

●   Was there any disruption to the postal or banking services?

Non-receipt of surcharge liability notice (SLN)

5.47   An SLN acts as a warning to businesses that if they fail to
submit further payments on time, within the period shown on the
notice, they will be liable to a surcharge. It must be received by the
business before any subsequent default can attract a surcharge. Customs

recognise that it is sometimes difficult to establish categorically that an SLN was received by the trader. Two basic points should be established before a decision is reached.

(1)   Was there a change of address during the relevant period?

(2)   Was the SLN issued with a tax assessment which was paid?

Illness/loss of key personnel

5.48   The following factors are taken into consideration when considering appeals of this type:

●   The precise date and nature of illness.

●   Is/was the illness serious enough to prevent the return and/or payment being rendered on time?

●   Could anyone else have provided cover in the trader's absence?

●   What steps have been taken to make alternative arrangements?

Computer breakdown/loss of records

5.49   Customs indicate that such breakdowns or losses are unlikely to provide reasonable excuse for more than one or two periods. Points to consider here are:

●   The precise dates of the computer failure/loss of records.

●   Extent and effect of the breakdown/loss.

●   Did the trader have a back-up system?

●   Did the trader notify his local office of the situation prior to the due date?

●   Did the trader estimate the tax due for the period and pay this before the due date?

Error on cheque

5.50   A cheque may be returned by a bank because of a difference between the amount stated in words and the amount stated in figures. In banking law that should not be returned by the bank. The *Bills of Exchanges Act 1882*, which requires the amount to be stated both in words and figures, contemplates the possibility of a discrepancy between the words and figures, and it specifically provides that where there is a discrepancy, the sum denoted by the words is the amount payable. It is common banking practice to return a cheque in those circumstances but the tribunal has accepted that as a reasonable excuse.

The tribunal will not accept as a reasonable excuse a situation in which the cheque is returned because the account holder has failed to sign it. That is a fault of the account holder and will not be accepted as a reasonable excuse.

Part 2: Practical Issues in Handling Investigations

Introduction

This part is intended to provide guidance in the practical issues relating to the handling of investigations of all types from start to finish. The approach will be to look at some general issues relating to the handling of investigations and then to look at specific issues that may arise during the five different types of investigation which are being considered. The format will therefore be as follows:

- Dealing with the initial approach (Chapter 6)

- Handling the opening meeting (Chapter 7)

- Progressing the investigation through to settlement (Chapter 8)

- Charity Commission investigations (Chapter 9)

- Inland Revenue FICO enquiries (Chapter 10)

- Inland Revenue FICO audits (Chapter 11)

- Inland Revenue employer compliance (Chapter 12)

- VAT (Chapter 13)

Trustees responsibility

At the start of this part the overall role and responsibility of the trustee body in controlling what happens in an investigation is re-emphasised. Their degree of involvement might vary according to the type of investigation, but they should always be aware of any investigation that is taking place and should always be consulted in the process of settlement.

Chapter 6

Coping with the First Approach

Introduction

6.1   The pattern for many investigations is set in the early days, and how the charity reacts in those early days can have a major effect on the overall outcome. Investigation work involving the Revenue authorities is very much a question of who has control of the board. With the Charity Commission, there may be less opportunity for control but that depends on the stage and nature of the inquiry being made.

This chapter looks at the key issues which trustees should consider in those early stages:

●   How will they become aware of the investigation?

●   How will they deal with the initial response?

●   What about using professional help?

●   How do they organise the succeeding stages of the enquiry?

The aim must be to minimise the impact of the inquiry on all the resources of the charity, because any inquiry will be a drain on the time and energy of the trustees, the staff who have to deal with it and possibly on the financial resources of the charity. If this is faced at the start it can help to clear the thinking about the strategy to be adopted.

Handling the initial approach

Charity Commission

Format of approach

6.2   The charity will be come aware of the interest of the Charity Commission when the Investigation section at the appropriate office contacts them to ask questions or to request a meeting. This will either be because the Commissioners have decided to carry out an evaluation exercise or because they have decided to go straight into an inquiry under *section 8*. In both cases it is likely that the correspondence will be addressed to the chairman of the trustee body who will need to decide on the appropriate response.

The person who receives the communication from the Charity Commission should acknowledge receipt of that letter immediately and indicate to the Commissioners that immediate action is being taken to convene a trustees' meeting. That will give the Investigation team some comfort, first that their letter has been received and secondly that it has provoked a response.

Notifying the trustees

6.3   Any approach from the Charity Commission which indicates some element of potential concern by the investigation section should be viewed with the utmost seriousness by the trustees. The number of cases that get reviewed each year is very small relative to the whole charity sector and the fact that one charity has been singled out in this way is significant. Allegations, however misguided, have to be answered, and the process needs to be put into effect as quickly as possible but also in as controlled a way as possible.

Assuming it is the chairman of the trustees who has received the letter, he or she needs to make other trustees aware of the situation as quickly as possible. (It is advisable for any trustee who has received correspondence from the Commissioners to contact all their fellow trustees – they must not assume that everyone will have received the same letter.) This is best done by calling a special meeting of the trustee body to discuss the response which should be made. Whether the chief administrative officer (CAO) is invited to attend that meeting may depend on the nature of the possible problems which are being raised by the Commissioners. If the allegations centre on the activities of the CAO, then they should not be invited to that initial meeting. A decision will need to be taken in such a case on whether the CAO should be suspended from their duties while the investigations are carried out. Professional advice should be sought on this point.

There may be particular awkwardness where the problems surround the activities of one of the trustees, particularly if that person is the founding trustee. In those circumstances it is likely that the Charity Commission will have taken steps to contact other trustees rather than the object of their concern. Those other trustees need to meet to discuss their action. The situation will be very unpleasant for all concerned but the other trustees need to collectively exercise their authority (possibly for the first time). They would be strongly recommended to seek professional advice before tackling the dominant trustee. If the other trustees fail to take any decisive action they may find that they simply reinforce the view that the Commissioners may have formed and cannot expect a great deal of sympathetic response from the investigation group.

No smoke without fire!

6.4   There will inevitably be a variety of reactions to the news of Charity Commission interest in the activities of the charity:

(1)   The view that such action could have been predicted and that the only surprise is that it has taken this long for any action to emerge. In these circumstances the trustees should seriously consider their own position immediately because they are almost certainly a contributory factor to the problem.

(2)   Genuine shock that any misdemeanour could even be contemplated or that there could be any grounds. This should galvanise the trustees to want to make their own full enquiry into what is going on and to get that moving as quickly as possible.

(3)   Indignation that anyone should make any complaint and that the whole thing is simply sparked by malice. This may be an understandable reaction because no body of trustees wants to think that they have allowed problems to arise and go unchecked. The appropriate reaction should be to ensure that action is taken to rebuff the complaints as quickly as possible.

In the case of point (3), the trustees should just stop to consider what could have caused the allegations to be made in the first place. It may be that someone is aggrieved at action taken (or not taken) and has simply made malicious remarks. There must be something that has caused the Charity Commission to react to those comments – possibly in the charity's accounts, annual report or some other documentation which lends some credence to the allegations. The trustees should consider all the possibilities and take some action to clarify the public (or maybe the internal) perception which people gain of the way they conduct the affairs of the charity.

The initial trustee meeting

6.5   The first meeting of the trustee body should consider the initial action which would be appropriate. This will obviously depend upon the precise allegations which are being made or the issues which the Commissioners are highlighting. Whatever the action (and some possible responses are set out below), it must be seen as being decisive in the relevant circumstances. There must not be any attempt to sweep matters under the carpet or to dismiss them as of no real significance. The reaction of the trustees will go a long way to colouring the views of the investigation team in the matter.

Some forms of action which may be considered are as follows:

- Where allegations relate to the activities of an employee, including the chief executive, then steps should be taken (after seeking legal advice) to suspend the employee immediately on full pay pending the outcome of the inquiry. The duties of the employee need to be covered and an initial explanation given to the other members of staff.

- Where allegations concern the activities of a trustee, that individual should be asked for an immediate explanation (although they may decline to give it until they have taken legal advice themselves) and they should be told that their role as trustee is being suspended and that they will take no further part in the activities of the trust until further notice. If this means that a new, albeit temporary, chairman is appointed then that action should be taken.

- If allegations concern the use of bank accounts, action should be taken with the bank either to freeze the accounts in question, or, if that is not practicable because the accounts are used for main charity activities, to amend the bank mandates so that fresh signatories are given power to control the account.

- Allegations concerning the activities of fundraisers will probably centre on the activities of those people and the terms of their relationship with the charity. It would be appropriate to suspend any agreement which is currently in place pending a review of the position. Again this action should be taken after legal advice has been obtained on the consequences of any suspension or unilateral cancellation of any agreement.

By the end of the meeting, the trustees should have agreed to make an appropriate response to the Charity Commission, and should have set in train an internal review, or a review by appropriate professional advisers, to look at the allegations.

The minutes of the meeting should be very detailed and should set out clearly the action which has been taken.

Response to the Charity Commission

6.6   As soon as possible after the meeting, the chairman of the trustee body (or the acting chairman if the allegations centre around the chairman), should write formally to the Charity Commissioners explaining the action which has been taken and to seek an early meeting with the investigation group to see how matters can be progressed. If professional advisers have become involved, this response could come from them.

Practical issues relating to the handling of a meeting are discussed in Chapter 7.

Inland Revenue – FICO

Format of approach

6.7   The approach from the Revenue will vary depending upon the type of enquiry being made. In the new self-assessment regime, the official start of any enquiry into the charity or any trading companies must come with a *section 9A* letter. This will go to the trustees with a copy to any professional adviser that the Revenue are aware of. The letter accompanying the *section 9A* letter should give the details of the areas of Revenue concern.

Routine issues relating to the accuracy of any tax repayment claim may be dealt with by letter – usually the Revenue will simply advise what charges they have made and why – or by means of a simple telephone call from the Revenue.

A decision by the Revenue to carry out an audit visit will be communicated by letter and will usually set out a date for the proposed visit. This needs to be acknowledged and if it is convenient, the arrangements should be confirmed. If it is not convenient then alternative arrangements should be made either by letter or telephone.

Notifying the trustees

6.8   Where the Revenue are commencing a formal *section 9A* inquiry there is no reason to take urgent action as with the Charity Commission opening, although if the covering letter suggests some serious problems are being raised that might put a different slant on the issue. The matter should certainly be put on to the next trustees meeting, but if that meeting is some time ahead, it might be sensible for the chairman to contact all trustees with a copy of the Revenue letter. It might be appropriate to raise the matter with the finance committee or whatever the relevant sub-group is called, but the matter should still be brought to the attention of all the trustees.

The enquiry might also involve the affairs of a trading subsidiary. In this case the existence of the enquiry should be brought to the attention not only of the trustees who are directors of the company but also all trustees who are not involved with the company and all directors of the company who are not trustees.

An approach on an incorrect repayment does not need any formal action although the trustee responsible for the financial controls might want to consider if the problem is symptomatic of something bigger.

Again a notification of an audit visit needs to be noted by the trustees but there is no need for immediate action by the whole trustee body. There should, however, be arrangements for a report to be tabled at the first trustees' meeting after the visit to consider the outcome of the visit. That way any problems which have arisen can be brought to the attention of the trustee body.

The need for internal review

6.9   If the *section 9A* enquiry looks as though it will go beyond a simple couple of queries that can be dealt with by correspondence, the trustees should consider either bringing in professional help to review the situation and ascertain the extent of the problem or to carry out a review internally. In either case a report should be made to the trustee body. This should also happen if the area of concern relates to a trading company.

Consideration at initial meeting

6.10   If the issues are straightforward there should be no need to take any action other than to note that an enquiry has been opened and any measures being taken. Wider discussion may be necessary if the enquiry is aimed at some key structural issues such as the relationship between the charity and a trading company or the question of whether charity income qualifies for tax exemption. If an internal review has been carried out, the findings of that review should be brought to the full trustee body so that they can consider if any action is needed, and decide on a formal response to the Revenue.

The key issues which will need to be thought through are:

(1)   whether professional advice is needed in connection with the enquiry;

(2)   whether any internal action needs to be taken to change existing procedures;

(3)   whether a request should be made to have a meeting with the Revenue.

Response to the Revenue

6.11   It is important that a reasonably early response is made to the Revenue particularly if they have asked for information. If they receive no early reply they may decide to take action to force in information by using the powers in *TMA 1970, s 19A*. This immediately hands control of the investigation back to the Revenue and is not to be recommended.

If more time is needed then you should explain to the Revenue what action is being undertaken and when you hope to make a full response. Keep a watch on the passing of time and if the proposed date passes make sure that the Revenue are kept informed.

Inland Revenue – employer compliance

Format of approach

6.12   The request for an employer compliance visit will usually be sent either to the payroll department or to someone involved in the administration of the charity. This might be the person who signs the Annual PAYE return (P35), or the person who regularly deals with the Revenue on employee-related issues.

Notifying the trustees

6.13   There is no need for urgent action to be taken by the trustees. They need to be advised that a compliance review is being undertaken and when and they may ask for a report back after the visit. The trustee responsible for this area of operation may be charged with oversight of the review.

Need for internal review

6.14   Once the Revenue have given notice of an intention to carry out a visit there is little that can be done to change matters. Certainly no attempt should be made to 'pretty up' the records – Revenue compliance officers are not stupid. However, some consideration should be given to the adequacy of the records which have been maintained because if there are any problem areas it may be prudent to bring these to the Revenue's attention at an early stage (see Chapter 7).

Responding to the Revenue

6.15   At this stage all that needs to be done is to acknowledge and confirm the arrangements or suggest an alternative.

VAT

Format of approach

6.16   The likely approach will be an advice that a control visit is to be undertaken. This will usually be directed at someone in the accounts department who is responsible for the completion of the VAT records or the submission of the VAT return.

Notifying the trustees

6.17   The same arrangements can apply as for an employer compliance visit. The trustees should be made aware of what is planned but do not need to take any immediate action.

Action at trustees' meeting

6.18   As for employer compliance issues, the trustees should not in any of these situations just assume that the process is routine and dismiss it.

Problems in PAYE records or VAT records can be a major concern in themselves but they can also be symptoms of something that that may be going wrong in other areas of the administration of the charity and trustees should always keep this in mind.

Response to Customs and Excise

6.19 Confirmation of the arrangements for the visit is all that is required at this stage.

Using professional advice

When is it needed

6.20 Trustees need to give serious consideration to the use of professional advice as soon as it becomes clear that matters are arising which are outside the normal routine of issues such as repayment claim errors or very routine PAYE or VAT compliance problems. The circumstances in which professional advice should definitely be sought are

(1) any inquiry or evaluation process by the Charity Commission;

(2) when it becomes clear that the Revenue at FICO are taking more than a normal interest in the tax affairs of a charity;

(3) when substantive issues emerge on a FICO audit such as the question of benefits under Gift Aid;

(4) when substantial issues arise on PAYE reviews;

(5) when substantial issues arise on a VAT control visit.

In all these situations there is a threat to the assets of the charity and the trustees need to be seen to be doing everything to protect those assets even at the ultimate cost of their own position if necessary – a trustee is deemed disposable, the assets of the charity are not.

Both the Charity Commission and the Revenue are happy to work with advisers. Both will make it clear that advisers are not to be used as an excuse for putting the blame elsewhere. They also make it clear that if they believe that the professional advisers are dragging their feet, they will revert back to the charity to continue inquiries or expect the charity to 'gee up' their advisers.

How do you choose?

6.21 The choice of an adviser is also very important. The accountant or auditor who provides the basic financial advice to the charity may do that job exceedingly well, but may very quickly get out of their depth in an enquiry situation. There will usually be two reasons for this:

(1) The technical arguments are quite specific to the charity sector. None of the traditional arguments come into the enquiry. Many accountants may be used to handling investigations that come down to issues of gross profit rate, or the drawings of proprietors or the private assets of the business owner, but will find arguments about trading or the use of trading companies very strange to them.

(2) The rough and tumble of the negotiating game can be one which many accountants find distasteful, and they may feel at a disadvantage through lack of practical experience. It helps to have someone who understands the arguments and Revenue techniques.

The same may apply to the choice of solicitor where a Charity Commission inquiry is under way. The solicitors who handle routine issues on charity property, for example, may not be the best to argue about the duties of trustees, or the complexities of fundraising legislation. If there are problems relating to a dominant trustee, solicitors who have been involved with the charity since its inception and who are therefore well known to the particular individual may have difficulty in maintaining an impartial or even a confrontational approach to the individual.

The author has been brought in on a number of cases where the existing accountants have felt unable to provide the specialist advice required and in one case where the incumbent auditors were part of the problem themselves. In all these cases the existing advisers have continued with their basic role of auditing and the author's involvement has ceased with the settlement of the enquiry.

The choice of a new adviser will come down to one essential point – the value of the service you are going to receive. This will show itself in the quality of the service and the cost. It does not necessarily follow that the cheapest quote should be taken. You need to establish a number of factors:

(1) What experience does the firm have in dealing with the type of problem you have? This needs to be experience not only in handling the technical issues but also an understanding of investigation techniques and practice.

(2) Is there one particular individual who has that experience – and if so will they be the person who will handle the case?

(3) How much personal involvement will that individual have or will they delegate work? (Delegation of routine work is perfectly acceptable and will keep costs down provided that the 'expert' takes overall control.)

Engagement process

Agreeing costs

6.22   Where a professional adviser is to be used, make sure that you are aware of the costs which can be incurred. Investigations of any kind are time consuming and, where professionals are concerned, time means money. Allow the professional adviser time to get a feel for the case and then ask for an idea of costs. They should be able to give an initial cost for carrying out a basic review or dealing with the first meeting. Beyond that, it may be difficult to estimate because much will depend on how the authorities react to the information supplied.

Professional firms usually base their charges on time and different grades of staff will have different charge-out rates. Typically a partner in a firm in London could be charged out at anything from £250 to £400 per hour, and outside London the rates could be from £150 to £250 per hour. Usually firms will discount their rates as far as charities are concerned. Make arrangements for fees to be rendered on a regular basis so that overall costs do not build up.

It is important to keep an overall eye on costs, and the adviser should do this as well. In very serious cases where the assets of the charity could be at risk there may be no alternative to proceeding with the inquiry. In most Revenue or Customs investigation cases there will come a point where it will be clear what the tax at issue actually is. At that point a decision may have to be taken as to whether a deal of some kind will be possible. At this point the trustees will want to set the costs of proceeding against the likely results and there is clearly little point in spending money on advice that is not going to save significant amounts. It is to be hoped that the adviser would make that clear and would make a strong recommendation even though they were losing potential fees as a result.

The arrangements with the adviser should be contained in a letter of engagement which will cover what work is to be done and set out other terms of engagement.

What is required?

6.23   Make it clear what you want the adviser to do – is it to provide advice on action to be taken or to take over the direction of the inquiry. This may depend on the nature of the inquiry.

Time and therefore costs can be saved by arranging for work to be done by charity staff. There is much that can be done internally especially if large amounts of information need to be extracted or analysed. It may be helpful to assign one person to work directly with the advisers – there is obviously an indirect cost in this in that the individual is being taken away from normal work but there will almost certainly be a cash saving.

It is also necessary to be clear from the outset how the adviser is to relate to the authorities in question. It must be remembered that ultimate responsibility for the inquiry rests with the trustees and nothing should be finally agreed without the trustees' consent. Within that constraint it is often sensible to let the adviser deal directly with the authorities without referring everything back to the trustees for approval. This can save time and costs and in reality the trustees do not lose anything. It is often the case that the adviser will establish informal links with the other side which can be useful in getting a feel for what is concerning them and what they will need to be satisfied. The trustees can retain their control by establishing a regular method of reporting by the adviser, either at trustee meetings or back through the chairman or some other nominated trustee.

Setting up the links

6.24   The adviser needs to know from the outset to whom they are responsible. It is recommended that on all points of principle they should relate directly to the trustees through the chairman or acting chairman. There is a case for setting up regular progress meetings or at least written progress reports. It will also be helpful as the case nears a conclusion for the adviser to attend a trustees' meeting so that all the trustees can be appraised of the state of the enquiry and the options available, enabling them to make an informed decision.

Example
The author was asked to become involved in a case where FICO were conducting a major review of the relationship between a charity and a group of trading companies and there were also other complications involving a profit-shedding deed of covenant. The trustees themselves were largely a new body having taken over from the two founder trustees whose activities lay at the root of the problems.

The working arrangements involved regular contact with the new chairman of the trustees and the chief executive. A number of meetings were held and regular contact maintained by telephone and letter. Much of the detailed investigation work was identified by the author but was prepared by charity staff under the direction of the chief executive. Towards the end of the enquiry, the author attended a trustees' meeting at which various scenarios for settlement were discussed. Much of the settlement work was done informally through discussions between the Inspectors at FICO and the author, although a major settlement meeting was held which was attended by the chairman of trustees and the chief executive.

Setting up a control group

Who should be involved?

6.25   A balance has to be struck between the need to settle the enquiry in the best way possible for the charity and to continue the work of the charity while the enquiry is running its course. This means that not everyone needs to be involved all the time and it may be sensible, subject to the issues discussed in 6.26 below, to set up a working group to handle the investigation.

Unless there are obvious conflicts of interest (i.e. the person concerned is themselves implicated in the investigation), the group should comprise:

- The chairman of trustees

- The chief executive

- The professional adviser

- The person who has administrative responsibility for the relevant area, e.g. payroll manager, accounts manager, director of the trading company, fundraising director, etc.

This group should meet on a regular basis, or at least communicate on a regular basis so that everyone knows what is happening, who is doing what and what the next likely action is going to be. The group should then report regularly to the trustee body.

Trustee responsibility

Accepting the responsibility

6.26   Nothing should be more certain in an investigation than that all the trustees take collective responsibility for the outcome and in consequence all must take an interest in the progress of the enquiry. Some of the trustees may not understand finance, or the legal issues because their real passion is for the activities which drive the objects of the charity, whatever those are. Those trustees must take their full responsibility seriously. They must ask intelligent questions and ensure that real progress is being made and maintained.

Creating the communications

6.27   Once an enquiry is under way, and in the case of PAYE and VAT inquiries it is clear following a review that there are issues which need to be dealt with and that a financial settlement is likely, then the enquiry should appear as a permanent item on the agenda for trustees' meetings. Such meetings should receive regular reports from one of the following:

- The chairman of trustees
- The leader of the steering group
- The professional adviser

These reports should cover:

- Action taken since the last report
- Areas where agreement has been reached since the last report
- Progress on the open areas
- Plans for action in the next period

The trustees should be prepared to comment on the actions taken and should endorse (or denote alternatives) for the plans which are being proposed. Such action should be recorded in the minutes of the trustee meeting.

Problems with a dominant trustee

6.28   The existence of a dominant trustee may be the key issue in a Charity Commission investigation, it can also be a major factor at the root of a FICO investigation or a PAYE review. The individual concerned must not be allowed to become involved in or to influence in any way the progress of the investigation. The remaining trustees need to assert their position and take effective control from the individual concerned. It may also in some cases be necessary to look at the influence the individual might exert over key employees within the charity which could lead to sensitive information being passed to the individual which could prejudice the action which might be proposed.

Chapter 7

The Opening Meeting and Inspection

Introduction

7.1 Once the initial shock of being the subject of an investigation has subsided, the trustees need to prepare themselves for the first face-to-face contact with the investigating authorities. In the case of the Charity Commission and FICO the meeting itself will be of critical importance in setting the tone for the rest of the investigation. With a FICO audit, an employer compliance visit or a VAT control visit the opening discussions will be part of a process which will also include an inspection of the relevant records. In this chapter consideration is given to how trustees should prepare for the meeting and visit and how they should actually conduct that meeting and visit. There are general comments which can be applied in all the situations but some specific points will be applicable to the particular visits.

Do you want to have a meeting?

7.2 An approach from one of the authorities for a meeting may provoke a negative response among the trustee body. There may be strong questioning as to whether there is a right to demand a meeting and what purpose such a meeting might have. It may be necessary to point out the following:

- The Charity Commission have the right of examination and this is effectively therefore a right to have a meeting. In any event, if the Charity Commission deem the matter serious enough to be holding an inquiry, the trustee body should regard the matter as serious enough to have a meeting.

- The Revenue and Customs and Excise have the right to carry out PAYE checks, Gift Aid audits and VAT control visits and so such visits cannot be put off indefinitely.

- Only in the area of FICO enquiries is there actually any real choice. The Revenue have no right to demand a meeting. Their internal guidance in the Enquiry Handbook recognises that there can be no demand for a meeting but then gives the following advice to inspectors:

'If the taxpayer refuses to attend, you will have to continue your enquiries by correspondence as far as possible and your only opportunity to question the taxpayer may occur at the hearing of any appeal against an amendment to the self-assessment or any assessments for earlier years you may eventually make.

If you do meet resistance to a meeting you should

● explain why you think a meeting is the best way of proceeding

● explain as clearly as possible what it is you wish to discuss

● suggest, where appropriate, that the cost to the taxpayer may be minimised by progressing the enquiry through a face-to-face meeting.

In some cases it may be worth pointing out that if your further enquiries lead to culpable omissions being established, then any added difficulty or delay caused by the taxpayer's refusal to answer reasonable questions could affect the mitigation of penalties. This would have to be sensitively handled and you would have to make it clear that you were not making unjustified allegations at this stage. You should also bear in mind that in some cases the taxpayer may be able to answer all questions through correspondence, without the necessity for a meeting.

You should ask the accountant to confirm that he has conveyed your views about the desirability of a meeting to the taxpayer.'

While it is undoubtedly true that a meeting can be expensive, especially if the professional adviser is present, it remains in the author's view, the most efficient way to get any investigation started. Correspondence takes time to prepare and can also be expensive. A meeting enables some probing to take place of where the Revenue are coming from. It can help to identify misunderstandings at a very early stage which would not be achieved by simply replying to factual questions in correspondence. It can also help to create the right kind of relationship with the Revenue which can be very useful in later stages of the enquiry.

Preparation for the visit

Preparation is the key

7.3   The guidance which the Revenue give to their own inspectors on handling the opening of an investigation can be summed up in the two words 'be prepared'. Inspectors are told as part of the preparation for an opening meeting that they should consider:

(1)   What is the purpose of the meeting?

(2)   What do they want to know?

(3)   Why do they want to know it?

(4)   What explanations will satisfy them?

(5)   What explanations will confirm them in a wish to dig deeper?

It can be helpful in Charity Commission and FICO inquiries for the individual being investigated to put themselves in the position of the investigator, in the light of the information they already hold, which may be limited to the accounts and return that have been submitted. If the subject of investigation were looking at his or her own activities would they have the same concerns?

The individual will then have an advantage because they know what other information they hold which might provide the solution to the investigators' problems. This information must be made available for the meeting and can be easily accessed if need be. If the investigator has landed on the 'winning square' and has asked the questions which they hoped he would never ask, then a damage limitation exercise will be needed, for which the preparations may be very different.

Don't panic!

7.4   A 'Corporal Jones' approach will not be any more helpful to the charity than it was to Captain Mainwaring! It is advisable to take a deep breath, and consider how best to approach the problem. If some of the action discussed in Chapter 6 has been taken, a considered approach can be adopted.

Where a records inspection is going to be undertaken, some review needs to be made of those records. If certain records are non-existent or in a mess, it would be a pointless exercise to create them, although a tidy up might help. The experienced compliance officer or VAT investigator will not be fooled! Try to look at the records from the point of view of an investigator who is looking for potential mistakes. Areas to focus on might be:

- In the case of Gift Aid – is the audit trail clear in respect of all payments; are there any potential benefit situations?

- On PAYE reviews issues such as casual labour, travel expenses and *ex gratia* payments are often problem areas.

- With VAT the question of the nature or value of supplies, partial exemption calculations, straightforward record-keeping and invoice production are worth looking at.

It can sometimes be useful to get an outside party, such as the accountant, to carry out a pre-inspection visit. Many firms have specialist staff, often previously employed by the Revenue or Customs, who can carry out such a review for a day or so and identify potential problem areas.

Anything to declare?

7.5   If a pre-inspection review throws up potential problems or if the individual knows already that there are problems waiting to be discovered, they should give serious consideration to making a disclosure to the officer carrying out the inspection. The question of penalties has already been covered in the preceding chapters, and the factors which can reduce penalties, particularly in Revenue investigations, are discussed in Chapters 10 to 12, but at this stage it is appropriate to remark that a significant element in the mitigation of penalties is the question of the degree of disclosure by the charity either in the case of repayment claim errors, or in respect of employer issues. A potential 20% of any penalty can be eliminated if errors are disclosed to the Revenue, and in simple terms that abatement will disappear if the Revenue make all the running and find all the problems.

The key question to be considered is whether to make a full disclosure to the Revenue of all areas where problems are apparent. It would be patently foolish not to disclose matters which the compliance officer will find without any difficulty. It may also be desirable to raise matters which are perhaps in a technical grey area, e.g. is a particular expense allowable, so that if there is a problem, the charity will at least have some credit for raising the issue voluntarily. However, the Revenue may take the view that the disclosure would not have made but for the prompting of a visit and so the disclosure is not fully voluntary.

Where should the meeting be held?

7.6   It was once traditional that meetings with the Revenue would always take place at the local tax office. In some situations that remains true but in the case of FICO, the Revenue would certainly expect to travel to a convenient location away from Liverpool for the meeting. The Charity Commission investigators would also expect to have a meeting away from their office. The two options which need to be considered are:

- The charity premises
- Neutral territory such as the offices of the professional adviser

Where it is likely that it will be necessary to refer to papers or possibly consult other people, then it will make sense to have the meeting on the charity premises. If for any reason the trustees want to keep the profile of the investigation low and not concern staff at the charity then the use of the adviser's office would be a sensible compromise.

Obviously where there is a FICO audit, an employer compliance visit or a VAT control visit, the only possible venue will be the charity premises.

Who should be there?

7.7   The other major issue to resolve ahead of the meeting or visit is to decide who will attend from the charity's side. This is very much dependent upon the actual roles which exist in the organisation and the precise nature of the meeting or visit. The overall impression to create is one of knowledge and competence and therefore it is necessary to have in attendance individuals who will know something about the issues involved.

Charity Commission meeting

7.8   This should be viewed as the most significant type of meeting and should be attended by trustees. It may be worth asking the investigator ahead of the meeting whether he or she would like all trustees to attend. If the matter is serious enough he may indicate that this should be the case, in which event all trustees, or at least as many as possible should attend. It would also be recommended that the chosen legal adviser should be present at the meeting.

Whether the chief executive or any other of the charity administrators attends will depend on the issues arising and the degree to which the individuals concerned may actually be involved in the investigation areas.

FICO investigation

7.9   The involvement of all the trustees is probably not necessary in this situation. If there is a working group set up for the purposes of controlling the investigation, the members of that group should attend. If there is no group, the chairman of trustees and the trustees with responsibility for finance should attend together with the senior administrator and the finance officer. Where it seems likely that the activities of a trading subsidiary will be included in the investigation, a director of the company who is not also a trustee should attend. Finally it is important to have a tax adviser present at the meeting so that they can hear the Revenue concerns and also make some initial judgments about the seriousness of the case.

FICO audit

7.10   Again the presence of a trustee is probably not needed. Many of these visits, particularly those involving churches, often take place at the home of the church treasurer who may also be a trustee. There is probably no need for anyone else to be in attendance, although the treasurer should have ensured that other trustees were aware of the impending visit

Employer compliance visit

7.11   At the very least the meeting should be attended by the person who has overall responsibility for payroll matters in the organisation, supported probably by someone from the accounts department who can deal with questions arising on the accounting records, cash book, etc. Ideally, assuming that the two people already mentioned do not have tax expertise, someone who has a knowledge of employee taxation should attend so that they can either provide answers on technical issues or prevent misleading answers being given.

It is probably not necessary to have a trustee present at the meeting nor the chief administrative officer, although the latter might consider attending the initial meeting or the post-inspection meeting.

VAT control visit

7.12   The key people here will be the person responsible for the accounting records and the production of the VAT returns. The senior finance officer should be present to deal with any major issues which might emerge from the visit. If they are unable to be there, those attending should be clear as to the level of authority they have been delegated to agree matters with the VAT Inspector.

Briefing staff

7.13   Staff in the accounts and payroll departments should be informed that the Revenue or Customs and Excise will be visiting, and they should be instructed to answer only factual questions relating to procedures, or action which has been taken. They should not seek to explain why they are asked to do things, and should be told that they must refer the compliance officer or Inspector to an appropriate person for further information. The Revenue in particular have no legal authority to ask questions. While no one would suggest that information should be withheld deliberately from the authorities, there can be dangers in people trying to give answers in situations where they do not really have an understanding of why or how things are done. Misconceptions can arise that can cause the authorities to take a different line to the one which the facts would require.

The opening meeting

Preparation

7.14   The importance of pre-meeting preparation has already been stressed and this careful approach should continue with the final preparations for the meeting itself. Three practical things to do are:

(1)   The meeting room should be comfortable for everyone – the meeting may become a lengthy one and it does not help to be in cramped conditions. It will be helpful to have plenty of table area to spread out papers. If use must be made of someone's own office, the desk should be made as clear as possible.

(2)   Immediately before the meeting time should be spent getting together all the papers that might be needed and they should be set out on the table so that they are easily accessible and their contents clear. It does not give a very good impression of an organisation if, every time some factual information is requested, someone has to shuffle through several files before finding the point. There should be someone at the meeting who knows their way around the papers and can find the relevant material when it is asked for.

(3)   Time should be spent with the professional adviser before the meeting so that there is an opportunity to clear any outstanding issues and exchange information on the latest developments.

The Revenue are also told to prepare before the meeting. In the *Inland Revenue Investigation Manual*, their advice is summed up as follows:

> 'Like many aspects of investigation work, your conduct of meetings should improve with practice and experience. However, a good meeting will have been well prepared and followed up. You should always
>
> ●   know exactly why you are holding the meeting, what you want to achieve, what information you want to obtain
>
> ●   prepare yourself thoroughly, so that you have mastered the appropriate law and all the relevant facts'.

The first five minutes

7.15   The first few minutes can be very important in setting the tone for the meeting and possibly for the whole enquiry. Practical issues to consider are:

●   When the visitors arrive, they should not be kept waiting unnecessarily. This can give the impression of disorganisation.

●   Before arranging for the investigators to come in, the charity representatives should check that everything is in place, and take a deep breath.

●   Someone should go to reception to greet the visitors rather than have them brought in by a secretary. This can help to break the ice a little.

●   Introductions should be made as they come into the meeting. If there are a number of people already in the room this can be rather bewildering especially if the introductions are rapid, so once everyone has taken their seats it is useful to recap on names so that everyone is aware of who everyone else is and what their roles are. It may be helpful to have tent cards showing each person's name placed on the table in front of them.

- There is no problem in offering refreshments, but it is not a good idea to go overboard. The Revenue certainly have strict rules about accepting hospitality. There is no problem with tea and coffee (and biscuits!). If the meeting is likely to go on over lunch, then arrange for sandwiches to be provided. The Revenue will probably record the fact in their meeting notes.

- The meeting will usually open with general courtesies. There is little point in being abrupt and discourteous to the representatives of the relevant authority. They have a job to do, and they should be treated in a civil way. They should, for their part, be well aware that they are not the ideal visitors!

Nerves are acceptable

7.16 The thought of meeting with an official from whichever department can be a daunting one, and even if the meeting is a prelude to a review, and there is no *prima facie* evidence of anything wrong, there is still going to be a feeling of nervousness. Arguably if there is not, if one feels totally relaxed there must be a real danger of saying or doing something silly. Nerves will provide that edge in thinking and responding.

Revenue Inspectors are certainly warned to expect nerves and are told that the fact that a person is nervous does not mean they are guilty. It is one thing for them to read that and another for them to put it into practice! They are told to try to put you at your ease and you should certainly do your best to keep feelings as much under control as possible.

The Revenue guidance does not say that the investigator may be nervous as well. The opening meeting is always important. A lot of preparation work may have gone on already, and the investigator may have built up a belief that there are questions to be answered and that he is justified in proceeding with his enquiry. All that belief could evaporate at the opening meeting when simple and clear explanations may be given for the problems which were concerning him and the prospect of a significant settlement recedes rapidly.

Nerves should never become aggression or rudeness on either side. In most cases involving charities the level of questioning should not get into the type of sensitive areas which investigations into traders can quickly stray on to, such as issues on private expenditure, sources of private capital and evidence of appropriation of funds. One may get frustrated with the line of questioning but it does not help to become aggressive. This applies to the professional adviser as much as to the charity representatives who attend the meeting.

The Revenue investigators are told to put the taxpayer or their advisers at their ease so that the earlier part of the meeting will be aimed at making them relaxed. This is fine, and any attempt to remove a confrontational approach must be welcomed, but whilst being relaxed, they should remain vigilant about the questions they are being asked.

Get any disclosure in first

7.17   If, as a result of the pre-visit preparation, areas have been identified which may cause problems, these should be raised at the outset of the meeting. This should be before the inspector or compliance officer launches into their formal approach. It is best to disclose possible problems on PAYE or expenses, or issues where there could be some alternative treatment. It might be that a discovery has been made of some donations where tax relief has been reclaimed but which should not have been treated as qualifying donations. If disclosure is made, it can be argued later that it was made without any prompting from the Revenue.

The opening

7.18   Precisely how the meeting opens will depend on the nature of the investigation. In the cases of a Charity Commission investigation or a FICO enquiry, the Inspector will already have identified the potential problem areas and they should begin by explaining their areas of concern. This should be followed by an opportunity for the charity representatives to explain how the issues have arisen as they see them. If they are aware of the general areas of concern ahead of the meeting it is sensible to have this statement prepared ahead of the meeting. If the alleged problems come as a complete surprise to them and an initial response is requested, it would be not unreasonable to ask for a brief time to consider the position before making any response. If a professional adviser is present, they could be consulted on how to reply. A short adjournment can be requested for the position to be discussed in a separate room. It is important not to be pressurised into giving an ill-considered response – Inspectors can give the impression that they want immediate replies which they will accept as initial reactions but may then quote back later in the investigation, statements made in the heat of the moment which turn out to be factually incorrect.

This opening part of the meeting is critical in determining the way the overall enquiry will proceed. It is a matter of control – initially this must rest with the authorities but it needs to be seen to move back towards the charity representatives and being pressurised at the start is not helpful.

Revenue Employer Compliance visit

7.19   At the opening meeting of an employer compliance visit, the Revenue officer will usually work through a basic questionnaire designed to cover all possible areas of investigation. Some of the opening questions will seem to be very general in nature, and will sound almost like polite chit chat, but they do have a serious purpose. For example the compliance officer will ask questions about the activities of the charity. This enables the compliance officer to build up a picture of the type of entity that he is dealing with, and to help identify some of the potential problem areas that he may come across which means that he can concentrate in the limited time available on the most fruitful areas.

The guidance given to compliance officers in the *Inland Revenue Employer Compliance Manual* states:

> 'Most employers are happy to talk about their business and may welcome the opportunity to ask you about any doubts and queries they may have about their tax affairs. Remember that educating the employer is an important part of a Compliance Officer's job.
>
> Your aim during these opening minutes should be to set the tone for the conduct of the review and to establish a rapport with the employer. Once you have obtained general information about the business you can move on to more specific questions about expenses and benefits.'

Charities are by their nature very different from the usual types of business that the employer compliance officer comes across and they may lack a real understanding of how a charity might work. Many of the common issues relating to staff incentives and benefits are not often present in charities, nor are there the usual issues relating to directors. The officer may need to be reminded of these basic points.

There will be general questions which will cover areas such as

- Staff:
  - How many are there?
  - How are they paid – monthly/fortnightly/weekly/at irregular intervals?
- Payroll:
  - Is it computerised, if so what software is used?
  - Who has access?
  - Who has authority to amend?
  - What are the back-up procedures?
  - How are tax rates input?
  - Does the payroll allow re-use of an employee consecutive number within a tax year?
  - Are leavers correctly processed?
  - Are spreadsheets used for casual expense payments?
  - Have there been any major payroll problems in the last year?

Specific areas which are likely to be covered in the initial questions will be:

- numbers of staff and volunteers used and, in particular, any issues relating to expenses for the latter;

- the business activities of the charity which might have an impact on employment issues such as shops, concerts and other events which might use paid casual labour;

- payment of travel expenses and other types of expense to employees whose general salary level may be lower than in commercial operations;

- overseas employment issues where the charity has overseas interests;

- use of consultants and specialists where employment status might be an issue.

The Revenue questionnaire covers a long list of items covering payroll matters, expenses and allowances and benefits in kind. This should be used selectively and should focus on key areas where there is likely to be a risk.

It may become tedious answering all the questions, but it is important to listen carefully to each question, and think before giving an answer. The implications of giving a quick answer to what looks like a simple question may become all too obvious as the investigation proceeds. This is especially true of the answer to the first question which is usually asked about payroll items: 'Are PAYE and NIC deductions made from all payments?'

The temptation at the start of the meeting is to want to create a favourable impression and therefore to answer 'yes'. But whoever is replying must be absolutely sure that they can. Otherwise, they should indicate that as far as they are aware, the tax implications of each type of payment have been taken into account. If there are problem areas which have not already been disclosed, this really represents the final opportunity to make anything like a voluntary disclosure, although the Revenue will probably argue, with some justification, that the matters were only disclosed because of the prompting in their question.

FICO audits

7.20   The initial discussion will centre around the accounting records and the procedures used for identifying and recording the receipt of 'qualifying donations' through to the completion of the repayment claims. The auditor will want a quick guide through the records so that they can carry out their own audit and will want to establish that the treasurer, or whoever is responsible for the records, actually understands what they should be doing. This will become more important under the new rules which will allow a much wider range of payments to come within the qualifying rules.

VAT control visits

7.21   Here again the initial discussion will centre on the nature of the records and the process used to establish if the person maintaining those records knows what they are doing. The VAT Inspector may also want to ask questions about zero-rating certificates and gain some background to the range of activities which the charity is undertaking.

The heart of the meeting

Keep your eye on the objects

7.22   Once the initial formalities are over, and the opening discussions have been completed, the meeting will settle down into a question and answer format, although from time to time there may be a discussion about the meaning of a particular term or the significance of a particular action or whether something is liable to tax or not. In the *Inland Revenue Investigation Handbook* at para 2301, Revenue officers are told to keep their eye on what the meeting is all about:

> 'Through the meeting you should bear in mind your objectives, and should avoid being steered away from them. There will be occasions when it is useful to let the taxpayer talk at length, but you should not allow him or her to ramble. You have asked for the meeting, and you are responsible for achieving your ends in a reasonable amount of time. You must remember that it will be costly for the taxpayer especially if accompanied by an agent. However, you should not be intimidated by that fact – the cost will be much more if the investigation drags on, especially if there has to be a further meeting to obtain information which could have been covered at the first meeting.'

The representatives of the charity need to do the same and concentrate on giving the answers which will allow the meeting to move forward. They need to beware of rambling into areas which are not really relevant to the points at issue, although if some background information might help the investigator to understand the overall position better, then this should be provided while making it clear why the point is being covered so that the investigator will not try to interrupt.

Official approach

7.23   The three authorities with whom a meeting may take place all put great stress on the importance of knowing how to conduct meetings. The Revenue have for a number of years run specific training for their investigators on how to conduct a meeting, Customs do the same and the Charity Commission are now also getting in on the act. In addition, of course, they will usually have had practical experience of running a number of investigation meetings. All of this puts them at a distinct advantage over the charity representatives for whom the experience may be totally novel.

The aim of the official training is to try to ensure that the investigator remains in control of the meeting throughout. Investigators are told, in their manual, not to become officious and to remain calm even if the tax-payer becomes abusive and angry, because this will enable them to retain control of the meeting. Specifically they are told:

- to adopt a confident and polite style;

- not be officious or hesitant;

- to use a conversational style;

- not to interrogate the interviewee;

- to treat the interview as an important and integral part of the inves-tigation and not as just a courteous preamble to the inspection;

- if they are using a formal *aide-memoire* (this is likely on employer compliance visits), they should use it intelligently;

- to adopt a flexible approach and tailor their enquiries to the nature of the business and the types of payments appropriate to it;

- not to adopt a rigid pre-set line of questioning.

Dealing effectively with questions

7.24   The Revenue guidance is to ask effective questions, and the fol-lowing advice is given:

(1)   ask simple, direct questions;

(2)   ask questions which invite more than a 'yes' or 'no' answer, i.e. 'open' questions;

(3)   listen carefully to replies and be prepared to repeat a question not fully answered;

(4)   follow up answers with supplementary questions;

(5)   challenge explanations which are inconsistent with probability, what the records show or other explanations given.

Bearing these points in mind, there are a number of practical tips which can be given to the charity representatives in these situations:

(1)   always listen carefully to the question being asked and try to find out if there is something more behind it;

(2)   try to give the fullest possible answer you can the first time, and if possible back it up by reference to examples or to your instructions or procedures;

(3)   if you don't know the complete answer, don't give a partial answer, it is better to say that you need to check out information before giving a full reply than to give a partial reply which later proves to be inadequate and which may cast doubt on the veracity or completeness of other answers you have given;

(4)   don't give answers which are simply wrong or try to defend the indefensible, accept that not everything may be as correct as you thought;

(5)   if questioning concerns the tax treatment of a particular item, e.g. whether a basic expense should have been taxed or whether a particular donation could qualify for Gift Aid, bear in mind that the Revenue will take account of the nature of the item and your own level of understanding, or the level of support that you have, in judging the adequacy of your reply;

(6)   your explanations in some grey areas are likely to be followed up by supplementary questions unless you anticipate them; the more probing that takes place, the more likely it is that the Revenue will get the upper hand on the particular point.

Role of the adviser

7.25   If the professional adviser is in attendance at the meeting what should be their role? The Revenue have their views (*Inland Revenue Investigation Handbook*, para 2310):

'When an agent is present, he or she may try to answer questions on the client's behalf. You should not allow this to happen – you need to hear what the taxpayer has to say. Tell the agent firmly but courteously, that whilst you appreciate that he or she is there to protect their client's interests, the purpose of the meeting is to hear from the taxpayer exactly how the business is run, etc. It is only the taxpayer who has the necessary first hand knowledge. However, this does not mean that you should stop the agent from asking the taxpayer to clarify any answer given to you.'

The view is acceptable as far as it goes. Yes the trustees will be the ones who will (or should know) the answers at first hand and it makes sense for the adviser to keep quiet and let them answer. A professional adviser may need to 'interpret' questions to enable their clients to make a sensible answer – the investigator may slip into tax or legal jargon outside the understanding of a lay trustee. The adviser should also be prepared to step in and tell the investigator when he believes that a question is irrelevant or totally out of order. Sometimes investigators will expect unreasonable levels of understanding from a taxpayer and the adviser may need to remind them at times that he is dealing with a layman working in a voluntary capacity. The adviser should be prepared to tell their client not to answer a particular question and to explain to the investigator why they have given that advice.

The main role of the adviser will be to provide guidance for his clients on the issues of principle emerging during the meeting. The adviser needs to keep up with every aspect of the meeting, listening closely to the questions and answers and trying to pick up the threads of the arguments being put forward.

Take notes of the meeting

7.26   Someone must take notes of the meeting. It is very difficult for those directly involved in the cut and thrust of the meeting to do this, so have someone there whose sole job is to produce the notes. At the end of the meeting the notes should be written up quickly, not necessarily in a verbatim format, but certainly in a way which makes very clear what answers and information were given, and what arguments were put forward. It is probably wise to retain the rough notes on file as well.

The Revenue in particular are told to take notes. Their instructions indicate that the detailed notes:

- should show the date on which the meeting took place and the names of all present;

- should be signed and dated;

- if drafted some days previously, this should also be recorded;

- should record details of any leaflets or other information handed to the taxpayer or agent during the course of the meeting;

- should be consistent in the use of titles, referring to the Inspector as 'Mr' or 'Mrs', and general reference to 'the taxpayers' is not acceptable.

The Revenue guidance states that copies of their notes should be sent to the taxpayer. This is a courtesy and there is no reason why this should not be reciprocated. In some situations the Revenue may ask the taxpayer to sign a copy of the notes. This is quite common in major investigation cases but should not be necessary in charity investigation cases. Such a request should be politely declined, although any glaring errors in the Revenue notes should be pointed out to them. Many firms of accountants adopt the policy of advising clients not to sign Revenue notes to provide a protection for clients. The Revenue like to suggest that this reluctance may stem from inaccuracies made in the statements given by the taxpayer at the meeting. Any such claims should be refuted.

Agree on action and responsibility

7.27   At the end of the meeting the action that each party is going to take should be agreed with the Revenue. This is particularly important at subsequent meetings as the investigation unfolds. When agreeing to provide further information or take some other action, it is important to be realistic about how long this will take. Things will always take longer than initially thought. The obvious desire to impress the investigator with a resolve to keep things moving has to be tempered with the practical reality of the time it will take to get things done. This may be particularly true if there are other pressures coming up such as the annual audit or the year end.

Co-operation is a factor in assessing the level of penalties in Revenue investigations and the speed of response is an element in judging co-operation. It is, however, better to deliver in the time stated than not deliver, and it is even better to deliver ahead of the time agreed. If the initial reaction is that a piece of information can be provided in six weeks, then by agreeing to provide it in eight or nine and then, delivering in seven weeks expectations will have been successfully exceeded.

It is a good idea immediately after the meeting to drop the investigator a line and confirm what has been agreed to be provided and by when. If information is going to be supplied by the adviser, they too should give realistic time limits and then deliver on or before time.

Experience rules

7.28   One final thought on matters to discuss at the opening meeting. In the course of the social conversation perhaps at the start of the meeting, it is useful to ask the investigator how long he or she has been doing this type of work. If the answer is that this is his or her first visit, the charity representatives can allow themselves an inward sigh of relief; but if he claims to have been doing the job for several years they should try not to let the disappointment show on their faces. Success at any kind of investigation work comes largely from experience. The good experienced investigator will be able to 'smell' a problem – he or she will know where to look and what to look for. The new investigator may appear to be more diligent, but in the limited time available, may simply not be able to identify the key areas.

The inspection

7.29   In the cases of employer compliance visits and FICO audits from the Revenue and VAT control visits, the opening discussions will be a preliminary to the review of records. There are a number of practical issues that should be considered.

Which records?

7.30   The charity representatives should try to ascertain ahead of the meeting which records the investigator will want to see. In the case of an employer compliance visit, it will usually be the records for the last complete tax year, although if the inspection takes place near to the end of a tax year, the review may cover the first six months of the current year. In the case of a FICO audit it will be the records relating to the last repayment claim. A VAT control visit will usually focus on the last quarter's return.

Where possible all the records should be gathered together in the same place as the investigator will be. Difficulty in finding current records will not create the right impression.

Where records are held on computer, printouts should be obtained of the key relevant information. The Revenue certainly are wary of interrogating taxpayer's computer systems. Alternatively someone should be available to obtain the records which are required at the time the inspection starts.

Where to hold the review?

7.31   It is sensible to find a room in which the investigator can work. They should be able to easily access the records they want and they know who to contact if they require other records.

Someone to answer questions

7.32   Someone should be available to answer routine questions relating to the records. This should be someone who has day-to-day responsibility for the completion of those records and understands them and how they are compiled. This person should be properly briefed and in particular they only give factual answers to factual questions. There are dangers in people expressing their own opinions. 'I have told them for years that this was a problem' is not the sort of statement that will help the argument!

End of visit meeting

7.33   At the end of the inspection of records the investigator should hold a debriefing meeting with the person who is controlling the investigation from the charity side. This should cover the areas of concern thrown up by the review and will give an opportunity for explanations to be provided. Those explanations should only be given if the person concerned can give a full and correct answer. Where they are not sure or need to think about the answer, they should decline to answer then but should promise a reply.

The person should make a list of all the issues raised by the investigator.

Immediately after the meeting

Reporting back to the trustees

7.34   As soon as practical after the opening meeting or visit there should be a formal report back to the trustees and a consideration of the issues by them:

- In the case of a Charity Commission inquiry, this meeting should record what the areas of concern are and what assurances the charity trustees have given. If all the trustees are present at the opening meeting, it would be sensible to hold a full trustee meeting immediately after the Charity Commission have left so that matters can be recorded whilst they are still fresh in minds.

- With a FICO enquiry a similar approach may be adopted, although it would be unlikely that all the trustees would have attended the meeting. A full report of the meeting should be prepared immediately and distributed to the trustees without delay. If there is no formal trustee meeting due, consideration should be give to calling a special meeting if the terms of the enquiry suggest that one is warranted.

- In the case of employer compliance visits, FICO audits or VAT control visits, a brief report should be filed giving details of any points of error which were raised and the likely cost relating to each in terms of a settlement. This should be considered at the first available trustee meeting. If the reviews show serious problems in records, these should be reported on and a plan to improve the position should be put forward. The potential amounts of tax at stake should also be calculated so that trustees have an early indication of the risks and costs.

Organising the follow-up

7.35   In some cases the meeting and the inspection may well end the investigation. That will be good news and no doubt a collective sigh of relief will be heard around the charity. In a significant number of situations there will be matters to be dealt with and a plan needs to be drawn up to deal with these. Responsibilities need to be allocated for dealing with the issues and a date set by which a response will be made. It also need to be decided whether the correspondence will be conducted by the charity directly or by the professional adviser.

Chapter 8

Progressing the Investigation Through to Settlement

Introduction

8.1   Having, with luck, survived the opening meeting and the inspection visit, the trustees move on into the period of the investigation which involves the really hard, detailed work of answering the issues raised by the authorities and seeking to reach a basis for a settlement. This may take several months, and in some situations can take a couple of years. Precisely what happens will depend on the specific issues in the particular case but a number of general features are usually present:

(1)   a considerable amount of research to provide information;

(2)   the gradual clearance of points – some by the charity accepting a liability, others by the authorities agreeing no liability;

(3)   the identification of points of law on which arguments are based (these will be discussed in Part 3);

(4)   the identification of issues on which agreement is not immediately apparent;

(5)   reaching a point of agreement which allows the case to be settled.

There will inevitably be regular exchanges of correspondence with the authorities and time delays may arise because of this. Meetings may be a regular feature to move things along and there may also be a need to seek advice from specialists. Paper will accumulate and the control of that paper is a problem in itself.

In this chapter we consider:

●   The practical control issues which are of general application

●   The tactical issues which need to be considered

●   The options in approaching a settlement

The first letter

The first letter after records inspection

8.2   The initial meeting and the records inspection may appear to have been very amicable. Some issues were found and dealt with, others needed some more research by the charity and on some the investigator wanted to go and have a think. Sometimes the tone may change when the first letter comes back from the Revenue or Customs. This letter will usually set out in detail the areas of irregularity uncovered at the visit. Hopefully it should contain no surprises, but sometimes additional items appear which were not discussed at the meeting. These may be items that the investigator simply forgot about, but will often be matters which they did not want to raise at the time until they had had time to think through the precise implications of what they had found.

It is likely that the letter will also set out the detailed computations of the tax which the investigator believes to be due as a result of the irregularities uncovered or their view of the tax treatment of particular items. This will apply for FICO audits, employer compliance visits and VAT control visits. This may well come as an unpleasant shock, because what appear at the final meeting to be small items, can add up to a large overall bill when aggregated together. Matters will be made worse of course, if the officer or Inspector decides to go back beyond the year reviewed and take into account potential liabilities for earlier years.

At this point the advice is 'take a deep breath' and take stock of the situation.

The first letter after an opening meeting

8.3   Where the case is an inquiry by the Charity Commission or a *section 9A* Revenue enquiry, the letter following the opening meeting may pick up the points dealt with at that meeting. It may remind the charity of the information it agreed to supply and may also contain the first Revenue or Charity Commission response to the arguments raised. This will need to be carefully considered and a response formulated.

Practical control issues

Taking a leaf from the Revenue's book

8.4   The *Inland Revenue Investigation Handbook* is the definitive guide for Inspectors carrying out investigations into taxpayer's affairs usually where there is evidence of omissions from returns and possibly some attempt at tax evasion. The approach it adopts is not directly referable to the type of investigation we are considering (hopefully) but some of the general principles which are expressed in the Handbook sum up the

Revenue's overall approach to investigation cases. Consider this general statement at the beginning of a section entitled 'Controlling the case':

'2500. General
It is essential to retain control of any investigation's progress and to be seen to be in control. You initiated the enquiry and certainly in its early stages have a greater interest in seeing matters forwarded. A taxpayer whose accounts are correct will usually want to see his or her affairs agreed quickly. A taxpayer who has evaded tax, on the other hand, may not see progress as being in his or her interest. He or she will be reluctant to attend interviews because of the concern that unknown facts might emerge or to co-operate in a process which could lead to the payment of additional tax and even interest and penalties. In some cases however a prolonged investigation in which you have discovered omissions can become wearing on the evader's nerves or those of his or her family, and they may want an early end to it.'

The guidance goes on to list the ways in which the Inspector should maintain control of the case – effectively there are ten commandments for successful control:

(1)   Have a well ordered file, so that you or any other investigator or manager can easily appreciate the up-to-date position and find all the relevant papers.

(2)   Do not cause any material delay in the case. If the ball remains in your court for long periods of time it is difficult to complain about delay by the other side.

(3)   Ensure that the taxpayer and his or her agent are always aware of what is expected of them. They should be aware of your right to be 'satisfied' and that any information you have requested is reasonable given your doubts about the accounts and the information already amassed (note that the basic right of satisfaction has now been superseded by the self assessment regime – but the right to enquire remains and the Revenue have the right to ask questions.).

(4)   Agree realistic timetables for action by any agent and check progress rather than waiting until a deadline has expired only to discover that nothing has been done.

(5)   Raise assessments promptly for all sources and years for which they are appropriate.

(6)   Try to bear in mind where you expect the case to go and what you need to know and do to get it there.

(7)   Use reminders as appropriate, but do not fall back on an endless stream of reminding letters. Be guided by your knowledge of the agent, the extent of the information called for and the progress

hitherto in the case. The telephone can be more effective than a letter. Some people will not act unless you take formal action.

(8) Use information powers and Commissioners' listings in cases where you do not receive prompt co-operation.

(9) Request payments on account once it is clear that duties have been unpaid.

(10) Act reasonably and courteously so that there are no grounds for the taxpayer to try to deflect the investigation by making a complaint.

Once the opening meeting is over, the chances of the charity being able to gain control, or at least to reduce the dominance of the Revenue, become greater and we need to consider how these features can be used to best account by the charity side and their professional advisers in all types of investigation.

Controlling the paper

A tidy file is the key to control

8.5   Investigation work will usually create a considerable amount of paper and it is vital that sensible file discipline is instituted from the start. Once it is clear that an investigation of some kind is under way, a separate investigation file should be opened. It is recommended that this be done by both the charity and its professional advisers. As far as the latter are concerned, the fact that this has been done should be noted on the cover of the main client files.

There should always be two files established:

(1)   a correspondence file

(2)   a working file which will best be established in a lever arch type file

Correspondence file

8.6   Correspondence accumulates rapidly in any investigation case and it is extremely important that it should be kept tidily and logically so that important items can easily be found. In a lengthy case it may be helpful to maintain an index of important correspondence showing

Date	Item	Notes

This should be used to record details of notes of meetings with both the client/adviser and the Revenue/Charity Commissioners/Customs and Excise as well as key letters to and from the client/adviser and to and from the authorities. This will help the process of review when the case is nearing settlement. The notes section can be used to indicate action needed or to supplement basic information. Inspectors are advised in their manual to number all correspondence and this may be a helpful practice to follow.

Working file

8.7   This is the heart of the investigation file. It will probably become necessary to hold papers in a lever arch file or indeed several files. It is vital that the indexes for such files are used so that no time is wasted tracking down key schedules. The working file will be used to store all the research that is done as well as, in the case of the accountant, holding the record of assessments appeals and payments on account.

It is likely that there will also be computer files containing spreadsheets and other documents which will form part of this file.

Draw up a control list

8.8   It is likely that, with the possible exception of a major Charity Commission inquiry, there will be a number of different strands to the investigation. This will almost certainly be the case with an employer compliance review and may also be the case with a VAT control visit. It is helpful at the outset to draw up a list of the investigation areas, probably using the headings in the Revenue or Contributions Agency letter, and to then keep this list as a working control so that the stage that each issue has reached can be monitored.

A record of open points should be kept on top of the correspondence, or the latest version of the action list, so that it is possible to see at a glance what stage the investigation has reached. This can be particularly useful if the client/adviser or the investigator phone unexpectedly.

Avoid delay

8.9   Someone needs to be given the task of keeping everyone on their toes. Time will run away if care is not taken and delays can be potentially expensive if they give the Revenue the impression that there is a lack of co-operation. It is suggested that there should be someone in both the charity and with the advisers who are given the roles and who agree to keep each other informed of progress.

The trustees themselves should of course keep an eye on progress through their trustee meetings and they should not be afraid to call people to account for delays which occur without good reason. If there are any blockages they should identify and clear them as quickly as possible.

One practical step which needs to be sorted out at the start is the process of dealing with correspondence where an adviser is involved. If they are going to deal with all the correspondence, but the trustees want to see all letters, this is going to cause delays unless the procedure is stream-lined. As an adviser, it begs the question as to why you are involved and what level of trust there is from the client if they expect to see every letter. The charity, having appointed the adviser should be prepared to let them get on with the job, certainly at this stage in the investigation without checking up on everything they are doing. The adviser will not commit the charity to a settlement without their agreement and after everything is over, the charity can look at the service it got from the adviser and decide whether they are going to pay them.

Know what is expected

8.10   It is vital that the investigator explains what he wants and why. The old doctrine of 'satisfaction' has now gone under self-assessment, and the Inspector should be able to state clearly what grounds he has for making enquiries in the first place and continuing those enquiries when information has been supplied. If the answers are not satisfactory, a clo-sure of the enquiry can be sought.

It is also important that if the information has to be requested from third parties, e.g. fundraisers, contractors, suppliers, that they too know what information is wanted and the timeframe within which it is wanted.

Realistic timetables

8.11   This was discussed in the context of the opening meeting and should remain a key factor throughout the investigation. It helps to be realistic in setting a timetable for action. It does not impress and Inspector to say that information will be supplied by a near date which is unrealistic. Having carefully worked out what is realistic, a couple of weeks should be added on for contingencies. This way, the initiative can be retained when the information is delivered ahead of the deadline.

Dealing with assessments

8.12   Both the Revenue and Customs have the right to raise assess-ments in appropriate situations. For the Revenue the raising of assessments will now only relate to 1995/96 and earlier in FICO inves-tigations but could cover more recent years in employer compliance cases (e.g. determinations under *Reg 49*). For Customs and Excise there is a three-year time limit for raising assessments. Where assessments are raised decisions need to be taken quickly about exercising the right to appeal (which does not commit the charity to formal action) and whether tax should be paid to minimise interest charges.

Where are we going?

8.13   The authorities may have their own objectives. The task of the charity and its advisers is to get the investigation settled for the lowest possible figure in the shortest possible time. This should not be forgotten!

The lowest possible figure, may not be the absolutely lowest figure possible. There will be situations where it may be necessary to strike a compromise to prevent further costs from building up. The adviser should be alive to this, but the trustees need always to keep in the forefront of their minds that they have the ultimate responsibility for the assets of the charity and those assets can be spent on tax and advisers' fees and in some cases the former may be a better option than the latter.

Use reminders

8.14   The investigator should not have to continually send out reminders of the action needed. He or she should be kept informed of progress either with regular letters or phone calls. It is helpful to make diary notes to do this on a regular basis throughout the investigation. It becomes vital where the investigation is falling behind the planned timetable.

Information powers

8.15   The Revenue and the Charity Commission both have formidable powers to require the production of information. Therefore, resisting requests for information should only be done with caution. If it is a reasonable request and one which could be reinforced by a statutory power little is gained in being obstructive – in fact this can be taken as a lack of co-operation and could cost money when penalties are finalised in a Revenue investigation.

Payments on account

8.16   If it is clear that tax has been underpaid, serious consideration should be given to making payments on account. Where necessary, send in the payment without being asked. This will have the dual effect of stopping the interest clock from running and also demonstrating co-operation.

Attitude under control

8.17   There is no need to be over aggressive towards the investigator – he has a job to do. Aggressiveness can be perceived as a sign of weakness and may simply cause the investigator to dig his heels in further. There may well be times in the course of the investigation when the investigator will exasperate the charity and the adviser. Inspectors can dig their heels in and not see the remotest possibility that the other side may have a valid point of view – VAT Inspectors and employment compliance officers are particularly prone to adopt this approach. The charity team must expect this and deal with it by firm argument and a determination to stand their ground and fight the point if it is worth it – becoming angry and frustrated is not the approach.

Pressure can be put on the investigator to take a more reasonable approach. He has superiors who may have an influence and failing that the Appeal Commissioners or the tribunal are means of securing a reasonable hearing.

Making progress through the investigation

Developing an approach

8.18   Each investigation is going to have its own issues and the main areas of contention in the different types of investigation that charities might face are discussed in the specific chapters which follow. There are, however, some general practical issues which can apply, with adaptation if appropriate in all types of cases. In some cases, particularly the employer compliance area, there could be a number of issues which have to be resolved, while in many cases there could be a single issue – the approach is essentially the same.

Charities themselves will only hope that they face a single investigation at worst, although the possibility of coping with the Revenue and Customs (albeit at different times) could be a realistic one. That makes the development of a strategy for handing investigations hardly worthwhile. Advisers, on the other hand, may find that they are involved in many different types of investigation and they will find it useful to build up experience and develop an approach which works from case to case. Much investigation work is down to experience – that is very true for the investigator and should also be true for those who work on the 'defence'. There are always lessons to be learned from each case and each situation should help to refine the approach for the future.

Correspondence or meetings

8.19   One of the key practical decisions is whether to continue the investigation by correspondence, at least until the final meeting, or to use regular meetings. There is no doubt that correspondence is the simplest way of proceeding to establish facts – written questions from the investigator met by the provision of information from the charity. At the start of the investigation that may well be the simplest way of proceeding. There will come a point sooner or later when all the relevant facts have been presented and the focus moves to the interpretation of facts. At that point, the use of meetings can become very important. Correspondence is an inefficient way of dealing with such issues – initial view expressed in letter 1, counter view in letter 2, further arguments in letter 3 and so on, and if there are many weeks between letters, the investigation just drags on and on. Far better to grasp the nettle and decide on a meeting to consider the arguments and see if progress can be made. It may take more than one meeting but the process should be considerably shorter.

Role of the adviser

8.20   If the accountant or solicitor is dealing with the investigation, the trustees should allow them to get on with the job as far as possible. A number of practical working issues will need to be established immediately after the opening meeting has been held with the investigator:

(1)   Who will act as the main point of contact between the investigator and the charity?

(2)   Assuming that this is the adviser, who from the charity side will act as the main contact for the adviser to co-ordinate the preparation of information?

(3)   Will the adviser need to clear all correspondence with the trustees? This is not a route which is recommended, it adds to delay and it indicates a lack of confidence in the adviser.

(4)   Will the adviser be able to fix up meetings with the investigator without anyone from the charity being present? This can be a useful way of making progress, although the adviser will not commit the charity to any agreement without detailed consultation.

(5)   What arrangements will be in place for regular briefings for the trustees from the adviser? At the very least the trustees should require a written report from the adviser for every trustee meeting with the option to require the attendance of the adviser if appropriate at significant stages.

Building your case

What are the issues?

8.21   Once the opening meeting has been concluded, and possibly the first letter received, the charity and its advisers will be in a better position to see what is involved and what lies ahead of them. At the first appropriate point they should sit down together, go through each issue and consider these questions:

●   What is the point that the investigator is making?

●   Do we agree with the interpretation they are putting on the point?

●   If yes, then what are the immediate consequences in that agreement in terms of tax payment or action which the Charity Commission might require?

- If no, why don't we agree and how are we then going to persuade the investigator?

- What are the realistic chances of success?

- Are all the facts relevant to a considered view out in the open?

- If not what facts do we need to bring out to support our view?

- What evidence can we produce to support those facts?

- Who is going to bring out those facts – the charity or the adviser?

From this review will come two further practical points which need to be cleared at this point:

(1)   What are the practical implications of the issues raised?

(2)   How is the gathering of the information going to be organised?

Implications of the issues

8.22   What the charity needs to know at this stage is and in particular what would be the impact on the charity if all the issues were decided in the favour of the investigator. This may involve the adviser in doing some calculations of the total tax which might be at risk on a worst case scenario, or spelling out the powers that the Charity Commission might decide to take. The trustees may not like what they hear but it should then govern the whole approach that they take.

The adviser may need to go through each issue and in addition to calculating the worst case scenario position, will also need to give some realistic odds on the chances of success. For example in the case of a an employer compliance visit, the view might be that some issues such as the use of casual labour are going to be difficult to argue because the charity has simply not applied the correct (or possibly any) procedures, on the other hand there may well be a realistic chance of defeating an argument that a particular worker should be treated as an employee.

The potential tax at stake may really crystallise the thinking of the trustee. The author recalls a case which he came into at a stage after the initial meetings with the Revenue, where he had his own initial meeting with the FICO Inspectors and was told that they expected the charity to settle for around £450,000. That figure would have wiped out the charity completely. The effect was to ensure that the trustees gave maximum co-operation in resolving the issues and in the end a deal was struck which settled the case for around £75,000 paid over a period of time in order to keep the charity going.

In Charity Commission cases the assessment of what is involved may mean some unpalatable decisions for the trustees such as taking a view on how to deal with a chief administrative officer who is the focus of inquiries, or even harder still how to deal with the founder trustee who is the real target of the inquiry. If action, such as suspension, needs to be taken it may be better for the charity to take it rather than have it imposed by the Charity Commission. Legal advice will be required and obviously alternative arrangements will need to be put into place to cover the situation.

Establishing the facts

Researching the facts

8.23   It is likely that at the start of any investigation, the investigating authority will have little in the way of hard facts. The inquiry may have commenced on the back of a consideration of the statutory returns which have been submitted, or comments made by a third party. In the case of a FICO audit, or an employer compliance visit or a VAT control visit, obviously there will have been a review of basic records from which certain conclusions may have been drawn. These records themselves may represent a tiny fraction of a wide range of documentation which could become part of the investigation. The starting point is therefore to consider what has been seen.

The next stage is to draw up a detailed list of what information should be available within the charity itself. The word 'should' is used because theory and practice may diverge dramatically. Documents may not have been kept because someone did not consider them important (in some cases because they were recognised as being vitally important and needed to be destroyed!), or the events concerned may have happened many years ago.

At this stage an attempt should be made to get together every possible piece of information. Some may turn out to be superfluous but it is better to eliminate it at a later stage. It may be helpful in some cases to have a number of different pieces of collaborative information. The sort of information which needs to be considered is as follows:

- Correspondence
- Minutes of trustees' meetings or committee minutes
- Agreements between the charities and third parties
- Accounting records
- Reports prepared by third parties
- Press cuttings
- Evidence that could be in the possession of third parties

Some examples of real situations will help.

Case 1

The issue concerned was whether the charity was carrying on an exempt trade for tax purposes. The evidence assembled involved going back to the origins of the charity almost 50 years ago and digging out minutes of general meetings as well as the basic founding documents. Current advertisements were found and basic current publications were obtained which set out what the activities clearly were.

Case 2

A FICO investigation on the relationship between a charity and a group of trading companies involved a detailed examination of the accounting records of all the entities to establish who had done what, and how loans between the bodies had evolved over a period of time.

Case 3

A FICO audit where a sample approach had been agreed involved a representative from the central body visiting a number of the churches concerned to look at specific deeds of covenant and how the payments had been treated in the accounting records.

Case 4

In an employer compliance case there were issues relating to travel expenses for one employee and the issue of categorisation of a couple of workers. The first issue involved unearthing a letter in which the chairman of the trustees had written to the employee agreeing that she could work from home and thus establishing the home as a base for travel purposes. In the second issue it was necessary to correspond with the two workers to establish from their evidence and activities that they were in business on their own account and that they could be treated as self-employed.

Case 5

This was a major VAT case on the alteration of a building (taken before the latest change in the law). The issues here involved speaking with the architect, examining plans of the building before and after the work, and getting photographs of the building before, during and after the work. As part of the exercise, the local VAT officer was invited to visit the building while work was going on so that he could see for himself the extent of the alterations.

It is necessary to establish who will obtain this information. The charity should aim to do as much as possible themselves because this will keep down the costs which can mount steadily if the professional adviser gets involved.

Interpretation of the facts

8.24   Having assembled all the facts, the adviser needs to consider what they tell him and whether any further work is needed before they are presented to the investigator. In some cases, particularly where accounting records are involved, it may be necessary to carry out some further analysis based on the records already provided. For example in case 2 above, a detailed review was carried out showing the effects of treating certain, clearly charitable, activities as having been carried out by the charity but which had, for some reason, been put through trading companies. This enabled an argument to be mounted that some of the money that the charity had loaned to the trading companies, which the Revenue were arguing was non-charitable expenditure, was in reality charitable expenditure.

It is important to present the facts obtained to the investigator in the most logical way. Sending in a summary of the facts with cross-references to the supporting documentation in a well presented file enables the investigator to see the relevance of documents more easily and also helps to create the impression of control. Simply sending a bundle of apparently unrelated documents with no clear guidance as to what each relates to is unhelpful from all angles.

Remember that no facts are being presented for their own sake. They are being submitted because they support a line of argument or effectively counter an argument that the investigator is pushing. The supporting letter should set out the conclusions drawn from the evidence and invite the investigator's agreement to the views therein. Care should be taken not to read too much into particular pieces of evidence. Some evidence may be helpful in establishing conclusively what was in the mind of the person at the time, some may simply be a possible pointer to that and will not of itself support a particular view. It is useful to put oneself in the position of an independent party who is seeing the evidence and hearing the arguments for the first time. What reasonable conclusions would they draw from what they see and hear? Remember that if the case is taken forward to an appeal tribunal this is precisely what will happen.

Building a legal argument

Introduction

8.25   As well as building up the factual picture consideration must be made of what legal support there may be for the arguments put forward:

Stage 1   what does the law say about the issue?

Stage 2   is there any other interpretation available on the law?

Stage 3   will involve trying to find any published cases that are relevant to the issue.

173

Stage 4   will be in using those cases to determine if any further evidence might be required

Stage 5   will be using those cases to support your argument

What does the law say?

8.26   What the relevant statute has to say on the point at issue should be identified at a very early stage. In some cases, such as the VAT legislation, this may be very explicit and detailed – the schedules on zero rating set out items and very detailed notes to add meaning to the items. In other cases the law may be using terms which are not defined in any detail at all. For example there is little in the way of detailed statute on the meaning of 'trade' for tax purposes.

There are some generally accepted rules for interpreting statutes, these include giving words and phrases their legal meaning where there is one but using the everyday meaning where no legal definition exists. For example there is tax legislation on the use of charitable funds which includes the concept of a loan being 'for the benefit of the charity'. This phrase is not defined in the legislation and so it is possible to use everyday definitions in support of arguments.

Is there other interpretation available?

8.27   In some situations there may be published guidance available that gives an indication of what interpretation the various regulatory authorities put on the legislation. This comes in the form of published guidance such as the various VAT notices and Revenue guidance on employment tax issues. It also comes in the internal guidance manuals that are available for the Revenue, Customs and Excise and now gradually for the Charity Commission. In all these sources you need to consider whether the view being put forward is supported by case law or whether it is simply a view which is as yet untested in the courts. Again using the example of 'benefit of the charity' which was mentioned in the previous paragraph, the Revenue say that in their view this means that the loan must carry a commercial rate of interest, must be secured and must have terms for repayment. This is a view based on advice the Revenue have taken but which has not been tested in the courts.

Customs and Excise are also prone to making pronouncements about the meaning of phrases and then finding that their view is not supported at tribunal.

Sources of cases

8.28   There are a number of sources of published cases to which reference may be made.

Decided cases on charity and trustee law

There is a substantial body of case law that has evolved on the role of trustees, the meaning of charity and the duties which attach to charity trustees. These will be available in published form as All England Law Reports or in other bound versions.

Tax cases

There are over 70 volumes of published tax cases which have come from the courts as a result of appeal cases taken to the General or Special Commissioners. There are not that many on charity tax issues but there have been some significant decisions on trading by charities. It may also be relevant to look at the cases which have established principles on employment taxation as well as general issues on trading.

Special Commissioners' decisions

There are now published decisions emerging from the Special Commissioners. It must be remembered that some of these will have gone on to decisions in the courts, and that others do not have the status of court judgments. They are, however, useful indications of the arguments that have been put and how those arguments were received.

VAT tribunal cases

There is a much more substantial body of VAT tribunal cases which has been built up. Many of these involve charities and they can be a useful source of argument and precedent.

VAT court cases

Some tribunal cases go through to the courts for further judgment and these add to the body of case law. Because VAT is a European tax there are cases that go through to the European Court of Justice and these have proved to be significant decisions in many areas.

In all UK court cases it must be remembered that House of Lords decisions are the highest level of authority. Any decisions made in lower courts in other cases are capable of being effectively set aside by the Lords.

Using cases to determine evidence

8.29   All cases need to be put into their own context and there are dangers in trying to draw too much out of them. It will be very unusual to find a case that has very similar facts – the best that can be done is to bring out the key features. A list of relevant cases should be drawn up and read. The key facts were that helped to decide the case should be established. The evidence should be studied to see if it can help to identify key items of evidence that should be drawn out in the case in question.

Using cases in argument

8.30   Some of the cases will have been decided in favour of the argument being put forward and others will have gone the other way. It is vital to try to associate the case with the successful arguments and to try to distance the facts from those in adverse decisions. The investigator will almost certainly be doing the same but of course from the opposite point of view.

Arguments about the meaning of cases are best carried out in meetings. Lengthy argument in correspondence is tedious and time consuming. It has to be accepted that in most situations there are shades of grey and not absolutes of black and white. Most of the cases have gone through the courts because of the grey. The investigator also needs to remember this and may sometimes need to be reminded of the fact.

Taking a second opinion

Why?

8.31   If the point at issue is one which has serious implications for the charity if lost, then it may be prudent for the trustees to consider taking a second opinion on the case before a decision is taken on whether to negotiate or fight. An adviser who realises the significance of the point involved should be prepared to suggest the same approach. This is in no way a reflection on the competence of the adviser, and should not be seen as a lack of confidence in their opinion. The adviser should see it as a measure of protection – if all goes wrong and the charity takes the view that the advice originally given was incorrect and decides to sue for professional negligence, there is value in having a second opinion to support the view the adviser has taken.

There is obviously a cost involved, but this must be set against all the other costs in the case and the financial risk to which the charity may ultimately be exposed.

Who?

8.32   There are two possibilities:

(1)   another adviser who has a proven reputation in the particular area;

(2)   a barrister who specialises in the area.

There are no hard and fast rules to determine the choice except that in many situations the authorities might give greater credence to a counsel's opinion. Investigation tactics are probably better dealt with by an experienced practitioner. The notes that follow deal with procedures for obtaining counsel's opinion but they can easily be adapted to deal with obtaining another professional opinion.

The process of obtaining an opinion

8.33   In cases where it is considered desirable to seek counsel's opinion, the reasons for this should be explained to the trustees and their consent should be obtained, ideally in writing. The cost will usually fall on the client, and they should be made aware of this. In exceptional cases where it is considered absolutely necessary to have an opinion but the client will not agree, it may be necessary to obtain the opinion at the expense of the adviser.

Selection of counsel

8.34   There are obviously many counsel to choose from. Usually the professional advisers will have several counsel who they use on a regular basis and who they are happy to recommend. Choosing for the first time is a little difficult and it may be sensible to ask around to find out if anyone has had experience of using counsel – some trustees (or other people working for the adviser) may have been involved in situations where counsel was used. Look to see who has represented charities in hearings on similar problems.

Preparation of brief

8.35   This is an important part of the process, and it is vital that a standard format is used so that counsel can easily see the points involved. The following headings should be used:

(1)   name of client;

(2)   facts – set out all the relevant facts with cross-references to any supporting documents, letters, etc. (if there are a number of documents these should be set out in a lever arch file and properly indexed);

(3)   point at issue – this should be simply stated;

(4)   your views on the point at issue, quoting statute and case law as appropriate (reference could be made to copy letters which set out the case);

(5)   the opposing view (if relevant), again quoting statute and case law (reference could be made to copy letters which set out the case);

(6)   the matters on which counsel's opinion is required – these should be clearly stated.

Contacting chambers

8.36   Before the brief is sent to counsel, it may be advisable to speak to the clerk to counsel to check on their availability to respond to the brief, particularly if time is of the essence. The clerk might also be able to give an indication of costs, but this will be more easily done once the brief has been submitted. Make it clear that you want that estimate before counsel proceeds. Costs are not usually excessive for an initial opinion – between £1,000 and £2,000, depending on the status of counsel used. (You will pay more for the opinion of a QC than for an ordinary barrister.)

The brief should be submitted to the clerk with a covering letter giving any relevant information about time pressures. Where matters are urgent, counsel should be asked to give an indication of when the opinion will be available and whether it would be desirable to have a conference.

Getting the opinion

8.37   There are various ways in which the opinion can be given. Conference in chambers is a method used for dealing with complex issues, especially where counsel considers that other facts may be needed. Conference should be attended by the professional adviser. The attendance of the trustees depends on whether counsel wants this, and in other cases whether the trustees wish to attend. The trustees should always be advised of any conference. Notes should always be taken at a conference and should be written up immediately afterwards. If counsel is not going to provide a separate written opinion they should be asked to 'settle' the notes of the meeting as effectively representing their opinion.

In other situations a written opinion will be received from counsel. If the original brief has been detailed enough, the opinion should not only cover the response to the situation as it currently stands but will also offer possible options for resolution and possibly a consideration of some wider issues that may not have been picked up at all. In case 1 at 8.23 above, counsel's opinion was eventually sought on the point of the exempt trading. The response received from counsel raised a line of approach which had not been previously considered by anyone, the Revenue included. A copy of the opinion was sent to FICO who terminated the investigation at that point.

When the opinion is received, the trustees should be advised of its contents, and its significance. It would be usual to take account of the opinion in the drafting of documents, etc. The next stage is to consider whether to fight or negotiate a settlement in the best interests of the charity.

A negotiated settlement

The decision to negotiate

8.38   At some stage in the enquiry, all the relevant facts will be out and the matters will turn to the interpretation of those facts and the consequences that flow from them. This is where negotiation really begins. It should be pointed out that the option to negotiate might not be a valid one in every case. In some Charity Commission investigations it may be clear that the position is so serious that the trustees have no choice but to do exactly as the Commissioners say and must implement their action plan.

In most Revenue, and indeed Customs cases, negotiation will be an option, although Customs and Excise do seem to show a lesser desire to negotiate than their Revenue colleagues. The investigator will have given an indication of the tax sum he or she is seeking and, for their part, the charity representatives should have some idea of what might be due. Some areas will simply be agreed either way as not negotiable, but eventually there will be issues which cannot be agreed as a matter of principle. There are then three choices:

- Agree the official position

- Fight the official position through appeal

- Find a compromise

A key determinant at this stage will be how much tax is actually at stake and the likely costs involved in fighting the point. Trustees have to remember that they are using the charity's resources to fight the point, and there has to be some consideration of the position of trustees if they continue to incur costs in fighting a matter on which very little tax actually rests. Even if they are not using a professional adviser, they are still tying up the resources of the charity in taking the case on.

Trustees also need to consider if the point is one which has implications for the future, or is simply an historic issue which will be finalised by a settlement. There is a much stronger incentive to seek a settlement in the latter situation.

It takes two to negotiate

8.39   The trustees are, however, only one party to the deal. The Revenue or Customs and Excise will have a view on how far they are prepared to take the case and an understanding of their position may help the trustees to decide on a course of action. The factors the authorities need to consider are:

- How long has the enquiry has been going on. The longer the time spent the greater the incentive to reach some sort of settlement. There are new cases to take up.

- How much tax is actually at stake on the case? The issue is one of costs versus revenue.

- Will any other cases be affected by the agreement? There are some issues where a dangerous precedent could be created by conceding a point to one charity. The charity world is one where the grapevine works well and the success of one charity in a dispute would be quickly passed around.

The point has already been made that the Charity Commission may decide that matters are so serious that there can be no room for negotiation on essentials. There may still be some room to negotiate on some of the detail.

Keep your options open

8.40   The option of going to the Commissioners or VAT tribunal should be kept open throughout the negotiation process which should be conducted on a 'without prejudice' basis so that any concessions that are made in the process of negotiation cannot be brought up in any formal proceedings at a later date.

Finding areas on which to negotiate

8.41   What is the basis for any negotiated settlement? This is obviously dependent upon the facts but a number of general options are possible:

(1)   It might not be possible to negotiate on the main point of principle because the case is weak, but it might be possible to reach a satisfactory deal on the question of interest and penalties. Ideally that the tax will be paid and the Revenue or Customs will not seek any interest or penalty.

(2)   There may be some area in calculating the tax bill where a compromise is possible. This will come out of the facts of the case and should be explored.

(3)   In some situations a clear opportunity may not be obvious, but it might be possible to construct a basis which will give the Inspector an opportunity to put the file away with a clear conscience. This may involve time spent going back over the facts and re-presenting the issues in a different way to establish a possibility.

(4)   The payment date can be used as a point for negotiation. Offering a slightly higher deal but with payment spread over a period of time may be a solution.

(5)   In some situations the issue may be how much the charity can afford to pay in order to both settle the issue and continue to provide a service. It is then a case of working back from there to make the figures fit. There is an element of 'emotional blackmail' in this but the Revenue will usually recognise a reality.

(6)   In the final analysis, it is usually possible to squeeze out a final small discount from the Revenue because there comes a point at which they will not want to lose a settlement to the case.

Don't expect a deal to be struck at the first meeting, it may take several meetings, a good deal of research and then some more meetings before the matter is resolved. The effort may be worthwhile.

Negotiation

8.42   In tax-related enquiries negotiations will fall into two areas:

- Definitive points at issue

- Penalties and the method of settlement

Successful negotiation is achieved when both parties leave the meeting believing that they have achieved what they set out to do. This means having realistic aims before discussion takes place. A review of facts and the law will have given an indication of the strengths and weaknesses of the case and any 'result' should be set against those issues.

Negotiation must mean being prepared to give way on some issues while maintaining a stand on others. Without a willingness to give up some ground there can be no negotiation and that willingness has to be there from both parties. The Revenue authorities are sometimes reluctant to give anything away at the start of a meeting and may have to be forced into a position where it is clear that they are going to have to concede some ground to achieve a result. Trustees must be realistically briefed ahead of the meeting to adopt a similar approach.

Preparation

8.43   The first meeting, called to consider a possible settlement of the contentious points, will be the most critical of the investigation. It is vital that detailed preparation is carried out. This should involve:

- a review of all the relevant facts and a clear understanding of the facts which are particularly helpful to the argument;

- a review of the legislation and the arguments already put forward, including consideration of the strengths of the argument but also the weaknesses and how these can be countered;

- if the trustees are not going to be represented at the meeting, briefing the adviser beforehand as to the extent to which he has room to negotiate – if there is a point beyond which the trustees are not prepared to go then that needs to be clearly defined;

- if the trustees are going to attend, making it clear who is conducting the meeting – the adviser should take the arguments using the trustees to emphasise points or to comment where appropriate;

- getting to the meeting before the other side and thus having time to collect thoughts, discuss any last minute issues and have all papers sorted out and ready.

Within the meeting

8.44   There should be little need for any formalities at this stage – it is likely that all parties will be well known to each other by now! The meeting should begin by setting out the stage the investigation has reached and what the issues are that require resolution. The arguments on both sides should be summarised and agreement from the other side confirmed. If there are any differences these should be cleared up at the start – it is pointless to spend time on lengthy discussion and then realise that both sides have been arguing on different points or without a real understanding of what is involved.

As agreement is reached on each point it is worth taking time to note that agreement and to clarify the consequences. That can be particularly important in something like an employer compliance review where there maybe a number of points being discussed and the parties are moving on to an overall settlement.

If 'time out' from the meeting is needed to discuss a point then it should be taken. This may be a better approach than leaving the matter to be resolved another day. It may also be necessary for the other side to do the same. The author was involved in a lengthy meeting involving charity representatives and two Inspectors, and on a couple of occasions the Revenue withdrew to consider proposals that had been made to settle.

If the adviser is in the meeting without charity representatives and the negotiations move beyond the parameters that might have been agreed beforehand, the adviser may find it preferable to take time to call the trustee representatives to try to clear the issue so that it can be resolved at the meeting.

Assuming agreement is reached on the substantive issues, at the end of the meeting it is worth taking the time to recap on those points so that there is no doubt what has been agreed. It may be advisable to get the points set out in writing either by the adviser writing to the Revenue and inviting them to confirm the points or vice versa.

If agreement is not reached at the meeting then it is likely that formal steps will have to be put in place to determine the issue. This is likely to involve the issue of assessments (if not already raised) and the proceedings for taking the case to Commissioners or VAT tribunal. It should be remembered that negotiation can take place right up to the time of any hearing. It may be sensible after the meeting to look at all the issues again and consider if the fight is really going to be worthwhile or whether there is a point of compromise. Keep the door open and you will often find that a settlement walks in!

Discussions on penalties

8.45   At the end of an Inland Revenue enquiry, after most, if not all, of the actual tax issues have been resolved, a meeting will be held to finalise the total liability which the trustees must meet. This will usually centre on the question of penalties and the degree to which the Revenue will use their authority to mitigate the level of penalties to be charged. The specific factors which need to be considered will be looked at in Chapters 10 to 12. As a general rule it is important to stress that this meeting must not simply be allowed to happen, and some preparation is needed. In particular:

(1)   Before any meeting with the investigator on the subject of penalties, everything that has happened should be reviewed and each abatement area considered in turn. In each area the points of strength for arguing a high abatement should be identified, and one should be realistic about the areas of weakness. These issues should be kept clearly in mind.

(2)   The investigator should be asked about the offer being sought on penalties. Although the investigator is unlikely to disclose the abatements being considered in particular areas careful questioning may elicit the key factors affecting his or her thinking.

(3)   The charity representative should be prepared to argue and be prepared to move but should always have in mind a maximum figure. The investigator will be working the other way and will have a minimum figure, which has probably been discussed already with his or her superiors.

(4)   If there is a case, it should be argued forcefully but not to the extent that it antagonises the investigator.

(5)   One should never allow oneself to be browbeaten by the investigator into accepting a figure which is unreasonably high.

Fighting the case at appeal

Is it worth taking the case to appeal?

8.46   Faced with a revenue authority which will not move on a point, the trustees can either accept the Revenue argument or fight the point. The factors which might influence that decision include:

●   The amount of tax at stake – the costs of fighting may not be worthwhile for a small amount of tax.

●   Whether there is a wider interest in the case – this may be the Revenue's reason for wishing to fight on even a small issue. The question is whether the trustees want to be the one to resolve the point. It is possible that some shared funding of costs might be possible in such a case.

- The opinion that the charity cannot be any worse off by appealing than they are now. If by going to appeal, the existing offers made in the case are all revoked (as they will be), then the charity runs the risk of being worse off by appealing. In other situations there may be no 'downside' risk because a defeat would not make the client's position any worse than it currently is, but a victory could significantly improve it.

What will it cost?

8.47   This will depend on who is going to take the case. There are three options:

- A representative of the trustees

- The professional adviser

- Counsel

Trustees taking their own case

8.48   There is nothing to prevent charity trustees taking their own case either before the Special or General Commissioners or a VAT tribunal. If the amount of tax at stake is relatively low but the trustees feel that there is a principle involved, this may be a realistic option provided there is a trustee who is prepared to take the case. The Commissioners and the tribunal will both be very understanding where a 'taxpayer' appears in person to conduct the case. They will accept that such an individual will not have a detailed understanding of procedures and will generally guide them through without, of course, losing their impartiality in the decision making.

In the Special Commissioners case of *Battle Baptist Church v CIR and Woodham* referred to at 3.30 above, it was the church treasurer who took the appeal before the Special Commissioners. He was a practising chartered accountant but had not taken an appeal case before. The author was able to give some advice ahead of the hearing and was on hand to offer advice at the hearing, but in fact the presentation of the case was very effectively and competently handled. The Special Commissioner was very patient and understanding in this case.

The time commitment involved in the preparation of a case is substantial and the trustees should only contemplate taking their own case if they are prepared to devote time to preparation. Obviously much depends on the complexity of the case, but even the simplest case is going to require several hours of preparation and may involve a number of days particularly if documents have to be prepared. The possibility of using a team of people from the charity would spread the load.

Professional adviser taking the case

8.49   Not every professional adviser has experience of taking hearings before Commissioners or tribunals and indeed may not have the competence to do so, whatever their technical competence in the field of inquiry. In considering the costs which will be involved the factors which should be taken into account are that:

- the hearing itself will usually take at least a day's worth of time for a partner and one other member of staff;

- the case requires detailed preparation which may entail:
    - interviewing witnesses and preparing their examination in chief,
    - reading statute law,
    - identifying and reading relevant case law,
    - preparing the opening statement,
    - drafting the closing statement,
    - time and cost in putting together bundles of documents;

- there will be general liaison time with the Revenue and the clerk over the actual arrangements for the hearing as well as preparing a statement of agreed facts with the Inspector and setting out the matter for determination;

- it might be necessary to seek a second opinion or counsel's opinion.

Even if the professional adviser can be persuaded to keep their costs down either by charging a flat fee or by using very reduced charge out rates, it is likely that an appeal hearing will cost several thousand pounds. Of course if the adviser would be prepared to take on the case for nothing so much the better.

Counsel taking the case

8.50   Counsel may be considered in more substantial cases where there are complex points of law involved. Counsel may already have been involved in the case by having been asked to give an opinion. Counsel should be asked to give a clear indication of his or her fee, which will cover all preparation for the case and appearing in the case. This will usually be charged on a daily basis and will obviously increase with the seniority of counsel chosen. In addition there may still be costs incurred by the professional adviser in:

- attending the hearing itself;

- preparation work on the case probably involving:
    - interviewing witnesses and preparing a statement of their evidence,

- general liaison with counsel on matters relating to the case,
- time and cost in putting together bundles of documents;
- general liaison time with the Revenue and the clerk over the actual arrangements for the hearing as well as preparing a statement of agreed facts with the Inspector and setting out the matter for determination.

Preparing the case – general points

Areas to consider

8.51 The notes which follow are intended to provide a general guide to anyone who is taking a case before the General Commissioners, Special Commissioners or VAT tribunal. There are a number of areas which should be considered as follows:

- Burden of proof
- Facts
- Evidence
- Organising the preparation
- Statement of agreed facts
- Checking the assessments
- The question for determination

Burden of proof

8.52 In tax appeals the burden of proof rests with the appellant, and so it is the appellant's side who must drive the appeal. The burden will be discharged by proving the case on a 'balance of probability' – it is not necessary to prove the case 'beyond all reasonable doubt' as in criminal proceedings.

Facts

8.53 The General Commissioners in particular are essentially a tribunal of fact. They can only base their decision on the facts that have been put to them. The legal argument is irrelevant if it does not relate to the facts of the case. An essential part of the preparation must therefore be to identify the facts which are important in the case, and then to determine whether those facts are contained in documents or can be adduced from the evidence of the appellant or others.

Evidence

8.54 Evidence can be presented in several ways:

- Documentary evidence can usually be presented by handing the document in. This will usually be the case where documents have already been sent into the Revenue as part of the discussions on the case. There is usually no requirement for a witness to prove a document.

- Oral evidence will usually be given primarily by the appellant, but it may be necessary to call other witnesses as well. Their testimony will be under oath. The Revenue have the right of cross-examination (often a crucial part of a hearing) and the Commissioners themselves also have the right to ask questions.

- Circumstantial evidence is defined as evidence of a fact not in issue but legally relevant to a fact in issue. It will usually be accepted by the Commissioners, particularly where no other evidence is available.

Organising the preparation

8.55　The preparation for the hearing needs to be structured and controlled. The starting point is to recognise that this is 'a whole new ball game' in the sense that all of the negotiations which have gone on to date are no longer relevant. It is therefore essential to start from scratch in building up the case, although some of the components may be more easily identified.

The basic preparation should be broken down into four broad parts:

(1) *Materials* – this will comprise the information on file in the form of accounts, correspondence and notes of meetings, from which the relevant facts which need to be established can be identified. It will also include the statute and case law relevant to the case.

(2) *Documentation* – this comprises the documentary evidence required such as contracts, items of correspondence, invoices, etc.

(3) *Examination* – this centres around the witnesses to be called and the evidence that they will give. At a later stage this will probably need to be put into question format.

(4) *Final address* – this represents the last word to the Commissioners and a skeleton of what is to be said should be prepared.

Two other important points need to be borne in mind throughout the preparation of the case

- The Commissioners, (whether General or Special) and the VAT tribunal will have no idea about any of the facts of the case. All they are likely to know is the name of the appellant and the date of the hearing.

- The General Commissioners will have little or no knowledge of statute law or case law. The number of contentious appeals they hear is very small, and it is safer to assume zero knowledge of the area being dealt with. A Special Commissioner will have greater experience and familiarity with the concept of statute and case law, but may still not be knowledgeable on the particular area. The chairman of the VAT tribunal will probably have some legal knowledge. (Chairmen of VAT tribunals sometimes also act as Special Commissioners).

Statement of agreed facts

8.56 This is sometimes referred to as an 'agreed statement of facts' which may imply that all the facts are totally agreed when in fact the interpretation of some facts may not be agreed. The statement of agreed facts should set out the sequence of events, e.g. on a particular date an asset was purchased, on a different date it was sold, etc.

This statement should be agreed with the Revenue, and it can then be presented to the Commissioners at the start of the hearing.

Checking assessments

8.57 It may sound excessive but it is worth checking first that all the assessments which are the subject of the appeal are valid assessments. There may be a hidden issue as to whether the assessment is on the correct person or was made at the right time. An assessment made out of time will require the Revenue to demonstrate fraudulent or negligent conduct.

Question for determination

8.58 This must be absolutely clear before the case goes to appeal. Agreement should be reached with the Inspector as to the form of words which sets out quite clearly what the point is, e.g. 'whether the costs of travelling from home to a site are allowable as a deduction for Schedule E under s 198 of ICTA 1988'.

Detailed preparation

Opening address

8.59 The opening address is critical because it represents the first opportunity to set out the case. Essentially it can be broken down into the following components each of which needs detailed preparation:

(1) *Statement of the facts* – what has happened, which facts are set out in the bundle of documents, which will be evidenced by witnesses.

(2) *The point at issue* – the address should aim to get this firmly into the Commissioners' minds.

(3) *The relevant statute law* – all the sections that are relevant to the case should be identified and set out before the Commissioners one by one.

(4) *The relevant case law* – only those cases which are going to assist the Commissioners in coming to their decision should be referred to or the charity representative should be aware of the cases which the Revenue are going to quote and should try to steal the Inspector's thunder by dealing with these cases first. It is usual practice to send a list of the cases to which reference is to be made to both the Inspector and the clerk ahead of the meeting.

(5) *How the facts and the law come together* – without repeating all the cases again it is necessary to demonstrate how the legislation and case law is relevant to the facts of the case. The overall objective on the point at issue must always be kept in mind and the contentions set out in a clear and concise way.

(6) *Closing summary* – The statement should be drafted in note form. It is dangerous to write it out in full because this can have an adverse bearing on the way it is actually presented.

Examination of witnesses

8.60   The selection of witnesses is crucial. The appellant will usually be called particularly if evidence of intention is to be presented. Other witnesses may be necessary to substantiate intentions and facts by being able to relate matters the appellant has discussed with them, or by adding information from their own knowledge of a business.

The first stage is to identify who might be called as a witness and to be clear what evidence they could actually supply and the relevance of that information to the case. The witnesses must be asked if they are willing to give evidence, which will include cross-examination, and a judgment will need to be made as to the ability of the witness to help the case. It is worth meeting each witness to go over their possible evidence and to probe them in the same way that an Inspector might cross-examine to see how good they really are.

A list of questions should be drawn up for each witness to let them see what is proposed. 'Leading' questions, i.e. those which direct an answer should be avoided. Witnesses are allowed to refer to writings and documents to assist them in giving their answers.

It is important to also consider the cross-examination by the Revenue. This will be a crucial aspect of the Revenue case for a number of reasons:

(1) it will be the Revenue's first appearance 'on stage' and they will want to make an impression;

(2) they will be seeking to shake up evidence which they don't accept;

(3) they will be trying to set the stage for their own later arguments and may have to elicit additional facts which they wish to use in their statement if they have not already been introduced – if they do not bring the facts out they cannot use them later;

(4)   they will be seeking to probe all areas of uncertainty and inconsistency in the stories being told by witnesses.

A good cross-examiner never asks a question to which he does not
already know the answer.

Final address

8.61   The next stage is to draft the final address. This should anticipate any arguments that the Revenue might use, although this will have
hopefully been taken account of in the opening statement. It is good
practice to have the final remarks written down. These should be a
restatement of the point at issue and a request that the Commissioners
decide that point in favour of the taxpayer.

Bundle of documents

8.62   This should be prepared with sufficient copies for the clerk and
every Commissioner. It should comprise the following:

- A statement of the point at issue

- A copy of the statement of agreed facts

- Copies of all relevant documents

- Copies of all statute law being referred to

- Copies of all tax cases being referred to or relevant extracts from
those cases

- Copies of relevant extracts from *Hansard* if appropriate

Each set should be clearly indexed with a list of contents, and should be
spirally bound if possible or alternatively set out in new ring binders.
The set should be labelled clearly 'Bundle of documents and other information relating to the appeal by (name of charity)'.

At the hearing

Before hearing begins

8.63   The charity representative should:

- arrive at the venue in plenty of time – ideally allowing himself an
hour before the start time;

- find the room for the meeting, and if the clerk is there introduce
themself;

- hand over to the clerk the bundles of documents they have prepared;

- check with the clerk whether the procedure is to stand during the
presentation of the case (*note* at the Special Commissioners parties
stay seated to present the case.);

- check where they are to be seated and set out all their papers so that they know where everything is and will not be looking for papers at a crucial time and ensure that their assistant also knows where the papers are;

- if the Revenue have arrived, make a point of introducing themself, especially if counsel or the Board's Solicitor are taking the case; and;

- check that all the people expected have arrived and give any witnesses a clear idea of when they are going to be called.

The running order

8.64   The order of events is usually as follows

- Introduction by the clerk and chairman
- Opening statement for charity
- Examination and cross-examination of witnesses for the charity
- Summing up of case for appellant
- Statement of case for Revenue or Customs and Excise
- Examination, etc. of any official witnesses (usually unlikely)
- Final reply for the appellant
- Commissioners' deliberation
- Commissioners' decision

Practical points to bear in mind:

(1)   All comments should be addressed to the chairman who should be referred to formally as 'sir' or 'madam'.

(2)   The opening statement should begin with an introduction to the charity representatives. It should be kept short and straight to the point.

(3)   To begin with the Commissioners should be referred to the bundle of prepared documents with a brief explanation of the contents, the order they are in and particular parts that will be referred to as the case proceeds.

(4)   The opening statement is then made as prepared earlier. It should be in note form and not read out. There will always be nervousness and the tendency will be to speak quickly – care should be taken to slow down and speak clearly. The Commissioners will be writing notes and will otherwise lose track of what is being said.

(5)   Where reference is made to documentation the Commissioners should be clearly directed to it and given time to look at it before proceeding. It is important that the story behind the appeal is

clearly told – these are the facts on which the Commissioners are going to have to make their decision and they will be interested in what has sparked the whole appeal.

(6)   When the witnesses are called, each one should be introduced, with an explanation of who they are and what function they have in the appeal. The questions should have been prepared beforehand and should be presented to them in the agreed order. Witnesses also get nervous and sometimes do not answer as clearly as they did at the practice session away from the hearing. If necessary they should be asked to repeat or to amplify an answer they have given which was not as clear as desired.

(7)   The Commissioners themselves may ask questions of the witness, either as the testimony proceeds or at the end. If those questions suggest that the Commissioners have failed to grasp a key area of the case, the witness should be taken through the relevant questions again, so that the point becomes clearer.

(8)   The charity representative has no direct control over the cross-examination but if the preparation has been done properly there should not be any questions that come as a surprise to them or to the witness.

(9)   Once the witnesses have finished the opening statement should be brought to an end. A potted summary should be presented and the Commissioners reminded of the point at issue.

(10)   The Revenue should have prepared their case, although they may have to revise it as they go along in the light of the evidence given. It is important to listen carefully to the Inspector's statement – it is not an opportunity to metaphorically 'nod off' with the job completed. Now is the time to identify any issues which should be rebutted in the closing statement.

(11)   The final statement should begin with a review of the points made by the Inspector. Arguments that clearly do not stand up should be rebutted and it is important to try to limit the damage of those statements which were knowingly pointed. It is unwise to denigrate the Revenue case or to use emotive words like 'ridiculous' to describe statements or opinions expressed by the Revenue.

(12)   The contentions made should be briefly summarised in a logical sequence that will leave them clearly in the Commissioners' minds.

(13)   Finally the point at issue should be restated and the Commissioners asked to uphold the appeal and take the appropriate action.

Commissioners' deliberation

8.65   The precise arrangements for this vary from hearing to hearing. At Special Commissioners and the VAT tribunal it is likely that the Commissioner will simply announce that he is going away to consider the matters and will deliver his decision in writing.

At General Commissioners the procedure may be that the Commissioners will decide to do the same and that will be the end of the proceedings. They may, however, decide to conclude the matter and will either retire to another room to make their decision, or will ask all parties to leave to allow them to deliberate.

In either event the charity representatives will find themselves with the Revenue side. Now is not the time to reopen all the issues again! Both parties will be tired and probably just relieved that all the effort is over.

If the Commissioners' decision is delivered verbally it will be the most nerve wracking part of the day! The parties should listen to the decision and note it down. They should not challenge it or make any comment on it in any way but should simply thank the Commissioners for their patience and their deliberation on the matter. If the decision is in favour of the charity, they can be magnanimous in their victory. The Inspector will be disappointed that his efforts have not been rewarded. If the case is lost the position should be accepted with grace and the Inspector congratulated on a case well done.

Immediately after the hearing the notes of the proceedings should be written up while matters are still fresh. The information may be important when a case stated is being prepared.

Learning from the investigation

8.66   Once the investigation is over, no matter how it is resolved, it is important that the trustees take stock of the situation. It is likely that they will not want to go through such a procedure again and they should look at what the investigation has told them about how they conduct the affairs of the charity and decide what they need to change to avoid similar problems happening again.

The checklists which are set out in Part 3 are intended to act as a guide to trustees in the areas covered. Time spent working through the relevant areas will not be wasted.

Chapter 9

Issues on Charity Commission Investigations

General

9.1   The nature of Charity Commission investigations tends to be very different to those conducted by the Revenue authorities. The Commissioners have much more direct power to take action and are quickly able to get to the heart of the problem and act decisively to correct it. The big monitoring issues may come after the basic remedial action has been put into effect.

The essence of the investigation is not to establish a quantum in terms of tax, as will be the case in Revenue and Customs investigations, but is essentially to ensure that the assets of the charity are protected and the work of the charity in its particular field is not impaired. Many of the issues are not therefore directly analytical but can be very subjective, therefore traditional investigation techniques are not applicable. The process will be one of seeing what is happening and what should in the opinion of the Commissioners be happening. The trustees and their advisers need to be considering if the difference between the two situations is a real one or simply one of perception. If the latter, then the course of the inquiry should be one to persuade the Commissioners that the risks they perceive to be present are not there. That is fundamentally more difficult to achieve that to analyse a tax issue and argue that there is no liability. The skills and techniques of negotiation in these circumstances are very different.

There will still be situations in which the Commissioners need to dig around and investigate transactions and the decision making process within the charity, and in those situations they may work with their colleagues in the Commission's support group and accountants group.

In this chapter we consider how an investigation might progress in relating to four particular areas of inquiry:

- Coping with personality issues
- Financial controls or lack of them
- Fundraising issues
- Trading companies

There will be many other topics of investigation but some basic principles will emerge from a closer look at these areas. The chapter will then look at the process of concluding an investigation.

Specific investigation areas

Personality issues

9.2 Issues relating to the role of dominant trustees or chief executives will always be difficult ones to handle, especially if the problem is compounded by a generally ineffectual trustee body who have allowed the problem to build unchecked and do not want to recognise it. The legal advisers in this case will have an important role to play in getting the trustees to take their role seriously or in pointing out the inadequacies to the Charity Commission and leaving them to take steps to replace the trustees.

The Charity Commission, having embarked on the investigation, will not stand back and see the problem continue as the inquiry proceeds. They will want to see positive action or they will take positive action. This has to involve the suspension or complete removal of the 'offending' individual.

Trustees will find that this type of investigation can be very difficult for them because it will inevitably show up the inefficiencies of the other trustees in failing to exercise proper control over the individual and therefore failing in their responsibility as trustees. The review is likely to look at the way the charity has been administered, the role of trustees' meetings and other decision-making matters.

Voice of Methodism Association

9.3 The Charity Commission published an abbreviated version of their inquiry report in this case on their website. The inquiry involved two separate but connected charities – The Voice of Methodism Association (the 'Association') and the VMA Board of Trustees (the 'Board'). The main object of the Association is essentially to defend the constitution of the Methodist Church and the main purpose of the Board is to advance the Association. Despite having so much in common, the progress of both bodies has been hampered by friction between them.

The Commission report that they were made aware of irregularities and a lack of proper governance in the charities which centred around the conduct of the Board secretary and trustee. There were three specific grounds for conducting the inquiry:

(1)   the failure of both charities to keep proper financial records or to produce any acceptable accounts in accordance with legal requirements;

(2)   allegations of dominance and financial and administrative mismanagement by the Board secretary;

(3)   the apparent difficulty in ascertaining who were the properly appointed trustees.

The investigators clearly spent considerable time digging among the records of the charities because they were able to identify at least 13 bank accounts in different parts of the country under the control of different individuals. They also looked closely at minutes of meetings and procedures and concluded that certain meetings and elections were invalid. The investigators asked for reliable accounts to be provided and a definitive membership list to be compiled. They also strongly suggested that the two charities should seek to find a basis for amalgamation.

The attempts to produce accounts got nowhere and simply reinforced the view that action needed to be taken. The two parties seemed to have continued to make allegations which re-emphasised the conflict. Many of the allegations centred around the Board secretary who was accused of financial misconduct and undue dominance.

The Commission were satisfied that there had been misconduct or mismanagement and that they needed to take action to protect the assets so they took the powers under *section 18* to:

(1)   freeze all identified bank accounts;

(2)   suspend the Board secretary;

(3)   appoint a receiver.

The actions of the receiver are described at 2.30 above. Following the receiver's report the Commission put together a remedial scheme under *section 18(2)* and details of that are discussed at 9.16 below.

Financial issues

9.4   Cases involving a lack of proper control over finances will be tackled by a review of the financial arrangements. The detailed investigation may involve a review of all fund accounts to ascertain who the controllers are and the uses to which the accounts have been put. This will require detailed analysis and probably a report to the investigator.

The Charity Commission accounting support are likely to become involved in this process.

One of the biggest charity fraud cases in recent years has involved a loss of £8.8m by the Salvation Army. An initial internal investigation by the solicitors and accountants stemmed the problem and also ultimately led to the recovery of all the lost funds. The Charity Commission started an inquiry in 1993 to look at the circumstances of the loss and to work with the Salvation Army to improve their financial controls and to ensure that the same thing could not happen again.

Sometimes reviews of financial aspects have to concentrate on small details. For example in a case reported in the Commissioners Report for 1991, the investigator found that an employee of the charity who had been appointed to look after its day-to-day finances, was one of three signatories to the charity's current bank account. That account operated with two out of three signatories on each cheque and the employee persuaded one of the other signatories, the secretary, to sign a number of blank cheques. It was discovered that one of those cheques had been fraudulently cashed.

The essential accounting requirement for all charities is that they should have accounting records which will allow them to ascertain the charity's financial position at any point in time. The existence of the records is a start, but these records will themselves only be of any use if there are proper controls in place to ensure that the information shown is complete. Charity income can come from many different sources:

- Donations of all kinds

- Endowments

- Appeals

- Fundraising activities

- Grants

- Legacies

- Subscriptions

- Trading activities

Within those groups, money can be received in the forms of cash, cheque, and credit card receipts. It can come in direct to the charity office, it can come in cash collecting boxes, it can come in through the Internet, it can come in from third parties. All of these sources and routes impose real control problems for the charity and the possibilities of leakages from the system are very real. The Charity Commission will expect the systems of the charity to be robust enough to cope with all the types of income they receive and if there are signs of weakness they will expect them to be strengthened.

Problems of this kind can often come to light not because of a deliberate fraud on the part of individuals involved in the charity, but because the activities of the charity have expanded so much and so quickly that the financial record-keeping and controls have not kept up. This is an area that trustees need to be constantly reviewing and will be looked at again in Part 3.

Roy Castle Lung Foundation

9.5   This has been the subject of a recent inquiry by the Charity Commission who published their summarised report on their website. The inquiry started with the trustees themselves who alerted the Commission to possible irregularities. They had their auditors look at the problems and their initial report was passed to the Charity Commission who decided to institute an inquiry which was to consider the events leading up to the resignation of the former chief executive and the foundation's general administration and governance.

The problems centred around the former chief executive, who failed to observe basic procedures and whose conduct, in the opinion of the inquiry, fell below the standard to be reasonably expected. Personal trips were made at the expense of the charity and other personal benefits were received such as substantial private use of a business mobile phone, and taking advantage of discounted facilities offered to the charity for its official purposes.

The inquiry looked at the accounting records and found that they were deficient in being able to ascertain the purpose of expenditure and concluded that they would have expected to find a more detailed and accurate system for a person in the position of the chief executive to justify the use of the charity's expenditure. The chief executive resigned and agreed to make good the non-business expenditure and the Charity Commission accepted this as a reasonable approach.

The Commission points the finger of blame at the trustees for their failure to exercise proper oversight and scrutiny in a number of areas of the operational management of the charity and in particular points to their failure to have any effective control over the activities of the chief executive. They point out that the charity had gone through a period of very rapid growth and that the fundraising skills of the chief executive had contributed to that growth. The Commission concluded, however, that rapid growth was not accompanied by sufficiently robust checks and balances and a supportive management culture.

Cases such as these are likely to require independent financial investigation. It can be argued that the existing auditors should not be involved because the existence of the problem may be one that they should have spotted. If they have spotted it and reported it to the trustees then the ultimate blame rests squarely on the latter group.

Fundraising issues

9.6   These cases may often involve other parties – either independent fundraisers or more usually the activities of a trading company controlled by the charity in terms of shareholding. The investigation detail will come down to examining the financial aspects of the arrangements and also the extent of the control which the trustees of the charity actually had over the activities of the other parties.

It can be expected that both the accounting and legal support teams of the Commissioners may become involved in such cases. There will also be some close working with the Inland Revenue on the activities of a trading subsidiary. Some of the specific investigation areas will centre on:

- Fundraising methods
- Fundraising costs
- Fundraising relationships

The growing use of professional fundraisers is a feature in all three of the above areas and the choice of such fundraisers is obviously critical. Most are diligent, professional people who are good at what they do and bring considerable financial benefit to the charities for whom they work. However, some are basically crooks who see charities as a soft touch and a means of earning easy money. For example in a case highlighted in the 1991 Report of the Charity Commission, the promoter of a lottery associated with a charity had diverted 40% of the funds raised through the lottery to his own benefit. He and his associate were jailed for two years on charges including deception, false accounting, false information and illegally applying lottery proceeds.

The procedures for dealing with professional fundraisers have now been codified in *Charities Act 1993* and there is much greater protection than in the past. It is still incumbent upon trustees to ensure that the arrangements they enter into are properly controlled and do not harm the charity in any way.

Fundraising methods

9.7   The Charity Commission in paragraph 4 of their leaflet CC20 'Charities and fund-raising' make it clear that the choice of methods of fundraising is one for trustees to decide upon. However, they go on to state that 'charities which are supported by donations need to be alert and sensitive to public opinion and criticism. Fund-raising methods which meet with disapproval can damage the charity and reduce public confidence in the sector as a whole'.

This is obviously an area where the public issue will be important. If members of the public feel that fundraising methods are aggressive or intrusive they will object, and charities involved may find themselves involved in an inquiry and will have to justify their methods or change them. This applies whether the fundraising activities are carried out directly by the charity or by professional fundraisers acting on behalf of the charity.

The Commission will accept that charities are in a competitive situation when it comes to getting funds at all. The statistics show that people are giving proportionately less to charities now than a decade ago, and in particular young people are giving less. There is also competition between charities for the limited funds available. In a world that is more aggressive than it used to be, charities or their fundraisers may feel that they have to adopt similar tactics to achieve justifiable charitable ends. The Charity Commission will need to be convinced. In *Charity Commission News 12*, published in spring 2000, the Commissioners included a short article entitled 'Fund-raising – manners make financial sense' and list suggestions received from funders and donors who had concerns about the ways in which they had been treated by fundraisers. The Commissioners point out that in a number of cases the people concerned had indicated that they would no longer be making donations to the particular charity. Those suggestions will be considered in Part 3.

Fundraising costs

9.8   A major area of Charity Commission concern is the costs of fundraising activities and ensuring that those costs are not excessive. It is not sufficient to argue that even a small part of the proceeds of a fundraising venture represent pure profit to the charity and huge expenses can therefore be justified. The Commission will accept that most fundraising ventures will incur costs of some kind – if only printing costs of leaflets or envelopes for a house-to-house collection. They will, however, expect that the costs will be kept to a minimum because that is what the public will expect as well. The man in the street making his donation of £1 will expect that the charity will be able to use most of that £1 for the work it does – if he finds out that 50% or more of that donation has gone in expenses he will believe that he has made his donation under false pretences and will rightly complain. In 1991 the Commissioners noted that in 19 cases they had investigated, the proportion of funds actually handed over to charities was less than 10% and that they had acted to prevent further fundraising and had frozen the relevant accounts. The position should be better after the enactment of *Charities Act 1993*, but there is still cause for concern.

Charities under investigation in this area will need to be able to justify the level of expenses that have been incurred. In particular they may need to justify the level of fees paid to external fundraisers and to consider:

- Why was that method of fundraising chosen if it was going to cost so much? There might be a justification in the extended publicity which an event generated, having a beneficial effect on donations in general.

- Were the costs of fundraising made clear in all the publicity? For example was it made clear that celebrities involved were making a charge, or that only a proportion of royalties was going to the charity, or that the costs of the fundraisers were a proportion of the proceeds?

- Were the costs of using external fundraisers lower than the costs of recruiting and employing people in a fundraising department?

Fundraising relationships

9.9   *Charities Act 1993* sets out the legal framework for relationships between charities and professionals. It covers the following areas:

(1)   legally enforceable agreements to cover fundraising;

(2)   disclosure of beneficiaries and remuneration;

(3)   repayment of donations made;

(4)   right of charities to prevent unauthorised fundraising;

(5)   penalties for making false statements.

The legislation applies to agreements between charities and professional fundraisers, and also to agreements between charities and other organisations referred to as 'commercial participators'. This covers in particular the relationship between charities and commercial sponsors. The Commissioners would expect now that any link with a professional fundraiser will be governed by an agreement which complies with *Charities Act 1993* and any charity which had failed to do this would be in serious trouble.

There are also signs that the Commissioners are becoming increasingly concerned that some relationships between charities and companies, while financially very attractive may be putting charity assets at risk. In particular they are concerned about the use of the charity name by the commercial concern. They state in leaflet CC20, para 43:

'A charity's name is precious. It is the means by which the charity is known and by which its reputation will be judged. We strongly recommend that trustees be careful how they allow it to be used, especially by a commercial participator during a promotional venture.'

The exploitation of a charity logo, many of which are very distinctive and well known, would fall into the same category.

Charities under investigation in this area will need to provide evidence to show that they have not harmed themselves by particular associations. This may actually prove to be very difficult and they will find themselves under some pressure to change arrangements.

Trading subsidiaries

9.10   Once all avenues for tax exemption either by statute or conces-sion have been exhausted, and it is clear that a profit is going to arise from any fundraising activity, it has to be accepted that a tax liability is going to arise. It is still possible to set up arrangements to ensure that the tax problem effectively disappears.

The route which is traditionally used is that of a trading company wholly owned by the charity. The company is in the scope of corporation tax but can effectively eliminate the corporation tax problem by arrang-ing for its profits to be paid up to the charity either by way of a deed of covenant or, more likely now, through Gift Aid. In both cases, the pay-ment is allowable as a charge for corporation tax purposes, leaving the company with no taxable profits and the charity in receipt of annual payments which are not in any way caught by the trading issues and are therefore basically exempt. As we shall see below there can be issues of concern in this for both the Revenue and the Charity Commission.

The areas of concern of the latter fall into a number of areas:

- The basic investment decision
- Funding arrangements
- The relationship between the charity and the company

The investment decision

9.11   There are two aspects to this:

(1)   Do the activities warrant the creation of a company?

(2)   Can the charity actually invest in the company?

There is a real danger of being swept away on a wave of enthusiasm for a project which in reality has no prospects of success or of contributing reasonable amounts of income to the charity. The time and expertise of the trustees should not be expended on peripheral fundraising compa-nies. Before a major venture is commenced, the charity trustees should draw up a clear business plan which can be used to justify the decision and will need to be produced in any investigation into this area. The make-up of this plan is discussed in Part 3.

There is little point in going to the cost of setting up a trading company if the likely profits are going to be small, the additional compliance requirements hardly make it worth the effort and it may be cheaper to pay a small amount of tax in the charity. The Charity Commissioners accept that where the activity is small enough, the trustees would not be considered in breach of charity law if they decided to incur a tax liabil-ity by leaving the trade in the charity. The Commissioners recommend taking professional advice on this point.

The usual structure will be a company limited by shares in which all the shares are held by the charity. In some cases it has been possible for a number of charities to get together to form a central trading vehicle. Again there are practical questions to consider including:

(1) Is shareholding in an unquoted trading company possible under the charity constitution?

(2) Is an investment in a trading subsidiary in line with the charity's current investment policy?

The charity will want to be the shareholder in what will be an unquoted company, and it is important to check that the governing instrument of the charity will allow funds to be invested in such a vehicle. The deed may have some specific prohibitions or may have a requirement that the trustees should invest only in sound funds, which may not include a new trading venture. Long-established trusts may have this problem, and it is always worth ensuring that when a new charity is created it has the power to make an investment in an unquoted company. In all cases the charity trustees should have before them a copy of the proposed business plan of the company, and need to be able to record that their decision to invest has been carefully thought through.

Funding arrangements

9.12   The initial funding of the company is a crucial area where considerable thought is required. One way in which this could be done is by putting in funds in the form of shares, but it must be remembered that the greater the shareholding by the charity, the greater is the risk to the funds of the charity. There are two other options – loans from the charity and outside funding.

The Charity Commission do not like to see large amounts of unsecured lending by a charity to its trading subsidiary. They regard such an arrangement as putting the assets of the charity at too great a risk. At the very least they would want to see that the charity trustees had seen all the business plans and cash flow forecasts of the company, and had recorded their reasons for making an unsecured investment clearly in their minutes.

Finding security for a loan in a trading venture may not be easy, but is a step which should always be carefully explored. If there are fixed assets, such as property in the company then any loan should, if at all possible, be secured on that property. Failing that, consideration should be given to taking a floating charge over the stock or debtors of the company. The Commisioners' preference is most definitely for secured rather than unsecured funding, because they are concerned that the charity trustees should be engaged in risk management. They recognise that this may not always be possible, and do not regard the policy as being written in tablets of stone.

The preferred option of the Commissioners is for some outside funding of the trading company. This could come from a financial institution such as a bank, but the bank will want to see evidence of the risks involved before parting with funds. This will certainly involve demonstrating that a coherent business plan has been put together, and that those involved in running the company are qualified to do so. Any such borrowing will involve a commercial rate of interest, which will usually increase with the level of risk that the bank manager perceives to be involved. The payment of interest should be built into cash flow forecasts. What the Commissioners would not want to see is the charity putting up any of its assets as security for external funding.

If a financial institution cannot be persuaded to fund the venture, there might be some individuals who are prepared to loan funds to the company. Any such loans should be direct to the company, and not made via the charity.

The continued funding of the company will also need to be considered, particularly if all profits are passed back to the charity. The tax issues will be discussed below but the Commissioners would also want to be satisfied that the charity was not continuing to put assets at risk. Certainly they would look very closely at the continued funding of a trading venture that made losses. It may be preferable to take a tax liability in the company and retain some profits rather than risk charity funds on further loans.

Relationship between charity and company

9.13   It is important that the relationship between the charity and the company should be kept distinct. It will often be the case that some of the trustees will also be directors of the company, but the two bodies should never be completely the same. There must also be on the board of the company people who have particular expertise in the areas of business in which the company is going to be active and who do not have a role as trustee. Trustees who are directors cannot receive any remuneration from the company.

The company will need to establish its own accounting records, and all transactions with the parent charity need to be carefully recorded. Care needs to be taken over the following matters:

- the financial structures of the charity and trading subsidiary ought to be kept separate;

- the separate identities of the charity and trading company should be made clear in all publicity material and in dealings with suppliers;

- the names of the charity and the trading company should be distinguished from each other to prevent confusion between the activities of the two organisations;

- the charity must not settle any debts of the company;

- the financial support required by the company must be carefully assessed with due regard being given to the non-cash commitments, such as shared staff and shared premises;

- the charity must not buy stock and donate it to the company.

Resolution of investigations

Remedial powers

9.14   As already stated, the aim of the Charity Commission inquiry is not to exact retribution on individuals or the charity or to seek financial redress. The purpose of any inquiry is to seek to protect the assets of the charity. It may be that in the course of achieving that objective, certain individuals may have to pay a price in terms of losing their role as trustee and possibly facing some public scrutiny through the publication of an inquiry report which names them.

The remedial powers available to the Commission are discussed in detail in Chapter 2 at 2.25 to 2.32. They represent a formidable array of weapons and allow the Commissioners to adopt an approach which can be tailor-made for the circumstances of each charity. Whether they use some or all of those powers, what the Commission aim to do at the end of an inquiry is to ensure that the charity concerned comes out of the process stronger and better equipped to carry out the objects for which it was established – it is not the aim to drive the charity out of existence.

Action plan

9.15   An integral part of this process is that the investigators seek to sit down with the trustees (either the existing trustees or new trustees that they have appointed) and agree an action plan with them which, when implemented, will put the charity back on track. They can offer the help of the support group within the Charity Commission to do this, particularly if the process requires any scheme to be prepared.

Obviously the contents of the action plan will vary from case to case and the beauty of the powers the Commission have is that they can be totally flexible. Charities must realise, though, that these are not soft options and are not ideas from a management consultant that they can accept or reject as seems appropriate. In reality these are requirements that must be implemented because if the existing body of trustees won't implement them, the Commission will find a group who will.

Voice of Methodism

9.16   This inquiry report has already been discussed at 9.3 above. The report having detailed the circumstances of the inquiry then sets out the remedial action which is to be put in place by means of a scheme using the Commissioners' powers in *Ch A 1993, s 18(2)(b)(ii)*. The elements of the Scheme were that:

- The two charities will become one under a single body of trustees.

- The objects of the new charity will simply restate the existing objects of the Association. (the Commissioners do not regard themselves as competent to determine doctrinal issues which lie at the heart of the objects.)

- The scheme will contain appropriate provisions for membership and subscription, and a membership list must be maintained. All members (and therefore trustees) of the newly-formed charity must be members or adherents to the Methodist Church.

- The trustees of the new charity will be elected from the membership and none of those individuals who have previously acted as trustees of either charity will be eligible for appointment

- The Scheme will either appoint the first trustees, whose duties will be to oversee the election of a committee in accordance with procedures to be set out in the Scheme, or, if it does not prove possible to identify sufficient individuals to form a body of trustees, the Scheme could appoint a small electoral board with responsibility for arranging an election of first trustees.

- Administration powers will be included in the Scheme.

Publicity

9.17   The Charity Commission have the power under *Ch A 1993, s 8(6)* to publicise the results of any inquiry. *Subsection (6)* states:

'Where an inquiry has been held under this section, the Commissioners may either

(a) cause the report of the person conducting the inquiry, or such other statement of the results of the inquiry as they think fit, to be printed or published, or

(b) publish any such report or statement in some other way which is calculated in their opinion to bring it to the attention of persons who may wish to make representations to them about the action to be taken . . .'

The Commissioners have always included notes about significant investigations in their annual report and have from time to time published some very detailed reports on inquiries. They are now making use of their website to publish details. These usually appear in the 'What's new' section of the site. The aim of the reports is not particularly to name and shame the charities and individuals involved. Certainly there is no intent to damage the charity because this would run counter to the purpose of the inquiry. Rather they want to assure supporters and beneficiaries that problems are under control and that the charity will be better able to carry out its objects. There is also a wider message to the charity sector that the problems discovered in one charity may be arising in others and the publication of the report should cause all trustees to pause and consider if they have similar problems. The final part of the report on the Roy Castle Lung Cancer Foundation actually sets out five quite clear lessons which all trustees need to take on board (see also 2.32 and 9.5).

Chapter 10

Inland Revenue FICO Investigations

General comments

10.1   The wide range of FICO investigations means it is difficult to make general comments on their approach. Major enquiry areas centre on the issues of trading and the use of trading companies and in particular the funding arrangements for such companies. These types of enquiry will inevitably involve a considerable amount of research, sometimes going back into the dim and distant past to look at the origins of the arrangements. One issue which is increasingly appearing as a feature in investigations is the use of legislation originally introduced in 1986 to curb the use of charities for avoidance purposes and, before looking at the more detailed investigation points, it will be helpful to explain the workings of this piece of legislation.

Restriction for non-qualifying expenditure

Definitions

10.2   The legislation which is now contained in *ICTA 1988, ss 505, 506 and Sch 20* had its origins in the perceived abuse of charitable status that was taking place in the late 1970s and early 1980s. The legislation was introduced after one false start in *Finance Act 1986*, but remains largely unknown by many involved in the charitable sector. It therefore comes as a shock to many when the Revenue use the legislation in calculating tax due in enquiry cases.

The legislation has created its own terminology and definitions, but there are four key concepts which have to be understood as follows:

(1)   Relevant income and gains – these are income and gains which would be taxable if not covered by *ICTA 1988, s 505* and income which is taxable irrespective of that section. Charities whose relevant income and gains in any chargeable period are less than £10,000 are outside the scope of the legislation. [*ICTA 1988, s 505(3)(a)*]. Where the Revenue consider that two or more charities are acting in concert in transactions aimed at avoiding tax, they

can give notice that the £10,000 limit is not to be applied. [*ICTA 1988, s 505(7)*]. Where the chargeable period is less than a year, the limit is reduced proportionately. Income from non-taxable sources, such as donations and legacies, is not taken into account as relevant income.

(2)   Qualifying expenditure – this is expenditure incurred for charitable purposes only. It does not include investments or loans. Expenditure on administration will qualify provided that it is reasonable in nature and amount. What will be subject to close scrutiny will be payments made to a body (not an individual) outside the UK. Such a payment will only be regarded as qualifying expenditure if the charity has taken reasonable steps to ensure that the payment has been applied for charitable purposes. [*ICTA 1988, s 506(3)*]. The Financial Secretary indicated in the course of the debate on *Finance Bill 1986* that the Revenue would look at this in the normal way.

In many cases the nature of the payments would be obvious but the Revenue could raise queries in other situations. They may require information about the activities and objectives of the overseas body or about the arrangements for earmarking the payment for a particular purpose or what it has been used for. It would, therefore, be prudent for all charities making payments overseas not only to carry out such checks but also to make sure that they have evidence to back their action.

Where a charitable payment is made after the end of a chargeable period but should properly be chargeable against the income of that period because of a commitment previously entered into, that payment will be qualifying expenditure.

(3)   Non-qualifying expenditure – in this case regard must be had not only to revenue-type expenditure but also to the nature of investments and loans made during the year. If items of investment or loan do not fall within the definition in the Act of a qualifying investment or a qualifying loan (*ICTA 1988, Sch 20*), the amounts involved will be regarded as non-qualifying expenditure. There are provisions to prevent a non-qualifying investment made, realised and reinvested being counted twice, although any profit element reinvested would become non-qualifying expenditure.

Qualifying investments which are not restricted to the UK, cover what might be termed approved investments such as those covered by *Trustee Investment Act 1961* (although mortgages are excluded), common investment funds, land and quoted shares. Bank deposits qualify provided they pay a commercial rate of interest and do not act as security for someone else to have a loan. Any other type of investment loan (including a mortgage) must be shown to be for the benefit of the charity and not for the avoidance of tax.

(4)   Qualifying loans – these loans are those not made by way of an investment where the loan is made either to another charity for charitable purposes only or to a beneficiary in the course of carrying out a purpose of the charity. A current bank account is also a qualifying loan.

Stages of action

10.3   Armed with the definitions and having clearly determined into which category all the income, expenditure and investment during the chargeable period properly fall, a formula must be applied to see if the tax relief is going to be restricted. This is best explained in stages.

Stage 1   Compare relevant income and qualifying expenditure. If the latter exceeds the former there can be no restriction of relief in the chargeable period, however, action may be required in respect of earlier years (see stage 7 below). If the relevant income exceeds qualifying expenditure proceed to stage 2.

Stage 2   Is there any non-qualifying expenditure for the year? If not there will be no restriction of relief. If there is proceed to stage 3.

Stage 3   Compare the excess of relevant income at stage 1 with the non-qualifying expenditure at stage 2. Tax relief on the excess is to be restricted up to the amount of the non-qualifying expenditure. There are provisions which will cause tax relief to be restricted where income is accumulated in a qualifying way and then used for non-qualifying expenditure. The restriction can be applied to income of a chargeable period which ended within the previous six years. Again the procedure is best explained in stages.

Stage 4   Does total expenditure (qualifying and non-qualifying) exceed relevant income? If it does not, no further action is required. If it does, proceed to stage 5.

Stage 5   Calculate the extent to which the excess expenditure is accounted for by non-qualifying expenditure. To the extent that it is, this is referred to as 'unapplied non-qualifying expenditure'.

Stage 6   Compare unapplied non-qualifying expenditure with non-taxable sums received during the period. If they cover the expenditure, no further action is needed. If an excess still remains, proceed to stage 7.

Stage 7   Take the excess back to a previous chargeable period (a later period in preference to an earlier one) where there was an excess of relevant income and treat it as a non-qualifying expenditure of that period and go through stages 1 to 3 again for that earlier period. If the excess expenditure is not used up, go back to another period where there was an excess of relevant income. If there are no years of excess relevant income, the excess expenditure is disregarded and cannot be carried forward to restrict relief in a later year.

The procedure is best illustrated by an example.

Example

Year 1
A charity has a deed of covenant income of £15,000 gross. It expends £7,000 on charitable activities, £3,000 on non-charitable activities and invests £5,000 in a Jersey bank account:

Stage 1	£
Relevant income	15,000
Deduct qualifying expenditure	7,000
Excess relevant income	8,000

Stage 2	
There is non-qualifying expenditure	3,000
Tax relief on excess relevant income restricted by	3,000

The charity will receive a tax repayment in respect of £12,000 of covenanted income.

Year 2
The charity has deed of covenant income of £15,000 and bank interest of £500. It spends £10,000 on charitable objects and invests a further £5,500 in its bank account:

Stage 1	£
Relevant income	15,500
Deduct qualifying expenditure	10,000
Excess relevant income	5,500

Stage 2
There is no non-qualifying expenditure.

The charity will receive a tax repayment on £15,000 of deed of covenant income and will not be taxed on £500 of bank interest

Year 3
The charity has deed of covenant income of £15,000 and receives a legacy of £5,000. It spends £16,000 on qualifying expenditure but also spends £14,500 on non-qualifying expenditure:

Stage 1	£
Relevant income	15,000
Qualifying expenditure	16,000

Therefore there is no excess of relevant income. Tax on deed of covenant paid in full.

Stage 4	£
Qualifying expenditure	16,000
Non-qualifying expenditure	14,500
	30,500
Deduct relevant income	15,000
Excess of expenditure over income	15,500

Stage 5	£
Unapplied non-qualifying expenditure	14,500

Stage 6	£
Deduct non-taxable income	5,000
Excess expenditure over non-taxable income	9,500

Stage 7
Take excess expenditure back to year 2 and treat as non-qualifying expenditure of that year. The excess relevant income of £5,500 is more than accounted for by excess non-qualifying expenditure of year 3 and an assessment would be issued on £5,500 gross.

There remains excess expenditure from year 3 of £4,000 (£9,500 – £5,500) this now goes back to year 1.

Excess relevant income in year 1 was £8,000 and non-qualifying expenditure now becomes £7,000 (£3,000 + £4,000). An assessment will be raised on £4,000 gross.

The overall position of the charity is as follows:

		£
Total relevant income		45,500
Deduct qualifying expenditure		33,000

		£	
Relief not given	year 1	7,000	
	year 2	5,500	12,500
Non-qualifying expenditure			17,500
Deduct non-taxable income			5,000
			£ 12,500

The effect has been to restrict tax relief by reference to the non-qualifying expenditure funded out of potentially taxable income.

Financial arrangements for trading companies

The root of the problem

10.4   The provisions allow the Revenue to take action when they find that a charity has been using its funds for purposes which the Revenue do not consider to be charitable. Most commonly this can arise in situations where a charity has a trading subsidiary. The need for a company usually stems from the fact that the charity wants to carry out trading activities which are not exempt from income tax – most typically activities which are primarily aimed at fundraising. The idea is that the company should trade in just the same way as any other commercial company but will pay its profits back to the charity in the form of a qualifying donation. In the past this would have been a payment under what was commonly known as a 'profit shedding deed' and following the changes to Gift Aid in *Finance Act 2000* is in future likely to be a Gift Aid payment. The Gift Aid donation is treated as a charge against the taxable profits of the company and reduces those profits accordingly (ideally to nil) and the receipt in the hands of the charity should be exempt as a qualifying donation. The charity has effectively received the profits of the trading activity in a non-taxable way.

If that arrangement is put into effect, the company will never be in the position to build up a reserve of profits to funds its development, and the charity will be continually required to keep putting in funds. In reality the same money could go round in a circular route of company profit → payment to charity → loan from charity to company. Unless some money actually comes to rest in the charity, the whole venture will be pointless.

The solution becomes a problem

10.5   This potentially circular system is one which concerns both the Charity Commission and the Revenue. The Revenue would look very closely at the anti-avoidance legislation described above which seeks to make the charity demonstrate that it has applied funds on qualifying expenditure – this obviously covers financing the work of the charity, but also allows for investments to be made. If the Revenue can show that funds have been made to non-qualifying items, they can restrict payments due to the charity, or if necessary charge the charity to tax.

One of the items in *ICTA 1988, Sch 20* which defines qualifying expenditure is related to loans made as investment. *Schedule 20, para 9* identifies as qualifying: 'Any loan or other investment as to which the Board are satisfied, on a claim made to them on that behalf, that the loan or other investment is made for the benefit of the charity and not for the avoidance of tax (whether by the charity of any other person)'.

The Revenue will focus attention on the phrase 'for the benefit of the charity' – a phrase which is not subsequently defined in the legislation. The Revenue argument is that they will not regard a loan to a trading company as being for the benefit of the charity unless three factors are present:

(1)   the loan is adequately secured;

(2)   a commercial rate of interest is charged;

(3)   there is a proper agreement showing the terms of repayment of the loan.

The Revenue view has not been tested in the courts and has not yet, as far the author is aware, been tested at the first point of appeal, the Special Commissioners. This approach is dogmatic and should be countered if at all possible. The relevant part of *Schedule 20* deals with investments but the Revenue are seeking to apply a commercial approach to the problem. They are content that under earlier provisions in *Schedule 20*, a charity can invest its funds in quoted companies, but any stockbroker would advise that the value of equities can fall as well as rise, and the recession has shown that even apparently strong companies can go to the wall.

The term 'benefit to the charity' is not defined in the legislation and therefore it is possible to consider the term in its everyday meaning. If it can be shown that the trustees took a decision to make the investment in the firm belief, backed by advice wherever possible, that the investment would yield a return to the charity and would not put charity assets at risk, then it should be accepted by the Revenue that the loan is for the benefit of the charity. If they wanted to restrict the meaning of benefit in the way they suggest, then they should have made that definition clear in the legislation

If the Revenue go down this route in an enquiry, it becomes important to look at the arrangements for funding the company. If loans have been used (and there are possible alternatives which need to be considered) then there should be evidence to show that the charity had taken advice on the making of the loans. In one case that the author was involved in, a charity was making loans to a company which was then investing in property development projects which were being run by companies under the control of the individual who had established the charity. The Revenue mounted an investigation into the loan arrangements and brought out the classic arguments on security, etc. A detailed review of the charity activities showed that before each loan was entered into, the trustees took independent advice from a property specialist, studied projections about the transaction and then decided if and how much they would invest. In the end, having wheeled out their basic arguments the Revenue after much discussion and a considerable period of time, decided not to pursue the point before the

Special Commissioners and an overall deal was negotiated to settle the enquiry.

Trading by charities

Introduction

10.6   The area of trading is probably one of the most contentious tax issues that charities have to grapple with, and it is likely to remain one of the main areas of focus for enquiries under the self assessment regime. There is a very detailed analysis on trading in Chapter 5A of *Tolley's Charities Manual* and the notes that follow here simply pick out the essential elements which charities need to consider. Some of the practical issues are dealt with in Part 3.

Trading is not a new tax issue for charities, there are tax cases on the subject going back almost a hundred years. Particular problems arise in the area of fundraising. Those problems have increased as charities have looked at different and more imaginative ways of raising funds to finance their activities. The real value of fundraising activities will be greatly diminished if tax has to be paid. It is not an exaggeration to state that when a charity is seeking to generate income, other than from investments and pure donations, *it is absolutely vital to give consideration to the question of trading*. The Revenue focus many of their investigations on fundraising activities and how they should be treated for tax purposes.

The tax exemption for trading has evolved over the last 75 years or so. The original tax legislation had no exemption for trading by charities. The latest part of the evolution occurred in the Charities Tax Review and finds its place in *Finance Act 2000*.

Identifying a trade

The legal position

10.7   Many charities would fail to take account of the possibility of trading because they are of the opinion that 'we are not trading because we are not a commercial body'. What matters from a tax point of view is not the type of body you are (except in certain cases) but what activity you are carrying on. The key question to consider is 'Does the activity we are undertaking amount to the carrying on of a trade for income tax purposes?'.

The Taxes Acts provide that the profits of a trade are to be taxed under what is known as Schedule D, Case I. [*ICTA 1988, s 18(3)*]. If asked to describe a trade, the man in the street would probably refer to the typical trading activities of major manufacturing or retail companies, or to the local 'tradesmen' such as the plumber, decorator, etc. If that was the extent of the definition there would be few problems, unfortunately the definition of trade is considerably widened by the provisions of *ICTA 1988, s 832*, which states that 'trade includes every trade, manufacture, adventure or concern in the nature of trade'.

This is a very wide definition because it brings into charge not only activities which are easily recognised as a full trade, e.g. a retail shop or a manufacturing activity, but the use of the phrase 'adventure or concern in the nature of trade' stretches the scope to include activities which have the characteristics of a trade, even if, as in some cases, there is only one purchase and sale.

Over the years the courts have established a number of so-called 'badges of trade', these are:

- **P**rofit-seeking motive
- **E**xisting trade connections
- **R**epetition
- **M**ethod of finance
- **I**nterval between purchase and sale
- **S**elling organisation
- **S**inheritance or donation – method of acquisition
- **O**perations pending sale
- **N**ature of asset

The bold letters give a useful mnemonic which serves as a reminder that if the characteristics are present, the Revenue have 'Permission' to tax as a trade.

Charities are not, however, commercial organisations – indeed an organisation could not be charitable if it had blatantly commercial objectives. A charity is established to carry out objects which meet one of the four heads of charity set out in the McNaghten doctrine (see 1.5). However, it will be clear from the description of the badges of trade that there are many situations in which a charity might be regarded as trading. There are other situations where, at first glance, the operations might not be regarded by the charity as a trade, because what is happening is that the organisation is doing the job for which it was established. It is always important to look a those activities and see if they amount to the carrying on of a trade. If they do then it is appropriate to consider the exemptions which might be available. It is extremely dangerous to assume exemption from the outset because if the assumption is wrong, an avoidable tax liability will have been created.

Examples of trading by charities

10.8   At this point it will be helpful to indicate some of the various types of activities of charities which could be regarded as trading – some such as fees received by a school will be quite obvious, others may not be.

Sponsorship

This is an important source of funds for many charities. If the sponsorship is nothing more than a straight donation, with nothing required in return, then there will be no question of trading. The sponsor could not, however, expect to get any tax relief against profit for their payment. For that reason, sponsors usually look for some tangible expression of their generosity – a prominent display of their name, the opportunity to advertise in the event programme or perhaps complimentary tickets to a function. Once this happens, the charity moves into a much greyer area where trading becomes a possibility.

Lotteries

Lotteries are undertaken for a clear profit motive. Sometimes their existence may be clouded by other factors, e.g. where part of a member's subscription is entered into a prize draw, with substantial cash prizes. It should be noted that if part of the ticket price is stated to be a clear donation, and the lottery is a private lottery, the Revenue will accept that the donation element is not taxable. It is important that the lottery costs, including prizes, should be covered by the non-donation element.

Charity shops

Such shops are a common feature of many high streets. To the extent that the shops sell only donated goods there will be no problem because the Revenue accept that the charity is simply turning donations in kind into cash donations. Many shops, however, buy in a variety of goods – sometimes by acquiring stock, in other cases operating an agency whereby, for example, a member of the public can sell clothing with the individual receiving a percentage of the sale proceeds. In any situation like this there will be a trading activity.

Christmas cards

Cards are now a common means of fundraising – they are sold in charity shops, and in special card centres. The activity is clearly a commercial one and is in competition with commercial card manufacturers.

Admissions

Charges for admission to museums, stately homes, and places of interest are receipts of a trade. Alongside that will usually go the sale of guidebooks, other publications and souvenirs of all types. All of these activities will be trading.

Conference centres

Centres providing holiday facilities or simply conference facilities will be carrying on a trade – they are acting in just the same way as hotels and commercial conference ventures. The same could apply to schools and colleges which let facilities during vacation time.

Affinity card schemes

These have been used by a number of charities, under which they allow their name to be used by credit card companies which produce specially designed cards. The key advantage for the credit card company is access to the membership of the charity who will be encouraged to use the card because the charity will benefit, both from their original take-up of the card and from their use of it. There are usually two transactions involved, first the licence of the charity name and logo which will not be regarded as a trading activity, and secondly the sale by the charity of its mailing list of members. That is a commercial asset and its exploitation will be regarded as a trading activity.

Fundraising events

These are commonplace; some are very small scale events, others use prestigious venues and operate on very commercial lines – both will be regarded as trading activities. A pop concert held at Wembley for a charitable purpose will be no less a trading venture than a similar event held to make a profit for the artistes.

Theatrical or artistic ventures

If these are run on commercial lines, they will be trading activities. They are no different in concept from commercial film making or theatres in the West End of London.

Recognising a trade

10.9   The Revenue may seek to argue that trading is taking place in the most unexpected situations and this can cause much time to be spent on fighting the point. In one case in which the author was involved, the Revenue had looked at the activities of a small private charity which had been party to some property transactions. The trust had been established by an individual who had some property interests as well as other commercial interests, and the objects of the charity were for the advancement of the Christian religion. The founder/trustee wanted to generate funds for the charity to purchase a property to act as a training centre. He had a property which he had purchased several years earlier and was able, after considerable difficulty, to find a purchaser. He could have sold the property and then transferred the profits to the charity under Gift Aid. He decided, however, to gift the property to the charity at the point of sale so that the charity appeared as the vendor and took the proceeds directly.

This was perfectly legitimate tax planning but the Revenue decided to argue that the transaction by the charity was an adventure in the nature of trade and wanted to tax it. They argued that there was minimal time between the purchase and sale (which was indisputable as far as the charity was concerned but ignored the time for which the property had been owned) and they regarded the previous property interests of the trustee as relevant. The latter were argued to be irrelevant as far as his role as trustee was concerned.

Considerable time was put into researching all the background to the transaction to show that the charity was not involved in negotiating the deal but was the passive beneficiary. In the end the Revenue decided not to pursue the argument although they did not actually concede the point, preferring to hide behind a statement that because of delays they would not proceed. The amounts involved were quite substantial and were certainly worth fighting for. The clear impression was that they were not willing to pursue the arguments on technical grounds.

Statutory trading exemption

10.10   The comments made above are intended to encourage a realistic view to be taken of activities which might be regarded as trading, rather than the offhand approach frequently adopted that 'we are a charity and don't need to be concerned about trading'. By the time an enquiry takes place, however, it may be too late to do anything. The only hope will be to try to demonstrate that the activity should benefit from the tax exemption for trading or the various extensions of that exemption which are no available.

The legislation in *ICTA 1998, s 505(1)(e)* provides:

'. . . exemption from tax under Schedule D in respect of the profits of any trade carried on by a charity, if the profits are applied solely to the purpose of the charity and either—

(i)   the trade is exercised in the course of the actual carrying out of a primary purpose of the charity; or

(ii)   the work in connection with the trade is mainly carried out by the beneficiaries of the charity.'

In considering whether exemption is possible under the primary purpose heading, the starting point must be to establish the primary objects of the charity clearly, as distinct from those activities which are peripheral to, or indeed help to finance, the primary objects. The objects should be clearly stated in the founding document of the charity, and it is important, when establishing a new charity which will have trading activities, to try to ensure that, as far as possible, any trading activities can be carried on within the primary objects.

Examples of situations which qualify for exemption under this heading are:

- a school, charging fees, which will be fulfilling the primary object of advancement of education;

- a charity for the advancement of religion which sells Christian books, or produces tapes of Christian music;

- a holiday centre established to provide special holidays for disabled people, or children from deprived areas, provided that the objects are within the general public benefit heading;

- the holding of an exhibition by an art gallery or museum in return for an admission charge;

- sales of tickets for a theatrical production staged by a theatre which has charitable status;

- the provision of healthcare services provided by a hospital in return for payment.

The exemption for work done by beneficiaries was introduced originally to provide exemption for the sale of work produced by disabled people, and its introduction in 1921, just three years after the end of the First World War, reinforces that. That type of activity would clearly still be relevant today, as would the sale of goods produced in third world countries and sold through aid shops or through mail order.

The clear task is to establish who the beneficiaries of the charity really are. That should be clear from the governing document but may not always be clearcut:

- In some situations the work may be done by both beneficiaries and also paid or volunteer employees who are not beneficiaries. Provided it can be shown that the greater part of the work is actually done by beneficiaries, there will be no problem.

- Where the charity makes a payment to the beneficiaries for their work, they will be treated as employees for tax purposes. Whether they cease to be beneficiaries will depend upon the terms of the employment. If those terms are such that the individuals are paid on a commercial basis, and no other benefits are provided, then the Revenue may cease to regard them as beneficiaries and remove the trading exemption.

Extending the exemption – ancillary activities

10.11   The Revenue recognise that there are some trading activities which do not fall within the strict primary purpose exemption, but which are so closely linked to the primary purpose that they can be treated as falling within the exemption. The problem is in identifying how close to the main activity the 'ancillary' activity needs to be to be brought within the exemption.

The approach which the Revenue adopt in practice is to look at the main exempt activities and to consider whether those activities cause the charity to have an obligation to provide other facilities or activities to people who are benefiting from the main activities. If the answer is that there is an obligation, then the activities relating to the meeting of that obligation are considered to be ancillary to the meeting of the main object and will be treated as within the main 'primary purpose' exemption.

An obvious example, which is quoted in the booklet, is the provision of accommodation to students by a school or college in return for rent. The letting of furnished and serviced accommodation is not the provision of education, which is the primary purpose of the school or college. The Revenue accept that, if the students are going to benefit from the educational facilities, they need to be resident on site, and the school is under an obligation to provide accommodation. The provision of that accommodation is an activity ancillary to the primary purpose and is therefore regarded as exempt.

Extending the exemption – peripheral activities

10.12 There may be trading activities which are predominantly fulfilling a primary purpose of the charity, but include activities which do not wholly satisfy that purpose. The hospital shop with access for the general public may be one example. Another example, which is quoted by the Revenue, is that of a shop in an art gallery or museum which sells a range of goods directly relating to the world of art or which are clearly educational, and which then begins to sell in addition items such as souvenir mugs or T-shirts, which could not, by any stretch of the imagination, be regarded as education. In those situations the Revenue will not regard the basic exemption for the main trade as being prejudiced, and will regard the non-exempt activities as falling within the exemption provided two conditions are satisfied:

(1) the part of the trade which is not within the primary purpose is small in absolute terms;

(2) the turnover of the part of the trade is less than 10% of the turnover of the whole trade.

Exemption for small trades

10.13 As part of the Charity Tax Review, the Revenue decided to extend the statutory exemption for trading to what are referred to in the legislation as 'small trades'. The object of the legislation is to allow charities to carry on some small scale trading through the charity itself rather than incur the costs of creating a limited company to avoid a tax liability. This area has not yet been subject to the Revenue enquiry regime and the comments below set out the basic rules and highlight some of the issues which should be considered.

It must be pointed out that the ability of a charity to trade in an area out-side its objects will be dependent upon the wording of its governing document. The Revenue guidance notes indicate that the Charity Commission have confirmed that where the governing document of the charity is based upon one of the model versions produced by the Commission, a charity may carry on activities which fall within the new tax exemption. The model contains the prohibition of 'any sub-stantial permanent activity', but the Commission are prepared to accept that exempt activity would not fall within this definition. Where the governing document does not follow the Commission models, it would be advisable to check it carefully and make sure that even small scale non-tax exempt trading would not cause a problem.

The new legislation, which is in *Finance Act 2000*, provides an exemption for trading income and also income which would be taxable under Schedule D, case VI where the income is applied solely for the pur-poses of the charity and either:

'(a) the charity's gross income for the chargeable period does not exceed the requisite limit or

(b) the charity had, at the beginning of the period, a reasonable expectation that its gross income for the period would not exceed that limit . . .'

The limits in the legislation are the greater of (a) £5,000 and (b) whichever is the lesser of £50,000 and 25% of all total incoming resources of the charity for the year. Points which charities will need to bear in mind are that:

- the exemption is a single one covering all non-exempt activities;

- the definition of incoming resources will only be relevant up to a total of £200,000, beyond that the £50,000 limit will be applicable;

- the Revenue are going to want to see some evidence before apply-ing the reasonable expectation test.

Exemption for fundraising events

10.14   Up to 5 April 2000 there was an extra statutory concession (C4) which the Revenue operated to exempt from tax the profits on what are termed 'small scale fund raising events'. This covered events such as bazaars, fetes, firework displays, etc. The concession was available pro-vided the events satisfied the following conditions:

(1)   the organisation or charity did not regularly carry on the activities;

(2)   the trading was not in competition with other traders;

(3)   the activities were supported because the public were aware that profits were going to charity;

(4)   the profits were transferred to a charity or otherwise applied for charitable purposes.

The VAT legislation has for a number of years provided exemption for all fundraising events which are not held on a regular basis. Exemption in this case means something very different – VAT is not charged on admission but no VAT can be recovered on expenses.

The Revenue have now amended their concession so that it follows the wording of the VAT exemption, which itself is being slightly amended. The approach now is that if the event qualifies for VAT exemption it will also qualify for income tax exemption, even though the term means something different! It is not clear why the Revenue have not taken the opportunity to make the exemption a statutory exemption rather than a concession.

The really significant change in the impact of the concession is in the size of the event that would qualify. With the new rules there is no size limit whereas in the past the Revenue would probably not have been prepared to stretch the concession to major events. Something like a charity football match at Old Trafford would not have qualified under the old rules but will qualify under the revised concession (unless it is one of at least 16 such games at the ground). The scope for charities in organising major fundraising events with tax-free profits has been considerably increased.

The VAT exemption in *VATA 1994, Group 12, Sch 9* will apply to:

'1. The supply of goods and services by a charity in connection with an event

(a)   that is organised for charitable purposes by a charity or jointly by more than one charity

(b)   whose primary purpose is the raising of money

(c)   that is promoted as being primarily for the raising of money . . .'

As with all VAT legislation in *VATA 1994, Sch 9* there are numerous notes which amplify the meaning of the exemption. Significant among these for the purposes of identifying events which qualify for the tax concession are:

(1)   The scope of an event is defined as including 'an event accessed (wholly or partly) by means of electronic communication'. [*Note 1*]. In other words an Internet event.

(2)   There is a maximum of 15 events of each type at the same location which can be exempt in any financial year of the charity. The limits apply to each charity or branch of a charity but are not to apply to what are referred to as 'small scale' fundraising events. Where a charity has branches the limit will apply separately to each branch as well as the national charity. [*Note 4*].

(3)   An event which brings in gross takings of less than £1,000 a time will be regarded as small scale and the legislation will allow each such event to be held much more regularly, with a maximum of a weekly event. [*Note 5*].

(4)   Exemption will not be permitted where the granting of an exemption would be 'likely to create distortions of competition such as to place a commercial enterprise carried on by a taxable person at a disadvantage'. [*Note 11*].

With careful planning, not least in getting the description and timing of the event right, a charity should be able to make many fundraising events fall within the exemption. The VAT rules do not take account of the size of the event and so it is likely that some events which the Revenue would not previously have regarded as within the extra statutory concession will now be exempt. The issues which charities might need to consider in this area are set out in Part 3.

Events which fall to be exempt under the concession will not count towards the turnover total for the small trading activities discussed earlier, although the turnover will count towards the total of incoming resources.

Enquiries

10.15   The author has seen a number of cases, many involving quite small charities where the Revenue have spent considerable time asking questions about fundraising events and activities. This has involved the charities concerned in having to research answers and also pay for professional advice. It is likely that this type of enquiry will continue as the new regime works its way through and charities need to be prepared to argue their corner.

Moving towards a settlement

The process of negotiation

10.16   Enquiry cases are inevitably going to involve considerable time in researching information, whether about the activities of a charity or its trading company. The purpose of the analysis must always be kept in mind and that will govern the detail of the work required. The paragraphs above give an indication of the key areas of investigation and the comments will help to focus on the areas which will need to be justified.

There will come a point where information has all been provided and hopefully the process can begin of negotiating the significance of the information. It has already been suggested in Chapter 8 that this process is probably best achieved through meetings, and in the author's experience this is an approach that the Inspectors at FICO are very happy to work with.

Just as it is sometimes advisable for the charity to seek independent advice on the subject of the investigation, so from time to time the FICO investigators need to seek advice from their technical specialists. Sometimes this advice will come from the technical advisers in Bootle who form part of the FICO team, but in some areas, particularly in relation to trading, it may be necessary to consult other specialists in the Revenue. For example in one case advice was sought from both the specialist on trading and also the specialist dealing with land transaction and in particular the application of certain anti-avoidance legislation which the FICO investigator thought was relevant. This process takes time, and the investigator should make it clear that there will be a delay whilst this process is pursued.

The result of that approach to specialists may well be that the enquiry closes. In some cases it might be followed by a request for more information. If that is the case, the nature of the information will give a clear guide as to the way the Revenue are moving in their thinking on the point at issue.

Keep the communication lines open

10.17   Throughout all this period it is important to keep the lines of communication open. While collating information communications with FICO should let them know the progress being made. If some information is proving particularly difficult, it may be worth asking just how important it is to the investigation. When the information has all been submitted, some time should be allowed for the investigator to have had a chance to deal with it and then it is worth calling to find out what is happening. If FICO advises that they are seeking advice then it may take several weeks before they get a response and then it will be appropriate to start chasing.

Reaching a conclusion

10.18   Obviously if the Revenue agree that the evidence backs up a particular case, that will bring an end to the enquiry and everyone can go back to a sense of normality. There are, however, three other scenarios which need to be considered:

(1)   Research may demonstrate that the Revenue may have a case after

all and the process becomes one of finalising the tax position in the best way possible and then having to consider the issue of interest and penalties where appropriate. This is discussed in more detail at 10.27 below.

(2)   Research may suggest that the Revenue do not have a case, but they maintain their position and the only way of resolving the issue is to have the matter heard by Special Commissioners. That process was discussed in some detail in Chapter 8 and is picked up again at 10.26 below.

(3)   The third possibility is that all the relevant information has been presented but the investigator persists in continuing with questions without taking any steps to resolve the argument. In that situation the new powers available under self-assessment may need to be considered and a completion application made. That is discussed at 10.19 below.

Completion applications

10.19   The new legislation contains an important provision which can allow the taxpayer to put pressure on the Revenue if they believe that the Inspector is keeping an enquiry going unnecessarily. Given that FICO enquiries are now under the self-assessment regime, that provision is available to charities and should be given serious consideration in circumstances where the investigation seems to be drifting along with no prospect of settlement either by agreement or through a formal hearing. The formal ending of an enquiry is by the issue of a completion notice from the Inspector and this application is a means of forcing that move.

At any time after an officer has given notice under *TMA 1970, s 9A* of an intention to enquire into a self-assessment return, and before the officer has issued a notice of completion of that enquiry under *TMA 1970, s 28A(5)*, the taxpayer has the right to apply to the Commissioners for a direction that the officer should issue a completion notice. The Commissioners are obliged to give such a direction unless they are satisfied that the officer has reasonable grounds for not giving a notice of completion – in other words the onus of proof is on the Revenue to show why they are justified in continuing with the enquiry. The direction must specify the period within which the notice of completion has to be given. [*TMA 1970, s 28A(6)*]. Proceedings under this subsection are to be heard and determined in the same way as an appeal. [*TMA 1970, s 28A(7)*]. This means in practice that either side can appeal to the High Court.

How is the application made?

10.20   The application can be made either direct to the clerk to the Commissioners or to the Commissioners via the district. It is recommended that the former route is used with a copy to the district. Inspectors are told that any application should be given priority.

When should the application be made?

10.21   There is no restriction on when an application should be made or indeed on the number of applications which can be made in any enquiry. There are some dangers in making applications too early or being seen to be persistent in making applications. The following are suggested as guidelines:

- An application should *not* be made immediately on receipt of the section 9A letter. The Inspector has a right to make enquiries and any application to complete will be a waste of time.

- An application should be considered where the Revenue have had detailed replies to letters and/or detailed information and have simply not replied within a reasonable period of time. It may be that they are taking advice (they may use this as a reason for keeping the enquiry open) but even if they are, an application may have the effect of making the specialist move a little quicker.

- An application should also be considered when it is believed that the Inspector has received all the information needed to settle the enquiry but is persisting in his enquiries.

- If an application is to be made, the investigator should be warned of this within a set period of time, say 28 days. That again might cause him to react to the situation and may prevent the need to actually take the hearing. If a hearing does go ahead, it will help to show that reasonable steps have been taken in the process!

The internal guidance given to Inspectors suggests that in most cases they should take the opportunity between receiving the application and having the hearing to process the case to a point where either closure is not a problem, or the Commissioners can be persuaded not to close.

Consequences of a Commissioners' direction

10.22   The giving of a Commissioners' direction under *TMA 1970, s 28A(6)* is not tantamount to the determination of an appeal for years before self-assessment. *Taxes Management Act 1970, s 28A(6)* does not give the Commissioners the right to accept the self-assessment as returned or to suggest any amendment to it. The Commissioners should not express any view as to the completeness or otherwise of the return or quantify any figure to be included in the self-assessment. They should simply, if they consider it appropriate, instruct the officer to complete the enquiry by a specified date.

Inspectors are warned that once the completion has passed they may correspond with the taxpayer or agent but must not make any more enquiries.

Issue of completion statement

10.23   The issue of a completion statement signals the formal end of the investigation. In cases where the Revenue are going to seek interest and penalties, they will continue to use the practice of a settlement by means of a letter of offer, which is discussed below. The *Inland Revenue Investigations Handbook* gives two basic forms of completion statement which can be used:

> **'No amendment to self-assessment necessary**
> 491   Where you have been able to determine that the return (or amendment) is correct and complete your notice of completion should reflect that conclusion. You should write to the taxpayer, with a copy to the agent, if there is one acting, incorporating the following standard terms in your letter.
>
> "Notice of completion under Section 28A(5) Taxes Management Act 1970.
>
> This letter gives notice that I have completed my enquiries into your [199 /9] tax return [into the amendment to your [199 /9] tax return made on . . . .].
>
> I have concluded that no amendment is needed to your self-assessment."
>
> You may of course wish to take the opportunity to add any further appropriate comments; for example, thanking the taxpayer for his or her co-operation, or drawing his or her attention to any points that need to be made (although in some cases these may need to be addressed to the agent instead). Where other years remain under enquiry you should point out that the notice does not affect the position for those years.'

In other cases the following wording will be used:

> 'Notice of completion under Section 28A(5) Taxes Management Act 1970
>
> This letter gives notice that I have completed my enquiries into your [199 /9] tax return [into the amendment to your [199 /9] tax return made on . . . .].
>
> In my opinion the amount of tax which should be included in your self assessment for that year is £ . . . . [I attach a computation showing how I have arrived at this figure [and an explanation of my conclusions]].
>
> An amendment form is enclosed to enable you to amend your self-assessment. You may amend it to the above figure or any other amount which you consider to be correct. Any amendment you make must reach me within 30 days from the date of this notice.

If I have not received your amendment by [date], or if I do not agree with it, I may amend your self-assessment to show the amount of tax which I think is correct. You will be entitled to appeal against any amendment to your self-assessment which I may make.

I have sent a copy of this letter to your agent [name]. You are advised to discuss its contents with him/her before making any amendment to your self-assessment.'

Action after receipt of completion statement

10.24 Where the Inspector's figures are being agreed, the charity should amend its self-assessment to the revised figures within 30 days. There is no standard format for this but it is suggested that it should:

(1) be in writing;

(2) be signed by the taxpayer (or by someone who could validly have signed the return, or someone who would, at the time the amendment was made, have had power to sign the return had it been made then, e.g. someone holding a power of attorney granted in the interim);

(3) give a clear indication of the terms in which the self assessment is to stand amended.

10.25 If the Inspector's figures are not agreed then various options are possible:

(1) Doing nothing – in this case the Inspector will have to issue a Revenue amendment, against which an appeal can be entered together with a postponement application

(2) Amending the self-assessment return including the charity's version of the figures – the Inspector has to decide whether to accept this, in which case he will do nothing further, or to issue a Revenue amendment in the figures he originally proposed. In the latter case an appeal can be entered together with a postponement application.

If it is clear that agreement is not being reached then this is the springboard for resolution of the matter before the Special Commissioners.

Special Commissioners hearing

10.26 Where it is clear that there is a basic disagreement on the points at issue, the use of a Special Commissioners hearing is the only route open to resolve the issue. The details of this approach and how it should be tackled are fully discussed in Chapter 8. It is a route which few charities actually go down (indeed it is a route that few taxpayers actually go down) and there seems to be a general fear about taking it. It is not an option to be taken lightly and obviously issues such as cost need to be taken into account, but it should be given serious consideration.

A number of cases start off down the road towards the Commissioners, but the very thought of going all the way can often bring a resolution of the case. The Revenue realise that there is a cost to them in taking a case and they will not want investigation resources tied up for a period of time on the preparation of a case. It is likely that the Inland Revenue Solicitor will also have to become involved. Asking for a case to be listed makes a statement of seriousness to the Revenue and will often force them to come to the table with a compromise, or to listen to a reasonable compromise. The more you move towards a compromise, the less likely it is that either side will wish to pursue the case to Special Commissioner level.

Settlements involving interest and penalties

10.27   Once the tax has been finally agreed, the settlement process will move on to consider the imposition of interest and penalties and this will involve further negotiation and opportunities to reduce the overall liability to the charity. Interest is largely a 'mechanical exercise' following the agreement of the tax, but the area of penalties is one in which there is plenty of room for argument.

The penalties which might be applicable are explained in Chapter 3 at 3.32 above. All of the penalties, whether for failing to notify chargeability or for errors on a return are tax based, i.e. the maximum penalty is related to the tax which now comes into charge as a result of the error. It is to that maximum that the Revenue apply the so-called abatements which will be discussed at 10.35 below. Before that, however, it is necessary to consider the Revenue's right to charge the interest.

Has an offence been committed

Failure to notify chargeability

10.28   Where the charity has not been issued with a return form and it has subsequently come to light that an exemption which the trustees thought they had, e.g. for trading income, is not actually available, the Revenue will probably seek to argue that the charity is guilty of a failure to notify chargeability. It should be noted that this is a simple offence, there is no requirement for any neglect or fraudulent conduct on the part of the taxpayer. The deadline to notify has passed and that deadline has not been met. Tax is due and a penalty follows.

There is one possible defence which needs to be considered and that is presented by *TMA 1970, s 118(2)* which states:

'. . . where a person had a reasonable excuse for not doing anything required to be done he shall be deemed not to have failed to do it unless the excuse ceased and, after the excuse ceased, he shall be deemed not to have failed to do it if he did it without unreasonable delay after the excuse had ceased.'

In the event of a failure to notify it is necessary to demonstrate the 'reasonable excuse' to avoid any penalty. The *Inland Revenue Investigation Handbook* gives instructions on how to deal with any reasonable excuse claim (extracts from paras 5062 and 5063):

> 'There are no absolute standards by which the words "reasonable excuse" can be defined. Generally, it can be said to be an excuse which sounds reasonable in the mouth of the person giving it, that is, the standard of reasonableness can vary according to the type, education, background etc of the taxpayer concerned. In every case of substance you should ascertain, as far as possible, the taxpayer's own reasons for his failure. This is best done in the course of an interview. The taxpayer, especially if he is unrepresented, must be made aware of the provisions of Section 118(2) TMA 1970 and their potential effect on the settlement. You must, of course, show that you are prepared to listen to the taxpayer and consider carefully what he is telling you.

> You will have to test the taxpayer's explanation against the information you already hold and you will be able to take into account events subsequent to the actual offence:

> Ignorance of the law is not a reasonable excuse. Where, however, the liability turns on a technical consideration which an unrepresented taxpayer might not appreciate . . . or on a disputed point of law, or a debatable view of the facts (for example, property dealing or an illegal activity) you will have to take a realistic view of the taxpayer's actions. The point may often in practice turn on your (or the Commissioners') view of the taxpayer's credibility as a witness.'

The issue which will be central here will usually be whether the charity and its advisers knew, or should have known, that a particular activity was not exempt. If the charity has no professional adviser that might be an easier point to argue, but it is not one which evokes a great deal of sympathy from Inspectors. The author has had a number of arguments with Inspectors over the years that where a liability arises as a result of the taxpayer accepting that they fall the wrong side of a liability line that might be drawn by a tax case and is therefore not clear-cut, no offence of failure to notify has been committed.

In one charity case, mentioned at 10.9 above, involving the transfer of property to a charity at the time of sale, the Revenue were prepared to argue that there had a been a failure to notify chargeability to trading income even though the transferor had returned the capital gains he had made on the disposal of the property. This line was disputed but in the end became irrelevant because the trading argument was dropped.

Charities and their advisers should always be prepared to argue the 'reasonable excuse' defence unless there really is no excuse, e.g. where advice was taken ahead of the event and trading was established. The key will be the extent to which the investigator is influenced by the final sentence in the quote above – how would the case look before the Commissioners?

Fraudulent or negligent conduct

10.29   The issue of 'fraudulent or negligent conduct' will arise in cases where an error has been made on a return. There is no definition in the Taxes Acts of 'fraudulent or negligent conduct' but charities need to be aware that the meaning covers a wide range of possibilities. At one end, fraudulent conduct would involve deliberately creating documents or records to falsify what had actually happened. At the other extreme, one can find a dictionary definition of 'negligent' which refers to 'lacking attention, care or concern'. It is in this latter area that most charities will (hopefully) find themselves. Issues which might fall to categorised in different shades of offence are set out in Chapter 3 at 3.33 above.

Each case must be considered on its merits (or possibly demerits) and the trustees or their advisers must be prepared to argue the point while accepting the reality that negligence is not a particularly heinous crime and can actually arise very easily.

If the eventual tax liability which is agreed relates to the issue of loans from a charity to a trading company which are agreed ultimately to be not for the benefit of the charity, should the Revenue then be able to take a penalty for an incorrect return which did not show the liability? Ignorance of the law is no excuse so the charity is deemed to have been aware of the legislation in *Schedule 20*, but are they guilty of negligent conduct by not recognising that they were not acting for the benefit of the charity when there is no definition of that term?

On the other hand, if the charity is engaged in a major fundraising campaign that operates directly through the charity and involves a wide range of activities that clearly amount to trading, there is little defence if the profit is treated as being exempt from tax when it is clearly taxable. There is sufficient publicity in Revenue and Charity Commission publications about trading for any trustee to be aware of the issue.

Once it is accepted that there is some degree of negligence the consideration turns to the mitigation of penalties where the gravity of the offence is one of the factors to be considered.

Mitigation of penalties

10.30   The law sets out the maximum level of penalty that can be charged, and the Revenue then have the discretion to mitigate that maximum by reference the facts of any case. The basic approach is to start with the maximum penalty of 100% and then to consider three areas of mitigation each of which carry a maximum percentage abatement which is deducted from the full penalty, The areas which are considered are:

- Disclosure – up to 20% abatement

- Co-operation – up to 40% abatement

- Size and gravity – up to 40% abatement

It is important to consider the factors that will influence the level of abatement in any case, so that some planning for penalties can be done at an early stage and appropriate steps taken to influence the Inspector's view.

Disclosure

10.31 The simple rule of thumb is that the more the Inspector finds for himself, the lower will be the abatement. This is why it is important that before the Inspector even comes to the charity, a review is undertaken to see if there are any issues that have been incorrectly dealt with and which need to be disclosed at the start of the first meeting. It is foolish to let the Inspector discover for himself issues which could have been disclosed to him. He may argue that it is only the thought of a visit that has prompted the disclosure and not any free desire on the part of the charity to disclose irregularities, but in the final analysis he will take any disclosure into account.

The guidance given to Inspectors at IH 5530 in the *Inland Revenue Investigation Handbook* is as follows:

'Circumstances will range from the extremes of—

- a complete and voluntary disclosure, made spontaneously by a taxpayer who has not been challenged and who has no reason to fear early discovery (when an extra 10 per cent should be given, making the maximum abatement 30 per cent); to

- no admission of irregularities even though the Commissioners have determined appeals against further assessments in the Revenue's favour (when no abatement for disclosure should be given).

Between these extremes there will be a variety of circumstances calling for differing degrees of abatements, including the following—

- A voluntary and complete disclosure by a taxpayer who has some reason to suspect early discovery;

- Full disclosure on challenge;

- A voluntary disclosure which turns out to be partial;

- Partial disclosure on challenge;

- Denial of irregularities on challenge, but disclosures subsequently made.

The list is not comprehensive and needs to be taken into account together with any other aggravating or mitigating circumstances. If there are no other relevant factors, it may be appropriate to allow 20 per cent for a case within the first two categories, and 5 per cent if the disclosure is very belated under the final category.

The extra 10 per cent abatement where there is spontaneous and complete disclosure will have the effect of franking part of the net penalty remaining after the other two elements have been considered.'

Co-operation

10.32   The key here is how quickly the enquiry proceeds to settlement. The Inspector will take into account the response time in dealing with queries, the willingness to have meetings, the avoidance of deliberate delays, and keeping to agreed deadlines. It is therefore important that where a professional adviser is used, the charity should ensure that they maintain the momentum of the enquiry. The Inspector should not view as lack of co-operation any time spent in reasonable argument on the points at issue – co-operation does not necessarily mean agreeing with everything the Inspector says!

Again the guidance that the investigator is given is in the *Inland Revenue Investigation Handbook* (IH 5535):

'It is not practical to lay down any fixed time limit to govern mitigation. It should, however, be possible to arrive at a relationship between the time that could have been taken and that which has actually elapsed, and between the co-operation which might have been expected and that which has been given. Against this background, you should bear in mind the presence in the case (or the absence from it) of the following features—

- General delay, prevarication and procrastination;

- Concealment of assets, piecemeal disclosures, and truthfulness;

- Number of Commissioners' meetings required to force progress;

- Necessity for making further normal and extended time limit assessments to force progress;

- Use of information powers;

- Persistence in unacceptable stories of gifts, cash hoards, betting wins, etc.;

- Necessity to have the liabilities determined by the Commissioners;

- Irregularities continuing during the course of the investigation;

- Post-appeal delays, for example, having to make an interest determination.

The fact that because a taxpayer has a genuine disagreement with you over the interpretation of a set of facts or the statute or has sought the intervention of Members of Parliament or other "external" authorities should not be regarded as lack of co-operation unless there can be shown to be a deliberate policy of obstruction, accompanied by clear evidence of attempts to mislead those authorities as well as the Revenue.'

Size and gravity

10.33   This will depend on the seriousness of the offence. Any attempt at fraud will be viewed very seriously and will result in a low abatement. At the other extreme, a simple mistake, while it may amount to negligent conduct, can be heavily mitigated. Where the error results in a large sum of tax becoming due, that should not mean a low abatement because that could come from one simple error. Where a large number of mistakes contribute to a large total tax bill, the Revenue may not be disposed to treat the charity lightly in this area.

Revenue guidance reflects that there are degrees of culpability which need to be considered in some kind of step arrangement. The *Inland Revenue Investigation Handbook*, IH 5540 goes on:

'In the normal course the abatement in cases in which fraud cannot be proved should not be less than 15 per cent. The range of abatements for such cases should be taken as 15 per cent to 40 per cent, with the lower figure reserved for the most serious cases in which culpability falls short of fraud, and the abatements for less serious cases scaled up accordingly within the range. A very serious case of negligence only will, therefore, normally qualify for an abatement in the region of, but not less than, 15 per cent. On the other hand, an offence which involves only a minor degree of negligence associated with muddle and confusion might, subject to size and circumstances, rate as much as 35 per cent. It should accordingly be rare for the full abatement of 40 per cent to be given, since normally, the existence of some offence should be reflected in the abatement. There may, however, be the exceptional cases of omissions, for example, where the taxpayer was aged or infirm where it may be appropriate to waive the penalty or include a nominal amount only.'

Putting it all together

10.34   The negotiations in any particular case will have to look at all the details and make realistic assessments of the worth of each in the abatement process. The discussion on penalties will take place usually at a meeting and the planning for that meeting will be important. The issues to consider for such a meeting were discussed in Chapter

8 at 8.45 above. In practice such meetings can take on a farcical air because the Inspector probably has a figure that he is prepared to accept and the charity and its advisers have one which they would be prepared to agree to and in reality the figures are probably not very far apart. There is, however, a ritual that seems to be gone through where the Inspector starts with a higher figure than he is prepared to accept and the charity starts with a lower one. Each chips away and in the end reach the numbers they first thought of. Both go away satisfied that they have negotiated the other up or down as the case may be!

Before going into a meeting it is important to be aware of two things:

- the maximum figure to which the trustees are prepared to go in an overall settlement;

- the value in cash terms of each penalty percentage.

If the Revenue will not come down to the trustees' maximum level there may be a need to adjourn the meeting to consider the options. This can be done by leaving the Inspector and going to another room to discuss the position. It may even be necessary to abandon the meeting altogether and take time to think about it. There is no need to be rushed into agreeing a figure which is considered to be excessive.

Ultimately it is up to the taxpayer to make an offer in settlement and this has to be considered by the Revenue. Usually this will be by a person who is senior to the investigator. If a lower offer is made the Revenue have three choices:

(1) they can accept the lower offer and get the case settled;

(2) they can reject the lower offer and go for a formal penalty determination;

(3) they can try to renegotiate a better offer.

It is always important to look at the situation from the point of view of the maximum amount the trustees are prepared to settle for overall and work back the penalty position from there.

Example
A position is reached where tax has been agreed at £79,000 and interest is agreed at £20,000. The trustees believe that the total settlement should be no more than £115,000. This would give a penalty of £16,000 which would represent 20.2%. If the Revenue are prepared to come down to that level or even lower so much the better. If not the other options to consider will be to:

- make a substandard offer and risk going to Commissioners for a penalty hearing which could lead to a higher figure;

- accept the position and increase the offer to above the Revenue's figure;

- agree to pay a sum that is below the Revenue level but not as high as the Inspector wants.

This latter approach is one that is always worth considering. If the offer is rounded down slightly, say to the nearest £1,000 or £500, the Inspector will usually be reluctant to take any action to seek to increase it.

There are no hard and fast tactics that can be advised in these cases. It comes down ultimately to a combination of the:

- facts of the case;

- willingness to do a deal;

- experience of the Inspector; and

- experience of the adviser or trustees in negotiating.

Penalty determination

10.35   If agreement cannot be reached on the level of penalties, then the investigator has the power to raise what is known as a penalty determination which sets out the figure he wants. This can be appealed against and an appeal hearing taken before the Commissioners who have the right to agree the investigator's figure, reduce it or increase it. There is therefore a downside risk in taking such an appeal.

Planning penalties

10.36   It can be seen that up to 60% of the penalty can be directly influenced by the action of the charity immediately before and during the enquiry, and full advantage should be taken of this in planning strategy for the enquiry. Issues like disclosure and co-operation should be borne in mind. Before contemplating any action the impact it might have on the penalty position should be considered. It might well change the decision.

Letter of offer

The basic letter

10.37   Once agreement is reached in a case where interest and penalties are involved, the Revenue will want to settle the matter using the letter of offer procedure. This is an arrangement which avoids the need to make a number of assessments. The charity agrees to sign a formal letter offering an agreed sum in settlement. This letter is sent to the Revenue and when they respond accepting the offer, the two letters form an enforceable contract.

There are standard wordings for the letter and the Revenue will usually supply a copy for the taxpayer to use. The basic wording for a letter for a company is as follows:

To the Commissioners of Inland Revenue

In consideration of no proceedings being taken against (insert the full style of the company) of (insert the full address of the Registered Office of the company)(hereinafter called 'the Company') in respect of the duties set out in the Statement below, which the Company acknowledges and agrees to be unpaid by reason, wholly or in part, of its default, or in respect of the penalties and interest to which the Company may thereby have become liable under the Taxes Acts, the Company hereby offers in respect of the said duties penalties and interest, the sum of £ . . . . ('the said sum')(of which £ . . . . has already been paid on account)*, to be paid within . . . . days of the date of the letter notifying the acceptance of this offer by you. If the said sum has not been paid by the day specified herein, then interest shall be payable upon any unpaid balance of the said sum, at the rate applicable from time to time for the purposes of Section 86 of the Taxes Management Act 1970 or any amendment or reenactment thereof, from that day. Any such interest shall be paid without deduction of Income Tax.

Statement of Duties unpaid by the Company

Year or accounting period	Duty	Amount

---

* The figure that would be inserted would be the total amount of the offer agreed including tax, interest and penalties.

Similar letters exist for charities which are trusts.

Time to pay

10.38   It is usual for the letter of offer to specify payment within 30 days of the date of the letter indicating Revenue acceptance. There might, however, be scope for some extension of that time limit, but this must be agreed before the letter of offer is signed. Where the charity is looking to pay in instalments, the Revenue will want a significant part of the final sum as a down payment and will also want to charge forward interest to cover the instalments. There are often reasonable grounds for considering a delay in payment, especially if the settlement is going to put a major strain on the cash resources of the charity. The Revenue are not going to wait forever for their cash, but they may be prepared to spread payments over six months with some forward interest. This gives the charity some time to pay, although it must be noted that if an instalment is missed then the whole sum remaining becomes due and payable.

It might even be possible to get a lower overall settlement by using the time to pay argument at an early stage. A high offer to pay over, say, six months could be proposed or as an alternative, a lower offer to pay within the 30 days. It might be worth a shot.

Chapter 11

FICO Audits

The basic approach

11.1 The methods of carrying out audits are described in Chapter 3 at 3.23 above. The inspection visit is followed by the publication of a report which will set out the irregularities, if any are found. Historically, these have centred on the validity of payments under deeds of covenant and to a lesser extent on Gift Aid payments. Following the changes in *Finance Act 2000*, it is likely that in future the arguments are going to focus on the new Gift Aid rules and a few key issues will be identified here. A detailed review of the new rules is in Chapter 6 of *Tolley's Charities Manual*.

The investigation approach must be to look critically at the arguments that are being put forward by the Revenue as to why a payment does not meet the conditions to be a qualifying donation and to see if evidence is available to counter those arguments. It has to be said that paperwork is the key in this area and it is always going to be difficult to argue a case without some written evidence.

New Gift Aid rules in outline

Introduction

11.2 The removal of the Gift Aid limit opens up all payments to the possibility of being treated as qualifying donations, and many charities must have been concerned when the idea was first suggested at the amount of paperwork that was going to be required. In addition, the Government was keen that donors should be able to make qualifying donations in any way which suited them, including by telephone and the Internet. The system of paperwork had to be flexible if the whole arrangement was not going to drown under a sea of paper, or become so unwieldy for charities to operate that they would simply not do so and thus lose the benefits which the new scheme offered.

The new paperwork is based on what is known as the Gift Aid declaration which has a number of significant differences to the old certification system as follows:

(1) The declaration can be in writing or it can be oral with a written record being made.

(2) It can relate to a specific donation, or a series of donations, or all donations or any arrangement that suits the donor.

(3) The charity is able to produce its own version although there are regulations which prescribe certain conditions which must be complied with. The Revenue have produced a model which can be used.

(4) The charity must ensure that it has an audit trail which enables all qualifying donations to be identified in the books from receipt onwards.

The rules are not particularly onerous but they must be complied with and charities will be foolish if they try to take short cuts. Once the system becomes established, charities will find it a much easier arrangement to operate and will be able to maximise the opportunities that the removal of the limit will bring.

The three key essentials which charities using the Gift Aid scheme will need to be sure about are:

● The Gift Aid declarations

● The audit trail

● The possibility of a benefit to the donor

Each of these will be considered in turn.

Gift Aid declaration

11.3 The Gift Aid declaration is the prime record. No repayment claim can be made without it and no matter how much paper is involved it must be obtained and retained. A number of practical issues arise:

(1) Charities need to ensure that they have a system in place for obtaining the declarations where donations are received. This can be important where donors respond to appeals and send in donations by post – there should be some automatic response arrangement to secure a declaration wherever possible. Consideration should also be given to this where large sums are potentially receivable through a sponsored event. One option is to ask the participant to collect in the money and Gift Aid declarations. An alternative would be for the participant to collect the money from their sponsors and then for the charity to follow up individual sponsors with pre-prepared information about Gift Aid and a pre – printed declaration for the donor to return.

(2) Where a charity holds an open-ended declaration it will need to retain that declaration for as long as it is making reclaims in respect of it. Charities could consider setting up a register of Gift Aid declarations which details all open declarations and could include information about the donor including:

    (a) change of name or address details;

    (b) the date the declaration was made;

    (c) the date the declaration was cancelled.

(3) Equally importantly it will need to ensure that it is able to 'capture' all donations made by the donor. Some may be easily identified from direct debits or standing order payments. Cheques can be identified and there must be a system for linking cash payments. It may be sensible have a record of donors for each tax year.

The audit trail

11.4 The Revenue guidance on the new Gift Aid procedures is quite clear:

> 'You must keep sufficient records to show that your tax claims are accurate. In other words, you must keep records that enable you to show:
>
> - an audit trail linking each donation to an identifiable donor who has given you a valid Gift Aid donation, and
>
> - that all the other conditions for the relief are satisfied.
>
> If you do not keep adequate records you may be required to pay back the Inland Revenue tax you have reclaimed, with interest. You may also be liable to a penalty.'

The position is quite clear and has not actually changed with the new rules. The existence of an audit trail has always been a requirement and has been carefully policed by the Revenue in the course of investigations of charity records.

Key elements of the trail

11.5 There is no legal list of what constitutes an adequate audit trail but the Revenue have published some general guidance. Much will depend of course on the size of the charity and the frequency and type of donations it receives. It is possible to identify the key elements in the trail and look at these in more detail to try to provide a guide to charities on the type of records they are keeping.

The audit trail should encompass the following:

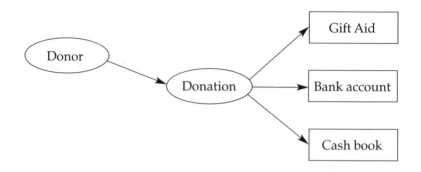

Tying donor to donation

11.6   This is the first key stage. There are two important elements: identifying the donor and clearly linking the donor to the donation.

The donor has to be identified by their name and address – this should present no problem as it is basic information that has to be put on to the written declaration and the written record. There is one situation in which care must be taken and that concerns cheques drawn on a joint bank account where one spouse may be a taxpayer and one not. The Revenue have indicated that in these circumstances they will regard the donor as being the person whose name appears on the cheque, etc. or who authorises the donation by credit card over the phone, so charities should ensure in such cases that it is always the same person whose name appears on the written declaration and that they are a taxpayer.

The link of donor to donation should be relatively easy where payments are by cheque or debit/credit card or by direct debit, because the name of the donor will appear on documentation of some kind. In the case of card donations or direct debit, that information will be on the charity bank statement or on statements received from credit card companies. In the case of cheques it might be advisable to take a copy of the cheque or at least to record the details of the cheque in the records.

Linking cash donations to donor will inevitably be the most difficult area and will be the area that will be scrutinised most carefully by the Revenue. It is therefore important that charities should consider adopting some suitable recording system and at the very least that those who handle cash donations for the charity should be told to ensure that they are meticulous in their recording of the origin of cash donations.

Cash book

11.7   This is a very important record particularly in the context of recording cash donations. Treasurers are going to need to be prepared to record more individual donations in the records to tie into the Gift Aid declarations and also the basic evidence of envelopes, sponsor forms, etc. If they do not want to record every single pound, but prefer to record a total collection, then they must be prepared to have subsidiary records such as sponsor lists or a list of Gift Aided donations showing names of donors. Either route should be acceptable to the Revenue.

Discipline and routine become the key and any individual who might be involved in the recording system, e.g. covering for staff holidays, must be aware of what is required.

Bank account

11.8   There are three important areas to keep a careful watch on

(1)   Bank statements should contain essential information, such as direct debits received, which can identify donors.

(2)   The bank statements will show the total sum banked on any occasion and some record needs to be maintained to ensure that details of all cheques banked are available. These may have been recorded on the paying in slip but this may not be returned by the bank so unless the paying in stub has been competed in full there should be a subsidiary record to show the individual cheques that make up the total banking.

(3)   Where sums are received from credit card companies, the full breakdown of these sums, showing donors' names should be retained.

Benefit to the donor

11.9   The concept of a benefit has been in the legislation since its inception in 1990, although it has to be said it is one of the less understood parts of the Gift Aid rules. Charities should have been looking at it closely in the past but will now need to pay it extra regard given the clear guidance which has been given by the Revenue.

The revised wording of the legislation in *FA 1990, s 25(2)(e)* includes as a condition of a payment satisfying the requirements to be treated as a Gift Aid payment that:

> '. . . neither the donor nor any person connected with them receives a benefit in consequence of making it or, where the donor or person connected with him does receive a benefit in consequence of making it the relevant value of the gift does not exceed the limit imposed by subsection 5A below and the amount to be taken into account for the purposes of this paragraph in relation to the gift does not exceed £250.'

If this condition is infringed, then the whole of the payment made falls to be excluded from the Gift Aid regime. Charities must, therefore, be aware of three important issues:

(1)   What constitutes a benefit?

(2)   Who are individuals who may be 'connected' to the donor?

(3)   What are the values of benefits which will cause a problem?

What is a benefit?

11.10   Benefits can arise in many different ways. At one level a charity may simply wish to give a donor some token of appreciation or acknowledgment for the their donation – that should generally cause few problems. At the other extreme a charity provides a positive incentive to a donor to make a donation – 'if you give us a donation above a certain figure we will give you something which is relatively small in relation to the donation but is nevertheless worth having'. In between comes the complex area of benefits that may result from the membership of a charity.

A benefit could take the form of goods provided. It could be in the form of services rendered. In some instances it could be something even more intangible. For example in the past the Revenue indicated that if an individual donor was released from a deed of covenant to allow them to make Gift Aid payments that could be a benefit because they had been released from a legal obligation. The Revenue have indicated that they will not be pursuing this line in the context of the new regime, but the example serves to illustrate the point.

Possible benefits which might be caught include:

- free or discounted services provided by the charity;

- donations linked to admission to fundraising events;

- benefits of membership (although not in the case of charities involved in preservation of buildings or conservation of wildlife where the benefit consists of right of free admission to view property or wildlife);

- support for charity workers;

- saving tax (in a decided case IHT was saved and that was deemed to be a benefit).

It is important to note that the benefit must be provided 'in consequence of making the gift'. This indicates that there must be a clear link between the making of the gift and the provision of the benefit. The benefit must be received as a consequence of making the gift. There must be some link between the making of the gift and the provision of the benefit, but the benefit does not have to be provided directly by the charity – it could come from a third party.

The phrase also indicates that the order of the events must be gift then benefit. This can be important where someone decides to make a donation to charity as a token of appreciation for some service received by themselves or a relative. For example the family of a patient who has been cared for in an hospice may decide to make a donation to that hospice after the death of their relative. There will be no problem in this case because the benefit which the relative received cannot be argued to be in consequence of the donation. If, however, they were to have made the donation during their relative's lifetime there would be an argument that the benefit of care was received as a consequence of the donation.

One further point to be noted is that there is no time limit between the donation and the benefit. The author has seen a case where an arts charity offered donors a number of benefits including the receipt of free tickets for performances a year and two years ahead. The Revenue confirmed in a discussion on this 'hypothetical case' that they would seek to invoke the benefit rules (assuming that the values were relevant). They also indicated that if the charity had made no mention of the free tickets in the publicity for the donations but had then decided that they would give all donors who gave above a certain level tickets for events there would not have been a problem.

Which individuals are caught?

11.11   If the person making the donation receives a benefit in excess of the limits, the gift is negated for Gift Aid purposes. The legislation goes further, however, and rules out benefits provided to people who are connected with the donor. The definition used is a wide one according to which 'a person' is connected with all of the following: 'An individual who is their wife or husband, or is a relative, or the wife or husband of a relative of the individual or of the individual's wife or husband. Relative means brother, sister, ancestor or lineal descendant'.

How do you value the benefit?

11.12   The test required by the legislation is not that there should be no benefit, but that the value of the benefits which are received in consequence of the gift do not exceed the specific limits. Before considering what those limits are, it is important to consider how a benefit is actually valued – in some cases this may be relatively easy, in others it will not. The Revenue guidance is not particularly helpful. It identifies the issue of goods or services provided to the public by the charity or someone else and makes the obvious point that an arm's length market value can be used. For example a theatre ticket given in return for a donation will have a clear market price, so does a meal provided at a gala dinner.

The basic value limits are imposed by a new *subsection 5A* inserted into *FA 1990, s 25*. These limits are banded as follows

Amount of donation	Value of benefits
Up to £100	25% of the value of the gift
£101 to £1,000	£25
Over £1,000	2.5% of the gift

These limits apply to each donation, and if they are exceeded, that donation fails to qualify as a Gift Aid donation. So, in simple terms, if a charity decided to hold a gala dinner and charged each person £50, the sums paid would not qualify for Gift Aid unless the actual value of the dinner which each person received was less than £12.50. That might be acceptable if the dinner concerned was a simple bread and cheese meal, but would probably not qualify if the dinner was at a four star hotel.

The limit used in the old legislation was 2.5% of the value of the gift with no banding so there is some improvement in the position for donations of under £1,000.

The new rules go further, however, and require a charity to annualise the value of benefits in certain cases. There is also an overriding limit of £250 which applies to aggregate donations from the same donor in the same tax year. These provisions will be considered in more detail.

Impact of annualisation

11.13   The concept of annualisation is introduced by a new *subsections 5B to 5D* in *FA 1990, s 25*.

Subsection 5B states that:

'where a benefit received in consequence of making a gift—

(a) consists of the right to receive benefits at intervals over a period of less than twelve months;

(b) relates to a period of less than twelve months; or

(c) is one of a series of benefits received at intervals in consequence of making a series of gifts at intervals of less than twelve months,

the value of the benefits shall be adjusted for the purposes of subsection 4 above and the amount of the gift shall be adjusted for the purposes of subsection 5A above.'.

In these circumstances both the value of the benefit and the value of the gift are annualised for the purposes of applying the *subsection 5A* limits.

Subsection 5C deals with another possible variation:

'Where a benefit, other than a benefit which is one of a series of benefits received at intervals, is received in consequence of making a gift which is one of a series of gifts made at intervals of less than twelve months, the amount of the gift shall be adjusted for the purposes of subsection 5A above.'

In this case it is the value of the gift which must be annualised but not the value of the benefit.

It is possible to summarise the four situations where annualisation is necessary as follows:

Category	Gift	Benefit
1	Single	Several received over an interval of less than 12 months
2	Single	Single but related to a period of less than 12 months
3	Series over less than 12 months	Series at intervals
4	Series over less than 12 months	Single benefit

Negotiating on single site audits

11.14   Where the FICO audit looks at a single charity it will be a matter for the trustees of that charity to negotiate a settlement with the Revenue. The actual review may have taken account of just one year but the Revenue may seek to use it to go back over a number of years and to review the repayment claims made. There are two areas for argument in this case.

Firstly why should particular payments be allowed? Obviously this will depend on the facts and the evidence available. Look carefully at the arguments that are being advanced and see how they might be rebutted. Issues relating to the audit trail and identification may be provable in other ways. It may be possible to reduce the potential value of benefits below the limit in the legislation or indeed to argue that there is no benefit at all.

The second stage is to consider the carry-back of the consequences of the first year. This should be relatively easy in the first few years of the new Gift Aid scheme because it is likely that there would not have been the level of Gift Aid donations in earlier years. This might remain an argument once the scheme moves forward. The other significant argument will always be that the issues found in the first year are peculiar to that year and would be unlikely to have been found in earlier years.

This could be the case, for example, with particular benefits received by some donors because the benefit was not available in the earlier years. The aim is to minimise the potential base that is being used for the carry-back calculation.

11.15

Example

The Revenue visit a church for an audit in 2005. The total tax reclaims in the last tax year 2004/05 amounted to £13,500. The auditor reviews all of these and finds some irregularities. These include:

- A donation of £500 (tax £140) made to support a church member going to Bible College. The donation, however, came from the individual's sister and should not qualify under the benefit rules

- Three donations where repayment was claimed but there is no evidence in the church accounts that enables the donor to be identified. The tax on these totals £800.

The auditor decides that on the basis of his review he wants £940 back from the church for 2004/05. He also decides that as the error rate is 7% (940 on 13,500), he is going to require repayment of a similar percentage of the tax repaid on claims for 2000/01, and subsequent years. The tax repaid in those four years totalled £40,000 and the auditor is looking for a settlement of £2,800 plus the £940.

The treasurer cannot argue about the benefit point for 2004/05 but he does make the point that there is clear evidence to show that there were no payments of a similar nature made in earlier years because the student in question only went to college in that year and no other student has been supported in a similar way. Of the other three payments, he manages to find evidence in the books of one of the payments because the donor is able to identify the precise date on which they made the payment by information from their own bank details. This is for tax of £280.

The impact of these adjustments is that the tax due for 2004/05 becomes only £660 and the sum to be used for extrapolation is only £520 or 3.8%. This reduces the reclaim for earlier years to £1,520.

Negotiating on multiple sites

11.16 It is noted in Chapter 3 that in some cases the Revenue have adopted a policy of dealing with audits on a sample basis. These are situations where one body, possibly a diocese, makes repayment claims on behalf of some or all of the churches in the diocese. This saves the individual churches making the claims and also reduces the number of claims the Revenue have to check through the repayment process. The audit approach which they like to agree is that they will visit a sample of churches and then want to extrapolate the results of the sample not only down the years, as in the example above, but also across the whole sample. There is no statutory basis for this – it is simply saving the Revenue time and money – but it could be an approach that is very expensive for the claim-making charity. The charity should actually consider very carefully if it is willing to accept this approach because, as the example below shows, it can have a significant impact on the central organisation and also possibly on charities that have been impeccable in their compliance.

The basic Revenue view is that if the sample is reasonable, any errors found can reasonably be extrapolated. This ignores basic rules of sampling error and makes the sweeping assumption that the same types of mistake must have been made across the sample. This may be true when looking at a machine process which might make errors but in this case individual claims are involved, recorded by a significant number of individual treasurers all of whom are aware of the system.

It is the author's view that charities in this situation should think very carefully before they agree to a sample approach like this. If the Revenue are not prepared to visit all the locations included in the claim then any extrapolation should be limited to the venues covered in the sample and not the whole population. After all, that would be the situation if each charity was visited individually.

Consider this example which is based on an actual case (names changed to protect the innocent).

Example
Barchester Diocese submitted a repayment claim on behalf of some 400 churches in the diocese. The claims made each year were as follows:

1993/94	£1,498,356
1994/95	£1,490,702
1995/96	£1,445,940
1996/97	£1,359,031
1997/98	£1,295,773
1998/99	£1,327,084
	£8,416, 886

The Revenue decided to sample check the claim for 1998/99 and it was agreed by someone representing the diocese that 15 churches should be visited and that an extrapolated result would be obtained. The visits took place and the auditors report was received. This showed the following results:

	Claim	*Errors*	*IR (%)*
Church 1	23,266	0	0.00
Church 2	11,666	0	0.00
Church 3	8,042	574	7.14
Church 4	15,474	92	0.59
Church 5	9,628	201	2.09
Church 6	15,167	369	2.43
Church 7	31,398	189	0.60
Church 8	12,968	0	0.00
Church 9	5,749	98	1.71
Church 10	14,732	457	3.10
Church 11	9,953	0	0.00
Church 12	13,486	222	1.65
Church 13	9,075	0	0.00
Church 14	12,224	219	1.79
Church 15	8,647	157	1.82
Total	201,475	2,578	1.53

On the basis of this sample, the repayments for earlier years were to be reclaimed to the extent of 1.53%, which meant a total repayment of £128,778.

The first point to note is that the Revenue percentage of 1.53% is the average percentage in the cases where errors were found. If the total value of errors is taken as a percentage of the total gross reclaim from the sample churches then the real error rate drops to 1.28% and the claim by the Revenue falls to £107,736, a drop of £21,000 which is more than significant. The Revenue argued for the validity of their original percentage but conceded the lower percentage after discussion. If a sample is to be used the results must be based on the whole sample not just the 'guilty' part of the sample.

Subsequent close scrutiny of the errors and some extra work by the centre enabled the Revenue to agree that the revised total error figure should be only £1,892, a percentage of 0.94%, reducing the total claim to £79,118.

Overall the negotiations reduced the Revenue claim by almost £50,000, but there remained a significant problem for the centre. They had to find the tax – the question was whether to take this out of some central fund or to seek redress from all the churches for whom they made the return. Spread over all 400 churches the cost would be £200 a church, but some churches which were not in the sample (and those that were shown by the sample to be all clear) could justifiably say that they had no liability. Why should they pay up for what is a statistical not a proven charge?

Moving to a settlement

Finalising the tax

11.17   In audit cases as we have seen above the usual approach of the Revenue is to go back over a six-year period, assuming of course that repayment claims have been made throughout that period. Their right to do so stems from their legal right to raise assessments within what is known as the ordinary time period. For accounting periods up to June 1999, the ordinary time limit was six years of assessment, now the limit is expressed as 'any time not later than five years after the 31st January next following the year of assessment to which it relates'.

So for a reclaim relating to 1999/00 the ordinary time limit will run to five years from 31 January 2001 and will therefore expire on 31 January 2006. Under the old rules the time limit for 1999/00 would have run to 5 April 2006.

The time limit is extended by TMA 1970, s 36 where there is fraudulent or negligent conduct:

> 'An assessment on any person (in this section referred to as 'the person in default') for the purpose of making good to the Crown a loss of income tax or capital gains tax attributable to his fraudulent or negligent conduct or the fraudulent or negligent conduct of a person acting on his behalf may be made at any time not later than 20 years after the 31st January next following the year of assessment to which it relates.'

This does of course mean that arguments about whether the charity is guilty of fraudulent or negligent conduct become significant if the Revenue are seeking to go back more than six years.

It is worth keeping a check on the assessment position in these cases because the Revenue can sometimes be caught out. Take the example used at 11.16 above. The earliest year that the Revenue have included is 1993/94. This particular year was in fact when the enquiry started, but the Revenue did not take any steps to protect their position for that year by raising an estimated assessment. (The practice of making protective assessments has been common in long running investigation cases for many years.) Once 6 April 2000 passed, the year 1993/94 fell 'out of date' and can only then be assessed under the extended time limit rule. The Revenue may believe that they have the power to do this because of the errors found, but ultimately they might have to defend that position in front of the Commissioners and also defend their approach on extrapolation. The point is worth making that the year 1993/94 should be excluded from the offer, to see what reaction that provokes from the Revenue.

Dealing with penalties

11.18   The issues relating to identifying whether there has been fraudulent or negligent conduct are discussed in Chapter 10 and the same broad issues apply to the settlement of FICO audits as to general FICO enquiries. Where mistakes have been made in repayment claims because of inefficiencies in the audit trail or because of benefit issues relating to the donor, the Revenue are going to argue that neglect has occurred. If a charity was caught having made clearly false repayment claims they could expect the Revenue to take a very serious view of the position.

When considering the mitigation of penalties, again the question of disclosure becomes important. Getting that in at the start of the audit visit can make a significant difference. Co-operation is particular to the circumstances of the investigation and one should always aim to get as near the 40% abatement as possible. The size and gravity abatement ought in most cases to be at least 30% unless something has gone very seriously wrong. Overall a 10%–15% penalty would be acceptable.

Letter of offer

11.19   In most cases where interest and penalties are involved, the Revenue will look to resolve the case by means of a letter of offer because this will save the paperwork of raising assessments for each year. The basic format of the letter of offer and other issues are dealt with in Chapter 10.

Chapter 12

Inland Revenue Employer Compliance

A variety of problems

12.1   The difficulty with employer compliance visits arises from the range of problems encountered! Every charity is different in terms of its workforce and the nature of payments that it makes. The activities of the charity may cause particular problems, e.g. the use of casual labour for performances or the problems of sending employees overseas. This section deals with the practical approach to some general problem areas that may feature in an employer compliance visit on a charity. Specific detail is available in Chapter 10 of *Tolley's Charities Manual* and some of the practical questions which charities should consider are set out in Part 3.

The general issues which will be considered here are:

- Problems with categorisation – is someone an employee or self-employed?
- Dealing with casual labour
- Payments and expenses
- Benefits in kind

Problems with Categorisation

12.2   The issue of whether a person engaged by the charity has to carry out work for it is an employee or a self-employed worker arises quite often on employer compliance visits. The use of 'consultants' has become commonplace, but the problem can arise in other areas as well. The status of a fundraiser and the status of an event organiser are both current issues. The use of one-man companies had become a problem and remains a problem for the person behind the company under the new so-called IR35 provisions, but it is no longer a problem for the user of the services and is not therefore an area which needs to be considered.

Identification

12.3   The question of status is one that the employer should not duck. It is vital that any situations where categorisation could be an issue should be highlighted at an early stage and a decision taken. It must be acknowledged that in many instances, it will be the erstwhile employer who instigates the move to self-employed status, because it saves the costs of the secondary (employers') NIC, which represents a real over-head to the employer.

A statement from a worker that he is self-employed, even if supported by a letter from his accountant, needs to be carefully considered but should not be accepted without question. It is possible that the circum-stances of the engagement in one particular situation may be very different from the norm, and each case must be considered on its own merits. What matters are the terms of the charity's relationship with the individual – they may be different to other working relationships and may mean that a different status is appropriate.

Obtaining advice

12.4   If in any doubt a ruling should be sought from the local Inspector. A full statement of the facts should be provided, even if some of them are not very helpful to the argument. If it turns out that the authorities have been misled, they cannot be expected to take a sympa-thetic view if they look closely at the situation in later years.

Tax offices are required to have an Inspector who is to be the 'nominated status officer' and whose task is to ensure that all cases requiring a ruling are dealt with by him. Instructions are clear that any decision made in writing is binding on the Revenue. The Revenue will not con-sider themselves bound by a decision where incomplete or misleading information was provided or where the facts have changed materially since the last ruling was made. In those circumstances they would feel entitled to backdate any change either to the date of the first decision or to the time when the material change occurred. Where the first ruling is regarded as being technically incorrect, the Revenue will seek to change it for the future but will accept the position for past years. The Revenue will not regard themselves as bound in any situation where a formal ruling has not been sought but the taxpayer has simply assumed a self-employed status.

In the meantime the charity should make it clear to the worker that advice is being sought, and until such time as a definitive ruling is received, tax will be withheld at the basic rate when payment is made. This does not have to be paid over to the Revenue, but could be held in a separate account so that if a positive ruling is received it can be paid to the worker, and in the event of a negative ruling funds are available to pay to the Revenue. If this route is not appropriate, some indemnity should at least be obtained from the worker that he or she will meet any tax due.

How will the problem be spotted?

12.5   Initial questioning may already have revealed that the charity uses self-employed labour, and the compliance officer may ask for specific information about payments made, and the circumstances of the engagement. Evidence of payments to 'contractors' will be available through a review of petty cash and creditor control procedures. Regular cash payments to individuals who are not employees will excite the attention of the compliance officer. Invoices on scrappy pieces of paper for 'consultancy services rendered' will make him dig deeper.

Dealing with the dispute

12.6   Having identified that there is a potential problem, the compliance officer will want to see evidence of the arrangements between the employer and the 'consultant', and to have full details of the amounts paid. The matter should then be referred by the compliance officer to the Inspector in the district that deals with the employer's tax affairs. An compliance officer has no authority to come to a decision on the status of a worker, and any attempt by them to do so should be resisted.

Once aware that the papers have been sent to the Inspector, it is advisable to either write to the Inspector or ask for a meeting to discuss the position. At the very least the charity's version of events should be set out at an early stage. The compliance officer may have made some mention of the charity's arguments in his submission, but he may not necessarily present those arguments with any real force.

In dealing with the Inspector the factors which are relevant to the question of status need to be considered and these are explained in more detail in Part 3. Each case must be considered on its own facts and it may be necessary to consult the individual concerned for further information. Bearing in mind that the circumstances under which they are engaged by other people may be very different to the circumstances of their engagement with the charity, a statement from the person or their accountant to the effect that they are self-employed cannot be wholly relied upon. The significant issues which are relevant in the case should be identified and those that give greatest support to the charity's arguments should be stressed while those that go against, should be minimised. It is a question of weighing up the arguments to find the factors that will help and others that will hinder.

If the Inspector can be convinced that the individuals concerned are genuinely self-employed, it is vital to obtain his written agreement to that situation. If he does not move from a position of regarding the individuals as employees then the strength of the case must be assessed and a decision taken as to the appropriate course of action from three possibilities:

- Agree the position

- Negotiate a compromise settlement

- Fight the point

Consequences of agreeing

12.7   In the worst case situation, if gross payments to a 'worker' who is in fact an employee, the employer will be required to account for tax and Class 1 NICs on all payments made notwithstanding they have no right to recover tax or NIC from the individual, and also ignoring the fact that the individual may have paid tax under Schedule D on that income. This stems from the basic requirement in *ICTA 1988, s 203, s 203 ICTA 1988* that the payer of income assessable under Schedule E has an obligation to deduct tax on the making of the payment. By accepting that the payment was of income assessable under Schedule E, the onus is on the employer to deduct tax. The Revenue will be able to go back up to six years, and include any payments made within that period. The precise calculation can be done on two bases, which could be described as a worst case scenario, and a worse worst case scenario.

(1)   Under the 'worst case scenario', the Revenue accept that the payment made represents the gross payment and calculate accordingly. If the payment was £100, then the calculation would assume that income tax has been deducted of £22 (at the 2000/01 basic rate of tax), employee's NICs of roughly £10, and employer's NICs of roughly £12. So in this situation, the total cost of using the 'consultant' has risen from £100 to £145.

(2)   Under the 'worse worst case scenario' the Revenue will argue that if the individual was paid £100, given that tax and NICs should have been deducted, it should represent a net sum. The calculation would then proceed on the basis that the gross sum paid was £130, leaving the employer with the responsibility of now paying over income tax of about £29, employee's NICs of about £13 and employer's NICs of about £16 – a total additional cost to you of about £58. It follows that this route should be resisted at all costs; the calculations should be carefully checked to make sure that it is not being slipped through.

Negotiating a compromise

12.8   If the employer has a weak case, they should put forward the argument that they will accept that the individuals concerned, who are still working for them, will be immediately treated as employees and that PAYE will be applied from the next payment. They should also offer to provide full details of all amounts paid to these individuals in the past so that the Revenue can ensure that they account for tax on that income. This approach has been adopted frequently in the past by Inland Revenue Special Officers, where they have done major investigations in the categorisation area. It reflects their view that they would rather seek a future income stream for the Revenue, than risk losing income by forcing an employer into financial difficulties, and even liquidation, by imposing a charge that could go back six years. The employer compliance officer may not be so enthusiastic, but it is an argument that should be pursued as part of an overall negotiated settlement.

Fighting the point

12.9   If an agreement cannot be reached, then the Inspector will need to raise a formal determination under Regulation 49 of the *PAYE Regulations*. This will either specify payments to particular individuals, or to a group of individuals, if the argument is one which affects a number. A determination is usually made for a tax year, and will be a determination of an amount of tax due. That determination is then treated as an assessment, and you should appeal against it and seek full postponement of the tax charged.

The dispute will be resolved by taking the argument to the General Commissioners. The employer will almost certainly need the co-operation of the individuals whose status is being contested, and it is important to ensure that this will be forthcoming before proceeding down this route. If the employer wins the case, that will usually end the matter. If the case is lost, the employer will of course have to pay the tax due, and there will also be an interest charge to pay, because a *Regulation 49* determination carries interest from 19 April after the year to which the determination relates, irrespective of when the assessment was actually raised.

Casual labour

The basic problem

12.10   Where an employer uses a large amount of casual labour, the problem of categorisation can take on a different dimension. It is easy to disregard casual labour by making the assumption that since there is probably no contract of employment, and since the period of engagement is usually for a short period of time, the individuals can be treated as self-employed and paid gross. The fact is that the short term engagement needs to be considered in just the same way as a long-term engagement, and if the factors point towards an employment, the casuals should be treated as such.

The paperwork involved in hiring casual labour is substantial, and the excuse is usually given that it is an unnecessary burden for short period engagements. Potentially that is a very expensive mistake, which could in theory cost £300 each time it is made.

The PAYE compliance officer will often spot the problem from the cash book, where a large number of cash payments may be shown as being made on a weekly basis, often with no receipt for them. The problem is common in businesses which use a large amount of seasonal labour, e.g. in summer, or at Christmas, or in the retail and service trades, particularly catering establishments and pubs. PAYE compliance officers going into such businesses will be aware of this and will be on the look out for consequent irregularities.

P46 procedure

12.11   The procedure for dealing with casuals is well set out in the Revenue publications available to employers. In the majority of cases, the individual coming to work will not have a P45, and therefore the procedures in *Regulation 28* will apply concerning form P46. This form has to be submitted by the employer.

Special rules apply where a student is being engaged during vacation periods. In that case, the employer should obtain a P38S signed by the student, which will allow payment to be made gross. It should be noted that this procedure is not applicable for weekend work by students who are at school during the week. In those cases the P46 procedure should be adopted.

Quantifying the problem

12.12   Assuming that the argument on employment status is lost, the painful part of the investigation will come in quantifying the tax liability. The compliance officer will usually compute a figure for one year based on the year reviewed, and should take into account the presence in the casual labour force of individuals who are not taxpayers, e.g. students. The calculation will then be taken back over a period of up to six years. When these figures are presented, the criteria which are being applied should be critically considered to see if they can be challenged. The strength of any challenge will depend very much on the evidence available. In particular the following factors should be considered:

- The development of the business – has it grown over the period or contracted, and how quickly? The movement may well have a bearing on the demand for casual labour.

- The pattern of the business – have activities changed over the years, particularly those which might use casual labour?

- What is the make up of the casual workforce – students, married women – and has this changed over the years

Cash payments and expenses

How are they discovered?

12.13   The compliance officer will usually go through a wide range of questions about the various allowances and cash payments, in the course of the opening part of the visit. This will enable him to identify areas that are going to be worth further investigation. If a staff hand-book or other similar publication exists, that may prove helpful to the compliance officer. Otherwise he will identify the cash payments made from his review of the cash book, and very often the petty cash vouch-ers. Items such as receipts for sandwich lunches are often found in this way.

The compliance officer will also want to see a standard expenses claim form, if such a thing exists, and will want to cover the procedure for authorising expenses claims. He may gain substantial amounts by focusing his review on the expenses claims of directors and other senior management, where the scrutiny may not be as rigorous as for ordinary employees. Again he will want to be aware of any standard expense amounts for subsistence, mileage, etc.

Resolving disputes

12.14   Once the main fieldwork has been completed and problem areas have been identified, arguments need to be resolved as to whether particular cash payments are taxable at all, or if taxable are wholly allowable. The starting point must be to go back to the basic principles discussed above and to ask whether the payments represent emolu-ments or earnings.

It is important that in any situation where a cash payment is being con-sidered for something which is not a normal part of the employees' duties, careful consideration should be given to the possibility of the payment being taxable. In fact it may be advisable to start from the premise that it would be taxable, and then to find a route to make it non-taxable. It is dangerous to adopt the approach that the term *ex gratia* can be translated as 'not taxable'.

The following approach should be adopted:

(1)   Is there any contractual obligation to make the payment? If yes, then it must be taxable.

(2)   Even if there is no contractual obligation on the part of the payer to make the payment, it is necessary to consider whether any

connection exists between the payment and the duties of the job.

> 'the test is whether, from the standpoint of the person who receives it, (the payment) accrues to him by virtue of his office; if it does it does not matter whether it was voluntary or whether it was compulsory on the part of the payer.' (*Herbert v McQuade, 4 TC 489*).

(3)   The money does not have to come from the employer, it can be paid by a third party, e.g. a customer as a tip. In this situation there will be no PAYE obligation on the employer, but there could be a requirement to notify the Revenue on form P35 that a payment has been received from a third party.

(4)   A payment will be treated as a profit arising by reason of the office or employment when it comes without any special conditions being laid down and without any regard to the personal circumstances or qualities of the employee.

Does section 198 apply?

12.15   If one accepts that the payments are taxable, the next step is to consider whether a *section 198* claim would succeed. This section is the basic expense section for Schedule E, but it is notoriously strict and a very difficult section to get around as many have found. Some of the expenses payments made, e.g. for travel expenses, often come under close scrutiny. The area of travel expenses has changed substantially in recent years and there are a number of important issues, such as what constitutes the workplace, which may be relevant. These issues are highlighted in Part 3.

Are the figures realistic?

12.16   Where the item under review is an expense payment, the key question to consider is how realistic the figures are. Is there a profit element and if so how much? How do the figures compare to published figures, e.g. civil service rates?

Is there scope for a concession?

12.17   If detailed technical arguments are getting tenuous, but it is strongly felt that the expense really is one which should incur no tax liability, it is worth checking to see whether the payments could fall within the scope of a published concession. If not, it might be worth considering whether there is a case for pressing for some form of concessionary treatment. After all, the existing extra statutory concessions were created in response to specific situations which merited special treatment.

Benefits in Kind

Identifying problem areas

12.18   The probing at the initial meeting will identify some areas of benefits that are going to be the subject of investigation. Others will arise from a review of purchase ledger items, including a review of invoices paid. One would expect to find few benefit problems within a charity, but from time to time issues do arise on matters such as the provision of accommodation, the provision of cars and possibly of other assets as well. If the charity allows the use of a credit card by senior employees it can expect that those bills will also attract close scrutiny.

Dealing with disputes

12.19   There will usually be considerable difficulty in arguing that benefits are not potentially taxable, given the wide scope of the legislation. The argument will have to centre on claiming that *section 198* is really in point and that the whole expense is a business expense.

It may be necessary to involve the employees or directors concerned in providing information, and they may take exception to this, particularly where they regard the company as being their own possession. Such situations need to be dealt with carefully but firmly, with the tax position being carefully explained.

The employer's duty

12.20   The duty of the employer is to identify the benefits and expenses and make a return of them on a P11D. They have no liability to pay any tax, and can tell the Inspector to arrange to raise assessments on all employees affected. The Revenue may argue that this will create a bad impression for their employees, who have received the benefits believing them to be tax free. The employer may decide to accept this argument and to accept liability to pay the employee's tax which will be calculated on a 'grossed-up' basis (see 12.21 below). But they do not have to be blackmailed into this approach and may decide that it is cheaper in the long run to let the employees know that they will face a liability and leave the Revenue to get on with the task of raising assessments. It can be argued that a charity, in particular, has no obligation to pick up employees' tax liabilities and that to do so would represent non-charitable expenditure.

Grossing up

12.21   Where grossing up is to apply, the Revenue assume that the value of the benefit given was net of tax, and so the tax liability that you have agreed to pay must be calculated on the net sum grossed up. The key is to establish the rate at which the grossing up should take place. Strictly the calculation should be done on an employee by employee basis to take account of individual tax rates. The Revenue may decide to calculate an overall figure based on a grossing up at either 40% or an 'average rate'. This should be challenged if a significant number of employees are in fact basic rate taxpayers.

The Revenue calculations proceed in three steps:

(1)   Value of benefit × tax rate = tax due

(2)   Tax due × (100/(100 – tax rate)) = grossed-up tax

(3)   Grossed-up tax × NICs rate = NICs due

The employer will be asked to pay the aggregate of (ii) and (iii). The Revenue will argue that the NIC liability arises because the employer is meeting a pecuniary liability of the employee, but this is debatable. It can be argued that a tax liability can only arise when an assessment has been issued, and in this case no assessment is being raised, in fact the employee, whose liability is supposedly being met, will be totally unaware of what is being agreed.

The overall settlement

12.22   There may be a number of issues involved in each investigation and the overall settlement that the Revenue will be looking for will be the aggregate of the individual items. In many instances the employer will be shocked at what the total can be.

Moving to a conclusion

Introduction

12.23   Once all the fieldwork and subsequent discussions on areas of dispute have been concluded, the Revenue will want to move the case towards a final settlement. There are a number of possible routes that this process can take, depending on the precise facts of each case, and which part of the employer compliance operation has been involved in the enquiry.

●   Failure to operate PAYE on employee remuneration – normally the responsibility of offices taking combined or PAYE only reviews and can include penalties.

●   Employee benefits – normally the responsibility of offices undertaking combined or Schedule E only reviews. Usually recovered by voluntary settlement with the employer with no interest or penalty.

●   Total or partial failure to operate PAYE on directors' remuneration – responsibility of offices conducting combined or Schedule E only reviews, may be settled by a Class VI settlement on the employer.

Non-recovery cases

12.24   There will be situations where all that comes to light in the course of the review is the fact that certain taxable benefits are being paid to employees for the first time, or the employer is proposing to make certain payments but is unsure about the tax treatment of those payments. In such cases, the Revenue will usually provide advice to the employer on the appropriate treatment to be given to the item. This will almost certainly be given verbally at the end of the field visit, but officers are instructed to provide written confirmation of any advice given, and employers should always ask for this. The employer than has some protection if on a later visit, a Revenue officer seeks to take a different view on the same point.

Open year adjustments

12.25   In smaller cases, it is possible that the only irregularities that are found relate to years for which no P35 has as yet been submitted at the time the review starts. This will normally mean that the irregularities relate to the actual tax year in which the review is taking place. It might also cover the immediately preceding year where the review visit takes place early in the tax year. Where the irregularities relate to cash payments being taxable, the Revenue will instruct the employer to make amendments to the deduction working sheet for either the last payment date for the current year or the final payment date for any earlier year.

Class 6 Settlements

12.26   Where it becomes clear that liabilities to tax on the employer are going to arise for a number of years, the Revenue will seek a different type of settlement which is based on a contract. This will also be used where in addition to tax, interest and penalties are going to be sought. The formal process is to seek a settlement by way of a formal letter of offer from the taxpayer which is accepted in writing by the Revenue. This exchange of letters then creates a legally enforceable contract which allows the Revenue to seek legal redress in the event of non-payment. The background to letters of offer is set out in Chapter 10.

The term 'class 6' is simply Revenue terminology and distinguishes a settlement on an employer from other types of investigation settlement.

Mitigating the penalty

12.27   The process of penalty mitigation for employer compliance cases is based on the same approach as for any Revenue investigation and again the details set out in Chapter 10 are relevant. The components of:

● Disclosure

- Co-operation

- Size and gravity

are the same. The *Inland Revenue Employer Compliance Manual* sets out some specific points that their compliance officers should bear in mind on abatement.

Disclosure

12.28 The Revenue guidance states that officers should take account of:

- whether the employer disclosed irregularity before they became aware that a visit was planned (a complete disclosure at this stage would justify a full 30% abatement);

- whether the employer made an immediate and full disclosure during the preliminary interview of irregularities which would not have been easily detected from the records (such an admission would qualify for a high abatement whereas piecemeal admissions as the review progressed would earn an appropriately reduced abatement);

- the extent of the disclosure (partial disclosures, say, where the full duration of an irregularity or all the individuals involved are not disclosed, will clearly earn a lesser abatement than full and complete disclosures).

The importance of considering a disclosure is emphasised yet again.

Co-operation

12.29 Guidance given to officers in the Revenue manual suggests that they should take into account the following

(1) the contribution made by the employer/contractor and/or agent to a prompt conclusion of the review, e.g. making early appointments and keeping to them, allowing unhindered access to records and so on;

(2) whether there was any attempt to conceal material facts or to mislead;

(3) the degree of acknowledgment of PAYE/NIC/SC failings (a rational difference of opinion, e.g. a status dispute, is not a lack of co-operation);

(4) help given with the extraction of data from records;

(5) the degree of reasonableness in agreeing to estimated computations;

(6) whether delays or prevarication on the part of the employer/contractor may necessitate formal recovery action, e.g. *SI 1993 No 744, Reg 49* determinations

(7)   whether, and if so at what stage, the employer/contractor 'came
clean'. Untruths during the preliminary interview would be difficult to redeem after irregularities had been discovered from the
records. *(Note: it is arguable that this is really a matter of discovery and
you should ensure that the Revenue do not seek to restrict abatement
twice for the same reason.)*

Gravity

12.30   The range of possible areas of investigation in employer compliance cases can make this a difficult area in which to identify the
degree of size and gravity. Revenue officers are told that there are a
number of general factors which they need to consider:

- The nature and seriousness of the irregularities. Where errors have
  been made as a result of an incorrect interpretation of the law, particularly if that was a grey area of law, this will be viewed less
  seriously than a deliberate, wholesale fraud or a situation where
  the employer has blatantly failed to act correctly. This will particularly be true where the employer is a small employer who may
  not have experience of employment tax issues, nor the resources to
  obtain detailed professional advice. A large employer with a tax
  department, or access to professional advice would not have much
  excuse. Ignorance of the law is in neither case any real defence.

- How the irregularities were carried out. If there is evidence that
  the irregularities have been carried out systematically less sympathy will be shown.

- How long the irregularities continued and their frequency and
  regularity. A one-off error would be viewed less harshly than regular systematic errors.

- The amounts involved. Account may be taken of absolute size,
  but the Revenue will also look at relative size both in relation to
  the employer and the employee. So a series of irregular payments
  totalling £4000 would be regarded as insignificant where the total
  payroll was say £1m a year than where the payroll was £40,000.
  Similarly an irregular payment which represented a substantial
  part of the remuneration of an employee would be viewed seriously. So too would a situation in which the culpable tax
  represented a substantial proportion of the total annual tax bill of
  the employer.

- The range of offences involved, from what is essentially a simple
  mistake of failure or commission, through to a blatant fraud. In the
  latter case an abatement of no more than 15% will be given.

Chapter 13

VAT Issues

Negotiating with Customs and Excise

13.1   Experience has shown that Tax Inspectors are generally prepared to look for some kind of compromise deal in order to get a case settled. It is often a pragmatic solution and one which needs to be carefully considered in every case. The Revenue certainly do not seem particularly willing to resort to the General or Special Commissioners to resolve matters. The time taken to get appeals to the latter body is often lengthy and the pressure to settle seems more attractive. This approach does not seem to be shared by VAT Inspectors who appear to be much more prepared to argue their point and to resort to the VAT tribunals. There certainly seems to be a regular flow of cases to the Tribunal and charities seem to account for more than their fair share of those cases.

It is possibly the fact that the VAT legislation, particularly in *Schedules 8 and 9* which set out the zero rating and exempt supply details, is much more precise (at least in Customs' opinion) in defining matters with its list of Items and then its detailed notes for clarification. If a word is there and that defines the area of zero rating then that is the end of the matter, if it does not then there is no relief. A spade is a spade and there are no other possible answers.

This opinion may be unfair to a number of VAT Inspectors who are prepared to accept that a wider definition may in some cases be possible, but it has been shown to be more the rule than the exception in the experience of the author. In one case it took three letters, including one to Customs head office to convince them that an old person could be disabled by reason of old age and that therefore the installation of a stair lift in an old people's home could be zero-rated.

In this climate it is important that charities are aware of some of the main issues that they may confront, although as with so many aspects of charity taxation, the sheer variety of types of charity makes sweeping generalisations very difficult. Again the reader will find much detailed material on VAT and charities in Chapter 11 of *Tolley's Charities Manual,* which is the longest chapter in the book! The notes here will summarise a few of the key issues on which disputes may arise. More of the background will be covered in Part 3.

The specific issues which will be considered here are:

- Business and non-business activities
- Welfare
- Partial exemption
- Education
- Admissions
- Fundraising events
- Aids for handicapped people
- Property issues

Business and non-business

13.2   The basic VAT legislation uses the phrase 'in the course or furtherance of a business carried on' to describe the sphere of activity within which VAT is chargeable. There is no comprehensive definition of business, just as there is no comprehensive definition of trade for income tax purposes. However, some guidance on the meaning is provided by *VATA 1994, s 94*.

Business includes 'any trade, profession or vocation' and so has a much wider scope than the income tax definition. [*section 94(1)*]. Any charity which is carrying on a trade for income tax purposes should therefore have no problem in satisfying Customs and Excise that it is carrying on some business activity.

The question of whether or not a charity is carrying on a business is one which is often at the centre of disputes between Customs and charities. The situation usually arises when there is either a large amount of VAT potentially payable by a charity – in which case Customs will try very hard to demonstrate that a business is being carried on – or where there is a large potential VAT recovery for the charity – in which case the charity will try to argue that it is carrying on a business and Customs will usually try to resist the claim.

Judicial guidelines

13.3   The courts, in their consideration of the meaning of 'business', have concluded that the word must be given its natural meaning and in one case (*C & E Commrs v Morrison's Academy, [1978] STC 1*) decided that the natural meaning was 'wide enough to include the deliberate carrying on continuously of an activity or activities, or an occupation or profession'. The concept of some degree of continuity derives from the phrase in the legislation 'in the course of' and in the *Morrison's Academy* case Lord Cameron commented as follows:

> 'The use of the words "in the course of" suggests that the supply must be not merely in sporadic or isolated transactions but continued over an appreciable tract of time and with such frequency as to amount to a recognisable and identifiable activity of the particular person on whom the liability is to fall.'

While much of the judicial comment on the meaning of trade for income tax purposes focuses on the 'profit motive' and commerciality, the court's deliberations on the meaning of business have specifically excluded the necessity to show a profit-making motive. One of the main arguments used by the taxpayer in the *Morrison's Academy* case was that the accounts of the venture were always drawn up to show a no-profit, no-loss situation. This was, however, rejected by the Court of Session with comments such as:

- 'I see no possible justification for the necessity of there being any "commercial element"'; and

- 'the absence of an objective of profit or gain should not and would not deprive the undertaking of the appellation of business'.

A very useful summary of the meaning of a business activity is given by Lord Cameron towards the end of his judgment that:

> 'it has every mark of a business activity; it is regular, conducted on sound and recognised business principles, with a structure which can be recognised as providing a familiar constitutional mechanism for carrying on a commercial undertaking, and it has as its declared purpose the provision of goods and services which are of a type provided and exchanged in the course of everyday life and commerce. Not only so, but to some extent the association is necessarily competing in the market with other persons and concerns offering precisely similar services to the same clients and customers.'

Tribunal decisions involving charities

13.4   Examples of decisions in tribunal cases involving charities reflect some of the extensions of these ideas:

- Provision of business services at non-commercial rates is a business activity (RSPCA).

- Investment activity without any direct involvement in the management of the entities is not a business activity (Wellcome Trust).

- The grant of a lease can be a business activity (Robert Gordon's College).

- Education can be a business (Royal Academy of Music).

- Small scale voluntary contributions do not make a business (Newtonbutler Playgroup).

- Charging scale fees is not a business (Arts Council of Great Britain).

Welfare supplies

Outside the scope

13.5   The area of what is generically termed 'welfare supplies' is one in which there has been considerable confusion and change in recent years. The precise definition of the term will be considered below in the context of the exemption which is now afforded by the legislation, but, in essence, 'welfare' can be seen as the heart of what is to many laymen the real meaning of charity.

Customs are prepared in some situations to regard the supply of welfare services as outside the scope of VAT. This will apply where welfare services are supplied, at significantly below cost, to distressed persons for the relief of their distress. This represents a significant concession by Customs, and, not surprisingly, they police it carefully. The term 'significantly below cost' is not defined in legislation, but is defined by Customs as supplies subsidised by at least 15%. To qualify, the service must be one of welfare services, as defined in the legislation, to an individual in need of welfare. Services provided to local authorities, etc. will not fall within the concession, even if they are supplied below cost.

In calculating the cost of the service, account is taken of all out of pocket expenses incurred by the charity in making the provision. No account is taken of capital expenditure, nor is any account taken of what it would cost a commercial organisation to provide the same service. It is actual cost and not notional cost that matters. Having ascertained cost, the charity must show that it deliberately subsidises that cost by at least 15%. Customs will not accept that the concession should apply if that result is achieved without any direct policy to achieve it. Finally, the service must be available to all those who need it, even those who can afford to pay for it, and without any conditions attached.

Exemption

13.6   Prior to the mid 1980s the concession set out above, was the only relief which Customs provided for charities supplying welfare services. Following a legal challenge, which successfully argued that Customs policy contravened the EEC Sixth Directive, Customs amended the UK legislation in 1985. That legislation is now in *Group 7, Schedule 9* as *items 9 and 10*:

'*Item 9* The supply, otherwise than for profit, by a charity or public body of welfare services and of goods supplied in connection therewith.

Item 10 The supply, otherwise than for profit, of goods and services incidental to the provision of spiritual welfare by a religious community to a resident member of the community in return for a subscription or other consideration paid as a condition of membership.'

To come within the exemption, three basic conditions must be satisfied:

(1)   the supply must be made by a charity or public body;

(2)   the supply must be made 'otherwise than for profit';

(3)   the supply must be of welfare services.

Issues which have been considered in cases include the following:

- where a surplus is ploughed back into the activity that will be regarded as 'otherwise than for profit' (Bell Concord Educational Trust);

- 'at a profit' is not the same as 'for a profit' (University of Edinburgh);

- an unexpected profit is nevertheless a profit (League of Friends of Poole Hospital);

- short-term holiday care for cancer patients was a welfare service (Macmillan Cancer Trust);

- supply of catering as ancillary to care is welfare.

Partial exemption

Basic issue

13.7   The basic concept of the recovery of all input tax assumes that:

(1)   all supplies are made in the course of carrying on a business; and

(2)   all supplies are taxable (standard- or zero-rated) and are not exempt.

Many charities, however, make supplies outside the carrying on of a business and will also make supplies which are exempt. Their ability to recover all the input tax they have suffered may be severely curtailed and as a result the level of funds they have available to meet their charitable objects may be reduced.

Inputs which are directly attributable to non-business activities cannot be relieved at all, and where an input is partly attributable to business and partly to non-business only a proportion may be allowed.

The distinction between taxable and exempt supplies is also crucial because only inputs attributable to taxable supplies can be allowed, although again a proportion of inputs attributable to both taxable and exempt supplies would be allowed. There are some provisions dealing with partial exemption which may in fact enable all inputs to be claimed even when there are exempt supplies and these are considered below.

Steps to be followed

13.8 Charities do therefore have problems in calculating allowable inputs and the steps to be followed by a VAT registered charity are:

Step 1 Classify all the activities of the charity as:

- outside the scope;

- taxable (both standard- and zero rated);

- exempt.

Step 2 Identify all the inputs on which VAT is borne and attribute, as far as possible, the input tax relating directly to each output. This is known as 'direct attribution'. VAT attributable to taxable supplies is fully recoverable. VAT attributable to non-business supplies would not be recoverable. The position on VAT on exempt supplies will depend on the application of the partial exemption limits. Where VAT is attributed to inputs which relate to all types of activity, these need to be apportioned. This latter item is known as 'residual input tax'.

Step 3 Consider the partial exemption position. The VAT rules allow all input tax on exempt supplies to be recovered where certain limits apply. Those limits have a dual test:

- the amount of input tax attributable to exempt supplies ('exempt input tax') must be less than an average of £625 per month; and

- the amount of exempt input tax must be no greater than 50% of the total input tax.

Step 4 Deal with the residual input tax. This has to be apportioned on a basis to be agreed with Customs and Excise. The 'standard method', prescribed by regulation is to apportion the residual input tax in the ratio of taxable supplies to total business supplies. This is referred to as the 'outputs' method because it focuses on the total value of supplies rather than on the actual input tax suffered. It is usually considered that this method is not to the advantage of charities which may have considerable outputs with no inputs at all. It is usually better to seek approval from Customs and Excise to adopt what is known as an 'input' method, taking the ratio of taxable inputs to taxable inputs plus exempt inputs.

Step 5   Total up the input tax recoverable, and compare to the tax payable to establish the net position.

Own schemes

13.9   There is some scope for charities to devise their own schemes for partial exemption and to submit them to Customs and Excise for approval. Regulations exist to allow formal agreement to the use of a special method. [*VAT (General) Regulations, SI 1972 No 1147*]. Where many activities are exempt or non-business a charity will usually suffer under the standard method. As well as the input method mentioned above, it might be possible to devise schemes based on non-financial criteria such as number of transactions, or floor area. This is where disputes can arise with Customs, and charities may wish to consider their options carefully.

Education

13.10   The supply of educational services is to be treated as exempt *Group 6, Schedule 9* and the basic exemption is set out in *item 1*:

   Item 1   The provision by an eligible body of—

   (a)   education;

   (b)   research, where supplied to an eligible body; or

   (c)   vocational training.

Customs have issued a detailed notice on 'Education' (notice 701/30). This sets out detailed guidance following the changes. The notice deals with a range of issues, but of particular interest are the examples that are given of what constitutes 'education' 'research' and 'vocational training'.

Definition of education

13.11   According to notice 701/30: 'Education means a course, class or lesson of instruction or study in any subject, whether or not that subject is normally taught in schools, colleges or universities and regardless of where and when it takes place.'

The guidance gives examples of what will and will not be regarded as education:

●   A separate charge for registration is part of the provision of education.

- Lectures, educational seminars, conferences and symposia, together with holiday, sporting and recreational courses is regarded as education.

- In the sports sector, education includes classes that are led and directed, rather than merely supervised. For example a local authority gymnasium will normally supply instruction in the use of equipment and in 'warming-up' techniques in a multigym, particularly when a person first enrols. This instruction, together with any assessment that forms part of it, is education. However, a charge to an individual to use the gym in a separate session where no instruction takes place, is not a supply of education.

- A charge for leisure sessions in a swimming pool where no instruction takes place, is not the provision of education. Staff are likely to be present for supervision on health and safety and insurance grounds but not to provide instruction. Under these circumstances, the charge is for admission and the use of facilities and is thus liable to VAT.

- A charge for admission to events such as plays, concerts, sports meetings and exhibitions, is not the provision of education. Exemption might still be available to charities under the fundraising rules.

Definition of research

13.12   The guide defines research as:

'original investigation undertaken in order to gain knowledge and understanding. It includes the use of existing knowledge in experimental development to produce new or substantially improved materials, devices, products and processes, including design and construction.'

Again examples are given of what does and does not constitute research:

- It excludes routine testing and analysis of materials, components and processes – as distinct from the development of new analytical techniques.

- It includes activities directed towards opening up new areas of knowledge or understanding, or the initial development of new techniques, rather than those directed towards mere quantitative additions to human knowledge. For example, if the aim the work is to discover a cure for a particular disease or improve an existing remedy, this is research, however, surveys of the incidence of disease are not.

- The fact that a project could have a specific commercial application does not necessarily prevent it from being seen as research.

- The following are examples of work that does not qualify as research:

  - management consultancy and business efficiency advice,

  - collection and statistical analysis of information,

  - market research and opinion polling,

  - writing computer programs, and

  - testing and analysis of chemicals, drugs and other goods.

However, some of these activities will qualify if they are supplied as part of a research project, e.g. if it is necessary to devise a specialised software program before carrying out the main tasks of a project.

Definition of eligible body

13.13   The key definition, dealt with by Note 1, covers the meaning of 'eligible body'. Included in the definition are obvious bodies such as

- schools;

- UK universities;

- institutions falling within the various Further Education and Higher Education Acts;

- a public bodies – government departments, local authorities etc.;

- bodies recognised under the British Council scheme for teaching English as a foreign language.

Less obviously, but significantly, the definition also covers:

'. . . any other body which is precluded from distributing and does not distribute the profit it makes and which applies those profits to the continuance or improvement of educational supplies.'

This wording could cause some problems for charities which might organise an educational conference, and aim at making a profit to plough back into other activities. If those other activities are not educational, such a conference will not qualify for exemption and, assuming the charity is registered, it will have to charge VAT. This may not be a problem if there are high inputs, e.g. hotel costs related to the conference, but the imposition of VAT may affect attendance.

Definition of vocational training

13.14   This covers training, retraining and the provision of work experience. It includes training for paid employment and also for voluntary employment in areas beneficial to the community as a whole – education, health, safety, welfare, and charity work in general. It includes courses, conferences, lectures, workshops and seminars designed to prepare those attending for future employment or add to their knowledge in order to improve their performance in their current work.

Customs took the view that the provision of services such as counselling, business advice and consultancy, which are designed to improve the working practices and efficiency of an organisation as a whole rather than to enhance the ability of individuals, was not vocational training. This view has been successfully challenged in a tribunal case

Admission charges

13.15 Where a charity organises a regular series of events where admission is paid, it needs to consider the VAT implications. The position has changed for one-off events and the comments in the remainder of this section relate to regular events. The basic principle is that a charge made to gain admission to any premises will be regarded as a standard-rated supply. Customs and Excise produce a leaflet on the subject (700/22).

Free admission but a collection taken

13.16 There are situations in which although admission (e.g. to a concert or sporting event) might be regarded as free, a collection is taken up at some stage during the proceedings. This will be regarded as a donation rather than admission, provided that entrance is guaranteed irrespective of whether or not a donation is made. The wording of publicity for such events must ensure that no element of compulsion is seen to exist otherwise VAT problems could arise.

Minimum admission charge

13.17 Some charities have very large fundraising events such as dinners, charity film premieres or major sporting events. The aim is that after covering the costs of staging the event surplus proceeds are donated to the charity. Where tickets are sold without any qualification they are regarded as admission charges and attract standard-rate VAT. It is possible to stipulate a minimum admission charge which would be standard-rated and to regard the balance as being a purely optional donation. Customs and Excise do, however, require that publicity should make it clear that a person paying the minimum admission charge will still be admitted even if he does not pay any donation. Care must be taken in fixing the level of the minimum payment. Customs and Excise will almost certainly want a realistic sum, e.g. they would be unlikely to accept £5 a head for a six course dinner at the Hilton Hotel, and it is also probably in the charity's interest to be realistic so that they are able to recover a greater proportion of their total input tax.

Admission to sports centres

13.18   Under the terms of the exemption, a non-profit making body operating a membership scheme has to tax at the standard rate all services supplied to non-members. However, any such body which is not operating a membership scheme, has to exempt sporting and physical education services supplied to all individual participants, e.g. where use is entirely on a pay-and-play basis.

Admission to cultural events

13.19   There is exemption from VAT for admission charges to certain cultural places and events. The exemption applies primarily to public bodies although a small number of charities may also be covered.

Where exemption does not disadvantage competing commercial bodies, public authorities are able to exempt the right of admission to their museums, galleries, art exhibitions, zoos, together with theatrical, musical and choreographical performances of a cultural nature. In cases where exemption would be financially disadvantageous to a public body and the body wishes to continue to tax admission charges, it is Customs' current policy not to compel the body to exempt. For example disadvantage may arise where exemption would cause local authorities to forfeit the right to recover the VAT paid on building, refurbishment and other capital projects.

The exemption also applies to a limited number of other non-profit making cultural bodies which charge for admission to the above-mentioned types of cultural activity or for associated fundraising events. However, the exemption only applies where the body covered is managed and administered, whether on a day-to-day basis or otherwise, by unpaid voluntary effort.

Fundraising events

13.20   The rules relating to fundraising events were changed as part of the Charity Tax Review and bring the VAT exemption into line with the income tax concession. Details of the VAT exemption are given at 8.39 above.

Aids for handicapped persons

13.21   *Group 12, Schedule 8* is an important provision in providing zero rating for a wide range of situations where medical and other supplies are made to handicapped people. The list of items is extensive and covers not only the provision of the aids but also costs linked to the provision of the goods. The stumbling block for many cases has been the requirement set out in the legislation that the goods should be solely for the use of a handicapped person. Customs consistently seek to argue that where any piece of work or equipment could benefit any individual, and not specifically a handicapped person, then zero rating should not be allowed. A whole raft of tribunal cases are testimony to the arguments which have been raised, often unsuccessfully, against that view.

Construction and alteration of buildings

Background to legislation

13.22   Most charities need premises from which to carry on their activities. For some charities (e.g. schools, residential homes, etc.), the need is absolute and specially designed or adapted buildings are needed. For other charities the need is for an administrative centre which can be in rented property and will in a number of cases be in someone's own residence. Many charities have been left with old buildings, often with listed building status, and the problems of the maintenance of such buildings represent a very real headache.

The practical problems have not been helped by the significant changes in the VAT legislation which have taken place particularly since 1984, when alterations to non-protected buildings became standard-rated. Following a decision of the European Court of Justice in June 1988 which stated that the UK had effectively been too generous in its use of zero rating and instanced the construction area as a prime example, legislation appeared in *Finance Act 1989* which made fundamental changes to the VAT treatment of construction. Although the legislation still gives some zero rating to charities, there are still a number of significant areas of uncertainty. The tribunals have been kept fully occupied dealing with cases relating to the interpretation of the 1989 legislation and in some areas further legislation has been introduced in an attempt to clarify the position.

Each case on its facts

13.23   There has been a steady flow of cases to the tribunals on what constitutes construction or alteration. The decided cases all relate to the pre-1995 legislation and Customs have taken account of the cases which they lost in framing the revised legislation. What is clear from those cases is that each situation must be considered on its facts. It is a case of considering the building which existed before any work was undertaken and the building that resulted from the work carried out. Charities which are considering building work which is not a clear-cut, green field construction would be well advised to take practical steps to build up a factual case in order to present an argument in the face of a challenge from Customs. The following practical steps are suggested:

(1) take extensive photographs or a video of the existing structure before work commences;

(2) make sure that all detailed architect's drawings and models are available;

(3) invite the local VAT officer to inspect the building before work begins and then during the construction process.

It is likely that in many cases the VAT at stake will be substantial, and there may be nothing to lose by taking the case to Tribunal. The facts will be all important and you must ensure that people like the architect are available to present evidence should that be required.

Zero rating for construction – the conditions

13.24 Zero rating is to be available on the first grant by the person constructing a building which is:

(1) designed as a dwelling or number of dwellings; or

(2) intended for use solely for a relevant residential purpose or a relevant charitable purpose.

Relevant residential purpose

13.25 This is defined in Note 4 and means use as:

'(a) a home or other institution providing residential accommodation for children;

(b) a home or other institution providing residential accommodation with personal care for persons in need of personal care by reason of old age, disablement, past or present dependence on alcohol or drugs or past or present mental disorder;

(c) a hospice;

(d) residential accommodation for students or school pupils;

(e) residential accommodation for members of any of the armed forces;

(f) a monastery, nunnery or similar establishment; or

(g) an institution which is the sole or main residence of at least 90% of its residents,

except use as a hospital, a prison or similar institution or an hotel, inn or similar establishment.'

With the exception of item (e) above, all the other activities could be provided by charities. It is significant that there is no mention in the note about business use and this is confirmed by Customs and Excise leaflet 708/4 'Construction: VAT certificates for residential or charity buildings' which states at paragraph 6: 'If a building or part of a building qualifies as a residential building then, whether or not it is used for business purposes, it is still eligible for zero-rating provided that the use is residential'.

Simple office accommodation, e.g. a warden's office, can be ignored in determining the status of the building but zero rating cannot apply to parts of a building such as a shop, gymnasium or swimming pool which are regarded as non-residential.

Relevant charitable purpose

13.26   The definition of 'relevant charitable purpose' is in Note 6 and states:

> Use for relevant charitable purpose means use by a charity in either or both of the following ways, namely:
>
> (a) otherwise than in the course or furtherance of a business;
>
> (b) as a village hall or similarly in providing social or recreational facilities for a local community?'

There is no restriction on the type of building. An office or warehouse could qualify. The key restriction is that relating to business use. The definition of business activities is no longer important only in considering the need to register for VAT. Note 6 does not set any minimum level of business activity by reference to turnover, it simply implies that zero rating will be lost if any business activity takes place in the building.

Problems can arise where a building is used indiscriminately for business and non-business purposes, e.g. a church hall may be used for worship but may also be let or hired out to groups and individuals. Such use can be ignored where business use is likely to take up less than 10% of the total time for which the building is normally in use.

Dealing with VAT disputes

An overview

13.27   The range of issues which could lead to a dispute between a charity and Customs and Excise are numerous and the examples given in the earlier part of this chapter are just some possible areas. Where there is a disagreement it may revolve around an interpretation of the law or the charity may accept that the interpretation they had made was incorrect but there are grounds for considering that the mistake was not a serious one. As indicated at the start of this chapter the art of negotiation is not as well practised in Customs as it is in the Revenue, and the charity may find itself in a serious dispute that it has to use formal channels to resolve.

The process of assessments and penalties are explained in detail in Chapter 5 at 5.31, 5.32 and 5.38 to 5.50 above, and that includes a view as to what constitutes a 'reasonable excuse argument'. What happens if the charity cannot accept the Customs view of the VAT treatment of the particular issue or wants to claim a reasonable excuse? The basic approach is to use the VAT tribunal procedure and that will be explained in more detail in this part of the chapter.

The general issues to consider in deciding whether or not to take a case to appeal are discussed in Chapter 8 and those issues apply to both direct and indirect tax appeals. The basic format of the tribunal hearings is also broadly similar to that of the Revenue Commissioners and again the general comments about preparation and presentation set out in Chapter 8 apply.

This section will consider:

• The organisation of the tribunal system

• How to make an appeal to the tribunal

• The types of tribunal hearing

• The issue of costs

The organisation of Tribunals

Legal basis

13.28 VAT tribunals are established under *VATA 1994, s 82 and Sch 12*. They operate under the aegis of the Lord Chancellor who also controls the General and Special Commissioners so that all the appeal bodies are independent of the government departments involved in the cases.

Location

13.29 There are three main VAT tribunal centres, these are in London (LON), Manchester (MAN) and Edinburgh (EDN). There are also provisions for cases to be heard at other centres around the country so that appellants should not have major distances to travel. Each centre deals with a specific list of local VAT offices. London and Manchester split England around Northamptonshire, with Northampton office cases being dealt with by London, but Coventry being dealt with by Manchester. The VAT offices in South Wales are dealt with by London and those in North Wales by Manchester. Edinburgh picks up all Scottish cases.

Personnel

13.30 The overall control of the VAT tribunals rests with a president who has to be a lawyer of at least 10 years' standing. There is a panel of chairmen who act in that capacity for each hearing. There are currently over 40 chairmen on the panel. There are also lay members who can sit on the tribunal to help the chairman on issues of fact but not on matters of law, which can only be dealt with by a chairman.

The tribunal members are supported by a unit which arranges hearings and keeps in contact with appellants.

Reports of Cases

13.31 VAT tribunal cases are reported in the public domain and form an important part of the body of material which can be used for interpreting legislation. They represent the first line of appeal and can be overruled by the courts but nevertheless give a guide as to what may or may not be possible. Cases are designated by their tribunal of origin using the abbreviations given in 13.29 above.

Making an appeal

Appealable matters

13.32 The list of matters which can be taken on appeal is set out in *VATA 1994, s 83* and include:

(1) the registration or cancellation of registration;

(2) the VAT chargeable on the supply of goods and services;

(3) the amount of input tax which may be credited;

(4) partial exemption claims;

(5) liability to a penalty or surcharge.

Condition of appeal

13.33 *Value Added Tax Act 1994, s 84(2)* requires that no appeal can be entered unless the appellant is up to date with all VAT returns and has paid the tax shown on those returns. An appeal against an assessment requires that the tax should have been paid on that assessment, although a claim can be made for exemption from this on the grounds of hardship. This may be relevant for charities involved in significant appeals, e.g. those relating to zero rating of buildings.

Procedure for making appeals

13.34 There is an official form, Trib 1, which can be used for making appeals to the tribunal, but the appeal can be made by letter instead. It must include the following details:

(1) the name and address of the appellant;

(2) the date (if any) with effect from which the appellant was registered for tax and the nature of his business;

(3)   the address of the VAT office from which the disputed decision was sent;

(4)   state the date of the document containing the disputed decision and the address to which it was sent;

(5)   the name and address of any representative;

(6)   attached to the letter, a copy of the document containing the disputed decision;

(7)   set out or attached to the letter, a document containing the grounds of the appeal, including in a reasonable excuse appeal, particulars of the excuse relied upon.

Once the notice has been served on the tribunal centre they will allocate a reference number which will include the tribunal name, the year the appeal was lodged and the tribunal reference number. The notice is not valid if sent to Customs and Excise, although it is usual courtesy to send a copy of the appeal to the VAT office.

Appeals must be made within 30 days of the date of the relevant decision. There are procedures available for making late appeals. An appeal once made can be withdrawn but the tribunal centre should be notified in writing as soon as possible, and if a hearing date has been fixed a telephone call should be made.

Types of tribunal hearing

13.35   There are three types of tribunal hearing:

Category 1 – tax evasion appeals

Category 2 – mitigation appeals or reasonable excuse appeals

Category 3 – other appeals

The third category of appeals are similar to the Commissioners hearings and the basic procedures discussed in Chapter 8 apply. The format of the hearing is similar.

Award of costs

13.36   If an appellants appeal is wholly or partly successful he can ask for an award of costs which would usually comprise

- accountants' fees for taking the case;
- solicitors' fees;
- barristers' fees.

Customs are also entitled to ask for costs if they win the appeal, but they rarely do unless the case has been extremely complex and involved large sums of money, making it comparable to a High Court hearing.

After the tribunal

13.37   The tribunal decision will bring the basic part of the case to a close. The losing party has the right of appeal to the High Court but only on a point of law. It is then a case of tying up the loose ends – paying the tax or surcharge if on the losing side, and perhaps basking in 15 minutes of fame if success has been achieved.

Part 3: Checklists

Introduction

In Parts 1 and 2 the background to investigations, the theory of what the authorities are able to do and the practical aspects of handling the various types of investigation are examined.

In this part some of the areas which might be the substance of the investigation will be looked at again. These are highlighted in Part 2 and there is much more about the background to these areas in *Tolley's Charities Manual*. The approach here will be to highlight the standards towards which charities should be striving and then, through a series of checklists, to set out the key questions which charities should be asking themselves.

There is a Peanuts cartoon in which Charlie Brown and Lucy are discussing problems and how they deal with them. In the final frame, Charlie Brown remarks that there is no problem so big that it cannot be run away from. It is not suggested that charities should run away from the problems of investigations, but it is true that the best way of dealing with an investigation is to avoid one in the first place. These checklists are intended to be an aid to that process.

The key areas covered are:

- General governance
- Financial governance
- Public accountability
- Trading, including the use of trading companies
- Fundraising
- Gift Aid
- VAT issues
- Employment tax issues

Sources of guidance

Introduction

There are a number of easily accessible sources of official information which charities can tap into for guidance in all these areas. Given the time and effort that the authorities put into making this information readily available, ignorance of its existence and the detail it contains cannot be regarded as an excuse.

Booklets

Charity Commission

The Commission publishes a long list of booklets that cover many aspects of the work of trustees. These are kept up to date as views change and you should always ensure that you have the latest version. The list of the latest publications is available at Appendix 5. All the booklets can be obtained from any of the three offices of the Commission and they are also accessible on their website.

Inland Revenue

The Inland Revenue do not publish many booklets specifically on charity tax. The existing publications that they have on deeds of covenant and trading are now out of date. They have produced some initial guidance on the *Finance Act 2000* provisions and leaflets IR64 and IR65 on giving to charity by business and individuals were issued in September 2000. It is understood that they are working on a new major guide for charities and that this should be available shortly.

Revenue booklets are available on many issues relating to employment tax matters. These are detailed at Appendix 5 and many of them can be accessed at the Revenue website.

Customs and Excise

Customs produce a wide range of VAT notices, including one specifically aimed at charities. These are updated on a regular basis and again a list of the main ones of interest to charities appears at Appendix 5.

Websites

All three departments have comprehensive websites which are kept up to date and contain not only the latest news but also much of the relevant background information which can be of real use to charities. All the sites are developing and it is likely that they will get bigger as time goes by. The addresses of each are:

> www.charity-commission.gov.uk

www.inlandrevenue.gov.uk

www.hmce.gov.uk

In addition there is a website called www.ukstate.com, produced by the Stationery Office which contains a wide range of official information including legislation and Parliamentary issues.

Manuals

In the spirit of open government, internal guidance manuals are now being made available. Much of the content may be for internal administrative consumption in the departments concerned but they do contain clear guidance to officers which can help in gaining an understanding of what the official view might be of a particular issue.

The Charity Commission operation guidance notes are being made available piecemeal and can be accessed from their website.

The Inland Revenue manuals have been in the public domain for a number of years now but only through commercial publishers. This has now changed and all the manuals are available through the Inland Revenue website. Most of the manuals are not going to be of particular interest to charities, but the main ones which may be helpful from time to time are:

- *Employer Compliance Manual* – deals with all aspects of employer compliance visits;

- *Enquiry handbook* – procedures on self-assessment enquiries;

- *Inspectors Manual* – covers issues like trading;

- *Investigation Handbook* – all aspects of investigations, mainly concentrates on traders but has interesting comments on interest and penalties;

- *Schedule E Manual* – all the theory of Schedule E. Includes guidance on particular types of employee e.g. ministers of religion, teachers.

Customs manuals are not as detailed as those of the Revenue. They are currently only available via commercial publishers. The main ones of interest to charities are:

V1-1	The User Guide
V1-3	Supply & Consideration
V1-4	Place of Supply
V1-5	Taxable person
V1-6	Business/Non-business
V1-7	Liability
V1-8	Land and property

Checklists

Governance Issues

Introduction

This series of checklists looks at the general role of trustees and the ways in which they should administer the charity. It is clear from reviewing notes of Charity Commission inquiries that many of the issues of maladministration can be laid directly at the door of trustees. The failure to take responsibility, the lack of direct control and, in some situations, being far too trusting of others, are all common causes of problems.

The checklists in this group are:

Checklist 1A – The governing document

Checklist 1B – Trustees

Checklist 1C – Trustee organisation

Checklist 1D – Trustee independence and integrity

Checklist 1E – Trustees and the appointment of employees

Checklist 1F – Other areas to consider

Checklist 1A – The governing document

The governing document should be clear in setting out its aims and rules, have legal powers necessary to achieve these and should be up to date.

Question

(1) When was the governing document drawn up?

(2) When was it last reviewed?

(3) Where is it?

(4) Do all trustees have a copy?

(5) What are the specific objects of the charity as set out in the document?

(6) Are those objects still relevant and achievable?

(7) If not, do we need to change the objects to make them relevant?

(8) Do the legal powers in the document need to be amended to enable the charity to function better?

(9) Are our membership requirements still relevant in terms of:
- Qualifications
- Subscriptions
- Rights of members
- Meetings of members
- Termination of membership
- Election of members

(10) Are the powers relating to the holding of land adequate?

(11) Are our investment powers wide enough?

(12) Is there power to amend the governing document easily?

Comment

Reviews need to be carried out periodically to ensure that all aspects of the document remain relevant.

The original should be kept in a safe place but copies should be available.

Every trustee should have a copy and know what is in it.

Many old charities may find that it has become impossible to fulfil very specific charitable objects established decades or even centuries ago.

Consider what the objects should be and take advice from the Charity Commission on how any changes should be implemented. It may be possible with the help of the Charity Commission to effect a merger with similar charities to achieve a more effective unit.

Powers that worked when the charity was small may be difficult to implement when the charity has grown or when external factors have changed.

This can be an area of great change and potential conflict if trustees and members do not agree. Qualifications should always be kept under review in the light of changing circumstances. A growing membership may find that they have less rights than they believe they should have. Tensions may also arise between a youthful membership and an older trustee body.

This may have been an area where little thought was given at the outset because it was never envisaged that land would be owned.

Investment opportunities are always changing and powers need to be kept under review. Consider in particular the powers relating to investment in unquoted companies if you have a trading subsidiary.

It should be possible to make simple amendments quickly and easily.

Checklist 1B – Trustees

The charity should be run by a body of people who are identifiable, accountable and take full responsibility for the resources of the charity.

'A trust is an office necessary in the concerns between man and man and . . . if faithfully discharged, attended with no small degree of trouble and anxiety . . . It is an act of great kindness in anyone to accept it.' Lord Hardwicke.

Question

(1) Can we identify who the trustees are?

(2) How many trustees should there be according to the governing document?

(3) Do we need to be able to appoint more trustees?

(4) Should we be reducing the number of trustees?

(5) Who are the current trustees and what expertise do they bring to the job?

(6) What areas of expertise do we need on the trustee body and do we have these covered?

(7) When were the current trustees appointed?

(8) What is the period of appointment of a trustee?

(9) Should we have a maximum term of office for trustees?

Comment

Trustees could have actual titles which vary according to the nature of the organisation, e.g.:

- Directors of a charitable company
- Trustees of a charitable trust
- Management committee of an association
- Governors of a school
- Deacons or similar body in a church.

It is therefore important that the group of people who are to be the trustees are identified at the earliest possible stage. They need to know because they carry the burden of responsibility.

This number might have been fixed when the charity was established and could now be inadequate for the needs of the charity. A large number of trustees need to be managed properly.

Is the current number too unwieldy for the efficient running of the charity? Should we be looking to create a core body of trustees?

Ideally a group of trustees should comprise a mix of people, all of whom have sympathy with the objectives of the charity, but who each can bring specific gifts, abilities and interests including business expertise. As far back as 1989 the Charity Commission was noting in its annual report that many trustees were simply not up to their job – good intentions did not necessarily make for an effective organisation.

The same issue but looked at from the other perspective. Key areas such as finance need to be present as well as people who have skills and experience relevant to the direct charity objects.

There can be dangers in having a trustee body that remains constant. They may not be alive to what is going on inside and outside the charity. Inertia can be dangerous.

Does this contribute to the problems of having long serving trustees?

This can force change. Consider a retirement age as well.

(10) Are all trustees in reality equal?

(11) What is the attendance record of trustees at trustees' meetings and committee meetings?

(12) Do we have a procedure for appointing new trustees?

(13) Do we have any checks to ensure that prospective trustees are not actually disqualified?

(14) Do we point out what potential trustees should consider?

(15) Is there any kind of induction programme for new trustees?

Checklist 1C – Trustee organisation

The trustees need to organise themselves in a way which enables the charity to run efficiently in achieving its objects and at the same time allows them to retain their overall responsibility.

Question

(1) How often are full trustees, meetings held?

Is there any evidence of a dominant trustee who actually takes all the decisions?

Trustees need to take all responsibilities seriously. If they are finding it difficult to devote sufficient time to the job they should not continue.

There should be a clear process which is established. It should not be possible for anyone to pack the trustee body with cronies. Consider what you need in the way of qualifications for a trustee taking into account any areas of expertise where you think you may be lacking.

Ch A 1993, s 72 sets out a list of circumstances in which an individual is disqualified from being a trustee of a charity. Those include individuals who have been convicted of any offence involving dishonesty or deception and anyone who has been adjudged bankrupt. A person who acts as a charity trustee whilst disqualified is guilty of an offence which could carry a prison sentence. [*Ch A 1993, s 73*]. Similar powers exist in Scotland by virtue of *LPMSA 1970, s 8*.

Kekewich, J said 'I think that when persons are asked to become new trustees, they are bound to enquire of what the property consists that is proposed to be handed over to them, and what are the trusts.'
They need to know all about the trust they are being asked to administer and what their precise duties should be. What time commitment is needed should also be made clear.

New trustees should be given a detailed rundown of the organisation and the activities of the charity. They should meet the key people and look at the main activities first hand. They should be taken through procedures such as the accounting arrangements, membership organisation, etc.. General training in trustee responsibility may be available locally. The Charity Commission produce a video and booklets which should be given to the new trustee.

Comment

Meetings need to be appropriate to the level of activity going on in the charity. Too short a period between meetings ties up resources in discussion. Too long can mean that decision making is either very slow or is delegated too much.

(2)   What are the procedures for circulating the agenda and sup-
      porting papers?

(3)   Who acts as chairman?

(4)   Is there a reasonable quorum required?

(5)   Are there clear procedures for preparing and circulating min-
      utes?

(6)   What arrangements exist for subcommittees:
      - What are they?
      - Are their functions clear?
      - Are their functions necessary?
      - What are the frequency of meetings?
      - How is membership determined?
      - What procedures exist for reporting back to the main
        trustee body?

Checklist 1D – Trustee independence and integrity

Trustees must always act only in the interests of the charity and its
beneficiaries. They must never put personal interests ahead of those of
the charity. They cannot benefit financially unless payment is legally
prescribed and is reasonable in amount.

'. . . what does the Lord require of you but to do justice, and to love
kindness and to walk humbly with your God?' Micah 6 v 8.

Question

(1)   What procedures exist for ensuring that trustees always declare
      an interest?

298

It must be recognised that not every point can be discussed in full detail and that papers need to be prepared to enable decisions to be made. Trustees need to have time to prepare for the meetings and therefore need to have the agenda and supporting papers in plenty of time to enable them to read them and be prepared with any questions. Trustees should not allow themselves to be rushed into significant decisions.

Are there clear procedures for appointing a chairman, and in particular are there procedures if the chairman is unable to attend?

The quorum should be such as to prevent a small cabal from pushing through decisions, but not so large that it becomes impossible to achieve and no decisions can be taken at all.

The minutes should record all the decisions if not the detailed discussions that took place. They should be circulated as quickly as possible after the meeting and should clearly denote any responsibility for future action. If the minutes are prepared by a secretary they should be approved by the chairman before being circulated.

Committees are usually a necessity but they cannot be a means of abdicating responsibility nor a means of securing control of the charity. Each committee must realise that it acts only under the authority of the main trustee body and is ultimately answerable to that body. Don't proliferate committees for the sake of it – if a committee has served its purpose get rid of it.

Comment

No trustee should take part in any discussion in which they might have an external interest. They should either withdraw from the room or stay but say nothing

(2) Are there any representative trustees?
i.e. trustees who are appointed to represent other organisations or parts of the charity, e.g. local authority trustees or staff trustees

(3) Are there any powers to allow trustees to be paid?

(4) Are any trustees actually paid other than expenses?

(5) What expenses can trustees claim?

(6) Do trustees understand the meaning of integrity in relation to their role?

(7) Is the founder of the charity still involved as a trustee?

Some trustees may be appointed, under the terms of the governing document, by particular bodies or organisations. This ensures that vacancies for the trustees are filled easily, and the governing body is balanced. It is important that such trustees do not become confused about their role and where their duties lie. The 1991 Report of the Charity Commission (para 42) adds this warning:

> '(Representative) trustees must act independently of the nominating body and act only in the best interest of the charity. They are not appointed to represent or pursue a sectional interest in the role or activities of the charity. Indeed there may well be occasions in the administration of the charity where such trustees may have to act in proper discharge of their trusteeship in a way which is in conflict with the interest of the bodies nominating them. In such circumstances the best interest of the charity must come first: this duty overrides all other considerations.'

This has been an area of considerable concern in recent years and is the subject of detailed review by the Charity Commission. The starting point is the basic premise that trustees of charities must not benefit in any personal way from their position. The office of trustee is not an office of profit. There can, in any event, be no possibility of payment being made unless the governing document of the charity permits it. The Charity Commission have indicated that they will only authorise remuneration of charity trustees in those circumstances where it can be shown to be both reasonable and necessary in the interests of the charity. The burden of proof in this lies with the trustees proposing it.

Assuming that this is legal it must be reasonable in amount. Special work by trustees can be remunerated where it can be shown that:

- the work was exceptional and not part of normal trustee duties
- the work is necessary
- payment is bona fide, e.g. trustee was not employed at a greater cost than would be charged elsewhere
- payment is commensurate with work done

It is not unreasonable for trustees to claim expenses such as travel expenses. These need to be clearly laid down and there must be clear procedures for making claims and determining who approves claims.

The key is always to consider what would a prudent and honest man do in any situation. Honesty goes beyond not running off with trust assets. There must never be an attempt to exercise a trust power that will also achieve some other non-trust purpose or benefit even if the interests of the beneficiaries are actually served.

The fact that a person was the founder of the charity should give them no more powers than any other trustee. The remaining trustees should ensure that they do not simply act as 'yes men' to the wishes of the founder.

(8) Are trustee decisions taken by a majority or on a unanimous basis?

(9) Do trustees take advice on key issues?

Checklist 1E – Trustees and the appointment of employees

Day-to-day functions of the charity may in practice be carried out by paid employees often under the overall control of a chief administrative officer or chief executive. Ultimately all employees are answerable to the trustees.

Question

(1) How many employees does the trust have?
How many are engaged on activities in direct fulfilment of the charity's objects and how many in general administration?

(2) Who is the senior employee?

(3) Is there a clear job description for the chief executive?

(4) What are the lines of responsibility between the CEO and the trustees?

(5) What is the appointment procedure for the CEO?

(6) How is the remuneration of senior employees determined?

(7) Who controls the expenses of senior employees?

There are pros and cons to each option. What is important is that no trustee should ever 'go along' with the majority for an easy life. Whatever decision making route is chosen, all trustees should remain responsible for the decision made.

Trustees should always take advice if they do not know how to proceed – that is what a prudent man would do in the circumstances. Having taken the advice, the trustee must then decide what action to take. Advice can be paid for out of the trust if it is advice relevant to the trust and not to the trustees personally. In cases of real doubt recourse can be had to the courts for guidance.

Comment

The absolute number is not relevant. What matters is that the number of employees is consistent with the resources of the charity to enable the objectives to be carried out. Care needs to be taken to ensure that those in non-charitable functions do not outnumber those working directly on charitable objects.

This must be clear. Their duties and lines of responsibility need to be spelled out so that there can be no doubt as to what they are required to do.

The CEO needs to be aware that they have a line responsibility to the trustees and it should be clear from the outset what authority is effectively delegated and what is directly retained by the trustees. Even delegated responsibility needs to be accounted for and there should be clear lines for reporting between the CEO and the trustees.

This should involve the whole trustee body although the initial work may be done by a working group. The CEO must be someone who will work with the trustees.

Again this needs to be a decision of the whole trustee body even though a recommendation may come from a committee.

Particular attention should be given to ensuring that effective systems exist for the authorisation of expenses for senior employees on matters such as travel, credit cards and telephones.

(8)   Are senior employees aware of the responsibility that they have for setting a standard in dealing with expenses and other use of charity resources?

Checklist 1F – Other areas to consider

There is a wide range of other issues which trustees need to consider. They are not dealt with in detail but it may be appropriate for trustees to draw up checklists to consider these areas.

Question

(1)   Insurance arrangements

(2)   Data protection

(3)   Human rights

(4)   Property

(5)   Investments

Everyone in the charity should share the responsibility for the resources of the charity and senior employees should set an example to more junior staff.

Comment

A wide range of insurances need to be considered including:

- Buildings and contents
- Computers
- Fixtures
- Employer's liability
- Public liability
- Fidelity guarantee covering fraud by staff.

Where databases of members and other information is held the implications of the various Data Protection Acts should be considered.

The UK has now embraced the European Community Human Rights convention and activities need to be compatible with that process.

There is a wide range of measures in the *Charities Act 1993* covering property transactions. These should be followed as appropriate.

If there are assets to invest are the provisions of the trust deed being followed and how does this relate to the various legal requirements?

305

Financial Governance Issues

Introduction

It is a fundamental requirement of charity law that the accounting systems of charities should enable the accurate financial position of the charity to be ascertained at any time. Financial governance goes beyond this – charities must deploy their resources correctly and there should be no opportunity for anyone, other than a beneficiary, to benefit legally or illegally from the resources of the charity. There are external controls which impose requirements and good financial governance means that these controls should be welcomed, not seen as an unnecessary imposition and interference.

The checklists in this group are:

Checklist 2A – General financial governance

Checklist 2B – Income controls

Checklist 2C – Expenditure controls

Checklist 2D – The audit and accounts process

Checklist 2A – General financial governance

'A well run charity understands the needs of its beneficiaries and users. It manages resources securely and economically and deploys them to the best advantage of its present and future users or beneficiaries. Funders, donors, supporters and users have a right to expect high standards of management and financial controls.'

Charity Commission *'Hallmarks of a Well-Run Charity'* (CC60)

Question

  (1) Is there a financial system in place which is fully adequate for the needs of the charity?

  (2) Is there a finance committee within the trustee body?

  (3) Who is responsible for the day-to-day management of the accounting function?

  (4) If the activities of the charity were to substantially increase over a relatively short period of time would the accounting system cope?

  (5) Apart from the general fund what other funds exist within the charity. In each case consider:

- What are the purposes of the fund?
- Are these purposes still relevant?
- Are the funds designated or restricted?
- Who has control of these funds?

  (6) How many bank accounts does the charity have? What are the signing rights in each case?

Comment

It is a legal requirement that the charity's accounting records must show and explain all transactions and be sufficient to:

- disclose at any time with reasonable accuracy the financial position of the charity at that time
- enable the trustees to prepare annual statements of accounts in accordance with accounting regulations.

Not necessary in small charities where the trustees will assume the full responsibility. If there is a finance committee are there people on that committee who are capable of understanding the accounting requirements?
This should be a standing item on the agenda of all trustee meetings.

This needs to be someone with the requisite experience or qualification. Their responsibilities should be clearly set out including in particular their lines of reporting to the trustees on financial issues.

It is not necessary that the system should carry so much spare capacity that it is inefficient, but times of rapid growth put the systems under the greatest strain and some slack that can be taken up may be useful.

There are dangers in having too many funds within the organisation. This can lead to people having access to money which others are not aware of with all the risks that this entails. Charities do not want money locked up in funds whose purpose has long since expired and which cannot be released for current needs.
Designated funds are funds which have no restriction on them but which have been earmarked by the charity for specific purposes. The charity can lift the designation when it wants.
Restricted funds are those which have very specific conditions attached which are legally binding on the trustees.

There are no hard and fast rules on the number of accounts, but common sense suggests that a proliferation of accounts will carry dangers. There should be dual signatory requirements over a specified amount and no signatory should ever sign a block of cheques, or indeed any single cheque which does not have the payee named.

(7) Who is responsible for the appointment of the auditor or independent examiner as appropriate?

(8) What factors are considered in the appointment of auditors?

(9) When were the auditors last appointed or re-appointed?

(10) Is there an annual budgetary process?

Checklist 2B – Income controls

Charities must have controls that ensure that all income, from whatever source, is accounted for in the books of the charity.

Question

(1) Are basic controls in place to ensure that all charity income has been recorded and banked?

(2) Are all incoming donations handled by at least two people?

(3) Are cash collections always supervised?

(4) Where possible, income from fundraising events should be checked against other available evidence.

This process may be delegated to an audit committee or the finance committee but it must also be considered by all the trustees. The danger of having anyone who might be connected, however loosely, to an employee or a trustee must be avoided at all costs.

Cost alone should not be the only factor. The cheapest audit is not always the best audit. You need auditors who are going to contribute something to the charity by commenting on what they see in the accounts and suggesting alternative routes for efficiency in all aspects of the charity's work, not simply its accounting function.

The process needs to be kept reasonably fresh. Inviting existing auditors to re-tender against other firms may help to refresh their ideas and approach.

The trustees should plan the work of the charity within the financial constraints of anticipated income and expenditure. To go forward on projects without having financial support in place or promised is dangerous and almost certainly a breach of trust because it puts trust assets at risk. Any budget should be based on realistic estimates of both income and expenditure.

Comment

The income of a charity comes from many diverse sources and basic controls are needed to protect everyone, including those who handle the funds.

This is a basic protection. The two people should not always be the same. There must be a segregation between the persons handling the cash and the person recording the cash in the books.

This is a notoriously difficult area especially where volunteers are being used to carry out street or house-to-house collections. Controls over collecting tins and the banking of cash from envelopes are very difficult but must be used. Where possible two people should be involved in the counting of any cash.

The same issues of cash collection arise, but in some cases it may be possible to check, for example, concert receipts against the number of tickets sold, or raffle proceeds against tickets.

(5)   Is a register of legacies maintained so that receipts can be tracked through?

(6)   Are there procedures for following through applications for grants, including ensuring that funds are used for the correct purpose?

(7)   What procedures exist for handling gifts in kind?

(8)   If the charity has a membership and subscription arrangements, are there proper records of members and controls in place to ensure that subscriptions are paid and recorded?

Checklist 2C – Expenditure controls

The charity must ensure that expenditure is always properly incurred, authorised and approved.

Question

(1)   Is all expenditure correctly analysed?

(2)   Are all payments made by cheque where appropriate with supporting evidence presented to the signatories?

(3)   Are there always two signatories to the bank account with alternative arrangements being made in the absence of one signatory?

(4)   If the charity makes grants are there proper controls in place over the application process and the subsequent payment of the grant?

(5)   What procedures exist to process expenses claims by trustees and to ensure that these are disclosed as appropriate?

(6)   Are transactions with parties connected to trustees disclosed?

Legacies now have to be accounted for as received. There can be a delay between being notified about a legacy and actually receiving it.

Applications for grants may take time and control needs to be maintained. Sometimes a grant maker imposes controls and the charity needs to ensure that they comply with wishes including making regular reports if necessary.

Donations sometimes come in non-cash forms and can themselves be very valuable, e.g. works of art. Procedures need to be in place to record receipt and value and where necessary to ensure that goods are kept secure.

Keeping membership records and cash recording separate will help. Getting subscriptions on to standing order or direct debit arrangements helps control.

Comment

Ensuring proper analysis enables meaningful accounts to be prepared quickly and budgetary controls to function effectively.

No cheque should be signed unless there is an invoice or some other documentation to indicate the payee and amount and the purpose of the expense.

Security in numbers should be maintained. If one signatory is going to be unavailable for any period of time a further signatory should be added on a temporary basis.

The grants paid must meet the charity objects. Steps must also be taken to ensure that the grants are from genuine sources and that the funds are used in the way the grant maker requires.

Trustees need to be whiter than white.

The existence of any connected party transactions must be disclosed in the accounts.

Checklist 2D – The audit and accounts process

The financial affairs of the charity should be presented to public scrutiny in a legally acceptable way.

Question

(1) Is the gross income of the charity under £100,000?

(2) Is the total income or total expenditure of the charity over £250,000 in the current year or was it over the limit in either of the two preceding years?

(3) Have accounts for the charity been prepared in accordance with the SORP?

(4) Do the accounts have proper regard for published accounting standards?

(5) Have the terms of the audit engagement been properly defined?

(6) What procedures exist to monitor problems found by the audit process?

(7) Should there be an internal audit function either within the charity on a permanent basis or hired in?

(8) Who is available to carry out any of the reviews covered by these checklists?

Comment

Accounts can be produced in a receipts and payments format where gross income is less than £100,000. Over that figure a full accruals basis must be used.

An audit is required.

This standard format is required for all charity accounts.

Although the SORP takes these into account as far as general principles are concerned, the accountant must have regard to all relevant standards.

There should be no doubt as to what is expected of the auditor and what will be presented to the auditor by the charity.

If problems are found they have to be identified and dealt with. Some may require urgent action, some may have a longer-term action plan. The audit should not be viewed simply as a legal obligation – it provides an external view of the charity (for which the charity is paying) and should be listened to and acted upon.

There is no legal requirement for this, but many charities accept the usefulness of this service as a means of demonstrating that they are serious about controls and efficiency.

Is there anybody there?

Public Accountability

Introduction

In their publication *Hallmarks of a Well-Run Charity* the Charity Commission give as one of those hallmarks that a well run charity should be 'open in the conduct of its affairs, except where there is a need to respect confidentiality'

One of the major impacts of the *Charities Act 1993* legislation is to make charities more accountable to the public, i.e. to those who support them and benefit from them. Some aspects of accountability such as the production of accounts and the annual report can be genuinely open and public, but there is also public accountability in terms of compliance with the tax regime which remains a confidential part of the charity's affairs.

There are two checklists:

Checklist 3A – Accounts and accountability

Checklist 3B – Tax compliance

Checklist 3A – Accounts and accountability

'Charities are favoured by the state and the public because their aims are for the benefit of the public. In return, charities are subject to the special regulatory system of charity law, which includes measures to ensure that charities are accountable for, and publicly report on, the use of their resources and the consequence of their activities.'

Charity Commission, *Hallmarks of a well run charity*

Question

(1) Is our income above £100,000?

(2) Is our gross income or total expenditure for the current year above £250,000. Was that level exceeded in either of the two preceding years?

(3) Are our systems able to ensure that the audit or independent examination can be completed within ten months of the end of our accounting period?

(4) Are we a registered charity with total income in excess of £10,000?

(5) Do we plan out the preparation and content of the annual report and see it as an integral part of the promotion of the charity?

(6) Would we consider entering our annual report for one of the various competitions that take place?

(7) Do we have any procedures in place to respond to requests from the public for copies of our report?

Comment

Above this figure accounts must be prepared on a full accruals basis. Below it the option is available to use a receipts and payments format.

If so, the accounts must be audited by a registered auditor. Below that level it is possible to use an independent examiner.

This is the standard that the Charity Commission expect to be adhered to. They can take steps to appoint an auditor if necessary.

Ch A 1993, s 45 requires all registered charities to prepare an annual report containing details of the charity's activities during the year and other information on the charity and its trustees.

The report should not simply be prepared for the benefit of the Commission, it is also an opportunity to let supporters or beneficiaries know what the charity has done in the year. A good report may help to attract new supporters and get the charity's message across more effectively to anyone interested in its work. The preparation of the annual report should provide the trustees with an opportunity to review the activities of the charity in relation to its objects and overall strategy.

There are awards for charity accounts and reports, which are setting new standards in presentation. Even if the trustees do not consider entering they should look at the reports and accounts that are successful and see what can be learned from them.

Charities must respond positively to any request from members of the public or commercial companies for copies of the latest accounts and annual report. The following practical issues should be noted:

- Any request in writing must be responded to within two months.
- A reasonable fee may be charged. This must do no more than reflect the costs of providing a copy.
- Whilst the only obligation is to send accounts, it is considered good practice to send a copy of the annual report.
- The latest accounts should be sent and this means the latest set to have been audited or examined.

(8)   Which charities are responsible for the submission of the annual
      return to the Charity Commission?

(9)   Did we comply with requests to submit returns in 1998 and
      1999?

Checklist 3B – Tax compliance

Although charities have substantial tax exemptions, they are still subject
to the administrative requirements of the tax system and need to ensure
that they can comply with those requirements.

Question

(1)   If the charity is a trust, has it received a tax return from the
      Inland Revenue for the last tax year?

(2)   If the charity is within the corporation tax regime has it received
      a notice to file a CT return for its last accounting period?

(3)   Are the trustees satisfied that all income and gains received by
      the charity are exempt from tax?

(4)   Is it clear who has responsibility within the charity for ensuring
      tax compliance?

(5)   Where tax repayment claims are made, is the person who signs
      those claims satisfied that exemption is available?

- The person asking for the accounts can use them as they wish, so the charity should point out any copyright which subsists.

Every registered charity (except those with annual income or expenditure below £10,000 p.a.) has to submit an annual return to the Commissioners at the same time as submitting their accounts. [*Ch A 1993, s 48*].

Hopefully yes. A failure to do so could have moved the charity well up the list of potential investigation cases and missing the next return could be very dangerous.

Comment

If yes that return must be completed and returned by 31 January after the end of the tax year concerned. (1999/2000 return to be filed by 31 Jan 2001). Failure to do so could lead to penalties and a possible investigation.

If yes, the return must be completed and returned within twelve months of the end of the accounting period.

The tax exemption is not a blanket one and is conditioned by the requirement that income must be applied for charitable purposes. If any income might fall outside the exemption, the charity should seek advice from a professional adviser or the Inland Revenue and if necessary advise the Revenue that there may be a potential tax liability.

If not, sort it out.

Don't treat the repayment claim as an automatic right. All the conditions need to be in place and it may be appropriate to subject a sample of claims to some internal scrutiny to check that they are valid.

Trading Issues

Introduction

The issue of trading is been highlighted in Part 2 as an area of investigative interest for both the Charity Commission and the Inland Revenue. It is also an area of interest to Customs and Excise because trading activities will mean business activities for VAT purposes.

An over-riding concern for charities in this area is to ensure that they have the right to trade. It will be assumed in the checklists that the trustees are satisfied with the position on this and are either carrying out the trade in the charity or have established a trading company for the purpose.

The checklists in this group are:

Checklist 4A – Identifying a trade

Checklist 4B – Is a charity trading?

Checklist 4C – Before embarking on any trading venture consider a business plan

Checklist 4D – Obtaining the benefit of the basic trading exemption for charities

Checklist 4E – Exemption for small trading activities

Checklist 4F – Fundraising events

Checklist 4G – Trading companies

Checklist 4A – Identifying a trade

The *Taxes Act 1988* defines a trade as including 'every trade, manufacture, adventure or concern in the nature of trade'. A charity should be able to identify whether the activities it is undertaking will fall within that definition.

Question

(1)　Is the activity being carried out to make a profit?

(2)　Is the activity linked to any existing trading activity?

(3)　Is the activity being repeated on any regular basis?

(4)　How is the activity being financed?

(5)　How long is the interval between the acquisition of goods and their sale?

(6)　Has an organisation for selling been established, e.g. a shop or mail order catalogue?

(7)　How were the assets now being disposed of acquired in the first place?

Comment

The presence or absence of a profit seeking motive is not necessarily conclusive, but it will be an important point to consider. A profit seeking motive may not be directly admitted, but it may, nevertheless, be implied from other features of the transaction. It must be present throughout the venture to be relevant.
Charities undertaking a fundraising activity will have some difficulty in showing that they did not carry it on for the purpose of making a profit. If they cannot do this, they will certainly face questions from the Charity Commission over the use of charitable resources.

If an activity is carried on which is loosely connected to some existing trading activity or experience, that will be a factor towards trading. This may not be a problem for charities initially, but could become a problem as activities develop.

While it is possible for a single activity to be treated as a trade it is more likely that an activity that is continually repeated would be considered as trading.

If an activity is funded by borrowing, the terms under which the money is borrowed – the loan period, rate of interest and security – will be important in establishing whether the activity is a trade. If the repayment period is very short or the interest rate is very high, the Revenue are likely to conclude that a quick sale will be needed to make any money out of the venture, and will argue strongly for trading.

The longer the period between the purchase of an asset and its sale, the less likelihood of a trade being involved. If however, the asset could be described as a 'commercial asset' the time period between purchase and sale will be irrelevant.

The existence of any selling organisation through a shop, advertisements, mail order or Internet site, will be a strong indicator of trading. Many charities operate such arrangements.

Where goods are purchased with a view to realise, there will be a strong presumption of trading. Where, however, an asset which has been inherited is sold, the argument will be that the inheritance is simply being turned into cash account. In the case of charities, where donated goods are often being sold through charity shops or at jumble sales, it is accepted that, although some of the other 'badges'

(8)   Are the goods modified in any way before sale?

(9)   What type of asset is being dealt in?

Checklist 4B – Is a charity trading?

A charity must always consider the badges of trade and then look at their implications in the light of the activities and objectives of the charity. Simply saying that the organisation is a charity will not achieve any tax exemption.

Question

(1)   Do the operations being carried out amount to a trade?

(2)   Did a profit emerge even though one was not expected?

(3)   Are all the profits being ploughed back into charitable activities?

are present, e.g. a selling organisation, all the charity is doing is to turn donations in kind into cash.

If an asset is changed or modified before sale, e.g. bare land has a property built on it, or even having planning permission granted, that would be an indication of trading. This can be a problem for charities with donated goods if they do something to the goods before sale.

This must be considered as one of the main factors. Some assets, e.g. works of art, give the owner no income but may give considerable pride of possession. Some assets, e.g. a property, may be let and generate an income. Some assets do neither, and only generate a benefit to the owner by being sold. These are referred to as 'commercial assets', and the acquisition and disposal of such assets will almost certainly be regarded as trading.

This can apply even where there is a single purchase and sale, with nothing done to the asset in the meantime. This is well illustrated by the case of *CIR v Fraser, (1942) 24 TC 498*. In that case a woodcutter purchased, via an agent, a quantity of whisky in bond, and two years later, without ever having taken delivery, he sold it. The profit he made was held to be trading profit. The judge said:

> 'the purchase of a large quantity of a commodity like whisky greatly in excess of what could be used by himself, his family and friends, a commodity which yields no pride of possession, which cannot be turned to account except by realisation, I can scarcely consider to be other than an adventure in the nature of trade.'

Comment

'If you do the operations of trading and make a profit, it seems to me that you are carrying on a trade.'
Rowlatt, J in the case of *Royal Agricultural Society of England v Wilson, 9 TC 62*

Whether a profit is sought or not, if a profit emerges it can be regarded as a trading profit.

'The profit can't be taxable because we are using it for a charity' is a very popular myth and one which can be very expensive.

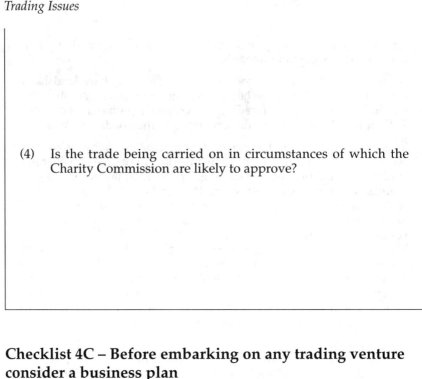

(4)   Is the trade being carried on in circumstances of which the Charity Commission are likely to approve?

Checklist 4C – Before embarking on any trading venture consider a business plan

No charity should engage in a trading activity which might put the charity assets at risk, even if the activity is tax exempt and approved by the Charity Commission. It is important to consider the key components of a business plan.

Question

(1)   What is the likely income flow from the project?

(2)   Where will that income be generated from?

(3)   What commercial competition is there in the particular area?

A clear distinction must be drawn between the earning of income and the paying away of that income. It is important to distinguish clearly between expenditure which is incurred in the earning of the income, and expenditure which effectively amounts to the paying away of the profits. The former will be allowable as an expense in calculating the profit (or loss) from the venture, whilst the latter has no immediate bearing on the tax position at all.

The Charity Commission are concerned that the activities, and hence the resources, of the charity are devoted to the objects for which the charity was established, and on the basis of which the Commissioners have allowed registration as a charity. They become concerned when the trading activities, as represented by turnover, begin to represent a diversion of the resources of the charity.

Look carefully at what the charity is supposed to be doing and ask how the trading activity fits into the achievement of those objects – if it doesn't and the trade continues to be run through the charity, all the benefits that go with charitable status are jeopardised.

Comment

The charity or fundraiser needs to consider the potential levels of income which could be generated from the activity. These projections need to be tested on a worst case basis before the venture proceeds. People with pet ideas always like to talk them up and make projections which may not be realistic.

Are these sources realistic or are assumptions being made that will not prove reliable? Can the proposed sources of revenue actually sustain the levels of income being proposed?

People will not always support charities just because they are there if there is a better commercial alternative. What can the charity do to make itself distinct – is there a unique selling proposition? Remember that just because commercial operations are in the area, it does not follow that they are being successful.

(4)   Have other charities tried the same activity – if so with what level of success?

(5)   Are other charities currently doing the same thing or something very similar?

(6)   What outgoings are likely to be incurred? Can any of these be covered by outside sponsors?

(7)   What labour will be required in the venture? Will they need payment? Are there enough volunteers available?

(8)   Will there be a large cash outlay needed before any income arises? A basic cash flow forecast is vital.

Checklist 4D – Obtaining the benefit of the basic trading exemption for charities

'One way in which trustees may be in breach of trust is by incurring an unnecessary tax liability' (Charity Commission booklet on Trading, para 5)

ICTA 1988, s 505 provides exemption for trading income where the income is applied for charitable purposes and either:

(a)   the trade is exercised in the carrying out of a primary purpose of the charity; or

(b)   the work in connection with the trade is carried out by beneficiaries of the charity.

The Revenue are prepared to extend the scope of this exemption for ancillary and peripheral activities. Charities should ensure that their trading activities will not fall outside these exemptions and so fall foul of the Charity Commission.

Talk to other charities about their experiences, especially if they are in different parts of the country. Find out why they are no longer pursuing the activity.

Should the charity be competing with other charities? This may depend on where the other charities are and how large the potential market is.

It is not only important to be realistic in talking down income, but also to consider the worst side of expenses. Test any assumptions that are being made. If sponsors are to cover the expenses consider whether they would want to be associated with the venture in the first place and if so, how do they want to be associated?

Labour intensive activities are going to add to the cost. Are the resources really available? Even if there are volunteers who can be called upon they may not feel that simply being involved in a trading venture is how they want to contribute their time and effort.

Most trading ventures have to have a period of expenditure before any income flows. If there is going to be a long delay before cash comes in how is that gap going to be funded? Reliable cash flow forecasts will help, but the risk to charity assets must be seriously considered. The typical 'dot.com' venture may sound cutting edge and may fit all the other features above, but the typical time lapse before generating income may make it too risky an area for a charity to contemplate.

Question

(1)   What is the prime purpose of the charity?

(2)   How does the trading being undertaken achieve that purpose directly?

(3)   Who are the beneficiaries of the charity?

(4)   Is the work done by beneficiaries alone or are there paid or volunteer employees involved as well?

(5)   Are there trading activities which have to be undertaken in order to carry out the main exempt activity?

(6)   Could the 'ancillary' activity be carried on as a stand alone venture?

(7)   Are there non-exempt activities which are developed alongside the main exempt trade but which are relatively small in relation to it?

Comment

Without this being clear in the governing document and in the minds of the trustees there are risks in trading outside those objects.

There must be a direct link between the trade and the charitable purpose. If the trading activity ceased, would the level of direct charitable activity undertaken be significantly reduced?

Again be clear on this. Where the charity makes a payment to the beneficiaries for their work, they will be treated as employees for tax purposes. Whether they cease to be beneficiaries will depend upon the terms of the employment. If those terms are such that the individuals are paid on a commercial basis, and no other benefits are provided, the Revenue may cease to regard them as beneficiaries and remove the trading exemption.

In some situations the work may be done by both beneficiaries and paid or volunteer employees who are not beneficiaries. Provided it can be shown that the greater part of the work is actually done by beneficiaries, there will be no problem.

The Revenue recognise that there are some trading activities which do not fall within the strict primary purpose exemption, but which are so closely linked to the primary purpose that they can be treated as falling within the exemption. The problem is in identifying how close to the main activity the 'ancillary' activity needs to be to be brought within the exemption.

The approach which the Revenue adopt in practice is to look at the main exempt activities and to consider if those activities cause the charity to have an obligation to provide other facilities or activities to people who are benefiting from the main activities. If the answer is that there is an obligation, the activities relating to the meeting of that obligation are considered to be ancillary to the meeting of the main object and will be treated as within the main 'primary purpose' exemption.

What starts off as an ancillary venture could become an activity with a life of its own. For example a theatre with a bar may decide to open that bar at lunchtimes or on evenings when there are no theatrical performances. That trade would no longer be ancillary to the theatrical productions.

There may be trading activities which are predominantly fulfilling a primary purpose of the charity, but include activities which do not wholly satisfy that purpose. In those situations the Revenue will not regard the basic exemption for the main trade as being prejudiced, and will regard the non-exempt activities as falling within the exemption provided two conditions are satisfied:

- the part of the trade which is not within the primary purpose is small in absolute terms, and

(8) Is the charity reliant on the peripheral income as a key part of its revenue?

Checklist 4E – Exemption for small trading activities

Finance Act 2000 provides an extension of the trading exemption to any activities which are not already exempt and fall within some very tight limits. Charities that wish to take advantage of this exemption should be aware of its limits.

Question

(1) Are there trading activities within the charity itself which are not covered by the basic exemption for trading even in its extended form to include ancillary and peripheral activities?

(2) Is the turnover from all such activities less than £5,000 in the charity's financial year?

(3) Is the turnover from all such activities greater than £50,000 in the charity's financial year?

(4) Are the 'total incoming resources' of the charity less than £200,000?

(5) Can the charity demonstrate that it had a reasonable expectation that its turnover from the non-exempt activity would not exceed the requisite limit?

- the turnover of the part of the trade is less than 10% of the turnover of the whole trade.

If the charity maintains that it could not do without that income, the Revenue are unlikely to consider it to be small in absolute terms. If they take that view then the whole profit from the trade, including the previously exempt part, will be regarded as taxable.

Comment

There could be small scale activities such as the sale of Christmas cards which are not included in the exemption but which are regarded as too small to justify the establishment of a trading company.

The profit will be exempt. But note the turnover exemption must be viewed as applicable to all the activities in aggregate – it is not an exemption for each type of non-exempt activity.

Subject to the 'reasonable expectation argument' (see (5) below) the profit if any will be fully taxable.

If yes, then the upper turnover limit will fall to 25% of those total incoming resources. The term 'incoming resources' has not been defined in the legislation. The Revenue say it has a very wide meaning and it will be in the interests of charities to define it as widely as possible where it is below £200,000.

The Revenue guidance suggests that it means the 'total receipts' for the charity from all sources. That would suggest that it should include all gross income – trading turnover rather than profit, gross rents rather than net rents – as well as income that would be non-taxable in all circumstances.

Where the turnover exceeds the limits, there is still a possibility that the trading could be exempt provided that the charity had 'a reasonable expectation' that its turnover would not exceed the limit. This could happen either because the turnover was underestimated or the incoming resources were overestimated. It will be necessary to convince the Revenue that the 'reasonable expectation' existed.

Checklist 4F – Fundraising events

Charities now have a much greater freedom to run fundraising events and make non-taxable profits following the extension of the extra statutory concession to cover any event that is exempt for VAT purposes and the widening of that VAT exemption. There are still pitfalls to catch the unwary and lack of care is not an excuse which the Charity Commission will have a great deal of sympathy for.

Question

(1) Is the fundraising being carried out through a regular activity such as the operation of a shop or bar?

(2) Has the event been organised and promoted extensively to raise money for the benefit of the charity?

(3) Where is the event being held?

(4) How many previous events of the same kind have been held at the location in the year?

(5) Is an event being run over several days?

(6) Is there a regular fundraising event held by the charity?

The Revenue have said that they will consider any evidence on this that the charity puts before them. This means that the charity must have that evidence in the first place – without evidence the charity will have little hope of succeeding. The precise type of evidence will vary from case to case.

Comment

This is not regarded as an event which in the opinion of Customs and Excise must be 'an incident with an outcome or result'.

This will bring the event within the basic provisions for exemption, subject to then meeting the other conditions. A social event which incidentally makes a profit will not be within the exemption.
Customs state that there must be evidence to show that the event was organised to raise funds. This might be through minutes of meetings, costings, correspondence, etc. The promotional material must clearly state that the event is a fundraising event and that those attending can be in no doubt as to its purpose.

Customs define the location as being the geographical area within which the activity takes place. Events held in special premises such as a sports ground or swimming pool will be regarded as held in a specific location. Where premises such as a playing field or community hall are used the place in which they are located will be regarded as a location.

The exemption can apply to up to 15 events of the same kind held in the same location. Where a 16th event takes place that ruins the exemption for all the previous 15 events as well as that 16th event.

Where an event is run over several days, Customs say it can be treated as separate events if there is a repetition of events on each day. If different concerts are held over a four-day festival it may be possible to argue that the event was a single event. The point is only going to be relevant if there is a danger of breaching the 15-event limit.

Regular events with a turnover of under £1,000 a week will not count towards the total of events.

(7) Is the event being organised a holiday event?

(8) Is the event being organised with any third parties?

(9) Is the event being organised by a professional fundraiser?

Checklist 4G – Trading companies

The use of a trading subsidiary to carry out permanent trading for the purpose of fundraising is an acceptable process but the charity trustees must ensure that such an investment does not in any way put the charity at risk and is organised in a way which will not lead to tax liabilities arising.

Question

(1) Do the investment powers in the charity deed allow an investment in an unquoted trading company?

(2) Have the trustees given consideration to whether, even if the deed allows it, they should be undertaking such an investment?

(3) What is the investment in the share capital of the trading company?

(4) Is the charity putting substantial loan capital into the company?

(5) Who are the directors of the company?

(6) Are any of the directors being paid?

The exemption cannot be applied to any event which could fall within the tour operator's margin scheme or might include the provision of two or more nights accommodation. Sponsored treks, mountain climbs, bicycle rides, etc. fall outside the exemption.

Take care that the only parties to the event are other charities, the trading subsidiary of a charity or what is known as a qualifying body. If a commercial body was involved in the organisation that would take the event out of the exemption.

The exemption will only apply if the charity is the principal in making the supply.

Comment

If they do not then the charity should not become involved without some change in powers agreed by the Charity Commission.

The trustees should have considered the business plan for the company together with financial forecasts and profit projections. They should also have considered whether such an investment would meet their current investment strategy.

Provided the investment is at a basic level, e.g. £2 or £100, the Charity Commission will not object.

The Charity Commission would expect any such investment to be within the investment powers of the charity and demonstrably a sound investment. Ideally there should be some security for the loan. The Commissioners' preference is for external commercial funding to be put in place.

The existing trustees of the charity should not all become directors of the company. There should be individuals on the board who are not trustees and trustees who are not directors.

No trustee/director should be paid. A company must not be a back-door way of receiving payment for acting as a trustee.

(7) By what name is the company known?

(8) Is there a common administration for the charity and the company?

(9) Are loans being made from the charity to the company as trading proceeds?

(10) Is a mechanism in place to transfer profits from the company to the charity?

(11) Are there procedures to ensure that the company files a corporation tax return and pays any CT due on time?

The names of the charity and the trading company should be distinguished from each other to prevent confusion between the activities of the two organisations.

The financial structures of the charity and trading subsidiary ought to be kept separate.
The separate identities of the charity and trading company should be made clear in all publicity material and in dealings with suppliers.
If charity staff are used in the administration of the charity, or there are shared expenses for offices, etc. there should be a charge from the charity to the company.

Watch for loans which might not be qualifying loans for the purpose of *ICTA 1988, Sch 20* and which might therefore invoke the anti-avoidance legislation and bring in a tax charge on the charity for not applying funds for charitable purposes.

This has historically been by deed of covenant, but is more likely now to be via Gift Aid. The payment must be made within nine months of the end of the company's accounting period. Consideration should be given to an amount which is less than the profits of the company but which might avoid the need to make loans back to the company.

Return needs to be filed within twelve months and any tax paid within nine months of the year end.

Fundraising Issues

Introduction

The Charity Commission, in its *Hallmarks of a Well Run Charity* points out that charities, both individually and collectively rely upon external support. They should be sensitive to external opinion particularly in the ways in which they raise money and advertise their activities.

In the 1985 Report of Charity Commissioners, para 75, the Commissioners noted a growing and worrying trend and warned charities against taking the view:

> '. . . that it does not really matter how funds are raised or how much profit is made by the non-charitable fundraiser so long as some money comes to the charity which it would not otherwise receive.'

The *Charities Act 1993* brought in a new regime to control fundraising, in particular the relationship between charities and fundraisers and between charities and commercial operations. The proposals relating to what will be known as 'public charitable collections' have yet to be fully implemented and so the existing rules still apply.

This series of checklists looks at those provisions as a means of establishing standards which are going to prevent the charity from incurring the wrath of the Commissioners. Of course the comments in the tax area also need to be considered. The following checklists are included:

Checklist 5A – Setting a fundraising strategy

Checklist 5B – Professional fundraisers

Checklist 5C – Links with commercial bodies

Checklist 5D – Public collections

Checklist 5A – Setting a fundraising strategy

Charities which are supported by donations need to be alert to public opinion and criticism. Time should be spent before undertaking any fund-raising to develop a strategy.

Question

(1)   What prompts the need for funds?

(2)   How much is needed?

(3)   Would it be possible to collaborate with other charities operating in the same field to meet the particular need?

(4)   What possible sources of funds might be available?

(5)   What will the fundraising actually cost?

(6)   Have fundraising costs been included in the charity budget?

(7)   What will the costs of fundraising be as a proportion of the total funds raised?

(8)   Have all the possible tax consequences of the fundraising activities been considered?

(9)   If fundraising is being carried out for a special project, what will happen if more money is raised than is needed?

Comment

Is it to fund a specific project or for the general work of the charity?

A more detailed and sustained strategy may be required and this may be done more efficiently through an in-house department which can be effectively controlled and costed.

It is not always necessary for charities to go it alone. The public sometimes wonder why charities appear to compete with each other to do the same things.

Funds could be available from government and local authorities as well as grant-making charities. These may obviate the need for a major fundraising campaign.

There are a variety of costs involved – printing, advertising, event organisation – as well as the costs of fundraisers. The costs of raising money for one project should not mean that another project does not happen.

If budgeting is to mean anything it should mean that costs which are not budgeted need to be deferred or a case made out for some exception and resources switched from elsewhere.

This can be a very emotive area as far as the public are concerned and has been a live area of investigation for the Commissioners.

Will the plans mean that a trading company is going to need to be established and can this actually be done? Issues raised in Checklists 4 will need to be reviewed.

The super success of a fundraising project needs to be covered in the promotional literature so that the trustees can deal properly with the extra funds if they arise. If this is not done the trustees will need to contact all donors and ask them what they want to be done with the donations which are in excess of target.

Checklist 5B – Professional fundraisers

Charities must ensure that professional fundraisers who work with them observe all the legal requirements imposed by *Charities Act 1993* and do nothing that would cause damage to the name of the charity.

Question

(1) Does the charity make use of the services of professional fundraisers?

(2) Is there a formal agreement in place between the charity and the fundraiser?

(3) How did the charity choose the fundraiser?

(4) Have fundraising plans been approved by the trustees before they are undertaken?

(5) Has the charity reviewed the records maintained by the fundraiser?

(6) Has the charity taken any action to stop any fundraising activity which they find offensive or which puts the charity at risk in any way?

(7) Is the fundraiser making clear to potential donors how much of the funds they are contributing are going to the fundraiser as remuneration?

(8) Is the charity aware of any fundraising which is being conducted without its permission?

Comment

A professional fundraiser is defined in *Charities Act 1993* and includes someone carrying on a fundraising business or who solicits funds for a charity for reward of more than £5 a day or £500 per annum.

This is a legal requirement (*Ch A 1993, s 59*) and the details of the agreement are set out in the *Charitable Institutions Fund-raising Regulations 1994*.

If a charity is going to become involved in fundraising using an outside agency rather than its own internal fundraising department, it should carefully check out the potential candidates. It should consider asking a number of firms to tender for the job and should ensure that all of them are at very least members of the Institute of Charity Fund-raising Managers (ICFM).

The trustees should agree to the principles of the arrangements which the fundraiser proposes and should be prepared to ask for anything to be changed which may otherwise tarnish the image of the charity.

The regulations require that records must be maintained in relation to each charity for whom the fundraiser acts. Trustees should arrange for these to be reviewed and checked from time to time.

There should be a continuous review of the fundraising that is taking place and at any time when the trustees think that matters are causing the charity harm they must step in and take decisive action.

This is a legal requirement. If the charity finds out that it is not happening, it should take firm action immediately.

Powers exist in *Ch Act 1993, s 62* to enable a charity to start legal proceedings.

Checklist 5C – Links with commercial bodies

A link with a major commercial organisation may appear attractive but there are a significant number of issues which a charity needs to consider to ensure that its name and integrity are protected.

Question

(1) Does the charity actually have the legal power to enter into a formal agreement?

(2) Is the charity happy for its name to be associated with the sponsor?

(3) Is the company happy for its name to be associated with the charity?

(4) Is the potential sponsor viable financially?

(5) Can the charity deliver its end of the deal?

(6) Do the parties see the relationship as a one-off or long term?

(7) What does the sponsor want out of the arrangement?

(8) Will the sponsorship be counterproductive?

Comment

Check the wording of the charity's governing document particularly if the arrangement is going to require the establishment of a trading company.

There can be problems where the association is with one company which is part of a large trading group which may have interests in other ventures which are in conflict with the objects of the charity.

The potential sponsor is looking to associate with an image and should ensure that there is nothing in the background which is going to dent that image.

It is worth carrying out a check of the company using Companies House or some credit reference agency. The charity does not want to find itself with a financial commitment which it has to take on because a sponsor has gone bust.

The commercial participator may well expect the charity to be involved in running events, mobilising support, etc.. If its staffing and administrative machinery is not up to scratch this may cause very real problems down the line.

It may be unwise to get into complex structures if the association is going to be a short-lived one.

Some sponsors may be happy to be involved simply because they like the 'feelgood' sensation. While one must never underestimate the philanthropic motive, it is likely that large scale sponsorship arrangements will only be entered into because there is also something in it for the sponsor. Some close questioning on this early on may help to determine whether the project is going to succeed and whether it is likely to be a short- or long-term arrangement.

Some potential donors may decide that if a large corporation is involved with the charity, then the charity has enough funds coming into it and therefore the potential donor's funds can be diverted to a more deserving cause. It also has to be accepted that not every donor will approve of the activities of the commercial participator, and may not wish to make donations.

(9) If it is an event which is being sponsored, who will control it?

(10) What are the funding arrangements?

(11) If an event is going to be held, who is responsible for health and safety issues?

(12) The charity should ensure that its logo is properly protected.

(13) What will be the tax consequences of the proposed fundraising?

Checklist 5D – Public collections

Traditional means of fundraising appealing directly to the public are still relevant but must be conducted in accordance with regulations and without causing offence to potential donors.

Question

(1) Has a licence for a house-to-house collection been obtained?

(2) Have the house-to-house collectors been issued with the requisite authority?

Ideally the charity will want to control the event, but the sponsor may want a large say in the organisation which may ultimately detract from the success of the event. On the other hand the commercial participator may find themselves having to throw personnel resources at the event simply because the charity does not have the ability to deliver.

Both sides need to ensure that the event has been properly costed, and realistic estimates made of the likely interest. The end result is then that more funding is needed or large amounts of expensive food, giveaways, etc. are left over and wasted. Both parties need to establish a realistic financial budget and ensure that each knows what they are contributing both to the running of the event and to the funding of any residual problem which may emerge.

Inevitably there must be precautions in place to ensure the safety of members of the public and employees of the charity and company and probably volunteers as well. It must be clear who is taking responsibility for this and for matters such as public liability insurance.

A number of charity logos are well known, e.g. the panda of the World Wildlife Fund, and they represent very valuable assets of the charity. The charity trustees must therefore ensure that any use of that logo by the commercial participator is properly controlled and licensed both as to the use and the period of use. A payment for the use of a logo will be treated as a royalty and this can be a very tax-efficient way of receiving the funds.

Consider the issues raised in Checklists 4.

Comment

The relevant legislation remains the *House to House Collections Act 1939* and various regulations under that Act. A licence has to be obtained from the District Council; in the City of London, the Common Council; and in the Metropolitan Police District, the Commissioner of the Metropolitan Police.

This requirement may be waived by the Home Secretary for national collections on behalf of national charities.

Collectors must be over 16 years old and must have a certificate of authority and a badge which they have signed.

(3)   Have these collectors been issued with instructions on how to carry out the collection?

(4)   Has the promoter arranged for another person to be present when the envelopes, etc. are opened?

(5)   Who is preparing the requisite accounts?

(6)   Is a street collection planned?

(7)   Have the street collectors been given instructions?

(8)   Have accounts been prepared?

Money must be placed in envelopes or sealed collecting boxes. Collectors must not annoy anyone. They must return their badges and authority together with the envelopes or boxes unopened.

This is a legal requirement. The money must be counted immediately and recorded.

Accounts have to be prepared and sent to the licensing authority within one month.

A license will need to be obtained if the collection is going to be held in a street which is defined as including any highway, public bridge, road, lane, footway, etc.. Collections on private premises such as railway stations, cinemas and theatres, do not require a licence but will require permission from the owner.

These include being over 16 years old. Remaining stationary on the pavement at least 25 metres from the nearest collector (unless collecting as part of a procession). Collectors must have written authority.

The regulations require accounts to be submitted to the licensing authority within one month (three months in London). The accounts must be certified by a qualified accountant.

Gift Aid

Introduction

The introduction of new rules on Gift Aid in the *Finance Act 2000* opens up a huge range of opportunities for tax-efficient giving. Charities may see the new regime as an opportunity to print money, or at least to divert considerable sums from the coffers of the Government into their own accounts. They should take care because the new regime has its 'small print' of conditions which may cause problems, and they should also bear in mind that the powers of the Inland Revenue to police the system efficiently have not in any way been undermined by the new rules.

The essence of the new system is one of flexibility. It is designed to cope with donations made in cash, by direct debit, by cheque, by credit card or by debit card. It will cope with donations made by handing over money in the church collection, by sending money through the post, by making a credit card donation over the telephone or over the Internet. It will cope with one-off donations, donations to be made over a specified period of time or all donations to be made to the same charity for the lifetime of the donor. In every case if the basic conditions are complied with, the charity will be able to uplift the sum received by a tax reclaim from the government.

These checklists cover the three key areas:

Checklist 6A – Declarations

Checklist 6B – Administration

Checklist 6C – Benefits to donors

Checklist 6A – Declarations

The working of the new system is based on a declaration given by the donor. Charities must ensure that such declarations are correctly completed.

Question

(1) Has the charity produced a master version of a written declaration?

(2) Has the charity produced alternative versions which can be used for specific types of fundraising?

(3) Is the charity encouraging regular donors to use an open declaration?

(4) Does the charity have procedures to notify donors of the total amounts they have paid in each tax year?

(5) Do charity workers dealing with telephone donations understand the rules relating to oral declarations?

Comment

The essential details which must be shown on the written declaration are:

- The donor's name
- The donor's address
- The charity's name or acronym
- A description of the donations to which the declaration relates
- A declaration that the donations are to be effective for Gift Aid
- A note explaining that it is a requirement that the donor must have paid sufficient tax to cover the tax on the donation
- The date of the declaration.

The Gift Aid declaration can be easily adapted to cover fundraising methods such as house-to-house collections and sponsored events as well as regular giving through standing orders.

Donations can be made on an open-ended basis using wording such as 'all donations I make on or after the date of this declaration' or 'all donations I make from this date until further notice'. These declarations would cover all future donations, but not any donations made in an earlier period. To cover these donations a wording such as 'all donations I have made since dd/mm/yy (cannot be earlier than 6 April 2000) and all future donations I make' would need to be used. Note it is possible to pick up earlier donations provided of course that these can be identified clearly as having been made by the donor.

This is not a legal requirement but there is a danger that open declarations could be overlooked by donors, and charities who hold them might want to remind donor's periodically that they are holding the declarations. The opportunity could be taken to remind donors of the sums actually paid in each tax year and to check at the same time that the donor remains a taxpayer (or at least is paying sufficient tax to cover the tax on the donations).

Where a donor makes a donation by credit card or debit card over the telephone this can be made into a qualifying donation provided a written record is made and sent to the donor. Charities which are operating this type of fundraising will need to ensure that the people handling the telephone calls are trained to maximise the opportunity and to ensure that the paperwork is correct.

The basic information which must go down on the written record at the time the oral declaration is made is as follows:

(6)   Are the charity's procedures for dealing with cancellations of declarations adequate?

- Donor's name
- Donor's address
- Charity name or acronym
- Description of the donations
- Declaration that the donations are to be treated as Gift Aid donations.

In addition the written record must show:

- A note explaining the requirement with regard to paying tax
- A note explaining the donor's right to cancel the declaration retrospectively
- The date on which the donor gave the declaration
- The date on which the written record is sent to the donor.

In practice it is likely that the donation details will relate to the specific donation being made on the telephone. The Gift Aid treatment can be dealt with by a Yes/No question to be asked by the telephonist. The form can be pre-printed so that the telephonist knows the information to seek over the phone and the record can be despatched as quickly as possible. The charity may want to have a system for checking the written records before they are sent out.

The donor has the right to cancel a declaration at any time, although the effect of the cancellation may differ according to the type of declaration. The notice of cancellation can be made however the donor chooses – it can be in writing, via e-mail, in a fax or during a conversation. In the latter case the charity may want to ensure that a written note is made of the conversation.

Where the declaration was made in writing, the cancellation takes effect from the date on which it is made and will apply to all donations received after that date or from a future date which may be specified by the donor. The latter may happen if the donor knows that in the following tax year they will not be paying sufficient tax to cover the tax on the donations – in that case the cancellation may be stated to take effect from 6 April next or some such wording. The donor cannot cancel a declaration in respect of a donation already made. If the donor discovers that they have not paid enough tax to cover the donation it is then too late and they must face the consequences as far as that donation is concerned.

Where the donor has made an oral declaration that can be cancelled within 30 days of the date on which the charity sent the written record. In this case the cancellation is retrospective and relates back to the time of the original declaration which therefore has no tax effect at all.

Checklist 6B – Administration

It is vital that a complete audit trail exists in the charity records for every Gift Aid donation.

Question

(1)   Are the procedures in place adequate to identify every donor?

(2)   Can each cheque or credit card donation be linked to a donor?

(3)   Are there procedures to link cash donations to a donor?

Comment

The donor has to be identified by their name and address – this should present no problem as it is basic information that has to be put on to the written declaration and the written record. There is one situation in which care must be taken and that concerns cheques drawn on a joint bank account where one spouse may be a taxpayer and one not. The Revenue have indicated that in these circumstances they will regard the donor as being the person whose name appears on the cheque, etc. or who authorises the donation by credit card over the phone, so charities should ensure in such cases that it is always the same person whose name appears on the written declaration and that they are a taxpayer.

The link of donor to donation should be relatively easy where payments are by cheque or debit/credit card or by direct debit, because the name of the donor will appear on documentation of some kind. In the case of card donations or direct debit, that information will be on the charity bank statement or on statements received from credit card companies. In the case of cheques it might be advisable to take a copy of the cheque or at least to record the details of the cheque in the records.

Linking cash donations to donor will inevitably be the most difficult area and will be the area that will be scrutinised most carefully by the Revenue. It is therefore important that charities should consider adopting some suitable recording system and at the very least that those who handle cash donations for the charity should be told to ensure that they are meticulous in their recording of the origin of cash donations.

Cash donated on the open plate or whatever system is used for cash offerings needs to be identified to donors who might have given open declarations or who might wish to Gift Aid for a one-off donation. The only way in which this can be satisfactorily done is through the use of envelopes.

Where cash comes in from sponsored events it is important that the sponsor lists provided to participants should have clear listing of the details of individual sponsors and the amounts that they have donated. Those lists should be retained for inspection. It might be sensible to record on the form the total cash received which should match the total of the individual details on the form and also agree with the basic cash book records.

Charities may receive cash donations through the post. Some may also enclose pre-printed forms included in newspaper adverts, others may have correspondence with them which will enable the donor to be identified. Both types of prime record should be retained.

(4)   Are donations recorded in the cash book or bank account as appropriate?

(5)   Are there standing procedures to ensure that a Gift Aid declaration is obtained for as many donations as possible?

(6)   Are all open-ended declarations retained?

(7)   Can all donations made by donors who have given open ended declarations be picked up through the charity's systems?

The cash book is a very important record, particularly in the context of recording cash donations. Treasurers need to be prepared to record more individual donations in the records to tie into the Gift Aid declarations and also the basic evidence of envelopes, sponsor forms, etc.. If they do not want to record every single pound, but prefer to record a total collection, then they must be prepared to have subsidiary records such as sponsor lists or a list of Gift Aided donations showing names of donors. Either route should be acceptable to the Revenue.

Discipline and routine become the key and any individual who might be involved in the recording system, e.g. at holiday time, must be aware of what is required.

There are three important areas to keep a careful watch on with bank accounts:

- Bank statements are all important and should contain essential information such as direct debits received which can identify donors.
- The bank statements will show the total sum banked on any occasion and some record needs to be maintained to ensure that details of all cheques banked are available. These may have been recorded on the paying-in slip but this may not be returned by the bank so unless the paying-in stub has been competed in full there should be a subsidiary record to show the individual cheques that make up the total banking.
- Where sums are received from credit card companies, the full breakdown of these sums, showing donors' names should be retained.

Charities need to ensure that they have a system in place for obtaining the declarations where donations are received. This can be important where donors respond to appeals and send in donations by post – there should be some automatic response arrangement to secure a declaration wherever possible.

Where a charity holds an open-ended declaration it needs to retain that declaration for as long as it is making reclaims in respect of it. Charities could consider setting up a register of Gift Aid declarations which detail all open declarations and could include information about the donor including:

- Change of name or address details
- The date the declaration was made
- The date the declaration was cancelled.

The charity needs to ensure that it is able to 'capture' all donations made by the donor. Some may be easily identified from direct debits or standing order payments. Cheques can be identified and there must be a system for linking cash payments. It may be sensible to have a record of donations for each donor for each tax year.

Checklist 6C – Benefits to donors

Charities must understand that if they provide a benefit back to the donor in excess of the permitted amount they will lose the Gift Aid relief on that donation.

Question

(1) Can the charity staff recognise a situation in which a benefit may have been provided?

(2) Is the benefit given in consequence of making the gift?

(3) If the charity is involved in the preservation of buildings or the conservation of wildlife, is it taking advantage of being able to use Gift Aid in respect of membership subscriptions and admissions?

(4) Are benefits to relatives being allowed to pass unchecked?

(5) Is the charity aware of the basic values of benefits which will cause a problem?

Comment

Benefits can arise in many different ways. At one level a charity may simply wish to give a donor some token of appreciation or acknowledgment for the their donation – that should generally cause few problems. At the other extreme a charity provides a positive incentive to a donor to make a donation – if you give us a donation above a certain figure we will give you something which is relatively small in relation to the donation but is nevertheless worth having. In between comes the complex area of benefits that may result from the membership of a charity.

A benefit could take the form of goods provided. It could be in the form of services rendered. In some instances it could be something even more intangible.

There must be a clear link between the making of the gift and the provision of the benefit. There must be some link between the making of the gift and the provision of the benefit, but the benefit does not have to be provided directly by the charity – it could come from a third party.

The phrase also indicates that the order of the events must be gift then benefit. This can be important where someone decides to make a donation to charity as a token of appreciation for some service received by themselves or a relative.

One further point to be noted is that there is no time limit between the donation and the benefit.

This important concession is set out in the legislation. The right of free admission is deemed not to be a benefit.

The benefit rules extend to situations where individuals connected to the donor receive a benefit. This covers:

'An individual who is their wife or husband, or is a relative, or the wife or husband of a relative of the individual or of the individual's wife or husband. Relative means brother, sister, ancestor or lineal descendant.'

The limits prescribed are:

- Donation up to £100, maximum benefit 25% of value of gift
- Donation £101 to £1,000, maximum benefit £25
- Donation over £1,000 maximum benefit 2.5% of value
- Overall limit of £250 benefit for aggregate donations from the same donor in the same tax year.

(6)   Are benefits provided over a period of time?

(7)   Is the charity aware that it can avoid the benefit problems by splitting the receipt between a payment for the benefit and a pure donation?

The rules on annualising benefits need to be considered to see if the specific limits or the overall aggregate are going to be affected.

Charities which want to go down this route for major fundraising events such as dinners or initiatives which offer free tickets for concerts, should make this option of a split arrangement very clear in the promotional literature for the event. The sums received from donors should then either be received as two distinct payments or should be accompanied by a letter or form which leaves no doubt that the benefit is being directly paid for.

Employment Issues

Introduction

There is a wide range of problems which can arise for the charity as an employer and it would not be appropriate to produce checklists here on all of them.

It is appropriate to consider how a charity should look at its total organisation to assess potential areas of risk in its systems which could cause problems in the event of employer compliance visits. The two technical areas that will be covered in this section are:

- Factors relating to the determination of an employment
- Issues relating to travel expenses

Checklist 7A – Assessing risk in employer compliance

Checklist 7B – Identifying employees

Checklist 7C – Travel expenses

Checklist 7A – Assessing risk in employer compliance

A charity that has duties as an employer should look at its organisation and procedures to ensure that there are no inherent risks of investigation.

Question

(1) How many employees are there?

(2) What is the geographical structure of the organisation?

(3) What authority is delegated to lower levels of management?

(4) Who is responsible for financial matters and who is responsible for taxation matters?

(5) Is there a central payroll?

(6) Do local/divisional managers have any discretion to make special payments or allowances?

Comment

This may be an obvious question. A harder one to answer could be 'how many employees should there be?' The more employees, the greater the risk that any single error could have a large impact.

The practical point is that the more widespread the organisation, then the harder it is to control from the centre, and the greater the likelihood of local situations being resolved by local decisions which may not always take tax into account.

Delegation without an awareness of tax problems can be a recipe for tax disaster. At the very least there might be a need to provide some training or support for people who have to exercise control over payroll matters at a local level.

If the answer is that it is the same person, then provided that person has a good level of tax knowledge relating to payroll issues, the level of risk should be reduced. If the functions are separate as will often be the case in larger organisations it is important that communications are good between the individuals or departments. Unfortunately, the tax role in many large organisations is primarily seen as a corporation tax role, and surprisingly few large organisations have designated payroll tax specialists at a high level in the organisation.

This will at least limit the areas which have to be reviewed, but one important factor to consider in a large organisation is how information is passed from local units. Does it follow a set route and timetable, or are there time delays which may mean a delay in recognising when a tax or NIC liability should arise?
If there is a central payroll it is likely that it will be computerised. This should eliminate many problems but it is a truism that a computer system is only as good as the data put into it. There are occasions where the sheer effort required can cause people to take short cuts, e.g. deciding to make a small cash payment directly instead of putting it through the payroll.

Local discretion puts a weakness into the compliance system unless it is backed up by support and training from the centre. Do these local payments have to be agreed in principle by higher authority and are there any standard procedures for reviewing the taxation consequences of any type of payment?

(7) How are payments made to temporary employees or casual labour?

(8) Are any payments made to individuals who are not employees and who render services to the employer?

(9) Are all creditors paid out centrally by cheque?

(10) Is there a staff handbook or similar document which sets out all the allowances and procedures for claim?

(11) Is there a standard expenses claim form?

(12) Is there scope for obtaining a dispensation?

(13) Is there regular contact maintained with the tax district that deals with the employees?

(14) Are all year end returns completed accurately and on time?

If the charity uses a lot of casual labour there should be clear procedures in place to ensure that the tax aspects are properly dealt with. This may not actually be a problem in organisations that use a substantial level of casuals, because it will be an acknowledged problem. Difficulties are more likely to arise in organisations which use casuals on a less frequent basis, or where particular branches are not used to handling such staff.
Identify who authorises the engagement of casuals and the payments to them, and ensure that they are fully aware of the P46 procedure.

Identify the use of 'consultants' and check that their status really is that of the self-employed (see Checklist 7B). Ensure that those responsible for engaging the services of these people are properly aware of the factors they need to consider. Where the situation is not clear cut, ensure that steps are taken to obtain the views of the local Inspector before gross payments are made.

If the answer is yes, this will make the review of these payments easier, and also the obtaining of information to complete the P11D. Check how often payments are made, and where original invoices are held.

Ensure that you have a copy and establish if all allowances and expenses are paid on the same basis across the organisation. Check, if local arrangements exist, that the tax consequences of any allowance have been properly considered.

Make sure that you have a copy. Check that the information required on the form is comprehensive. Establish too that procedures exist for requiring vouchers or receipts in support of expenses claimed.

This can reduce the amount of work required in completing forms P11D by getting the Revenue to agree that certain payments, e.g. travel expenses, are wholly allowable. The procedure for getting a dispensation is relatively straightforward and should be seriously considered.

Make sure that any new developments are discussed with them, and clear the unusual with them. It can avoid problems later.

Failing to completing the P35 and P11Ds by the time limits brings you to the Revenue's attention and they will assume that your systems are not up to much.
Make sure that there are no silly mistakes on the returns – the P35 is run through a standard check by the National Insurance Office and if there are mistakes this can set off an investigation.

Checklist 7B – Identifying employees

The charity must be able to identify those workers who are employees and operate tax procedures correctly. Failure to do so can lead to a substantial liability to tax and National Insurance.

This checklist is based on the guidance given to Revenue staff with additional comments, using the numbering appearing in that guidance.

Question

'Employer's' business

1(a) What is the 'employer's' business; what service does he provide or what does he make? If it is a large organisation, what is the business of the particular section using the worker?

(b) Are there other workers doing similar duties? If so, are they employed or self-employed? If employed what are the differences in the terms of engagement?

(c) Has the worker previously been an employee of the 'employer'? If so when was the change and what are the differences in the terms of engagement?

Nature of job

2 What is the worker's job description; what sort of job did he agree to do?

Engagement of worker

3(a) How was the job obtained? If it was advertised is there a copy of the advertisement or can they give you a description of what was said?

(b) Was the worker interviewed? What information was he given about the job?

(c) When he first started who did he report to and what instructions was he given? What did he do on his first day, starting with the moment of arrival at the place of work and ending with the cessation of work?

Comment

This is a factual question requiring a factual answer. The Inspector needs to understand how the business of the employer operates so that he can establish how the worker fits into the overall scheme of things.

It is difficult to sustain a situation in which people doing the same job are categorised differently. It does not of course follow that all must be treated as employees – possibly they should all be treated as self-employed. Look closely at any differences in the terms of engagement and try to identify if the differences are in fact real.

This is a crucial question. If nothing has really changed then it will be difficult to argue a change of status. Sometimes this situation arises when a worker retires and is re-engaged in a similar capacity – make sure that there are some significant changes in the terms of engagement, e.g. no fixed hours, a change in payment arrangements, etc..

The Revenue will ask questions of both sides. You need to ensure that a consistent line is adopted.

Clearly if the job advert is phrased in terms which are clearly indicative of an employment then it will be essential to explain why the reality was different.

The same comments apply.

The reality of the working arrangement must match the theory set out in the advert or interview.

Contract

4(a)   Is there a written contract or correspondence concerning the engagement or were handbooks or other literature issued to the worker? If so obtain copies.

(b)   If there is no written contract, or the written contract did not cover the full terms of the engagement, what oral agreements were made between the parties?

(c)   Are there any aspects of the job which were not covered by either a written contract or oral agreements but which the parties understood would apply, possibly because of recognised practices or conventions within the particular trade or knowledge gained from previous working relationships?

Control and right of control

5(a)   What parts of the work are or can be checked by a supervisor or manager? If work is substandard can the worker be told to do it again?

(b)   What code of practice, working rules, regulations, etc. has the 'employer' laid down on any aspect of the work or the behaviour of the worker?

(c)   Who decides what is to be done?

The existence of a written contract, while not conclusive as to the nature of the arrangements, will be strong evidence. That evidence can only be overturned if the reality of the arrangements is directly contrary.
The existence of handbooks or franchising agreements, for example, will also be examined.

This can only be ascertained by asking both parties. In some cases the answer may be set out in additional correspondence so do not be surprised if the Revenue ask to see the correspondence which passed in the course of finalising arrangements.

The legal definition of a contract of employment refers to the contract being 'written or oral, expressed or implied' and this question is aimed at identifying the final two aspects. There may be circumstances where working arrangements are prescribed by industry practice or agreement.

As indicated earlier, this used to be considered as one of the prime factors in establishing an employment – if a 'master servant relationship' existed then it was considered difficult to dispute the existence of an employment. The inference in the questions is that if the answer to any of the questions 5(a) to 5(o) below is the employer, then an employment must exist, but this may not be the case.
What the Revenue are looking for in reality is the right of control. There may be situations in which the worker is left to get on with the job because they are perceived as having the initiative to work unsupervised and to make sound decisions. The Revenue would still look to see if the employer had the right to control that worker even if the right was not exercised.

Work done by a self-employed worker may still be subject to quality assessment and he or she may be required to do the work again. A key supplementary question would be: At whose expense is the work put right? If it is at the worker's, then that could be a significant factor pointing to self-employment.

A self-employed consultant could be subject to conditions as to standards and behaviour, particularly while on the 'employer's' premises.

This question has really to be concerned with the detailed doing of the job. If there is detailed direction by the employer then it will be hard to refute the existence of an employment. One of the key factors in the decision in the case of *Stagecraft Ltd v Minister of National Insurance 1952 SC 288* was that the theatrical producers in the case could require a variety comedian to play parts as required by their productions.

(d) Can the worker be moved from job to job if priorities change?

(e) Who decides where the job is to be done?

(f) How much work is carried out on the 'employer's' premises; if not all, where is it done and who decides this?

(g) Who decides when the work is to be done?

(h) Are there set hours?

(i) If there is any flexibility over hours what are their limits?

(j) What arrangements are there for meal breaks, holidays?

(k) What notification does the worker have to give the 'employer' about absence due to illness?

How the work is to be done:

(l) Who tells the worker how to do the work or could tell him if necessary?

(m) What written or oral instructions or other guidance have been given either when the worker first began or since?

(n) Has the worker a particular skill or experience which means no one needs to tell him how to do his job?

(o) If the worker can use his discretion over what, when, where and how work is to be done, who can overrule his decision if necessary?

Personal service

6(a) Must the worker do the job himself or can he send a stand-in or use helpers?

The clear inference is that in these circumstances the worker has no real independence and will be an employee. Again in the *Stagecraft* case the ability of the producers to transfer the comedian to any of their theatres was a factor in determining an employment.

If this is decided in advance by mutual agreement, the issue is neutralised.

The inference is that if the worker is on the premises there is more control. In these days of modern communications this question really has little relevance. A worker can spend their time at home linked by computer to the office – they may be an employee, or they may be self-employed.

This can be mutually agreed.

This will be a factor pointing to an employment. A self-employed person should be able to determine their own hours within any overall agreed deadline for completion.

These will be factors towards an employment.

Much will depend on the nature of the job and the skills and knowledge of the worker.

The setting up of a job specification may not amount to control.

If the answer is 'yes' the other questions in this part are probably irrelevant.

Even if there is such a person it does not imply the existence of an employment.

This can be an important area where services are being provided.
The ability and right to provide a substitute can be a strong factor pointing towards self-employment. It can diminish arguments on control and it can enhance arguments that the worker is a person in business on their own account. In an Australian case the Privy Council noted that 'power of unlimited delegation is almost conclusive against the contract being a contract of service'.
It should be noted that there may be circumstances in which a contractor is required to provide personal services – that of itself will not negate the existence of a self-employment.

(b)   If it is claimed stand-in's or helpers can be provided:

(1)   Was there a specific provision to that effect when the contract was agreed?
(2)   In what circumstances can they be provided?
(3)   Who makes the decision to engage them?
(4)   What restrictions are imposed on their use by the 'employer'?
(5)   Who recruits them?
(6)   Who pays them?
(7)   Who is responsible for their performance?
(8)   Have any ever actually been provided; if so how often and in what circumstances?

Provision of equipment

7(a)   What equipment is necessary to do the job – what is its approximate cost?

(b)   Who provides the equipment?

(c)   Who is responsible for the cost of its upkeep, running costs, fuel, insurance, etc.?

Financial risk, etc.

8(a)   Has the worker invested any capital in his business?

(b)   Is there any chance the worker might make a loss on the contract entered into with the 'employer'?

(c)   Does the worker have to meet the costs of any expenses, e.g. office facilities, telephone, stationery?

(d)   Can the worker increase the profit element in his remuneration in any way other than by working extra hours?

(e)   Does the worker pay for special insurance cover such as public liability?

Payment arrangements

It is easy to get bogged down in detailed argument in this area. In reality, this aspect is often inconclusive. There are many types of employee who are paid on the basis of results and there are many self-employed people who charge on a time basis, e.g. by the day.

Questions (5) to (7) here are the most important. If the worker makes the payments, this is a strong pointer towards self-employment.

This will be a significant factor where the relevant equipment is expensive. The fact that a worker may provide their own stationery would not be evidence of self-employment. The Revenue are most concerned to identify the equipment which is fundamental to the carrying out of the job. However, as the *Lorimer* case demonstrates, it may not be sufficient, to establish employment that the key, expensive equipment is provided by the user of the service.

Simply setting up a £2 company will not be sufficient. This could be significant in connection with question 7 above. The Revenue acknowledge that where the individual risks his own money he will almost certainly be regarded as self-employed.

An absence of financial risk does not always mean an employment. An example would be a member of an orchestra who played sessions. In a couple of cases, such individuals have been held to be self-employed largely on the grounds that they remained freelance musicians pursuing their own profession and maintaining their own individual reputations even when working in an orchestra.

If there is, this should be a strong pointer towards self-employment.

Again a strong pointer towards self-employment.

This is looking at the ability to manage business and profit.

Again a strong pointer towards self-employment.

9(a) On what basis is pay calculated (e.g. hourly, weekly, by the piece, etc.)?

(b) How were the pay arrangements fixed in the first place?

(c) Is overtime paid?

(d) To what extent do payments fluctuate?

(e) What is the frequency of payment?

(f) Who is responsible for making payment?

(g) Is a car or mileage allowance paid?

(h) Is payment made for expenses?

(i) Does the 'employer' provide free transport?

(j) Does the 'employer' provide any benefits for the worker?

(k) Does the worker issue invoices and receipts?

(l) Is the worker registered for VAT and does he charge the employer VAT?

Holiday pay, sick pay, pensions

10(a) What paid holidays is the worker entitled to? Would he be entitled to statutory sick pay or any other pay if off sick?

(b) Does he belong to the firm's superannuation scheme or has the 'employer' made any pension arrangements for him?

Exclusive services

11(a) Does the worker provide similar services concurrently to any other firms? If so obtain details.

(b) Is the worker precluded from providing his services to anyone else for the duration of the contract with the employer? If he is, exactly what is the restriction?

(c) If there are no restrictions is there any scope for the worker to work for others, namely does he work full-time for the employer?

A rate for a job would be a key pointer towards self-employment.

Only relevant if the same arrangements continue. Watch for subsequent changes.

Strong pointer towards employment.

Supplementary question is why?

Payment on completion of job or at agreed stages would be a pointer towards self-employment.

Links to (k). If the payment is made automatically by the employer then that would be regarded as a strong indication of employment. If it is triggered by an invoice then the emphasis moves. Watch for situations in which the issue of an invoice is really a sham.

Not helpful unless it is a method of calculating agreed travel costs.

Depends what the expenses are. If they are incurred in the performance of tasks required under the contract then there is no reason why the employer should not pay them. Disbursements are a common feature of many professional invoices. Arrangements should be clear from the outset.

Of limited application.

Again of limited application.

See comments at (f) above.

May not be conclusive evidence of self-employment. Were Customs told the same details as the Revenue?

A 'yes' answer to either question would be very damaging to a claim to be self-employed.

Don't assume that this means they are self-employed. Each set of arrangements needs to be considered. They could all be employments.

If there is no restriction that would be a potential factor towards self-employment although this would be considerably stronger if there was evidence that work was actually carried out for other people. The existence of a restriction does not necessarily mean an employment.

Is the worker part and parcel of the organisation?

(This links back to question 1.)

12(a)   What is the organisational structure within the business; how does the worker fit within it; who is he answerable to; is he responsible for the work of any other workers?

(b)   Is the task self-contained (i.e. does the worker offer a specific service or produce a particular item)?

(c)   Does the worker present himself to customers as a representative of the organisation?

(d)   Has he a business card and if so how is he described on it?

Right of dismissal

13(a)   Does the 'employer' have the right to either fire or suspend the worker and in what circumstances?

(b)   Is the worker entitled to a period of notice?

(c)   If the work has ended why did it do so and what notice was given.

Statement of intention

14   Was the nature of the engagement stated at the outset? Do both parties to the contract agree on its nature?

'Mutuality of obligation'

15   If it is claimed that the 'employer' is under no obligation to offer or accept further work:

(a)   How is work offered and accepted?

(b)   Do the pay records suggest work is in fact done continuously?

(c)   How often has work been refused?

(d)   If work is refused will the 'employer' offer work in the future?

Casual and short-term engagements

16   Does the worker provide similar services to many engagers? If so:

(a)   Obtain a list of all engagements over the previous 12 months showing for each engagement name of engager, dates between which engaged, nature of engagement and approximate earnings.

(b)   Establish how engagements are obtained and to what extent any business organisation (office, staff, phone, equipment, etc.) exists in relation to the individual's work when viewed overall.

Could be a problem if the worker fits into a specific job title in the hierarchy. The fact that he is responsible for the work of others is not conclusive of employment.

Helpful towards self-employment.

These two factors are linked. A business card showing a job description within the employer's organisation and bearing the employer's logo, etc. would be a strong factor towards employment.

Contract for services, i.e. self-employment, would usually specify some clause for termination including a period of notice.

A question of fact in any set of circumstances.

Helpful only when the other factors are giving a confusing picture. A statement that the worker is self-employed will not hold if the reality is the reverse.

The essence of a contract is that each party should have obligations to each other. The issue is one which the Revenue instructions seek to play down and to debunk from a tax perspective. The Revenue instruction to Inspectors is not to consider this point at all unless the engager or worker raises the subject. It is likely to be of greater significance in the context of casual labour.

These questions look at the worker's side of the operation.

Background. Remember each engagement could be an employment.

If the responsibility is on the worker and they incur expenses in obtaining jobs that would be a helpful factor towards self employment. It was a specific factor in the *Lorimer* case.

(c) Establish the nature of additional expenditure incurred as a result of this pattern of working (e.g. incidental to obtaining and carrying out the work).

(d) To what extent does the individual influence the rate of pay received (e.g. is there any evidence of tendering for work)?

Longer-term part-time engagements

17 If the engagement is part-time in nature is it related to any existing business of the worker? If so:

(a) Ascertain the exact nature of the existing business and how the part-time engagement fits in with that business.

(b) Establish the approximate number of hours spent working in that business per month (excluding the part-time engagement) and how many hours per month will be spent on the part-time work.

(c) Establish the approximate monthly income from the business activities (excluding the part-time work) and the monthly income from the part-time work.

(d) Establish how the other business engagements are conducted and see to what extent this differs from the part-time work.

Checklist 7C – Travel expenses

The rules relating to the allowance of travel expenses changed in 1998 and charities should be aware of the new rules and of the extent to which they are now able to make tax-free payments of travel-related expenses to their employees.

General issues on travel expenses

Question

(1) Is there a section in our staff handbook relating to travel and subsistence?

(2) How do the mileage rates that we pay compare to the Inland Revenue Authorised Mileage Rates?

If work is simply taken at the rate proposed then that would be a factor towards employment. Evidence of tendering would be a helpful pointer towards self-employment.

The key evidence will be the existence of other factors indicating that the worker is engaged in a business on their own account. What the questions are seeking to establish is if the arrangements with the employer are being carried on quite genuinely as part of that business or whether they should be viewed as distinct. In the latter situation it must be considered whether the arrangements constitute an employment.

Comment

If not you should have one. If you have a section has it been updated to reflect the post April 1998 position? Have the new arrangements been communicated to employees?

If your rates are higher, you should be taxing the excess. If your rates are lower, you should be advising employees that they can claim the difference from the Revenue.

(3) Does our claim form for travel and subsistence need revision in the light of the 1998 changes?

(4) Do we have a dispensation for travel and subsistence? If we do, does it need updating for the post-1998 situation?

The new rules

The key issues which need to be considered under the new rules are:

● Travel in the performance of the duties

● Defining a permanent workplace

● Identifying a temporary workplace

Travel in the performance of the duties

This is allowable, but remember that home to work travel is still not allowed.

Question

(1) Do we have employees who are on standby? If so what is the nature of the standby? Do we pay them travel if they are called in?

(2) Do we pay home to work travel in any other situation?

(3) Are there any employees who work for more than one company in our group? Do we actually have a group structure or are there associated companies?

(4) Do we have employees working on joint projects with other employers?

Quite likely that it will.

If you don't have a dispensation you should get one. It will save a large amount of work. If you do, then contact the tax district to get the dispensation updated particularly if expenses which were not previously allowable are going to be allowed under the new rules.

Comment

Just because someone may be required to come into work outside normal hours it does not make home to work travel allowable.

Can you demonstrate that duties actually begin before the employee leaves home?

This will inevitably be taxable! Watch out for situations when employees are asked to come in for very specific reasons, e.g. to work on an urgent project. Also watch out for local managers taking uni-lateral decisions.

If they travel between places at which each employment is exercised, that will be allowable.

Watch the definition of a group which a company is a 51% subsidiary of a parent or where there are two 51% subsidiaries of the same parent. Associated companies under common control will not qualify and travel between employments will not be allowed.

Travel will be allowable.

Defining the workplace

Question

(1)   Can we identify the workplace of each employee?

(2)   Do we have any procedure for checking on the reason for any journey?

(3)   Can we identify the permanent workplace for each employee?

(4)   Could an employee have more than one permanent workplace?

Does the employee regularly perform a significant part of their duties at the location?

Would people expect to be contactable at both locations?

Do they have office and support facilities at each location?

Do we pay travel costs between the locations?

(5)   Are there employees who regularly attend a depot or base from which they perform their duties or at which they receive their allocation of work?

(6)   Are there employees who have their duties defined by reference to a geographical area?
Do they attend at different places in the area but none of those places could be regarded as a permanent workplace?

Comment

A workplace is defined as 'a place at which the employee's attendance is necessary in the performance of the duties of their employment'. It will become necessary to determine if the workplace is permanent or temporary.

Is the journey necessitated by business or is it primarily a private journey with an incidental business purpose?

This is defined as 'a place which the employee regularly attends in the performance of the duties of the employment' and is not a temporary workplace.

The Revenue regard 'regular' attendance as being frequent, following a pattern, and being at a place which the employee attends for the whole of their period of employment.

There could be some employees who work at more than one location under arrangements which could make more than one location their permanent workplace.

The Revenue would regard 40% of time as significant.

Points towards permanence.

Points towards permanence.

Travel costs from home would be ordinary commuting and taxable.

The depot will be the permanent workplace and travel from home to the depot will be ordinary commuting.

The travel from home to the edge of the area is ordinary commuting.

All business travel within the area will be allowable.

All business travel to places outside the area will be allowable.

Identifying a temporary workplace

Questions

(1) Are there employees who have regular visits to the same location?

Are their duties there of limited duration?

Is each visit a self contained task?

Is there evidence to back up the argument for a temporary workplace?

(2) Are there employees who have been seconded on a full-time basis to a location for a period of continuous work?
Is it intended that they will be there for more than 24 months?

Is it expected that they would be there for the whole of the period of their employment?

If they have been seconded on a part-time basis will they spend more than 40% of their time at the location

(3) Was the original intention to spend more than 24 months at the location?

Was the original intention to spend less than 24 months but has this now been changed so that more than 24 months will be spent at the location?

Has any change of location of work had a substantial effect on the actual journey to work or the cost of that journey?

Comments

Don't immediately assume that the place is a temporary workplace.

A 'yes' answer would be helpful.

Again a 'yes' answer points to temporary.

The more often the employee visits the same site, the more likely it is that the Revenue could raise the argument. Look for evidence of project records, diary notes, etc..

The law says that where an employee attends a place for continuous work for more than 24 months, that cannot be a temporary workplace.

If yes, that will be a permanent workplace. However, if they are likely to move on to another place, e.g. another client's premises, that will be temporary.

The definition of 'continuous work' includes the phrase 'to a significant extent' which the Revenue have indicated means more than 40% of the time. So if an employee spends more than 40% of time for a period expected to exceed 24 months at a location that will be a permanent workplace.

The location will be a permanent workplace up to the date of the change of intention and temporary thereafter.

The period up to the time of the change of intention will be treated as temporary. Only from the date of change of intent will the place become a permanent workplace.

A move from a secondment in London to another secondment in the same area of London would not cause a break in the period of working.

VAT Issues

Introduction

As with employment tax issues, VAT is a huge subject and there are so many possible areas of interest that numerous checklists would be needed. A few key areas of more general interest across the charitable sector are included. Charities with very specific areas of interest can review the relevant Customs and Excise VAT guide or look in Chapter 11 *Tolley's Charities Manual* for some initial guidance.

Checklists included are:

Checklist 8A – Basic VAT questions

Checklist 8B – Business activities

Checklist 8C – Partial exemption

Checklist 8D – Land, building and construction

Checklist 8A – Basic VAT questions

VAT is a subject that charities cannot ignore. There are potential opportunities and also potential risk areas and a general awareness of the key issues is vital.

Question

(1) Are the supplies that we are making within the scope of VAT?

(2) If they are, do we need to register for VAT as a matter of law?

(3) Should we in any event consider registration?

(4) Do the supplies that we make fall within any of the special rules which relate to charities?

(5) Do the goods or services that we purchase fall into any of the special rules which relate to charities?

(6) Are we able to recover all the VAT that we suffer on goods and services that we purchase?

(7) Should we be looking at ways of ensuring that we recover as much VAT as possible?

Checklist 8B – Business activities

Charities need to be able to identify if the activities they are engaged in could be regarded as business activities for VAT purposes. This could mean a need to register if supplies were standard-rated and over the registration limit. It might also adversely affect the ability to benefit from zero-rating on new building work.

Question

(1) Is there a clear element of continuity in the activity?

(2) Is the charity deliberately planning to make a profit?

Comment

This means identifying that the supplies are first of all supplies made in the course of a business (see Checklist 8B).

Registration is necessary if the supplies are taxable at the standard rate and exceed the current limit for registration.

It may be possible to consider registration even if supplies are below the threshold. This should only be considered if it is likely that there could be a substantial recovery of input tax and no extra administrative work.

There are special rules which provide exemption or zero-rating in areas such as fundraising, education and welfare.

This can be important where goods are being acquired for the handicapped or supplies of equipment are being made to eligible establishments. Advertising services also benefit from zero-rating. The whole area of new building offers opportunities to benefit from zero-rating and is covered in Checklist 8D.

Exemption unfortunately means no recovery of VAT, but zero-rating can be very useful.

Making sure that the partial exemption rules work as much as possible in the charity's favour is an important area of VAT planning.

Comment

A single transaction will not be sufficient.

This will be very helpful, but the absence of a profit motive cannot be detrimental.

(3)   Is the activity regarded as a trade by the Inland Revenue?

(4)   Is the activity conducted on clear business lines?

(5)   Are we providing a service which is not one commonly provided in the commercial sector?

(6)   Can we demonstrate that you are in competition with other traders?

(7)   Is there a clear link between the making of the supplies and the payment?

Checklist 8C – Partial exemption

Many charities find their ability to reclaim VAT is very limited. Looking closely at the rules for partial exemption can sometimes show opportunities for improving the position.

Question

(1)   Can more of the activities be brought into the definition of taxable activities (preferably zero-rated) from being either outside the scope or exempt?

(2)   Could a better result be obtained by creating two organisations?

(3)   Have we tried to ensure that inputs are attributed as far as possible to taxable supplies, or failing that fall into the residual input tax pot.

(4)   Have we looked to find the best method of apportioning the residual pot?

If it is, it will be regarded as a business for VAT purposes unless it is only a single transaction of purchase and sale.

Make sure that there are similarities between the way the charity's activities and other similar activities in the commercial world are conducted.

This will be a difficult area in which to convince Customs that a business is being carried on.

This will be helpful.

This will be helpful even if this is not on a commercial basis.

Comment

This will improve the direct attribution of inputs as well as having a major effect on the percentage used in connection with residual inputs.

For example, the non-business activity could be carried on in one charity, with the minimum of taxable inputs so that there is a low irrecoverable amount there, while the taxable activities with relatively high inputs, could be carried on in either another charity or possibly a trading subsidiary which can be fully taxable.

Leaving inputs attributable to exempt or outside the scope supplies seriously damages recovery of inputs.

Don't be coerced into using the output method. Be prepared to find the best method and persuade Customs to accept it.

Checklist 8D – Land, building and construction

Charities need buildings and in many cases have been left with premises that need work or alteration. There are specific rules which can help charities to achieve zero-rating for some of this work but there are substantial pitfalls which need to be planned around.

Question

(1)   Is the building a new construction?

(2)   Is the work the conversion or alteration of an existing building?

(3)   Is the work a construction of an annexe?

(4)   Is the building going to be used for a relevant residential purpose?

Comment

Subject to issues relating to use there should be zero-rating of the cost.

The rules on zero-rating are now very limited because the legislation states that an existing building will only cease to be an existing building when:

- demolished completely to ground level; or
- the part remaining above ground consists of no more than a single facade or where a corner site, a double facade, the retention of which is a condition or requirement of statutory planning consent or similar permission.

Although the legislation removes the construction of an annexe from zero-rating, there is an exception where the annexe is intended for sole use for a relevant charitable purpose and:

- is capable of functioning independently from the existing building; and
- the only access or, where there is more than one means of access, the main access to:
  - the annexe is not via the existing building and
  - the existing building is not via the annexe.

This is defined as:

- a home or other institution providing residential accommodation for children;
- a home or other institution providing residential accommodation with personal care for persons in need of personal care by reason of old age, disablement, past or present dependence on alcohol or drugs or past or present mental disorder;
- a hospice;
- residential accommodation for students or school pupils;
- residential accommodation for members of any of the armed forces;
- a monastery, nunnery or similar establishment; or
- an institution which is the sole or main residence of at least 90% of its residents,

except use as a hospital, a prison or similar institution or an hotel, inn or similar establishment.

(5) Is the residential accommodation used only on a short-term basis?

(6) Is the building or part of the building used for business purposes by a charity?

(7) Could the building be described as a village hall?

Tribunal decisions have indicated that this will still qualify for relief. In ordinary English 'residential accommodation' merely signifies lodging, sleeping or overnight accommodation. It does not suggest the need for such accommodation to be for a fixed or minimum period.

The tribunal has also decided that a building could be residential accommodation without being a person's residence.

The legislation does not set any minimum level of business activity by reference to turnover, it simply implies that zero-rating will be lost if any business activity takes place in the building.

Problems can arise where a building is used indiscriminately for business and non-business purposes, e.g. a church hall may be used for worship but may also be let or hired out to groups and individuals. Such use can be ignored where business use is likely to be less than 10% of the total time the building is normally in use.

This will allow zero-rating.

Distribution of work for each office of the Charity Commission based on charity's area of benefit/operation

LONDON OFFICE	LIVERPOOL OFFICE	TAUNTON OFFICE
National and overseas charities where the correspondent is based in:	**National and overseas charities where the correspondent is based in:**	**National and overseas charities where the correspondent is based in:**
All the Boroughs in the Greater London area.	Cambridgeshire	Bedfordshire
	Essex	Buckinghamshire
	Norfolk	East Sussex
	Northamptonshire	Hertfordshire
	Suffolk	Kent
		Surrey
		West Sussex
National, local and overseas charities based in:	**National, local and overseas charities based in:**	**National, local and overseas charities based in:**
Bedfordshire	Cheshire	Bath & North East Somerset
Brighton and Hove	City of York	Berkshire
Buckinghamshire	Conwy	Blaenau Gwent
Cambridgeshire	Cumbria	Bournemouth
East Sussex	Darlington	Bridgend
Essex	Denbighshire	Caerphilly
Greater London	Derby	Cardiff
Hertfordshire	Derbyshire	Carmathenshire
Luton	Durham	Ceredigion
Kent	East Riding of Yorkshire	City of Bristol
Milton Keynes	Flintshire	Cornwall

Appendix 1

LONDON OFFICE	LIVERPOOL OFFICE	TAUNTON OFFICE
Norfolk	Greater Manchester	Devon
Northamptonshire	Gwyneed	Dorset
Suffolk	Hartlepool Borough	Gloucestershire
Surrey	Isle of Anglesey	Gwent
West Sussex	Kingston Upon Hull	Hampshire
	Lancashire	Hereford & Worcester
	Leicester	Isle of Wight
	Leicestershire	Merthyr Tydfil
	Lincolnshire	Monmouthshire
	Merseyside	Neath Port Talbot
	Middlesbrough	Newport
	North Lincolnshire	North Somerset
	North East Lincolnshire	Oxfordshire
	North Yorkshire	Pembrokshire
	Northumberland	Poole
	Nottinghamshire	Portsmouth
	Powys	Rhondda, Cynon, Taff
	Redcar & Cleveland	Somerset
	Rutland	South Gloucestershire
	Shropshire	Southampton
	South Yorkshire	Swansea
	Staffordshire	Torfaen
	Stockton-on-Tees Borough	Wiltshire
	Stoke on Trent	Vale of Glamorgan
	Tyne and Wear	
	Warwickshire	
	West Midlands	
	West Yorkshire	
	Wrexham	

Annual Return (AR8)

Registered Charities, Annual Return

Charity Database Division, PO Box 241, Liverpool L69 3XQ
Helpline **0151-703-1515** (6 lines) Fax 0151-703-1564
Internet Address: http://www.charity-commission.gov.uk

FINANCIAL YEARS ENDING ON OR AFTER 28 FEBRUARY 1999

AR8

Completion Notes

❶ You are legally required to complete Section 1 of this return if the charity is registered with us and either the gross income or the total expenditure of the charity is over £10,000, in the financial year covered by this return. You are, in addition, legally required to complete section 2 if either the gross income or total expenditure exceeds £250,000 in the financial year.

Please refer to the reverse of the letter accompanying this return for guidance on how to calculate gross income and total expenditure.

❷ We are issuing this form to all registered charities - including those that appear from our records to be small - because we do not know when issuing it whether the gross income or the total expenditure of a charity in the financial year covered by the return is over £10,000. **If both the gross income and total expenditure in the year is £10,000 or less you should not complete this form.**

❸ All the questions relate to the financial year covered by this return, unless stated otherwise. The financial year covered by the return will be that ending on or after 28 February 1999. If the charity's financial year ends before 28 February 1999, you should complete a form AR7 which should already have been sent to you. If you need another copy of AR7 please contact our Helpline.

❹ Mae'r ffurflen flynyddol hon ar gael yn Saesneg neu yn Gymraeg. Os ydych wedi derbyn fersiwn Saesneg, ond byddai'n well gennych lenwi'r ffurflen yn Gymraeg, cysylltwch â'n Llinel Gymorth a bydd fersiwn Cymraeg yn cael ei anfon atoch. (This annual return is available in English or Welsh. If you have received an English version but would prefer to complete the return in Welsh, please contact our Helpline and a Welsh version will be sent to you.)

❺ This annual return must be sent to us **within 10 months** of the end of the financial year to which it relates. However, where we have agreed to extend the period for transmitting the annual report and accounts for that year, the period for sending back this return is similarly extended. If your return has not been received by the due date we will issue one reminder. The Commission has statutory powers to act for the protection of charities and may exercise those powers where charities which should send a return fail to do so.

❻ Trustees who are required to send a completed return to us but who, without good reason, persistently refuse to do so, or who give answers which they know or suspect are untrue or misleading, may be committing an offence.

❼ **Failure to complete and send back this annual return if you appear to be legally required to do so (see Note 1 above) may be taken as evidence that the charity has ceased to exist, no longer operates, or no longer meets the minimum requirements for registration and this may lead to steps being taken to remove the charity from the Register.**

❽ Please enter all financial amounts **in sterling** to the nearest £.

❾ Where there is no information to be entered in a particular box please enter 'None'.

❿ Information entered in this return in boxes with a **double** border may be recorded on the register and be open to public inspection. Information entered in boxes with a **single** border may be recorded on the register, but, if it is, it will not be available for public inspection.

⓫ Please bring the contents of this annual return to the attention of all the charity's trustees. Please seek advice if you have any doubts about how to complete it. You may wish to keep a copy of your completed return.

⓬ If the charity has ceased to operate, please send this form back with a letter explaining the circumstances.

⓭ If you need any assistance in completing this return please contact our Helpline on 0151-703-1515.

REGISTERED NUMBER

MAIN CHARITY NAME

1

Section 1

- You should only complete this form if your gross income or total expenditure exceeds £10,000 in the financial year.
- Please note that Y or N can be used as acceptable abbreviations of YES and NO when completing either Sections 1 or 2.

Financial Year

❶ Please show the financial year that this return covers:

Financial year **Start**

Financial year **End**

❶ The financial year should end no earlier than 28 February 1999 (see Completion Note 3).

Gross Income and Total Expenditure

❷ Please extract the following information from the accounts prepared for the financial year:

Gross Income £

Total Expenditure £

❷ Please refer to the reverse of the letter accompanying this return on how to work out gross income and total expenditure.

In all cases please take the figures from the charity's accounts.

The Statement of Recommended Practice on Accounting by Charities recommends that, in certain circumstances, a charity should, in addition to its own accounts, prepare consolidated (or group) accounts for itself and its subsidiary undertakings such as connected trading companies. The figures should not be taken from any such consolidated accounts.

For the meaning of **"connected trading company"** see the notes to question 9.

The gross income and the total expenditure figures should be calculated for the whole of the financial year shown above even if the actual period is longer or shorter than a year (in some cases this may be as little as 6 months or as long as 18 months).

Internal Management

❸ a Those who examine accounts **may** from time to time produce a report concerning weaknesses in accounting and internal control systems.

Has the charity received a report during the financial year, or on the accounts prepared for the financial year, from an auditor, reporting accountant, or independent examiner concerning any material weakness in its accounting and internal control systems?

Please answer YES or NO

b If YES to **Question 3a**, has action been taken to deal with it, at any time before the date you complete this form?

Please answer YES or NO

❸ If further information is needed, please see our leaflet CC8: Internal Financial Controls.

Fund-raising

❹ a Does the charity engage in fund-raising efforts?

Please answer YES or NO

If YES please answer the questions below.

b Please state the gross amount received from all fund-raising efforts.

£

c Does the charity make use of professional fund-raisers?

Please answer YES or NO

d Does the charity make use of professional fund-raising consultants?

Please answer YES or NO

If the answer to either Questions 4c or 4d is YES:

e How many professional fund-raisers/consultants did the charity make use of during the financial year?

NUMBER

❹ a If further information is needed, please see our leaflet CC20: Charities and Fund-raising.

b "The gross amount received from fund-raising efforts" includes:

- solicited gifts (eg gifts which result from direct mailing, telephone canvassing, public collections, sponsorship arrangements);
- the proceeds of sale of goods or services (eg income from lotteries and competitions and charity shops);
- money received from the National Lottery Distribution Fund.

It does not include:

- gifts by will;
- unsolicited gifts;
- membership subscriptions;
- any investment income;
- gifts or dividends received from connected trading companies;
- income received from central or local government funds or from other statutory funds.

For the meaning of **"connected trading company"** please see the notes to question 9.

c The term **"professional fund-raiser"** does not include a trustee or an employee of the charity. The term is defined in Part II of the Charities Act 1992.

d The term **"professional fund-raising consultant"** means any person who is paid to advise the charity about its fund raising. It does not include a trustee or employee of the charity, nor does it include anybody within the statutory definition of professional fund-raiser. However, if the consultant carries out a fund-raising business or does more than merely provide advice, that person is likely to be a professional fund-raiser, even though his is not actually raising funds for the charity and the requirements of Part II of the Charities Act 1992 may apply. If this is the case please answer Yes to question 4c.

2

Fund-raising (continued)

f Does the charity have a formal written agreement with each of the professional fund-raisers/consultants?

Please answer YES or NO

g Are any of the professional fund-raisers/consultants paid on a commission basis?

Please answer YES or NO

Cash Balances

5 a Please state the total amount of all **cash on hand** and held in bank or building society **current account balances** at the end of the charity's financial year.

£

b Please state the total amount of **cash held on deposit** (for example in a bank or building society) at the end of the charity's financial year.

£

Trustees and Trustee Benefits

6 a Please state the number of trustees the charity had at the beginning and end of the financial year.

BEGINNING   **END**

b Please give the total of the amounts paid or payable **to or for the benefit** of trustees, or people, or bodies connected with them. Please divide the amounts into the categories below and include both direct and indirect payments. Please include amounts paid or payable from the funds of any company or other institution connected with the charity, as well as payments from the charity's own funds.

i) Payments of trustees' expenses.

£

ii) Amounts paid or payable to trustees for any professional services provided to the charity or to any company or other institution connected with the charity.

£

iii) Amounts paid or payable to trustees for any other services provided to the charity or to any company or other institution connected with the charity.

£

iv) Loans made to trustees.

£

v) Other amounts paid or payable to trustees.

£

c Has any property of the charity, or of any company or other institution connected with the charity, been purchased by a trustee or person or body connected with that trustee?

Please answer YES or NO

d At the end of the financial year was the charity, or any company or other institution connected with it, owed money by any of the trustees, or by any person or body connected with any of the trustees?

Please answer YES or NO

5 a **Cash and current account balances** at the charity's regional offices and branches should be included here. Include here interest-bearing current account balances.

b **Cash on deposit** includes any interest-bearing deposits of money (other than interest-bearing current account balances which should be shown under 5(a)).

6 a If further information is needed, please see our leaflet **CC11: Remuneration of Charity Trustees.**

b Do not include items purchased by trustees for the benefit of the charity (eg stationery, equipment, supplies) that are reimbursed by the charity at cost.

i) These are expenses which trustees incur in carrying out their duties **as trustees** and include for example travel, meals, accommodation and telephone costs.

ii) This includes any payments for consultancy and other professional services provided by trustees to the charity.

iii) This includes salary, wages, honoraria and other earnings in employment, as well as payments to trustees as contractors. It also includes pension provisions and compensation for loss of office.

v) **Other amounts** include, the cost of purchasing trustee indemnity insurance, payments for the purchase of goods or property, etc.

c/d The following are **"connected with"** a trustee:

i) the trustee's spouse";

ii) the trustee's children, parents, grandchildren, grandparents, brothers and sisters and their spouses";

iii) the trustees of any private trust of which the beneficiaries or potential beneficiaries include the trustee or anyone mentioned in (i) or (ii);

iv) business partners of the trustee or of anyone mentioned in (i), (ii) or (iii);

v) firms or businesses (not including those which are wholly owned by one or more charities) in which the trustee and anyone mentioned in (i) to (iv), taken together, has or have a substantial interest.

"Spouse includes someone living with another as their husband or wife.

Substantial interest means the ownership of at least one-fifth of the shares in the company or the ability to direct how at least one-fifth of the voting power in the company is exercised.

For the meaning of **"connected company"** please see the note to question 9. **Other institutions** will be connected with the charity in the same circumstances.

3

411

Trustees and Trustee Benefits (continued)

● Have any services been made available by the charity, or any company or other institution connected with the charity, to a trustee, or to a person or body connected with a trustee?

Please tick the appropriate box

i) No services used by trustee or connected person/body.

ii) Services used generally by beneficiaries or members of the charity and used by a trustee, or connected person/body, as one of them.

iii) Services used by a trustee or connected person/body otherwise than as one of the beneficiaries or members of the charity.

Occupation of Functional Property

❼ If any part of the functional property owned by the charity was not occupied by it please state who occupied that part of the property and whether or not they paid rent.

	Occupied at **full** rent	Occupied at **reduced** or nil rent
Another charity		
Charity s clients or beneficiaries		
Anyone else		
Not occupied by anyone		

Land and Buildings

❽ a If the charity **acquired** any freehold or leasehold land or buildings from any of its trustees, or from people or bodies connected with any of its trustees, please state the total amount paid.

£

b If the charity **occupies** any land or buildings belonging to any of its trustees, or to people or bodies connected with any of its trustees, please state the total amount paid in respect of that occupation.

£

● **Services** includes the use of land and buildings and motor vehicles. Services made available generally to the beneficiaries of the charity includes the services provided to local inhabitants of a village hall or recreation ground charity.

If a charity has allowed a trustee the residential use of property which it owns then the third box should be ticked.

❼ **Functional property** is land or buildings owned by the charity and used primarily in furtherance of its charitable objects. It does not include land or buildings used primarily for investment or fund-raising purposes.

Owned includes ownership as tenant or lessee (ie leasing or renting land or buildings) as well as freehold ownership. But a charity which merely has a licence or permission to use property is not the owner of it. If a charity has regular use of a building or part of a building on say one day a week, it is probably a licensee. **Primarily** means more than half of the total area being used, for more than half of the time available.

Occupied at full rent means that the total amount which is paid for the use of the land, under the agreement between the charity and the occupier, is the highest amount which the charity can reasonably obtain for that use, from any occupier. The amount which can reasonably be obtained may be affected by planning restrictions, or covenants in the charity s own title document which restrict the charity s freedom to use or let the property.

A trustee who occupies the functional property of the charity for his/her own benefit should never be treated as doing so as a client or beneficiary for the purposes of this section. The "Anyone else" category should be used.

Please tick as many boxes as are needed to reflect the charity s circumstances.

❽ **If further information is needed, please see our leaflet CC33: Acquiring Land.**

a To identify people or bodies connected with trustees, please see the notes to question 6.

b Please include rent or licence fee, any premium or capital payment and all other payments made under the tenant s covenants in the lease or under the terms of the licence, for example on repairs/improvements to the property etc.

Dealings with Connected Companies or Connected Trading Companies

9 a Does the charity have any companies connected with it?

Please answer YES or NO ◯

If YES, is any connected company a connected trading company?

Please answer YES or NO ◯

If YES please answer the questions below

b Please state the total cost of the charity's shares in its connected trading companies, as at the end of the financial year.

£ ◯

c Has the Inland Revenue at any time been asked to confirm that any of these shares which were acquired on or after 12 June 1986 are qualifying investments?

Please answer YES or NO ◯

d Has the Inland Revenue **accepted** these shares as qualifying investments?

Please answer YES or NO ◯

e Give the total outstanding balance of loans owed to the charity by connected trading companies as at the end of the financial year (from the accounts)

£ ◯

f Has any money originally loaned to a connected trading company not been repaid, but has instead either been subscribed by the charity for the issue of new shares in that company (ie converted to share capital) or written off?

i) Converted to share capital?

Please answer YES or NO ◯

ii) Written off?

Please answer YES or NO ◯

iii) If the answer to either of these is **YES**, was the action approved by the trustees?

Please answer YES or NO ◯

g Please give details of total amounts due at the end of the financial year to the charity from connected trading companies excluding loans.

The total amounts due to the charity.

£ ◯

h Please give the following details about all the charity's connected trading companies

i) Total turnover.

£ ◯

ii) Total profit or loss on ordinary activities before taxation. (Losses should be shown by placing figures in brackets).

£ ◯

iii) Total amounts transferred to the charity.

£ ◯

9 a The company may be limited by shares or guarantee. A **connected trading company** means any company which is connected with the charity but is not itself a charity. A company is connected with a charity if the charity:

- owns at least one-fifth of the shares in the company; or
- can direct how at least one-fifth of the voting power in the company is exercised; or
- can otherwise ensure that the affairs of the company are conducted in accordance with its wishes.

If further information is needed, please see our leaflet CC35: Charities and Trading.

b The "total cost" means everything spent by the charity either in purchasing shares in its connected trading companies, or in making subscriptions for share capital in its connected trading companies.

c/d A qualifying investment in a connected trading company is an investment which the Inland Revenue is satisfied is made for the benefit of the charity and not for the avoidance of tax and is defined in part 1 of Schedule 20 of the Income and Corporation Taxes Act 1988.

f Where provision has been made in the accounts of the charity for the partial or total non-repayment of a loan which the charity has made, the loan should be treated as "written off".

g This could include amounts owing to the charity for goods and services provided, or service charges, or as a result of charging expenses of the company to the charity.

h i) Please give the overall totals of:

the turnover; and

profit or loss

of all the trading companies which are connected with the charity for the last complete financial year ending on or before the last day of the financial year of the charity

ii) For present purposes profit or loss on ordinary activities should be calculated **before** deducting any gifts made to the charity (eg under deed of covenant or Gift Aid) but **after** deducting any payments of interest on loans from the charity.

iii) By deed of covenant, Gift Aid, dividend or any other means. Transfers by deed of covenant or Gift Aid should be treated as having been made by the company in the financial year in which they are treated for tax purposes as having been made.

End of **Section 1.** If neither the charity's gross income nor its total expenditure was over £250,000 in the financial year, then please ignore **Section 2,** but complete the declaration on **Page 8.**

413

Appendix 2

Section 2

Please note that Y or N can be used as acceptable abbreviations of YES and NO when completing Section 2.

The questions in this section are only for charities having a gross income or total expenditure in the financial year in excess of £250,000.

Details of Expenditure

10 Please show the breakdown of the total expenditure figure given in the answer to **Question 2 Section 1:**

Expenditure directly relating to the objects of the charity.

£

Expenditure on fund-raising and publicity.

£

Expenditure on the cost of managing and administering the charity.

£

Information on Assets and Funds

11 a Please give the following details from the charity's balance sheet:

Total Endowment Funds (A)

£

Total Restricted Income Funds (B)

£

Total Unrestricted Funds (C)

£

Total of All Funds (D=A+B+C)

£

b Please break down the **TOTAL Funds** (D above) into the following categories of asset and liability:

Intangible Fixed Assets (E)

£

Tangible Fixed Assets for use by the Charity (F)

£

Investments (G)

£

Total Current Assets (H)

£

Total Assets (I=E+F+G+H)

£

Short Term Liabilities (J)

£

Long Term Liabilities (K)

£

Total Net Assets (I-J-K=D)

£

10 Please copy these figures from the charity's accounts. If you require further guidance on what items of expenditure to include under these headings please refer to The Statement of Recommended Practice on Accounting by Charities paragraphs 92 and 93.

11 a **Endowment funds** are funds which the trustees are legally required to invest or to keep and use for the charity's purposes. These funds may be **permanent endowment** where the trustees can spend only the income which the funds produce, or **expendable endowment** where the trustees are entitled to convert the entire fund or any part of it into income and then spend it.

Permanent endowment means property which cannot be spent as income, because:
- the terms of the charity's governing document prevent that property being spent; or
- the person who gave the property to the charity directed that it should be kept for use by the charity, or that it should be invested to produce an income for the charity.

Restricted income funds are funds which ought to be spent within a reasonable time of receipt, but only for a particular purpose within the wider purposes of the charity.

Unrestricted funds are all other funds, which ought to be spent within a reasonable time of receipt, but may be spent for any purposes of the charity, at the discretion of the trustees.

If further information is needed, please see our leaflet CC19: Charities Reserves.

b Please add E, F, G & H together to give item I (total assets).

If the charity's balance sheet includes a provision for liabilities and charges, please divide the between items J and K, according to whether these are short term or long term liabilities.

6

414

Contingent Liabilities

12 Please extract from the accounts the total amount or estimated amount of any contingent liabilities of the charity at the end of the financial year:

£ ⃝

13 A liability is contingent if it is subject to a condition that exists at the balance sheet date where the outcome is dependent on one or more uncertain future events.

Investments and Loans

13 a Does the charity at the end of the financial year have any investments, or outstanding loans it has made by way of investment? (Please exclude investments in, and loans to, connected trading companies).

Please answer YES or NO ⃝
If **YES** please answer the questions below.

b What was the approximate market value of all the charity s **investment properties?**

£ ⃝

c What was the approximate market value of the charity s **financial investment portfolio?**

£ ⃝

d What was the approximate market value of the charity s largest single holding in its **financial investment portfolio?**

£ ⃝

Please give details as at the end of the financial year.

e What was the charity s gross investment income for the year?

£ ⃝

f If, at the end of the financial year, the financial investment portfolio included shares in, or loans to, unlisted companies or loans to individuals or unincorporated bodies, what was the total amount paid or subscribed for such shares, and/or loaned as at the end of the financial year?

£ ⃝

g At the end of the financial year did the charity have any outstanding contractual rights or obligations under derivatives?

Please answer YES or NO ⃝

Management of Investments

14 a Does the charity use the services of an independent investment advisor?

Please answer YES or NO ⃝

b Do the trustees delegate their investment powers to an investment manager?

Please answer YES or NO ⃝
If **YES** please answer the questions below.

c Is the investment manager paid by commission?

Please answer YES or NO ⃝

d Is the investment manager paid by a fee?

Please answer YES or NO ⃝

e How much was the investment **manager** paid during the year?

£ ⃝

Please complete the Declaration overleaf.

13 If further information is needed, please see our leaflet CC14: Investment of Charitable Funds: Basic Principles.

For the meaning of **"connected trading company"** see the notes to question 9.

a **Investments** means any assets held which are intended to produce continuing benefit to the charity in the form of income or capital gains. This includes land and buildings, government or other securities, loans, common investment funds, unit trusts, shares in a public or private company and bank or building society deposit accounts. Investments may also include cash held temporarily as part of an investment portfolio.

b **Investment properties** means land and buildings other than functional property (see question 7).

c/d **Financial investment portfolio** means investments in government or other securities, loans, common investment funds, unit trusts, shares in a public or private company. Do not include bank or building society deposit accounts which have already been reported under question 5b.

e Give the total income from all investments defined above (including deposit accounts) for all funds: endowment, restricted and unrestricted.

f This question relates to loans made as investments and **not** to loans made in furtherance of the objects of the charity. **Unlisted companies** are companies the shares of which are not listed on a stock exchange which is recognised for the purposes of section 841 Income and Corporation Taxes Act 1988. **Unincorporated bodies** include trusts, associations and partnerships.

g **Derivatives** are financial instruments the value of which is dependent on the price movements in one or more underlying investment assets or in interest rates. Examples include options, futures and interest rate swaps. Units in common investment funds and unit trusts are **not** derivatives and should **not** be included in this section.

14 b This means giving an investment manager authority to make and change investments on behalf of the charity without asking the charity trustees even when changes are reported later.

Appendix 2

Checklist

You must complete this return if the charity is registered with us and either the gross income or the total expenditure of the charity is over $10,000 in the financial year covered by this return. You are also required to send us copies of the trustees' annual report and the accounts of the charity. It would be helpful if you would **please enclose them with this return** if you have not already sent them to us. Please tick the relevant boxes to show which you are sending to us with this return.

Trustees Annual Report	Not enclosed				
	Already sent	Brief Report (income $100,000 or less)		Full Report	
Annual Accounts	Not enclosed				
	Already sent	Receipts and Payments Accounts and Statement of Assets and Liabilities	Statement of Financial Activities and Balance Sheet		Other Form or Account
Examination Report	Not enclosed				
	Already sent				
	No Report required	Independent Examiner	Audit Exemption Report		Audit Report

Declaration

We need accurate information to do our work. Please take care to check that the information you are giving us is correct.

The completion notes on Page 1 of this return show whether and when charity trustees are required to complete this form, and send it to us. Trustees who are required to do so but who, without good reason, persistently refuse to send a completed form to us, or who, in the form, give answers which they know or suspect are untrue or misleading, may be committing an offence.

I certify that the information given in this form is correct to the best of my knowledge and **has been brought to the attention of all the trustees.**

Signed, by one trustee on behalf of all trustees

Date

Title and Full Name
(Please use BLOCK CAPITALS)

TITLE

FULL NAME

ADDRESS

POSTCODE

Please give the name and telephone number of someone we can contact if we need to clarify any of your answers.

CONTACT NAME

DAYTIME TELEPHONE NUMBER

For office use only:

A		B	
C		D	
E		F	
G		H	
I		J	

416

Charity
COMMISSION
for England and Wales

Registered Charities - Database Update 1999/00
Charity Database Division, PO Box 241, Liverpool L69 3XQ
Helpline **0151-703-1515** (5 lines) Fax 0151-703-1564
Internet Address: http://www.charity-commission.gov.uk

Completion Notes

❶ Trustees of all registered charities have a legal duty to notify us of any changes in the particulars entered in the Register. Completing this Database Update form is a convenient way of doing this.

This form is **NOT** part of the charity's Annual Return ARB and only charities with either gross income or total expenditure over $10,000 in their financial year are obliged to complete an ARB. **However, unless you complete this Database Update form showing details of your gross income etc we will not know whether your charity is over the £10,000 threshold.** If you don't complete this form you may receive reminders.

❷ This form contains an extract of the particulars of your charity that we hold on the register of charities. Please check these particulars carefully.

• If all the preprinted information is still correct you need only complete the Gross Income and Total Expenditure boxes on page 2, and the declaration on this page.

• If there are changes needed please indicate these in the space(s) provided and then sign the declaration.

When you have done this, please return the form to us. If you also need to complete an annual return, it would be easier for us if you returned both documents at the same time, together with a copy of the relevant annual accounts and the trustees' annual report.

❸ Although most of the particulars on the Register are open to public inspection, there are some that are available

only to our staff. Some key registration particulars which are open to public inspection are also available on our internet site address, as above.

❹ Charities can seek a dispensation to exclude the Principal Address and/or Trustees Names from their annual report. If a dispensation has been given we will also exclude this information from the Public Register and our internet site. If you would like more details please contact our Helpline on the telephone number above.

❺ Space is provided for changing the details of the charity correspondent and of trustees. If you are changing a post code, telephone number or name only, please show the change in the space(s) provided. For changes to any other part of the address please confirm the address again in full.

❻ Mae'r ffurflen hon ar gael yn Saesneg neu yn Gymraeg. Os ydych wedi derbyn fersiwn Saesneg ond byddai'n well gennych gwblhau'r ffurflen yn Gymraeg, cysylltwch â'n Llinell Gymorth a bydd fersiwn Cymraeg yn cael ei anfon atoch. (This form is available in English or Welsh. If you have received an English version but would prefer to complete the form in Welsh, please contact our Helpline and a Welsh version will be sent to you.)

❼ **If you require any help at all in completing this form please do not hesitate to contact our Helpline on 0151-703-1515.**

ALL REGISTERED CHARITIES SHOULD COMPLETE THIS FORM.

Declaration

I certify that the information given in this form is correct to the best of my knowledge.

SIGNED _____   DATE _____

FULL NAME _____   TEL NO: _____

Reminder! *Have you entered the Gross Income & Total Expenditure figures on Page 2?*

Main Charity Name/Number & Company Registration Number

Main Charity Name/Number - *Our records show your Main Charity name is as shown here. If you have recently changed your name, please enter the new name in the box below. Also, if you haven't already done so, please send a copy of the resolution or other document by which the name was changed.*

_____

Company Registration Number

If the number is wrong or missing please enter the correct details here: ⬚⬚⬚⬚⬚⬚⬚⬚

If a number is shown but the charity is not a Registered Company please tick this box ⬚

417

Appendix 2

**This form should be completed for the Financial
Year Ending between 28 February 1999 and 27 February 2000.**

If either is wrong, please enter the correct details here:

Financial Year **Start**

Financial Year **End**

Our records show your next financial year will end on:-

If this is wrong, please enter the correct details here:

Financial Year **End** *(Day & Month)*

We cannot process your form unless you provide details of your Gross Income & Total Expenditure, therefore please provide the following information.

**Gross Income and Total Expenditure for the above
Financial Year**

*Details of how to calculate these figures are provided on the
reverse of the covering letter that accompanied this form.*

Gross Income **(to nearest £)**   £

Total Expenditure **(to nearest £)**   £

Charity s Working Names

Charity s unofficial names (if it has any) -

Some charities like to use a working name as well as their main name. You can enter a
working name here (if you have one) and this may help the public to trace your charity on
our public register.

Please cross out any name that is no longer used or requires amendment.
Please write in details of amendments beside the relevant preprinted information,
and add any new names below the preprinted details.

Charity Contact Details

Charities which have been granted dispensation from disclosure of their principal address should **NOT** complete this section, but notify us
separately of any change in either their principal address or the name and address which appears on the Public Register. For more detailed
advice on how to request a dispensation please contact our **Helpline** on **0151-703-1515.**

THE INFORMATION IN THIS SECTION WILL BE OPEN TO PUBLIC INSPECTION

This is the postal address that we and the public will use to contact the
charity.

This address should be the charity s principal address. If the charity
is a registered company this will be the registered address.

In other cases it can be the charity office or the name
and address of an individual.

Please see completion note 5 if you are changing any
part of the address.

If the details are incorrect please enter the correct details here.

FULL NAME

ADDRESS

POST CODE   **TEL NO**

Charity s Web Site/E-mail Address

If this is wrong, please enter the correct details here:

2

418

Trustees - ALL REGISTERED CHARITIES SHOULD CHECK ANY PREPRINTED DETAILS SHOWN ON THIS PAGE.

Below are details of the trustees we currently know about. We only need details for a maximum of 50 trustees, so continuation sheets may be enclosed. Please check the list(s) and if any amendment is needed to a name, post code or telephone number just complete the relevant amendment box. For changes to any other part of the address please write the address in full again. If a trustee is no longer acting tick the No longer trustee box.

If we have omitted the names of any trustees who have been acting for some time don t make any entries on this page, **please enter their details on page 4** (we will then enter these onto our database). Also if we show more than one entry for the same trustee please tick the No longer trustee box by the entry you want us to delete. (It is possible that the same trustee could be listed twice due to a variation in the initials used.)

Please use page 4 to advise us of the details of any new trustees.

The details provided should apply to the trustees in post at the date you complete this form. **We will not make available to the public the addresses or dates of birth of any trustees.** We need the date of birth for identification purposes.

Amendments

NAME

ADDRESS

POSTCODE

TEL NO   DATE OF BIRTH

No longer trustee

Amendments

NAME

ADDRESS

POSTCODE

TEL NO   DATE OF BIRTH

No longer trustee

Amendments

NAME

ADDRESS

POSTCODE

TEL NO   DATE OF BIRTH

No longer trustee

Amendments

NAME

ADDRESS

POSTCODE

TEL NO   DATE OF BIRTH

No longer trustee

Amendments

NAME

ADDRESS

POSTCODE

TEL NO   DATE OF BIRTH

No longer trustee

3

419

Appendix 2

NAME		NAME	
ADDRESS		ADDRESS	
	POSTCODE		POSTCODE
TEL NO	DATE OF BIRTH	TEL NO	DATE OF BIRTH
NAME		NAME	
ADDRESS		ADDRESS	
	POSTCODE		POSTCODE
TEL NO	DATE OF BIRTH	TEL NO	DATE OF BIRTH
NAME		NAME	
ADDRESS		ADDRESS	
	POSTCODE		POSTCODE
TEL NO	DATE OF BIRTH	TEL NO	DATE OF BIRTH
NAME		NAME	
ADDRESS		ADDRESS	
	POSTCODE		POSTCODE
TEL NO	DATE OF BIRTH	TEL NO	DATE OF BIRTH
NAME		NAME	
ADDRESS		ADDRESS	
	POSTCODE		POSTCODE
TEL NO	DATE OF BIRTH	TEL NO	DATE OF BIRTH

4

420

Trust and Estate Tax Return

Income for the year ended 5 April 2000

Inland Revenue

TRUST AND ESTATE CHARITIES

Fill in these boxes first

Name of trust

Name of charity, if different

Tax reference

If you want help, look up the box numbers in the Notes on Trust and Estate Charities.

Claim to exemption

- Charity repayment reference — **7.1**

- Charity Commission Registration Number or Scottish Charity Number — **7.2**

If the trust is a charity are you claiming exemption from all tax on all or part of your income and gains? — YES / NO

Have all income and gains that you are claiming to be exempt from tax been, or will they be, applied for charitable purposes? — YES / NO

Return period

- Are you returning information for the **year ended 5 April 2000?** YES / NO

- If 'No', what period does this Return cover?

  Period begins **7.3** / / and ends **7.4** / /

- Are accounts to be enclosed with the Return? YES / NO

  If 'No', explain why **7.5**

Repayments

	Income Tax	Transitional relief
• Amount already claimed on form R68 or R68(MGA)	**7.6** £	**7.7** £
• Total repayment/payment due	**7.8** £	**7.9** £
and		
• further repayment/payment due	**7.10** £	**7.11** £
or		
• amounts overclaimed	**7.12** £	**7.13** £

Income on which you are claiming exemption

Non-exempt amounts should be entered in the appropriate parts of the Return.

• Total turnover from exempt trading activities	**7.14** £
• Investment income	**7.15** £
• UK land and buildings income	**7.16** £
• Deed of covenant	**7.17** £
• Gift Aid or Millennium Gift Aid	**7.18** £
• Other charities	**7.19** £
• Legacies	**7.20** £
• Other donations	**7.21** £
• Other, for example, commissions, fees, small fund raising	**7.22** £

continued over

SA907

BMSD 12/99net   Trust and Estate Tax Return ■ Charity Pages TCH1

Expenses as included in the charity accounts

- Trading costs **7.23** £ _____
- UK land and buildings **7.24** £ _____
- All general administration costs **7.25** £ _____
- All grants and donations made in the UK **7.26** £ _____
- All grants and donations made outside the UK **7.27** £ _____
- Others (not entered elsewhere on the Return) **7.28** £ _____

Assets

	Disposals in year	Held at 5 April 2000
Tangible fixed assets	**7.29** £	**7.30** £
UK investments (excluding controlled companies)	**7.31** £	**7.32** £
Shares in, and loans to, controlled companies	**7.33** £	**7.34** £
Overseas investments	**7.35** £	**7.36** £
Loans and non-trade debtors		**7.37** £
Other current assets		**7.38** £

- Were all investments qualifying investments, and were loans made qualifying loans, within Part I or II of Schedule 20 ICTA 1988? **YES** **NO**

- Value of any non-qualifying investments and loans **7.39** £ _____

- Number of subsidiary or associated companies you control at 5 April 2000 **7.40**

Claim

I claim exemption from tax

7.41

Signature   Date

Print name in full here

Status or capacity in which you are signing

7.42

Additional information

Corporation Tax Return CT600 and CT600E

1

Inland **Revenue**

Company Tax Return
Form CT600 (1999) Version 1
For accounting periods ending on or after 1 July 1999

This form (or an Inland Revenue approved substitute version of it), together with any relevant *Supplementary Pages*, must be used whenever a company is required by form *CT603 Notice to deliver a company tax return (the Notice)* for any period ended on or after 1 July 1999. This form sets out the information we need and provides a standard format for calculations. Please complete the 'Company information' immediately and then read the notes on page 2 before completing any other sections.

Company information

Company name

Company registration number *(if registered)*

Reference - *as shown on the Notice*
/ /

Address - *If different from that shown on the Notice*

Postcode

Period covered by this return *(cannot exceed 12 months)*
From *dd/mm/yyyy*
/ /

To
/ /

Before you begin completing the form, read the notes on page 2 and then go to Section 1 on page 3 as this will help you decide whether you need to obtain and complete any of the Supplementary Pages which form part of the return. Fill in the 'Summary' and 'Declaration' below once you have completed the relevant sections, and before you send back the return to the issuing Tax Office.

Summary of return information

Put an 'X' in box if 'Yes'

Are you making a repayment claim
· for this period?

· for an earlier period?

I attach

· accounts for the period to which this return relates

· accounts for a different period

Put an 'X' in box if 'Yes'

Are you filing more than one return for this company now?

Are you seeking approved investment trust company status under S842(1) ICTA 1998?
Attach a schedule showing how the company has met all the conditions. See note 26

· if no accounts, say why not

I am sending you the following completed *Supplementary Pages* as part of the return form
Put an 'X' in appropriate box(es)

Loans to participators by close companies (CT600A)

Controlled foreign companies (CT600B)

Group and consortium (CT600C)

Insurance (CT600D)

Charity (CT600E)

Declaration

Warning
Giving false information in the return, or concealing any part of the company's profits or tax payable, can lead to the company and you being prosecuted.

Declaration
The information I have given on this form and the accompanying Supplementary Pages is correct and complete to the best of my knowledge and belief.

Signature

Date *(dd/mm/yyyy)*
/ /

Status

Name *(in capital letters)*

Except where a liquidator has been appointed, any person who is authorised to do so may sign on behalf of the company. A photocopy of a signature is not acceptable.

BMSD 6/99

CT600 (1999)

Appendix 4

Important points

- As soon as you receive the **Notice to deliver a company tax return (the Notice)** make sure you obtain all the *Supplementary Pages* you need. The information on page 3 in Section 1 should help you decide which you will need and how to get them. Please contact the Tax Office shown on the *Notice* if you need more help.

- **Members' clubs, societies and voluntary associations** may only need to complete the *Company information, Summary* and *Declaration* sections on page 1, and the short calculation on pages 4 and 5. Note 1 in the *Company Tax Return Guide (Guide)* gives more detail about what to complete but our leaflet *'Clubs, societies and voluntary associations' (IR46)* gives more information and includes an example of a completed form *CT600*. The leaflet is available from any Inland Revenue Enquiry Centre or Tax Office (see 'Inland Revenue' in your local Phone Book).

- **'Company' includes** every kind of body, club, society, association or organisation that is chargeable to corporation tax, whether or not it is incorporated.

- **Please do not** make an entry where the company did not have the item specified in the return form. Complete the boxes with whole figures only, except where pence or decimals are indicated.

- **The Guide** and the further notes on this form will help you complete this return.

Which sections you need to complete

After reading the notes on this page, start at Section 1.

All trading companies must complete Section 2. All companies must then complete either the Short Calculation (Section 3) or the Detailed Calculation (Section 4). The notes at the beginning of each Calculation will help you decide which one is appropriate.

Complete Section 5 if you want to claim capital allowances.

Complete Section 6 if, in this period, the company has any of the losses or excess amounts listed there. Group companies must also show the maximum amounts available for surrender by way of group or consortium relief.

Complete Section 7 if there is a repayment claim attached to this return.

If the company charges directors' remuneration in the accounts please complete Section 8.

What to do when you have completed the return

When you have completed the appropriate sections make sure you give us all the information requested on page 1. Once you have done this, sign and date the *Declaration* and send the **whole** form to us. Attach any supporting calculations, claims or surrender documentation. Send them along with the relevant completed *Supplementary Pages*, company accounts and, where prepared, directors' and auditors' reports. Note 3 in the *Guide* advises you of the date by which you must do this (the filing date).

It is a good idea to keep a copy of the completed return for your own records.

You must pay any tax outstanding that you calculate is due. A payslip is attached to the *Notice*. Note 20 in the *Guide* tells you about payment dates.

Do not send back the *Guide* but please keep it for reference purposes.

When we receive the return - *see note on page 12 of the Guide*

When we receive your completed return we will process it, based on your figures, and record the amount you have shown in the return as the tax due for this period. At this stage we will acknowledge receipt of the return.

The *Guide* tells you the time limits by which you can amend the return, and the time limits applying to us for correcting or enquiring into it.

Remember

- **Interest is charged on tax paid late.**
- **The company may be liable to penalties if its return is late or incorrect.**

Section 1: Which *Supplementary Pages* must be completed?

This page will help you decide if you need any *Supplementary Pages*. The notes in the *Guide* will also help you. Most company agents have supplies but if you do not have an agent, or your agent does not hold stocks, please call the CTSA Orderline on 0845 300 6555, or fax on 0845 300 6777. Make a note of the name and form number of the *Supplementary Page(s)* you want before calling. The CTSA Orderline is open 7 days a week between 8am and 10pm.

If you need further help please contact the Tax Office shown on the *Notice*.

Members' clubs, societies and voluntary associations are unlikely to need any *Supplementary Pages*.

Close companies

If the company is close and made a loan, or loans, to an individual participator, or associate of a participator, in the return period which has not been repaid within the return period, **you must complete** the detailed calculation on pages 6 to 8 and the *Loans to participators by close companies Supplementary Pages (form CT600A)*.

See Note 2 in the *Guide* for the meaning of 'close company', 'loan', 'participator' and 'associate'

Controlled foreign companies (CFCs)

If, in this period, the company had an interest of 25% or more in a foreign company which was controlled from the UK, **you must complete** the *Controlled foreign companies Supplementary Pages (form CT600B)*, and, if there is a charge under S747 ICTA 1988, the detailed calculation on pages 6 to 8.

Further guidance on CFCs is available - see *'Other publications of interest'* on page 12 of the *Guide.*

Group and/or consortium companies

If the company is claiming or surrendering any amounts under the group or consortium relief provisions for this period **you must complete**

- Section 4, the detailed calculation on pages 6 to 8, if you are claiming group or consortium relief
- Section 6 on page 9 if you are surrendering relief and
- the *Group and consortium Supplementary Pages (form CT600C)*.

Insurance companies and friendly societies

If, in this period, the company or society

- made claims under Sch 19AB ICTA 1988 to provisional payments (including notional repayments in respect of tax on gilt interest) or
- has entered into business in the accounting period which it treats as overseas life assurance business (OLAB)

you must complete the detailed calculation on pages 6 to 8 and the *Insurance Supplementary Pages (form CT600D)*.

Charities

If, in this period, the charity is claiming exemption or partial exemption from tax **you must complete** any relevant section of the *CT600* for taxable income and the *Charity Supplementary Pages (form CT600E)*.

Section 2: Turnover of the company

You must complete this Section if the company has trading or professional income.

Members' clubs, societies and voluntary associations that do not trade outside their membership need not complete this Section.

Investment companies and Unit Trusts need not complete this Section.

Turnover

1	**Total turnover from trade or profession** *Enter the total for this return period. See note 4*	**1** £
2	**Banks, building societies, insurance companies and other financial concerns** *Put an 'X' in this box.*	**2**

This is the end of Section 2. Please now complete either Section 3 on pages 4 and 5, or Section 4 on pages 6 to 8.

4 CT600 (1999) Version 1

Section 3: Short calculation

You may complete this section if it covers all the entries you need to make and any entry is less than £10 million.

In all other cases, or if you prefer, complete Section 4 instead. You should enclose explanations and calculations of any figures you have estimated or which are not immediately recognisable from the company's accounts. If you include a valuation you should state from where you obtained it. The figures to be entered are those adjusted for tax purposes, after deducting capital allowances and adding balancing charges, where appropriate. **References to *notes* are to those in the *Guide*.**

If the company is close and has made loans to an individual participator, or associate of a participator, in this period that were not repaid within the period, you need to complete Section 4 instead.

Please note that certain numbered boxes are missing from the short calculation.

Income

3 Trading and professional profits
See note 5. Complete Section 6 if there is a loss

   3 £

4 Trading losses brought forward claimed against profits
Only include losses made in the same trade. Include charges treated as losses. **Do not enter an amount larger than is needed to cover the profits in box 3.** *See notes 5 and 6*

   4 £

5 Net trading and professional profits
If box 4 equals box 3, enter '0'. Leave this box blank if there are no trading profits in box 3

   box 3 minus box 4
   5 £

7 Profits and gains from non-trading loan relationships
Include bank, building society or other interest, and any other profits and gains even if tax has been deducted. You will need to complete the 'Detailed calculation' at Section 4, and Section 6, if you have deficits on non-trading loan relationships from this, earlier or later accounting periods to include. See note 8

   7 £

8 Annuities, annual payments and discounts not arising from loan relationships and from which income tax has not been deducted
Exclude any amount included in box 7

   8 £

10 Income from which income tax has been deducted
Enter the gross amount before tax and exclude any amount included in box 7. See note 9

   10 £

12 Income from UK land and buildings
Enter the amount net of allowable expenses. Complete Section 6 if there is a loss. See note 10

   12 £

13 Annual profits and gains not falling under any other heading
Enter amount net of losses. Complete Section 6 if there is a loss. See note 7

   13 £

Chargeable gains

14 Gross gains
See note 11. Complete Section 6 if there is a loss

   14 £

15 Allowable losses including losses brought forward
Do not enter an amount larger than the amount of gross gains shown in box 14. *See note 11*

   15 £

16 Net chargeable gains
If box 15 equals box 14, enter '0'

   box 14 minus box 15
   16 £

19 Profits before other deductions and reliefs

   total of boxes 5, 7, 8, 10, 12, 13 and 16
   19 £

Deductions and reliefs

26 Trading losses of this or a later accounting period
& under S393A ICTA 1988
27 *Put an 'X' in box 26 if amounts carried back from later accounting periods are included in box 27. See note 12*

   26   **27** £

30 Profits before charges

   box 19 minus box 27
   30 £

31 Charges paid
This figure must not exceed profits shown in box 30. See note 13

   31 £

Corporation tax profits

33 Profits chargeable to corporation tax

   box 30 minus box 31
   33 £

Carry forward the figure in box 33 to the box at the top of page 5

Appendix 4

Section 3: Short calculation continued

Profits chargeable to corporation tax *Enter the figure from box 33 on page 4*   £

Tax calculation If you claim tax is chargeable at the small companies' rate, or if you are claiming marginal small companies' relief, complete boxes 34 - 38. If there are no associated companies, franked investment income or foreign income dividends, please enter the financial year(s) in boxes 35 and 37, and '0' in boxes 34, 36 and, if necessary, 38. *See note 15*

34 Franked investment income and foreign income dividends arising in the period covered by the return. *See note 15* **34** £

35 - 38 Number of companies associated with this company in the/each financial year(s) covered by this return *Exclude this company. See note 15*

Financial year *(yyyy)*	Number of associated companies
35	**36**
37	**38**

39 - 59 Corporation tax chargeable *See note 16*

Financial years beginning 1 April *(yyyy)*	Amounts of profit	Rates of tax *See note 31*	Tax
39	**40** £	**41** . %	**42** £ p
49	**50** £	**51** . %	**52** £ p

box 42 plus box 52

59 Corporation tax chargeable   **59** £ p

Reliefs and deductions in terms of tax

60 Marginal small companies' relief *Attach your computation. See notes 15 and 16*   **60** £ p

62 Advance corporation tax (restricted if necessary under S239(2) ICTA 1988) *See note 17*   **62** £ p

total of boxes 60 and 62

63 Total reliefs and deductions in terms of tax *Cannot exceed box 59 amount*   **63** £ p

box 59 minus box 63

68 Tax chargeable   **68** £ p

69 Income tax deducted from gross income included in profits *Do not include deductions used to cover income tax for which the company was liable to account to the Inland Revenue on payments it has made. See note 18*   **69** £ p

70 Income tax repayable to the company *Complete if box 69 is greater than box 68. Also complete Section 7*   **70** £ p

box 68 minus box 69

72 Tax payable *Enter '0.00' if you have completed box 70. See note 20* **This figure is the amount of your self-assesment**   **72** £ p

Tax reconciliation

73 Deductions under the Construction Industry Scheme *Enclose forms SC60/CIS25. See note 19*   **73** £ p

box 73 minus box 72

74 Construction industry deductions repayable *Complete Section 7*   **74** £ p

75 Tax already paid (and not repaid) *Exclude amounts entered in boxes 69 and 73. See note 21*   **75** £ p

box 72 minus boxes 73 and 75

76 Tax outstanding *This amount is payable to the Accounts Office. See note 23*   **76** £ p

box 75 plus box 73 minus box 72

77 Tax overpaid *Complete Section 7*   **77** £ p

Indicators

79 Put an 'X' in this box if the company should have made quarterly instalment payments under the Corporation Tax (Instalment Payments) Regulations 1998 *See note 20*   **79**

80 Put an 'X' in this box if the company is within a group payment arrangement for this period   **80**

This is the end of the Short calculation.

6 CT600 (1999) Version 1

Section 4: Detailed calculation

Complete this section if you have not completed Section 3. You should enclose explanations and calculations of any figures you have estimated or which are not immediately recognisable from the company's accounts. If you have included a valuation you should state from where you obtained it. The figures to be entered are those adjusted for tax purposes, after deducting capital allowances and adding balancing charges where appropriate. **References to *notes* are to those in the *Guide*.**

Income

3 Trading and professional profits
See note 5. Complete Section 6 if there is a loss

3 £

4 Trading losses brought forward claimed against profits
Only include losses made in the same trade. Include charges treated as losses. **Do not enter an amount larger than is needed to cover the profits in box 3.** *See notes 5 and 6*

4 £

5 Net trading and professional profits
If box 4 equals box 3, enter '0'. Leave this box blank if there are no trading profits in box 3

box 3 minus box 4

5 £

6 Profits and gains from non-trading loan relationships,
& exchange fluctuations and certain financial instruments
7 *Include bank, building society or other interest, and any other profits and gains even if tax has been deducted. Also include intra-group income under S247(4) ICTA 1988 which represents interest on loan relationships. Put an 'X' in box 6 if income is stated net after carrying back deficits on non-trading loan relationships. Complete Section 6 if there are net deficits. See note 8*

6   **7** £

8 Annuities, annual payments and discounts not arising from loan relationships and from which income tax has not been deducted
Exclude any amount included in box 7

8 £

9 Overseas income within Sch D Case V
Complete Section 6 if there is a loss

9 £

10 Income from which income tax has been deducted
Enter the gross amount before tax and exclude any amount included in box 7. See note 9

10 £

11 Intra-group income under S247(4) ICTA 1988 election where tax has not been deducted
Exclude any amount included in box 7

11 £

12 Income from UK land and buildings
Enter the amount net of allowable expenses. Complete Section 6 if there is a loss. See note 10

12 £

13 Annual profits and gains not falling under any other heading
Enter amount net of losses. Complete Section 6 if there is a loss. See note 7

13 £

Chargeable gains

14 Gross gains
See note 11. Complete Section 6 if there is a loss

14 £

15 Allowable losses including losses brought forward
Do not enter an amount larger than the amount of gross gains shown in box 14. *See note 11*

15 £

16 Net chargeable gains
If box 15 equals box 14, enter '0'

box 14 minus box 15

16 £

Deductions specifically from non-trade profits

17 Losses brought forward against certain investment income

17 £

18 Non-trade deficits on loan relationships (including interest), exchange fluctuations and certain financial instruments brought forward
See note 8. Amount cannot exceed total of boxes 7, 8, 9, 10, 11, 12, 13 and 16

18 £

total of box 5, and the net sum of boxes 7 to 13 and 16 minus boxes 17 and 18

19 Profits before other deductions and reliefs

19 £

Carry forward the figure in box 19 to the box at the top of page 7

CT600 (1999) Version 1   7

Profits chargeable to corporation tax *Enter the figure from box 19 on page 6*   £

Deductions and reliefs

20 Losses on unquoted shares   **20** £

21 Management expenses under S75 ICTA 1988   **21** £

22 Interest distributions under S468L ICTA 1988 *See note 29*   **22** £

23 Schedule A losses for this or previous accounting period under S392A ICTA 1988 *See note 10*   **23** £

24 Capital allowances for the purposes of management of the business *S28 CAA 1990. Investment companies only. Complete Section 5*   **24** £

25 Non-trade deficits for this accounting period from loan relationships, exchange fluctuations or certain financial instruments *See note 8*   **25** £

26 Trading losses of this or a later accounting period
&   under S393A ICTA 1988
27 *Put an 'X' in box 26 if amounts carried back from later accounting periods are included in box 27. See note 12*   **26**   **27** £

28 Non-trade capital allowances *S145(3) CAA 1990. Complete Section 5*   **28** £

total of boxes 20 - 25, 27 and 28

29 Total of deductions and reliefs *This figure must not exceed profits shown in box 19*   **29** £

box 19 minus box 29

30 Profits before charges and group relief   **30** £

31 Charges paid *This figure must not exceed profits shown in box 30. See note 13*   **31** £

32 Group relief *This figure must not exceed box 30 minus box 31. Complete and attach the 'Group and consortium Supplementary Pages'. See note 14*   **32** £

box 30 minus boxes 31 and 32

33 Profits chargeable to corporation tax   **33** £

Tax calculation If you claim tax is chargeable at the small companies' rate, or if you are claiming marginal small companies' relief, complete boxes 34 - 38. If there are no associated companies, franked investment income or foreign income dividends, please enter the financial year(s) in boxes 35 and 37, and '0' in boxes 34, 36 and, if necessary, 38. *See note 15*

34 Franked investment income and foreign income dividends arising in the period covered by the return. *See note 15*   **34** £

35 - 38 Number of companies associated with this company in the/each financial year(s) covered by this return
Exclude this company. See note 15

	Financial year *(yyyy)*	Number of associated companies
35		**36**
37		**38**

39 - 59 Corporation tax chargeable *See note 16*

Financial years beginning 1 April *(yyyy)*	Amounts of profit	Rates of tax *See note 31*	Tax
39	**40** £	**41** · %	**42** £ p
	43 £	**44** · %	**45** £ p
	46 £	**47** · %	**48** £ p
49	**50** £	**51** · %	**52** £ p
	53 £	**54** · %	**55** £ p
	56 £	**57** · %	**58** £ p

total of boxes 42, 45, 48, 52, 55 and 58

Carry forward the figure in box 59 to the box at the top of page 8   **59** £ p

433

Appendix 4

Section 4: Detailed calculation continued

Corporation tax chargeable *Enter the figure from from box 59 on page 7* £ _____ p

60 - 63 Reliefs and deductions in terms of tax

60 **Marginal small companies' relief**
Attach your computation. See notes 15 and 16 **60** £ _____ p

61 **Double taxation relief**
Exclude any amount included in box 67 **61** £ _____ p

61A Put an 'X' in this box if box 61 includes
an Underlying Rate relief claim **61A** ____

62 **Advance corporation tax (restricted if
necessary under S239(2) ICTA 1988)**
See note 17 **62** £ _____ p

63 **Total reliefs and deductions in terms of tax**
Cannot exceed corporation tax chargeable amount in box 59 *total of boxes 60, 61 and 62* **63** £ _____ p

64 - 78 Calculation of tax outstanding or overpaid

64 Net corporation tax liability *box 59 minus box 63* **64** £ _____ p

65 **Tax payable under S419 ICTA 1988**
&
66 *Complete and attach the 'Loans to participators by close companies
Supplementary Pages'. Put an 'X' in box 65 if you completed box A11
in the Supplementary Pages. Copy the figure from box A13 to box 66* **65** ____ **66** £ _____ p

67 **Tax payable under S747 ICTA 1988**
Enter the total figure of tax from the 'Controlled foreign companies Supplementary Pages' **67** £ _____ p

68 Tax chargeable *total of boxes 64, 66 and 67* **68** £ _____ p

69 **Income tax deducted from gross income included in profits**
*Do not include deductions used to cover income tax for which the company was
liable to account to the Inland Revenue on payments it has made. See note 18* **69** £ _____ p

70 **Income tax repayable to the company**
Complete if box 69 is greater than box 68. Also complete Section 7 **70** £ _____ p

71 **Advance corporation tax on foreign income dividends and
set off to the extent that corporation tax is otherwise unpaid**
See note 22 **71** £ _____ p

72 **Tax payable**
Enter '0.00' if you have completed box 70. See note 20
This figure is the amount of your self-assesment *box 68 minus boxes 69 and 71* **72** £ _____ p

Tax reconciliation

73 **Deductions under the Construction Industry Scheme**
Enclose forms SC60/CIS25. See note 19 **73** £ _____ p

74 **Construction industry deductions repayable**
Complete Section 7 *box 73 minus box 72* **74** £ _____ p

75 **Tax already paid (and not repaid)**
Exclude amounts entered in boxes 69, 71 and 73. See note 21 **75** £ _____ p

76 **Tax outstanding**
This amount is payable to the Accounts Office. See note 23 *box 72 minus boxes 73 and 75* **76** £ _____ p

77 **Tax overpaid**
Complete Section 7 *box 75 plus box 73 minus box 72* **77** £ _____ p

78 **Tax refunds surrendered to the company under S102 FA 1989**
Enclose a copy of the joint Notice. See note 24 **78** £ _____ p

Indicators

79 Put an 'X' in this box if the company should have made quarterly instalment
payments under the Corporation Tax (Instalment Payments) Regulations 1998
See note 20 **79** ____

80 Put an 'X' in this box if the company is within a group payment arrangement
for this period **80** ____

This is the end of the Detailed calculation.

CT600 (1999) Version 1   9

Section 5:   Claims for capital allowances and details of balancing charges You

You must complete this section if you want to claim capital allowances. You should also show balancing charges taken into account in Section 3 or 4 calculations. Show details of qualifying expenditure on which writing-down allowances may be claimed. even if you do not want to claim any allowances for this period. *See note 25.*

Notice of expenditure on machinery and plant *See note 25*

81 Expenditure on which first year allowance is claimed	**81** £
82 Qualifying expenditure on long-life assets	**82** £
83 Qualifying expenditure on other assets	**83** £

Charges and allowances included in calculation of trading profits or losses

	Balancing charges	Capital allowances
84 - 85 Cars *Including leased out and 'expensive' cars*	**84** £	**85** £
86 - 87 Machinery and plant - long-life assets	**86** £	**87** £
88 - 89 Machinery and plant - other assets	**88** £	**89** £
90 - 91 Industrial buildings and structures *Including qualifying hotels, and commercial buildings and hotels in enterprise zones*	**90** £	**91** £
92 - 93 Other charges and allowances *For example agricultural buildings, mineral extraction, scientific research, patents*	**92** £	**93** £

Charges and allowances not included in calculation of trading profits or losses

	Balancing charges	Capital allowances
94 - 95	**94** £	**95** £

Section 6:   Losses, deficits and excess amounts

Complete this section if the company has incurred, in this period, any of the losses or deficits shown below, or if it has, for this period, any of the excess amounts shown below. Companies that are proposing to surrender any amount as group or consortium relief should also complete the second column. *See note 27.*

		Arising	Maximum available for surrender as group relief
96 - 97	Trading losses Case I *See note 5*	*calculated under S393 ICTA 1988* **96** £	*calculated under S393A ICTA 1988* **97** £
98	Trading losses Case V	*calculated under S393 ICTA 1988* **98** £	
99 - 100	Non-trade deficits on loan relationships *See note 8*	*calculated under S82 FA 1996* **99** £	*calculated under S83 FA 1996* **100** £
101 - 102	Schedule A losses *UK land and buildings. See note 10*	*calculated under S392A ICTA 1988* **101** £	*calculated under S403 ICTA 1988* **102** £
103	Overseas property business losses Case V	*calculated under S392A ICTA 1988* **103** £	
104	Losses Case VI	*calculated under S396 ICTA 1988* **104** £	
105	Capital losses	*calculated under S16 TCGA 1992* **105** £	
		Excess	
106	Excess non-trade capital allowances *Excess over income in period*	**106** £	*calculated under S403 ICTA 1988*
107	Excess charges *See note 13*	**107** £	*calculated under S403 ICTA 1988*
108 - 109	Excess management expenses	*calculated under S75(3) ICTA 1988* **108** £	*calculated under S403 ICTA 1988* **109** £
110	Excess interest distributions	*calculated under S468L(7) ICTA 1988* **110** £	

435

Appendix 4

Section 7: Overpayments and repayment claims

Complete this section if you are claiming a repayment. If you have completed boxes 70, 74 and 77 in Section 3 or 4, attach your calculations. Do not forget to put an 'X' in the appropriate box of the *Summary of return information* section on page 1. *See note 28.*

Please note there is no box 113 in this section.

111   **Repayment of corporation tax**
Include construction industry deductions
repayable and enclose forms SC60/CIS25

111	£		P

112   **Repayment of income tax**

112	£		P

114   **Repayment of advance corporation tax**
See note 22

114	£		P

Bank details (for person to whom the repayment is to be made)

Repayments of corporation tax (but not income tax, advance corporation tax or construction industry deductions) can be made quickly and safely by direct credit (BACS) to a bank or building society account.

You should provide details of the account which is to be credited. If the details are those of the nominee you want to receive the repayment, remember to complete the authority overleaf.

Name of bank or building society

115	

Branch sort code   **Account number**

116				117	

Name of account

118	

Building society reference

119	

Signature

120	*Except where a liquidator has been appointed, any person who is authorised to do so may sign the BACS details on behalf of the company. A photocopy of a signature is not acceptable.*

Name *(in capital letters)*

120A	

CT600 (1999) Version 1   11

Section 7: Overpayments and repayment claims continued

Repayment claim

121 The following amount is to be repaid

121 £   p

either

122 • to the company   122

or   *(put an 'X' in either box 122 or 123 but not both)*

123 • to the nominee in the authority given below   123

124 The following amount is to be surrendered under S102 Finance Act 1989, and

124 £   p

either

125 • the joint Notice is attached   125

or   *(put an 'X' in appropriate box)*

126 • will follow   126
Repayments of advance corporation tax cannot be surrendered

127 Please stop repayment of the following amount until I send you the Notice

127 £   p

Payments to a person other than the company

Complete the authority below if you want the repayment to be made to a person **other than the company**. The Inland Revenue reserves the right not to make a repayment to a nominee and will not normally make a repayment to an overseas nominee.

I, as *(enter status - company secretary, treasurer, liquidator or authorised agent, etc.)*

128

of *(enter name of company)*

129

authorise *(enter name)*

130

(enter address)

131

Postcode

Nominee reference

132

to receive on the company's behalf the amount due.

Signature

133

Except where a liquidator has been appointed, any person who is authorised to do so may sign the BACS details or an authority on behalf of the company. A photocopy of a signature is not acceptable.

Name (in capital letters)

133A

This is the end of Section 7

Appendix 4

Section 8: Directors' remuneration - optional section

Please complete this section if directors' remuneration is charged in the accounts supporting this form *CT600*.

Attach a continuation sheet if you need more space.

Company name

134	

PAYE District	**PAYE reference**
135	136

Accounts for the period From *(dd/mm/yyyy)* to	**Remuneration claimed as a deduction in the accounts** *Show total figure for all directors*
137 / / 138 / /	139 £

Date when accounts laid before the company in general meeting or, if resolved not to lay accounts, the date on which the accounts were approved by the directors

140	/ /

Analysis

Net remuneration voted after adjustments

Enter the net figure of remuneration after deducting employers' National Insurance contributions, employers' and employees' superannuation contributions and any benefits which have been included in the accounts' figure

141	Name of director	National Insurance number	Salary	Bonus, fees or commission
			£	£
			£	£
			£	£
			£	£
			£	£
			£	£
			£	£
			£	£

Put an 'X' in here if a continuation sheet is used | 142 | |

143	Adjustments to reconcile the analysis above with total accounts' deductions claimed - please give details

	£
	£
	£
	£
	£

Date of commencement or cessation of directorship during the period of account

144	Name of director	National Insurance number	Date commenced	Date ceased

438

1

 Inland **Revenue**

Information

Charity Name

Tax reference

/   /

Period covered by these *Supplementary Pages* *(cannot exceed 12 months)*

From *(dd/mm/yyyy)*   **To**

/   /   /   /

Important points

- *These **Supplementary Pages*** will form the Charity's claim to exemption that its income and gains have been applied for charitable purposes only.
- **Please enter** '0' where appropriate.
- **How often** you are asked to make a return will depend on the extent and nature of your activities.
- ***These Pages***, when completed, form part of the company's return.
- ***These Pages* set out** the information we need and provide a standard format.
- ***These Pages* are covered by** the Declaration you sign on page 1 of the form CT600.
- **The warning shown on the form CT600 about prosecution, and the advice about late and incorrect returns, and late payment of tax also apply to these Pages.**

You need to complete these *Supplementary Pages* if

the Charity claims exemption from tax on all or any part of its income and gains.

Claim to exemption

This section should be completed in all cases

Charity repayment reference

Charity Commission Registration number; or Scottish Charity number *(if applicable)*

During the period covered by these *Supplementary Pages*:
Put an 'X' in the box if 'Yes'

- The company was a Charity and is claiming exemption from all tax on all or part of its income and gains

- All income and gains are exempt from tax and have been, or will be, applied for charitable purposes only

or

- Some of the Charity's income and gains may not be exempt or have not been applied for charitable purposes only, and I have completed the form *CT600*
  See Note 7 on page 2 of these Pages

I claim exemption from tax

Signature

Date *(dd/mm/yyyy)*

/   /

Name *(in capital letters)*

Status

Except where a liquidator has been appointed, any person who is authorised to do so may sign on behalf of the company. A photocopy of a signature is not acceptable.

BMSD 6/99

CT600E Charity Supplementary Pages

Appendix 4

Notes to help you complete the Charity Supplementary Pages

Repayments (Boxes E1/E1a and E2/E2b)

1. In Boxes E1/E1a:
    - Enter the amount of income tax and transitional relief claimed on forms R68 for the period covered by these Pages.
    - This should relate only to income arising in the period.
    - Do not include amounts claimed for earlier periods.

2. In Box E2/E2b enter the total amount due for income received in the period on which the Charity can claim.

Trading income (Box E5)

3. Enter details of the turnover of trades, the profits of which will be exempted by S505(1)(e) ICTA 1988.

    If the charity has carried on a trade during the return period which falls outside the exemption, complete the *Short* or *Detailed calculation* on the form *CT600*. Do not include in the calculation sources of income which are otherwise exempt from tax. Also complete the *Summary* and *Declaration* on page 1 of the form *CT600*.

Other sources (Box E13)

4. Enter details in Box E13 of the total income received from sources other than those included in the boxes above. If the amount in Box E13 includes income which is assessable under Case VI of Schedule D (for example, the profit from a single transaction or isolated service of some kind, which do not amount to trading under Case I of Schedule D), then complete the *Short calculation* in the form *CT600*, entering the income assessable at box 13. Also complete the *Summary* and *Declaration* on page 1 of the form *CT600*.

Investments and loans within Sch 20 ICTA 1988 (Box E26)

5. Qualifying investments for the purposes of S506 ICTA 1988 are specified in Part I, Sch 20 ICTA 1988.

    Qualifying loans for the purposes of S506 ICTA 1988 are specified in Part II, Sch 20 ICTA 1988.

    Any loan or other investment not specified may be accepted as qualifying where the loan or other investment is made for the benefit of the charity and not for the avoidance of tax (whether by the charity or any other person). Any claim must first be approved by Financial Intermediaries and Claims Office (FICO).

Investments and loans made outside Sch 20 ICTA 1988 (Box E27)

6. If the charity has made any investments or loans which do not fall within Sch 20 ICTA 1988 and no claim is to be made, enter the total of such investments or loans in Box E27.

Restriction of relief for non-qualifying expenditure.

7. Relief under S505(1) ICTA 1988 and S256 TCGA 1992 may not be available.

    The Charity should attach a calculation of restriction of relief under S505(3) ICTA 1988 and send it with this return. If you need help with this calculation please contact the FICO technical helpline. For Charities in England, Wales and Northern Ireland the telephone number is 0151 472 6046. For Charities in Scotland the telephone number is 0131 551 8643.

Subcontractor payments

8. If the Charity has made payments under the Construction Industry Scheme enclose forms SC60/CIS25.

Repayments

Enter details of repayments/payments for income arising during the period covered by these Supplementary Pages

See Notes 1 and 2 on page 2 of these Pages

		Income Tax	Transitional Relief
E1/E1a	Amount already claimed in period using form R68 or R68(MGA)	**E1** £	**E1a** £
E2/E2b	Total repayment/payment due	**E2** £	**E2b** £
and either			
E3/E3c	Further repayment/payment due *Where E2/E2b is more than E1/E1a*	**E3** £	**E3c** £
or			
E4/E4d	Amounts overclaimed in period *Where E1/E1a is more than E2/E2b*	**E4** £	**E4d** £

Information required

Enter details of any *income* claimed as exempt which is received from the following sources. Enter the figure included in the Charity's accounts for the period covered by these Supplementary Pages

Non-exempt amounts should be entered on the form CT600 in the appropriate boxes

Source	Amount
E5 Enter total turnover from exempt trading activities *See Note 3 on page 2 of these Pages*	**E5** £
E6 Investment income *Exclude any amounts included on the form CT600*	**E6** £
E7 UK land and buildings *Exclude any amounts included on the form CT600*	**E7** £
E8 Deed of Covenant *Exclude any amounts included on the form CT600*	**E8** £
E9 Gift Aid or Millenium Gift Aid *Exclude any amounts included on the form CT600*	**E9** £
E10 Other Charities *Exclude any amounts included on the form CT600*	**E10** £
E11 Legacies	**E11** £
E12 Other donations	**E12** £
E13 Other sources (for example, commissions, fees, small fund-raising) *See Note 4 on page 2 of these Pages*	**E13** £

Enter figures of *expenditure* as shown in the Charity's accounts for the period covered by these Supplementary Pages

Source	Amount
E14 Trading costs *In relation to exempt activities in box E5*	**E14** £
E15 UK land and buildings *In relation to exempt activities in box E7*	**E15** £
E16 All general administration costs	**E16** £
E17 All grants and donations made within the UK	**E17** £
E18 All grants and donations made outside the UK	**E18** £
E19 Other expenditure not included above, or in calculating figures entered on the form *CT600*	**E19** £

Continued on page 4

Appendix 4

Continued from page 3

Charity Assets	Disposals in period (total consideration received)	Held at the end of the period
E20 Tangible fixed assets	**E20** £	**E20a** £
E21 UK investments (excluding controlled companies)	**E21** £	**E21b** £
E22 Shares in, and loans to, controlled companies	**E22** £	**E22c** £
E23 Overseas investments	**E23** £	**E23d** £
E24 Loans and non trade debtors		**E24e** £
E25f Other current assets		**E25f** £

E26 Put an 'X' in this box if all investments and loans made by the Charity in the accounting period were qualifying investments or loans within Part I or II of Sch 20 ICTA 1988. *See Note 5 on page 2 of these Pages*   **E26**

E27 Value of any non-qualifying investments and loans. *See Note 6 on page 2 of these Pages*   **E27** £

E28 Number of subsidiary or associated companies the Charity controls at the end of the period   **E28**

What to do when you have completed these *Supplementary Pages*

Follow the advice shown under 'What to do when you have completed the return' on page 2 of the form CT600.

Appendix 5

Useful Publications

Charity Commission publications

CC2	Charities and the Charity Commission (Dec 1999)
CC3	Responsibilities of Charity Trustees (Sept 1999)
CC3a	Responsibilities of Charity Trustees: a Summary (Aug 1999)
CC4	Charities for the Relief of the Poor (July 2000)
CC6	Charities for the Relief of Sickness (Mar 2000)
CC7	Ex Gratia Payments by Charities (Jan 1995)
CC8	Internal Financial Controls for Charities (July 1999)
CC9	Political Activities and Campaigning by Charities (Sept 1999)
CC9a	Political Activities and Campaigning by Local Community Charities (Feb 1997)
CC10	Annual Report for 1998: a Summary (May 1999)
CC11	Remuneration of Charity Trustees (Oct 1999)
CC12	Managing Financial Difficulties and Insolvency in Charities (July 2000)
CC13	The Official Custodian for Charities' Land Holding Service (Mar 1995)
CC14	Investment of Charitable Funds: Basic Principles (Aug 1995)
CC14a	Depositing Charity Cash (Aug 1999)
CC18	Use of Church Halls for Village Hall and Other Charitable Purposes (Mar 1996)
CC19	Charities' Reserves (June 1999)
CC20	Charities and Fund-Raising (April 2000)
CC20a	Charities and Fund-raising – a Summary (Sept 1999)
CC21	Registering as a Charity (May 2000)
CC22	Choosing and Preparing a Governing Document (Aug 2000)
CC23	Exempt Charities (July 1999)
CC24	Users on Board: Beneficiaries who become trustees (Mar 2000)
CC25	Resolving Charity Disputes: Our Role (Mar 2000)
CC27	Providing Alcohol on Charity Premises (July 1996)
CC28	Disposing of Charity Land (June 1996)
CC29	Charities and Local Authorities (Apr 1996)

CC32	Trustee Investments Act 1961: A Guide (Aug 1999)
CC33	Acquiring Land (Mar 1995)
CC35	Charities and Trading (Apr 2000)
CC36	Making a Scheme (Sept 1999)
CC37	Charities and Contracts (Jan 2000)
CC38	Expenditure and Replacement of Permanent Endowment (Apr 1994)
CC40	Disaster Appeals (Aug 1994)
CC43	Incorporation of Charity Trustees (June 1999)
CC44	Small Charities: Alteration of Trusts, Transfer of property, Expenditure of Capital (May 1999)
CC45	Central Register of Charities (Nov 1995)
CC47	Inquiries into Charities (Feb 2000)
CC48	Charities and Meetings (Aug 1999)
CC49	Charities and Insurance (June 1996)
CC50	Getting in Touch with the Charity Commission (June 1996)
CC51	Charity Accounts: The New Framework (June 1999)
CC52	Charity Accounts: Charities under £10,000 Threshold (Apr 1999)
CC54	Accounting for the Smaller Charity (Sept 1999)
CC55	Accruals Accounting for the Smaller Charity (Sept 1999)
CC56	The Carrying out of an Independent Examination Directions and Guidance notes (Mar 1996)
CC57	Receipts and Payments Accounts Pack (July 1998) Introductory Notes
CC57(a)	Accounting Statement
CC57(b)	Independent Examiner's Report on the Accounts
CC57(c)	Trustees' Annual Report (Accompanying Receipts and Payments Accounts)
CC58	Accruals Accounts Pack (July 1998)
CC58(a)	Accounting Statement (Accruals Accounts)
CC58(b)	Independent Examiner's Report on the Accounts
CC58(c)	Trustees' Annual Report (Accompanying Accruals Accounts)
CC 60	The Hallmarks of a Well-Run Charity Mar 1999

Inland Revenue publications

CB1 **Setting up a charity in Scotland** (Feb 1999)

NE1 **First steps as a new employer**
Thinking of taking someone on? We have set up a special Helpline for new employers to help you find your way around the Pay As You Earn (PAYE) system. (Apr 1999)

IR46 **Clubs, Societies and Associations** (Jan 2000)

IR56 **Employed or self-employed? A guide for tax and National Insurance**
This can help you decide whether or not you are employed or self-employed, an area that causes a lot of confusion. It also tells you how tax and National Insurance affect you, whatever your employment status. (Apr 1999)

IR64 **Giving to charity by business. How businesses can get tax relief**
Companies and individuals in business can get tax relief for payments made to charity. This leaflet describes how the relief is given. (Sept 2000)

IR65 **Giving to charity by individuals**
If you are thinking of making a gift to charity, this booklet shows you how changes which came into effect from 6 April 2000 make tax effective giving easier. (Sept 2000)

IR69 **Expenses payments and benefits in kind. How to save yourself work**
This explains how employers can apply for a 'dispensation notice' to remove the need to report expenses payments on forms P11D. The leaflet includes an application form. (Apr 1999)

IR72 **Investigations. The examination of business accounts**
What happens if your accounts are selected for investigation? This leaflet describes how we select accounts to investigate and how a tax assessment is worked out. (May 1995)

IR73 **Inland Revenue investigations. How settlements are negotiated**
What happens at the end of an investigation into someone's tax affairs? This describes our approach to reaching an agreement if there is an amount owing. (Jan 1994)

IR109 **Employer compliance reviews and negotiations**
This leaflet explains what happens at the end of an employer compliance review. It describes how we reach an agreement if we feel you have to pay us anything following the review and what happens if we cannot reach an agreement. (Mar 2000)

IR128 **Corporation tax pay and file. Company leaflet**
A simple guide that gives a brief outline to the rules for paying corporation tax. (July 1993)

Taxation of company cars from 6 April 1994. Employers' guide
This leaflet has been replaced by IR172.

PAYE Settlement Agreements
This leaflet is for employers who make expenses payments to their employees or give them benefits in kind. (Apr 2000)

IR160 **Inland Revenue enquiries under Self Assessment**
This leaflet explains what happens at the end of an enquiry into your tax return. (Dec 1999)

IR173 **Tax credits – a summary for employers. Working Families' Tax Credit and Disabled Person's Tax Credit**
This leaflet is for all employers who operate a PAYE scheme (other than a simplified scheme for domestic staff). So, if you are an employer and you deduct income tax and/or National Insurance contributions (NICs) from the pay of any of your employees you should read this leaflet. (Dec 1999)

480 **Expenses and benefits. A tax guide**
This booklet explains the tax law relating to expenses payments and benefits received by directors and employees. It tells you which expenses payments and benefits are taxable and which are not. It describes, among other things, dispensations, the use of cars, and entertaining expenses. (Apr 2000)

490 **Employee Travel. A tax and NICs guide for employers**
This guide describes the tax and National Insurance contributions (NICs) treatment of business travel by employees. It covers business journeys made on or after 6 April 1998. The rules which apply before that date are set out in the 1999 edition of booklet 480 (see above). (Jan 1998)

Customs and Excise publications

Level 1 Introductory

Group Treatment	700/2	(Sept 1999)
Registration for VAT: Corporate bodies organised in divisions	700/3	(Mar 1998)
Registration for VAT: Non-established taxable persons	700/4	(Mar 1997)
Should I Be Registered for VAT? (Also available on cassette and in large print from your advice centre)	700/1	(Apr 2000)

Level 2 VAT Basic information

Filling In Your Return (inc. Updates 1 and 2) (Also available in large print from your advice centre)	700/12	(Sept 1995)
How to correct VAT errors and make adjustments or claims	700/45	(Jan 2000)
Keeping Records and Accounts (Also available in large print and as a video (from your advice centre) and accompanying booklet)	700/21	(Mar 1995)
Liability Law	701/39	(May 2000)
The Ins & Outs of VAT (Also available in large print from your advice centre)	700/15	(Mar 1995)
The VAT Guide	700	(Mar 2000)
VAT Notes		
VAT Notes No 1 2000		(Mar 2000)
VAT Notes No 4 1999		(Dec 1999)
VAT Notes No 3 1999		(Sept 1999)
VAT Notes No 2 1999		(June 1999)
Welcome to VAT (video and booklet)		(1995)

A

Admissions	700/22	(Oct 1989)
Advertising (by Charities) and goods connected with collecting donations	701/58	Draft
Annual accounting (Updates 1 and 2)	732	(Jan 1996)

B

Bad debts – relief from VAT	700/18	(Dec 1997)

C

Cancelling your registration (inc. Update 1) (Also available in large print and audio cassette format from your advice centre)	700/11	(Apr 2000)
Capital goods scheme – input tax on land, computers and buildings acquired for use in your business	706/2	(Apr 1990)
Cash accounting	731	(Mar 1999)
Charities (incl. Update 1) (Also available	701/1	(Jan 1995)

H

Health

Drugs, medicines and aids for the handicapped: liability with effect from 1 January 1998	Info Sheet 6	(1997)
Hotels and holiday accommodation (inc. Update 1)	709/3	(Apr 1993)

L

Land and Property:

Land and Property (inc. Updates 2 and 3)	742	(Dec 1995)
Land and property: law	742C	(Nov 1995)
Letting of facilities for sport and physical recreation	742/1	(Mar 1990)
Lotteries	701/28	(Mar 1997)

M

Motor Vehicles:

Motoring expenses (inc. Updates 1 and 2)	700/64	(May 1996)

N

New Deal Programme	Info Sheet 3	(1999)

P

Partial exemption	706	(Feb 1999)
Payments on Account	700/60	(Nov 1996)
Place of supply of services	741	(Sept 1998)
Printed and similar matter	701/10	(Oct 1999)

R

Reduced rate for the installation of energy saving materials	Info Sheet 1	(2000)
Registered social landlords (Housing Associations etc)	708/5	(Sept 1997)
Reliefs for people with disabilities (Also available in large print and on cassette from your advice centre)	701/7	(Aug 1994)
Relief from VAT on bad debts	700/18	(Dec 1997)
Requirement to give security to Customs & Excise	700/52	(Mar 1996)

Retailers:

Retail schemes (inc. Updates 1 and 2)	727	(Aug 1997)
Bespoke retail schemes (Update 1)	727/2	(Aug 1997)
How to work the Point of Sale scheme (inc. Updates 1 and 2)	727/3	(Aug 1997)
How to work the Apportionment scheme (inc. Updates 1 and 2)	727/4	(Aug 1997)
How to work the Direct Calculation scheme (inc. Updates 1 and 2)	727/5	(Aug 1997)

S

Sponsorship (Update 1)	701/41	(July 1995)
Sport and physical education (Updates 1 and 2)	701/45	(Apr 1994)
Staff (Update 1)	700/34	(May 1994)
Subscriptions to political, religious, patriotic, philosophical philanthropic and civic bodies (exemption of)	Info Sheet 11	(1999)

T

Tour Operators/Travel Agents

Changes to the Tour Operator's Margin Scheme from 1 Jan 1996	Info Sheet 5	(1995)
Tour Operator's Margin Scheme	709/5	(Feb 1998)
Trade unions, professional bodies and learned societies (inc. Update 1)	701/33	(Aug 1997)

V

VAT civil evasion cases: Trial of a new approach to investigations – Statement of practice	Info Sheet 4	(Aug 2000)
VAT liability law	701/39	(May 2000)
VAT: New Deal Programme	Info Sheet 3	(1999)
VAT notices having the force of law	747	(Feb 1998)
VAT relief on the installation of energy saving materials	Info Sheet 9	(1998)

Y

Youth clubs	701/35	(July 1995)

Level 4 VAT What you can expect from HM C&E

Administrative agreements entered into with trade bodies	700/57	(Apr 1999)
Artificial separation of business activities: Statement of practice	700/61	(June 1997)
Civil evasion penalty investigations: Statement of practice	730	(Dec 1994)
Confidentiality in VAT matters (tax advisers) – statement of practice	700/47	(Feb 1993)
Default Interest	700/43	(Dec 1993)
Default surcharge (inc. Update 1)	700/50	(Apr 1997)
Default Surcharge: incorrect rate of assessment	Info Sheet 7	(1995)
Late registration penalty	700/41	(Apr 1995)
List of VAT Business Advice Centres	700/66	(Jan 1999)
Misdeclaration penalty	700/42	(Dec 1993)
Treatment of VAT repayment returns and VAT repayment supplement (inc. Update 1)	700/58	(June 1998)

VAT civil evasion cases: Trial of a new approach to investigations – Statement of practice	Info Sheet 4	(Aug 2000)
VAT enquiries guide	700/51	(Mar 1993)
VAT input appeals: luxuries, amusements and entertainment (inc. Update 1)	700/55	(July 1993)
What if I don't pay?	930	(Dec 1999)

INDEX